History of the Justices of the Peace

History of the
Justices of the Peace

by

Sir Thomas Skyrme

KCVO, CB, CBE, TD, JP, DL, MA

Of the Inner Temple, Barrister-at-Law

Volume I
England to 1689

Published by Barry Rose and the Justice of the Peace
Chichester
England

ISBN No.
1 872328 45 8

British Library Cataloguing in Publication Data
Skyrme, *Sir* Thomas
  History of the Justices of the Peace
  Vol. I
  1. England. Magistrates. History
  I. Title
  344.20716

ISBN 1-872328-45-8

Typeset by Countrywise Press, Chichester
Printed and bound by BPCC Wheatons

CONTENTS

Table of Statutes and Ordinances   ix

Introduction   xix

Preface   xxv

Acknowledgements   xxxv

Abbreviations   xxxix

Chapter I
Origins   1
  Saxon and Norman Influence   1
  Appointment of Keepers of the Peace in times of crisis - Edict of 1195   5
  Development of the Keepers   10

Chapter II
Transformation of Keepers into Justices 1327-61   15
  Statute of Westminster 1327   15
  Fluctuating fortunes of the Keepers   16
  Appointment of the Keepers   18
  Establishment of the Quorum   20
  The Plague: Labour and financial crisis   22
  The Earlier Courts   24
  The General Eyre   28

Chapter III
The First Justices   31
  Statute of Westminster 1361   31
  Beginning of Quarter Sessions   34
  Commission of the Peace   38
  Executive Officers of Quarter Sessions   40
  The Clerk of the Peace   41
  Remuneration of Justices and Clerks   46

Chapter IV
The Fifteenth Century
  Consolidation and Expansion   48
  Trade and Industry   49
  Class distinctions   59
  Roads, waterways and bridges   60
  Criminal jurisdiction   61
  Work of justices out of sessions   63
  Supervision by superior courts   64
  Savagery of the times   65
  The Wars of the Roses   66
  Language used in legal documents   72
  Establishment of the Tudor monarchy   72

Chapter V
The Counties Palatine   74
  Chester   75
  Durham   80
  The Duchy of Lancaster   87

Chapter VI
The Early Tudors 1485-1558
I - The New System of Government 107
    The new regimé 107
    Supervision by the higher courts and by the Council 109
    The Commission of the Peace 116
    Lord Lieutenant 120
    Deputy Lieutenant 122
    Clerk of the Peace 122

Chapter VII
The Early Tudors 1485-1558
II - Functions, Organization and Procedure 128
    Powers of the justices out of sessions 129
    Quarter Sessions and discretionary sessions 133
    Appeal 137

Chapter VIII
The Elizabethans'
Establishment of Royal Authority through the Justices of the Peace ... 163
    Beginning of the justices' text book 164
    Quarter Sessions 169
    Work out of sessions 172
    Sentencing 173
    Assizes 176
    The rulers of the counties 177
    Appointment 180

Chapter IX
The Seventeenth Century 1603-1688 206
    The first Stuarts 211
    Civil War, 1642-1646 219
    Restoration 228
    Routine duties 238
    The justices' officers 254
    JPs in other lands 255

Chapter X
The Cities and Boroughs 256
    Justices of the Peace in towns prior to 1835 256
    Municipal reform of the nineteenth century
    The twentieth century 281
    Remaining differences between borough and county benches ... 302

Index to Volume I xli

TABLE OF STATUTES AND ORDINANCES
CITED IN VOLUME I

Statutes were formerly cited according to the regal year of the monarch's reign. The Acts of Parliament Numbering and Citation Act 1962 provided that from the beginning of 1963 statutes should be numbered by the calendar year and not by the regnal year in which the session of Parliament was held. Modern Acts also have short titles by which they are cited, in addition to the year. In the following table all modern Acts are shown in this way under short title and calendar year, but a larger number of earlier enactments are given in the old style with regnal years to meet the wishes expressed in certain other countries beyond the United Kingdom. In these cases the name of the statute is given only in those instances where it is usual to refer to it in this manner. In every case the calendar year is also shown (the date being in accordance with the Julian calendar until 1582 and thereafter with the Gregorian).

Date	Citation _Name_	Page
1072	Ecclesiastical Ordinance	26
1166	Assize of Clarendon	2, 27
1176	Assize of Northampton	27
1258	Provisions of Oxford	8
1275	First Statute of Westminster, 3 Edw. I, c. 15	133
1285	Statute of Nisi Prius, 13 Edw. I, c. 30	29
1285	Second Statute of Westminster, 13 Edw. I, st. 1, c. 47	61, 156
1285	Statute of Winchester, 13 Edw. I, c. 6	11-13, 29, 38, 81
1327	Statute of Westminster, I Edw. III, st. 2, c. 16	15, 16, 81
1328	Statute of Northampton, 2 Edw. III, cc. 1-7	17, 38, 81
1330	Statute of Westminster, 4 Edw. III, c. 2	17, 133
1344	Statute of Westminster, 18 Edw. III, st. 2, c. 2	20, 21, 81
1349	First Ordinance of Labourers, 23 Edw. III	23
1350-51	25 Edw. III, st. 3, c. 4	61
1351	Statute of Labourers, 25 Edw. III, st. 2	42, 58, 145
1361	Statute of Westminster, 34 Edw. III, cc. 1-11	31-4, 35, 38,

		42, 56, 81, 133
1362	36 Edw. III, st. 1, c. 12	34, 134
1363	37 Edw. III, c. 19	59
1368	42 Edw. III, c. 3	37
1369	42 Edw. III, c. 6	34
1370	45 Edw. III, c. 2	61
1382	5 Rich. II, st. 1, c. 7	130
1383	7 Rich. II, c. 5	57
1388	12 Rich. II, c. 3	57
1388	12 Rich. II, c. 4	54
1388	12 Rich. II, c. 6	58, 144
1388	12 Rich. II, c. 7	57
1388	12 Rich. II, c. 10 (Statute of Cambridge)	46-7, 57, 69, 90, 123
1389	13 Rich. II, c. 9	50
1389	13 Rich. II, c. 12	52
1389-90	13 Rich. II, st. 1, c. 8	54, 56, 68
1389-90	13 Rich. II, st. 1, c. 9	36
1389-90	13 Rich. II, st. 1, cc. 10, 11	51
1389-90	13 Rich. II, st. 1, c. 13	59
1389-90	13 Rich. II, st. 1, c. 19	61
1390	14 Rich. II, c. 7	40, 46-7
1391	15 Rich. II, c. 2	130
1394	17 Rich. II, c. 9	61
1394	17 Rich. II, c. 10	39
1399	1 Hen. IV, c. 12	61
1402	4 Hen. IV, c. 11	61
1403-4	5 Hen. IV, c. 3	63
1403-5	5 Hen. IV, c. 10	63
1406	7 Hen. IV, c. 7	52
1406	7 Hen. IV, c. 17	57
1409-10	11 Hen. IV, c. 4	58
1409-10	11 Hen. IV, c. 6	51
1409-10	13 Hen. IV, c. 7	63, 130
1414	2 Hen. V, st. 1, c. 4	136

1414	2 Hen. V, st. 1, c. 7	71
1414	2 Hen. V, st. 2, c. 1	63, 69, 119
1421	9 Hen. V, st. 1, c. 11, & st. 2, c. 8	54
1423	2 Hen. VI, c. 7	52
1423	2 Hen. VI, c. 17	53
1423	2 Hen. VI, c. 18	55
1424	3 Hen. VI, c. 1	36
1427	6 Hen. VI, c. 3	54, 56
1429	8 Hen. VI, c. 7	70
1429	8 Hen. VI, c. 9	130, 170
1430	9 Hen. VI, c. 9	61
1433	11 Hen. VI, c. 8	36
1433	11 Hen. VI, c. 12	53
1433	11 Hen. VI, c. 17	145
1439	18 Hen. VI, c. 11	69-70
1441	20 Hen. VI, c. 8	62
1441	23 Hen. VI, c. 1	62
1444	23 Hen. VI, c. 9	132
1444	23 Hen. VI, c. 12	56
1461	1 Edw. IV, c. 2	40-1, 61
1464	4 Edw. IV, c. 1	51, 68
1464-5	4 Edw. IV, c. 8	68
1472	12 Edw. IV, c. 1	68
1472	12 Edw. IV, c. 7	61
1477-8	17 Edw. IV, c. 1	140
1477-8	17 Edw. IV, c. 3	58
1477-8	17 Edw. IV, c. 4	51, 68
1482-3	22 Edw. IV, c. 5	68
1483	1 Rich. III, c. 3	62, 133
1485	1 Hen. VII, c. 7	145
1485	1 Hen. VII, c. 8	141
1487	3 Hen. VII, c. 3	133
1487	3 Hen. VII, c. 4	146
1487	3 Hen. VII, c. 5	...
1487	3 Hen. VII, c. 9	148

1487	3 Hen. VII, c. 16		72
1488-9	4 Hen. VII, c. 12		114, 115, 138
1488-9	4 Hen. VII, c. 16		141
1491	7 Hen. VII, c. 3		145
1495	11 Hen. VII, c. 2		142
1495	11 Hen. VII, c. 3		161
1495	11 Hen. VII, c. 4		132, 145
1495	11 Hen. VII, c. 7		161
1495	11 Hen. VII, c. 15		114, 130, 132
1495	11 Hen. VII, c. 22		146
1495	11 Hen. VII, c. 23		141
1495	11 Hen. VII, c. 24		114
1495	11 Hen. VII, c. 25		114
1496	12 Hen. VII, c. 5		132
1503-4	19 Hen. VII		149
1503-4	19 Hen. VII, c. 4		143
1503-4	19 Hen. VII, c. 10		157
1503-4	19 Hen. VII, c. 11		145
1503-4	19 Hen. VII, c. 12		142, 148
1503-4	19 Hen. VII, c. 13		161
1511-12	3 Hen. VIII, c. 3		162
1511-12	3 Hen. VIII, c. 5		160
1512	4 Hen. VIII, c. 1		161
1514-15	6 Hen. VIII, c. 2		143
1514-15	6 Hen. VIII, c. 3		146-7
1530-1	22 Hen. VIII, c. 5	Statute of Bridges	132, 154, 270
1530-1	22 Hen. VIII, c. 10		151
1530-1	22 Hen. VIII, c. 12		126, 149
1531-2	23 Hen. VIII, c. 2		132
1531-2	23 Hen. VIII, c. 4		140
1531-2	23 Hen. VIII, c. 7		158
1532-3	24 Hen. VIII, c. 1		140
1532-3	24 Hen. VIII, c. 3		146
1532-3	24 Hen. VIII, c. 4		141

1532-3	24 Hen. VIII, c. 6		146
1532-3	24 Hen. VIII, c. 7		142
1532-3	24 Hen. VIII, c. 10		142
1533-4	25 Hen. VIII, c. 11		145
1533-4	25 Hen. VIII, c. 13		141
1533-4	25 Hen. VIII, c. 17		162
1535-6	27 Hen. VIII, c. 5		76
1535-6	27 Hen. VIII, c. 10		119
1535-6	27 Hen. VIII, c. 20		152
1535-6 1533-6	27 Hen. VIII, c. 24	Act of Resumption	74, 82, 83, 95, 117, 118
1535-6	27 Hen. VIII, c. 25		144, 149, 150, 188
1536	28 Hen. VIII, c. 10		152
1539	31 Hen. VIII, c. 14		152
1540	32 Hen. VIII, c. 1		132
1540	32 Hen. VIII, c. 7		152
1540	32 Hen. VIII, c. 13		142
1540	32 Hen. VIII, c. 43		77
1541-2	33 Hen. VIII, c. 6		162
1541-2	33 Hen. VIII, c. 9		144
1541-2	33 Hen. VIII, c. 10		134
1541-2	33 Hen. VIII, c. 13		77
1542-3	34 & 35 Hen. VIII, c. 1		152
1542-3	34 & 35 Hen. VIII, c. 3		145
1542-3	35 Hen. VIII, c. 5		153
1542-3	35 Hen. VIII, c. 8		140
1542-3	35 Hen. VIII, c. 17		132, 142
1545	37 Hen. VIII, c. 1		119, 122, 123
1545	37 Hen. VIII, c. 7		134
1547	1 Edw. VI, c. 3		132, 149, 150
1547	1 Edw. VI, c. 4		153
1548-9	2 & 3 Edw. VI, cc. 9, 11		140
1548-9	2 & 3 Edw. VI, c. 15		146, 147
1548-9	2 & 3 Edw. VI, c. 19		140
1549-50	3 & 4 Edw. VI, c. 1		120

1549-50	3 & 4 Edw. VI, c. 5	120, 130
1549-50	3 & 4 Edw. VI, c. 10	153
1549-50	3 & 4 Edw. VI, c. 16	150
1549-50	3 & 4 Edw. VI, c. 21	146
1551-2	5 & 6 Edw. VI, c. 1	153, 154
1551-2	5 & 6 Edw. VI, c. 3	153
1551-2	5 & 6 Edw. VI, c. 4	153
1551-2	5 & 6 Edw. VI, c. 5	141
1551-2	5 & 6 Edw. VI, c. 6	139
1551-2	5 & 6 Edw. VI, c. 9	153
1551-2	5 & 6 Edw. VI, c. 14	140, 141,146
1551-2	5 & 6 Edw. VI, c. 25	119, 132, 142
1552-3	7 Edw. VI, c. 5	146
1552-3	7 Edw. VI, c. 7	140
1553	1 Mary, st. 2, c. 2	153, 154
1553	1 Mary, st. 2, c. 3	130
1553	1 Mary, st. 2, c. 12	130
1554-5	1 & 2 Philip & Mary, c. 2	139
1554-5	1 & 2 Philip & Mary, c. 3	154
1554-5	1 & 2 Philip & Mary, c. 4	151
1554-5	1 & 2 Philip & Mary, c. 5	139
1554-5	1 & 2 Philip & Mary, c. 13	133
1554-5	1 & 2 Philip & Mary, c. 14	139
1555	2 & 3 Philip & Mary, c. 3	141
1555	2 & 3 Philip & Mary, c. 5	150, 151
1555	2 & 3 Philip & Mary, c. 8	156, 157, 194, 250
1555	2 & 3 Philip & Mary, c. 9	144
1555	2 & 3 Philip & Mary, c. 10	133
1555	2 & 3 Philip & Mary, c. 11	140
1555	2 & 3 Philip & Mary, c. 16	140, 147, 300
1558-9	1 Eliz., c. 1	200
1558-9	1 Eliz., c. 2	154, 173, 200
1558-9	1 Eliz., c. 13	196
1558-9	1 Eliz., c. 16	130, 172
1562-3	5 Eliz., c. 1	201

1562-3	5 Eliz., c. 3		188
1562-3	5 Eliz., c. 4		173, 197-8
1562-3	5 Eliz., c. 5		196
1562-3	5 Eliz., c. 7		197
1562-3	5 Eliz., c. 12		142
1562-3	5 Eliz., c. 13		195, 250
1562-3	5 Eliz., c. 14		131, 173
1571	13 Eliz., c. 2		201-2
1571	13 Eliz., c. 13		142, 196, 198
1571	13 Eliz., c. 19		197
1571	13 Eliz., c. 25		132, 173
1572	14 Eliz., c. 5	Act for the Punishment of Vagabonds and for the Relief of the Poor and Impotent	188-91, 194
1575-6	18 Eliz., c. 3		91, 173, 190, 191, 193
1575-6	18 Eliz., c. 10		195
1580-1	23 Eliz., c. 1		173, 202
1580-1	23 Eliz., c. 10		172
1584-5	27 Eliz., c. 13		123
1584-5	27 Eliz., c. 14		173, 196
1584-5	27 Eliz., c. 29		190
1586-7	29 Eliz., c. 5		190
1588-9	31 Eliz., c. 7		168, 199, 200
1588-9	31 Eliz., c. 10		190
1588-9	31 Eliz., c. 11		130, 172
1588-9	31 Eliz., c. 12		172
1592-3	35 Eliz., c. 1		173, 202
1592-3	35 Eliz., c. 2		202
1592-3	35 Eliz., c. 4		192
1597-8	39 Eliz., c. 2		190, 191, 196
1597-8	39 Eliz., c. 3		138, 191
1597-8	39 Eliz., c. 4		172, 173, 175
1597-8	39 Eliz., c. 16		173
1597-8	39 Eliz., c. 17		192

1597-8	39 Eliz., c. 20		173, 196
1598-8	39 Eliz., c. 21		192
1601	43 Eliz., c. 2		191, 248
1601	43 Eliz., c. 3		190, 192, 193
1601	43 Eliz., c. 7		172
1601	43 Eliz., c. 10		196
1603-4	1 James I, c. 27		241
1609-10	7 James I, c. 4		241
1609-10	7 James I, c. 5		242
1609-10	7 James I, c. 11		241
1623-4	21 James I, c. 12		242
1625	1 Charles II, c. 1		241
1627	3 Charles I, c. 1		241
1627	3 Charles I, c. 24		142
1642-60	Acts and Ordinances of the Interregnum		225-6, 250-1
1662	14 Charles II, c. 4	Act of Uniformity	232, 233
1662	14 Charles II, c. 2		299
1662	14 Charles II, c. 12	Settlement and Removal Act	247, 271, 298
1662	14 Charles II, c. 6		252
1662	14 Charles II, c. 10		243
1662	14 Charles II, c. 12		241
1663	15 Charles II, c. 1		252-3
1664	15 Charles II, c. 13		243
1664	16 Charles II, c. 3		243
1664	16 Charles II, c. 4	Conventicle Act	233
1664	17 Charles II, c. 2		209, 233
1670	22 Charles II, c. 1		233-4
1670	22 Charles II, c. 12		252, 299
1670-1	22 & 23 Charles II, c. 7		240
1670-1	22 & 23 Charles II, c. 20		240
1673	Test Act		235, 237
	29 Charles II, c. 7		234-5
1688	1 William & Mary,	Great Seal Act, c. 21	120, 123
1690	2 William & Mary sess. 2, c. 8		299

1692	4 William & Mary, c. 24	136
1695-6	7 & 8 William III, c. 32	260
1696-7	8 & 9 William III, c. 17	299
1698	10 William III, c. 5	270
1698	10 William III, c. 12	242
1698-9	11 William III, c. 23	270
1702	1 Anne, c. 2	181
1713	12 Anne, st. 1, c. 18	271, 298
1715	Riot Act	99, 129
1755	28 Geo. II, c. 32	270
1765	6 Geo. III, c. 34	270
1788	28 Geo. III, c. 65	270
1798	38 Geo. III, c. 58	94
1805	45 Geo. III, c. 59	100
1821	Act	272
1832	Reform Act	274
1834	Central Criminal Court Act	293, 297, 300-1
1835	Municipal Corporations Act	79, 84, 100-1, 264-5, 268, 273-8, 282-3, 287, 294
1836	Durham (County Palatime) Act	83, 85, 86
1839	County District Constabulary Act	80, 99
1846	County Courts Act (12 & 13 Vict., c. 69)	264
1849	Indictable Offences Act (12 & 13 Vict., c. 70)	294
1849	Summary Jurisdiction Act	294
1849	London Reform Act (11 & 12 Vict., c. 43)	131, 294
1851	14 & 15 Vict., c. 55	297
1854	15 & 16 Vict., c. 50	46, 270
1873-5	Supreme Court of Judicature Acts	86, 101, 301
1877	Crown Office Act	276
1877	Prisons Act	299
1882	Municipal Corporations Act	84, 118, 268, 276, 282, 285
1886	Oxford University (Justices) Act	118
1888	Local Government Act	25, 293
1889	Palatime Court of Durham Act	86

1901	Demise of the Crown Act	181
1910	Licensing (Consolidation) Act	299
1920	Mayor's and City of London Court Act	293
1925	Criminal Justice Act	301
1933	Children and Young Persons Act	295
1933	Local Government Act	282
1938	Administration of Justice (Miscellaneous Provisions) Act	104
1949	Justices of the Peace Act	101, 104, 264-5, 279, 283-6, 295, 297
1956	Criminal Justice Administration Act	278
1962	Criminal Justice Administration Act	278
1963	Children and Young Persons Act	277
1964	City of London (Courts) Act	293
1968	Justices of the Peace Act	33, 286, 297
1971	Courts Act	79, 86, 104-5, 279, 280, 287, 294, 298, 301
1972	Local Government Act	86, 287, 297
1973	Administration of Justice Act	79, 105, 287, 297
1987	Crossbows Act	143

INTRODUCTION

"THE COMMISSION OF THE PEACE has always been regarded by Continental writers as amongst the most unique and distinctive features of the English Constitution."[1] It is "perhaps the most distinctively English part of our governmental organization."[2] The office of Justice of the Peace was conceived and developed in England and its history has been closely interwoven with that of English society for the past 800 years. In the course of time it was transported with varying degrees of success to other territories, both within the British Isles and in other parts of the world. Nowhere except in Wales did it become deep-rooted or maintain so vigorous a growth as it did in the land of its origin where, in spite of striking changes - social, political, economic and governmental - the importance of the Justices of the Peace has been inevitable and omnipresent.

The Justices of the Peace did not make a sudden appearance upon the stage of history. Their story is one of gradual development, starting with tentative, spasmodic experiments in methods of maintaining order in times of crisis. The process was then expanded to meet further needs arising from new economic, administrative and judicial problems. In its early stages the office developed from a mixing of diverse ingredients, some emanating from the prevailing conditions in England at the time, while others reflected earlier institutions dating back to the Anglo-Saxons.

It is important to view the justices against the background of the times in which they lived and worked. Their roots lie deep in the history of the people of England. Their creation and development were the outcome of political, social and economic conditions which prevailed at each stage in their history. The earliest embryo of the Justice of the Peace is to be found towards the end of the twelfth century in the appointment of certain officers whose primary function was to preserve order during exceptional times of crisis. The term "Justice of the Peace" was not, however, established until nearly two centuries later when it was applied to the holders of an office which, in response to new, unprecedented circumstances, involved judicial and administrative as well as purely police functions. From then onwards the justices were subject to a continuing process of adaptation and adjustment to meet the challenge of the frequently changing climate in which they lived and performed their duties. This constant moving with the times ensured their continued survival for a further 600 years to

1. ELG, The Parish and the County, p. 294.
2. F.W. Maitland, *Collected Papers,* ed., H.A.L. Fisher, Cambridge Univ. Press, II, 1911, p. 470.

the present day.

A notable feature of the system was that it was based upon the voluntary, part-time, unpaid service of the landed gentry in the shires and of prominent citizens in the towns. They were influential men with local ties and involvement who, for the most part, took a close personal interest in the affairs of their area and of its population. In this respect they represented a movement away from feudal traditions and they were in marked contrast to the centralized royal bureaucracy which was established in other countries.

The history of the Justices of the Peace in the shires is distinct from, although similar to, that of the officers who performed equivalent functions in the boroughs. The two need to be treated separately until the nineteenth century when they were merged in the course of local government reform.

The birth of the Keepers of the Peace, who were the precursors of the justices, coincided with the emergence of a new, influential middle class, composed of the landed gentry and of the leading citizens of the towns, from whom they and the justices who succeeded them were drawn. They were a section of the community which had been involved for some time in the management of local affairs and their interests lay in loyalty to the King, who could generally rely upon them for support against baronial aggrandisement and for the maintenance of law and order in their localities. The office of the keepers and of the justices was compatible with English tradition with its emphasis on the unpaid service of responsible members of the local community. The fact that an effective source of such citizens was readily to hand in the increasingly powerful middle class placed the seal upon the successful establishment and subsequent development of the system. Had this ingredient not been present it is reasonable to suppose that the English phenomenon of amateur judges and administrators would never have become established; still less that it would have survived the vicissitudes of so long a period. This supposition is supported by experience in other territories. Justices of the Peace on the English model were introduced into Scotland in 1609 when the Crowns of the two countries were united, but the system never flourished there as it did south of the Border, and this seems to have been due partly to the absence of an effective middle class between the clansmen and their chiefs in the Highlands or between the nobles and the peasants in the Lowlands.

Although the status and power of the justices varied considerably from time to time, it is true to say that throughout most of their history they played a prominent and, for a period, highly influential role, not only in the administration of justice, but perhaps to an even greater degree in the social and political history of the country. The rudiments of local government were in the hands of the justices by the fourteenth century and by the Tudor period virtually the whole of the administrative machinery of the country was operated through them. From this time there was also a steady increase in their jurisdiction out of Quarter Sessions, often requiring the presence of only two justices. Until the Commonwealth, when they suffered a temporary eclipse, they were subject to a varying amount of supervision and discipline by the Privy Council, but after the Restoration they became in effect the rulers of the land, generally unaffected by government intervention. Not only were they the undisputed governors of their local territories, but large numbers also sat in Parliament and were prominent on the national stage where they were in the forefront of the newly developing party political system. In this national sphere they played a leading role in the formulation of government policy. This close association between Parliament and local administration through the justices was without parallel in any other country.

The eighteenth century saw a decline, although this was more pronounced in the urban areas than in the rest of the country. In London, where the deterioration had had the most serious consequences, the justices were largely replaced by a new system of full-time, professional magistrates. Nevertheless, when in the nineteenth century almost all the administrative and executive functions of the justices were transferred to new, elected local government authorities, these changes were inspired more by the prevailing spirit of reform than by any general dissatisfaction with the lay magistrates. During this period the justices ceased, for the most part, to be involved in two of the three spheres of responsibility in which they had previously played the major role. As peace-keepers they had been responsible since the Middle Ages for the apprehension and prosecution of criminals. This function was transferred to the new police authorities, although the justices retained a direct interest through their representation on the standing joint committees. In the area of local government almost all their work, except for licensing, was assumed by the new, elected borough and county councils.

Some contemporary authorities in the nineteenth century doubted whether the Justices of the Peace would survive the amputation of their governmental and peace-keeping functions. These doubts proved to be unjustified. Having been deprived of their administrative and police work, the justices devoted themselves to their judicial functions which, from the last quarter of the century, were steadily expanded. This led to a great number of indictable offences which were previously triable only with a jury being brought within the summary jurisdiction of Petty Sessions. Even in London, the powers which had been removed from the lay justices when stipendiary magistrates were introduced were restored and extended in the mid-twentieth century. Suggestions were occasionally made for the replacement of the justices by a universal system of professional magistrates, but none of these proposals received serious support. Instead, the duties and responsibilities of the justices continued to increase under successive governments. The linking of the ordinary citizen with the administration of justice was part of the national heritage deeply ingrained in the way of life of the English people which could not be uprooted.

The process continued of adapting the magistrates to a rapidly changing environment and in 1948 a Royal Commission made a number of far-reaching recommendations for raising the standard of those appointed justices and for improving their efficiency and that of their courts. Almost all these recommendations were implemented and there followed an impressive improvement in every aspect of the justices' work which was reflected in greater approval by Parliament and the public and resulted in still further increases in the justices' burden.

The system of Justices of the Peace was a peculiarly English institution. Created in England by the Plantagenets, it was extended to Wales by Henry VIII in the sixteenth century as part of his policy of establishing control over that country. Soon afterwards the same process was followed in Ireland, though far less successfully. At the beginning of the seventeenth century King James, with a view to strengthening royal authority, introduced Justices of the Peace into Scotland, where again they did not thrive to the extent that they did south of the Border. Finally, in the seventeenth and eighteenth centuries the system was introduced into other lands, usually in the wake of colonization, but nowhere did this achieve the remarkable results that were manifest in England and Wales. Even in these two countries there has been considerable diversity in the system as it operated in different areas, and it is difficult to give a precise and formalized picture of the office as a whole. In addition to the peculiarities of the London area and of the counties palatine there have been variations between many of the other counties, between boroughs and between urban and rural areas. Even today, there are some marked differences in the composition of urban and rural benches and in the way in which they perform their duties, notably in the treatment of offenders. Again, as will be seen, the Welsh experience revealed certain distinctive patterns as the system developed in the Principality. An attempt has been made in the following pages to embrace the whole of this varied patchwork in so far as this is reasonably possible.

There are few surviving institutions of any kind which can claim a continuous history of at least 800 years. Fewer still have had a profound influence for an appreciable time upon the communities in which they operated. It cannot be claimed that the influence of the JPs has invariably been for the good; on the contrary there have been periods when it was positively retrograde and disruptive. Yet the behaviour of this remarkable body of persons is always of interest in that it reflects the society in which they operated. Moreover, some of what are generally regarded as the more attractive features of the way of life in the people of the land of their origin have owed much to the peculiar English system of Justices of the Peace.

PREFACE

MY INTEREST in the history of the Justices of the Peace began while I was an undergraduate at Oxford and heard some remarks by Sir William Holdsworth, author of the *History of English Law* and Vinerian Professor at the University. He commented upon the important role which justices had played throughout many centuries and he drew attention to what he clearly regarded as a regrettable lacuna in that there was no comprehensive history of the Justices of the Peace and their work from their origins to the present day.

It was indeed the case that there was no such work existing at that time, and it remains largely true to the present day, although there have long been signs of increasing interest in the subject. The history of the Justices of the Peace has been neglected save in so far as it has been accorded an ancillary role in the discussion of other principal issues. Until recently there has been remarkably little original research, considering the importance of the subject, and even now the work which is being done is on a minor scale.

When Holdsworth made his comments in 1932 the most comprehensive work on the history of the justices was C.A. Beard's *The Office of Justice of the Peace in England,* which had been published in 1904, but this was based entirely upon limited written sources and it did not take the story beyond 1600. Moreover, Beard made little reference to the peculiar position of the boroughs and the counties palatine, and he did not touch upon the translation of the system into territories beyond England. There were earlier writers such as Gneist, Reeve, Pike and Stephen but their works were based on incomplete information. H.M. Cam's admirable studies do not cover all aspects of the subject, while in Blackstone the justices are ancillary to the main theme. Sidney and Beatrice Webb covered some parts of the area very thoroughly in their various works but only during a period of two hundred years, and here again their study was limited to England and Wales; moreover they, like many others, based their conclusions upon limited and sometimes biased evidence. Before the Webbs there were numerous textbooks for justices during the sixteenth, seventeenth and eighteenth centuries, beginning with Marowe's *Reading* of 1503 and the *Boke* of 1506 and continuing until Burn's *The Justice of the Peace and the Parish Officer* whose last edition was published in 1869. It has been estimated that no less than 57 editions or issues of treatises for justices were printed between 1506 and 1599 alone. Many of these give a detailed contemporary account of the justices' functions and they are indispensable to the historian, but they contain little about the personnel of the commissions and they provide only a limited picture of the environment in which the justices operated. Holdsworth's own *History of English Law* gives an excellent account of their functions in so far as they fall within the framework of legal administration, but when dealing with the magistracy he was obliged to concentrate on certain areas only of the broader JP landscape.

The most scholarly works that were written during the first part of the twentieth century on the Justices of the Peace were those of Bertha Putnam. Professor Putnam, like her colleague, Nellie Neilson, was on the faculty of Mount Holyoke College in the United States, but both spent long periods researching medieval records in England. They belonged to a new generation of distinguished American scholars who became engaged in the study of English medieval history. After the publication in 1908 of her first book *The Enforcement of the Statutes of Labourers during the First Decade after the Black Death 1349-1359* (Columbia University Studies), Miss Putnam devoted most of the rest of her life to the Justices of the Peace from the transformation of the keepers into justices between 1327 and 1380 until the end of the sixteenth century. She indulged in a vast amount of original research in the course of which she opened up entirely new fields and made a number of important discoveries which included the identification of indictments and Assize rolls recording sessions of the early keepers and justices. She also carried out a detailed examination of the manuals for justices published in the fifteenth and sixteenth centuries which I have mentioned above. Almost all of Miss Putnam's treaties, however, relate to the period before the reign of Elizabeth, and moreover, as she herself readily admits, there was still much material which she did not have time to explore. She was therefore unable to observe some essential factors such as the inclusion of the Assize justices in the Commissions of the Peace from a much earlier date than she supposed; a matter of considerable substance as it weakens to some extent the supposition of rivalry between the lawyers and the early Justices of the Peace, which has always been assumed to have been a key issue in the fourteenth century.

A notable development has occurred during the past 50 years when there have been far more attempts than before to conduct detailed studies of specific matters in certain periods. This can be attributed partly to a keener interest in the research of medieval manuscripts but it is also due to the much greater availability of material, especially from the seventeenth century onwards. Many original manuscripts can now be examined for the first time and these, together with a perusal of the relevant statutes, give an accurate though confused picture of the justices and their functions from the late sixteenth to the nineteenth century. A feature of this new expansion of interest is that although some of the recent monographs have been written by British scholars, such as Lionel Glassey's *Politics and the Appointment of Justices of the Peace 1675-1720,* the majority of the authors, like Beard and Putnam themselves, were American. We are indebted to them for a number of superb works published during the past 20 years on the justices in the sixteenth to eighteenth centuries, especially those by Thomas Barnes, J.S. Cockburn, J.H. Gleason and Norma Landau. Perhaps the fact that the United States is the land of my mother and her forbears and the one in which I received my early education is accountable, at least partly, for my own fascination with the subject.

My interest in the Justices of the Peace started to lapse after I began to practise at the Bar, in spite of sometimes being on my feet in magistrates' courts, and I felt no inclination to embark upon a profound study of their past history. Such a task would obviously have been formidable and I had no time to devote to the essential research. Suddenly the scene changed dramatically when, near the end of the Second World War, my service in the army ceased abruptly and at the same time I was forced to abandon all hope of being fit enough to return to my practice. The dismal prospect was unexpectedly brightened by an invitation to join the small, personal, legal staff of the Lord Chancellor. Almost from the start I became involved *inter alia* in the appointment and removal of Justices of the Peace, and my entrée coincided with the establishment of the Royal Commission on Justices of the Peace of 1946-48 which was to lead to fundamental changes in the office of magistrate. From then onwards, for some thirty years, there were no innovations or variations in the magisterial system in the United Kingdom, whether statutory or administrative, in which I was not involved to a greater or lesser extent. During the whole of this time I was responsible, as Secretary of Commissions, for the Justices of the Peace throughout England and Wales and for shorter periods in Scotland and Northern Ireland. To enable the Secretary of Commissions to understand the problems facing his flock it was customary for him to serve as a justice himself, and I was therefore appointed a magistrate soon after I assumed office. I sat regularly for the next four decades and in the course of time became chairman of both Petty Sessions and Quarter Sessions. Appropriately, I was finally compelled to retire under the age limit which I had been instrumental in introducing. Somewhat earlier I had left the Lord Chancellor's Office and served for a term as Chairman of the Council of the Magistrates' Association of England and Wales and also as President of the Commonwealth Magistrates' and Judges' Association.

I make these immodest references to my career not with a view to impressing the reader but to explain why I not only became absorbed in the theme of Justices of the Peace but was also forced to the

xxviii   *History of the Justices of the Peace*   Vol. I

conclusion that I had a duty to record the fruits of my unique experience and opportunities. In addition to knowledge acquired from service in the Lord Chancellor's Office I found numerous papers relating to justices packed in the Victoria Tower and in the cellars of the House of Lords which had not as yet been examined for historical purposes, and in some cases had not been viewed at all for more than a generation. For some time after the War there was also a vast amount of manuscript material which was still stored away in old country houses, many of which I had occasion to visit in my official capacity. I am deeply indebted to my many hosts throughout the United Kingdom, especially the Lords Lieutenant of counties, not only for their generous hospitality but also for showing me so much fascinating material which had been accumulated by their ancestors. At the same time I also came to know the county officers who were responsible for the keeping of local archives, and they too could not have been more helpful in drawing my attention to relevant records. These exceptional opportunities continued though on a lesser scale when, after ceasing to work for the Lord Chancellor, I travelled the country as Chairman of the Magistrates' Association; while my search for enlightenment among the atavistic magistracies in overseas territories was facilitated by the assistance I received from those I met through the Commonwealth Magistrates' and Judges' Association.

In spite of the opportunities with which I was presented during my perambulations of Great Britain, there still remained much material stored away in private collections which I never saw; but here again I was fortunate in being able to benefit from the enormous opening-up of resources which began soon after the War. Until then, apart from what could be gleaned from the private collections, the historian was obliged to rely upon limited sources, mostly Parliamentary documents, and in the later period, pamphlets, periodicals and anecdotal evidence contained in works of fiction. Very little information was available on the detailed operation of magisterial work both in and out of court. The revolutionary change which took place after World War II was due to the establishment and rapid development of the county Record Offices in which archives of county affairs were assembled, calendared and made easily available to the researcher. These now include invaluable records of the justices' functions, particularly those performed in Quarter Sessions, and later in Petty Sessions. A number of the offices have issued useful guides to their sessions records with full and helpful introductions. Some of these are highly informative, such as the volumes of Warwick County Records, edited by S.C. Ratcliff and H.C. Johnson, which contain numerous citations from Quarter Sessions' order books and indictment books in the seventeenth century. In addition to sessions' records and formal public documents, county offices have become the depositories for a multitude of other classes of papers both private and official, including ecclesiastical and manor court records, many of which give an intriguing insight into contemporary administration of justice. The records of Petty Sessions give a vivid picture of the every-day life of the community and in themselves constitute a social history of the times. Additions are still being made to these county collections as bundles of papers are found in private houses or in the vaults of solicitors' offices; the latter have been particularly prolific in manor court rolls which the lord of the manor had long ago deposited with his lawyer.

A major difficulty which still faces the historian is that a substantial quantity of manuscript material remains in private hands while what has found its way to the county Record Offices is scattered throughout the country. There is no national record of all manuscript material, and the researcher needs to spend an appreciable amount of time in each county in order to carry out a complete job. Moreover, the county offices contain few early documents - theirs are mostly from the seventeenth century onwards and none before the sixteenth, though within this period they cover a wide area and include calendars, certificates, indictments, jury lists, precepts, petitions, presentments, recognizances and various memoranda. Early manuscripts must be sought in the national institutions, particularly the Public Record Office, the British Museum and the British and Bodleian Libraries. The PRO have stacks of medieval documents which still need exploration. They hold numerous records of early Commissions of the Peace, and also earlier Commissions of Labourers which are of particular interest because a study of the origins of the Justices of the Peace requires an examination of their predecessors, the Justices of Labourers and the Keepers of the Peace in the twelfth and thirteenth centuries. The lists of Commissions of the Peace and of the numbers of justices during their first three hundred years which are shown in the Appendices in vol. III are all taken from the original documents in the PRO. The Office also includes among its essential manuscripts writs, indictments and Assize and gaol delivery rolls for the fourteenth and much of the fifteenth century, but the practice which arose later of destroying files which were no longer required caused records to become fragmentary from 1460. From 1361 until the seventeenth century the appointments of Justices of the Peace are normally to be found in the patent rolls, the *dorses* of which contain many formal copies of commissions, although there are some complications which are explained by Bertha Putnam in an article published in 1927 in the *Bulletin of the Institute of Historical Research*. They are in chronological order which makes discovery of the places for which they are issued a rather laborious task, but there are five lists of justices in alphabetical order of counties between the reigns of Henry VIII and James II (PRO ref. C 193/12). Lists of justices' names, showing which were members of the *Quorum*, are given in the *Libri Pacis* which are to be found in many collections both public and private. The *Libri*, however, most of which are for years between 1558 and 1688, do not contain the commissions. When one comes to the eighteenth century the Crown Office docket books, which run from 1595 to 1949 in 22 volumes, seem to be the only source for the commissions, which were in Latin until 1733 except during the Interregnum. During the first two centuries of their history the commissions were obscure and confusing because there were frequent changes of form and the wording often did not comply with the statutes currently in force. In the Middle Ages the Crown, when issuing commissions, did not regard itself as being strictly bound by Parliamentary legislation, and the documents reflected the whim of the King and his ministers. It also seems to have been quite common for the name of a justice which appeared in a commission to be omitted from a subsequent commission purely in error. Moreover, in addition to the commissions, extra duties were often imposed on the justices by letters close and letters patent. Further, the commissions were in general terms and were interpreted differently by the justices themselves in different areas and at different times. It is not surprising to find therefore that the early justices sometimes acted beyond the powers which the commissions were intended to confer.

In addition to the obvious printed sources such as *Statutes of the Realm,* Rolls of Parliament and the State Papers which contain numerous instructions to the justices, one needs to study many other documents particularly the pipe rolls, the sessions rolls and the order books. Some of these, however, are misleading in that they depict only part of the picture. The order books and indictment rolls, for example, give the names of justices attending the sessions but often do not include all those who were present. The pipe rolls, which extend from the twelfth century to 1832, contain the annual records of the sheriffs for the payment of the justices' wages, but for one reason or another many of those who came to sessions were not included. Moreover there was no entry in a pipe roll if no wages were paid to the justices, which seems to have occurred fairly frequently. In Cumberland and Westmorland there is no record of wages being paid before the sixteenth century. In addition to the pipe rolls some records of wages paid to Justices and Clerks of the Peace are contained in indentures which are among the sheriffs' accounts. Apart from these the estreats of fines and amercements paid into the Exchequer often contain the names of the justices who were present at each session and some of these survive from the thirteenth century.

As to the work that the justices performed, quantities of court records survive even from the early years, but they are severely limited in the information they provide, references to each case being confined to a brief statement of the facts and the court's decision. Fortunately this can often be supplemented from incidental sources such as *The Paston Letters*, but it must be recognized that this is circumstantial evidence which has to be treated with caution.

When I embarked, perhaps rashly, upon my project I was astonished at the depth of sources still unfathomed, and it was clear that I could not hope to research them all even with assistance. I have therefore concentrated upon the essential elements and upon an explanation of the many diverse factors which have played a significant part in the formation and development of the system, such as the traditional involvement of laymen in the administration of justice, the close relationship between Quarter Sessions and Assizes in early times and the remarkable ability of the lay justices to adapt to a constantly changing world. The history of the Justices of the Peace in England, and to a large extent in Wales, is closely related to almost all aspects of the history of the country and its people, and I have therefore endeavoured to place the facts in perspective within their contemporary environment.

There has been severe censure of the Justices of the Peace at many points in their history, especially during the eighteenth century. Much of the criticism could be justified by modern standards, but it is essential that these matters be related to the environment of particular times and places. If judged against the background of the ages in which they lived it seems doubtful whether any other contemporary groups or institutions would have proved to be more creditable or efficient. Although there were numbers of individual justices who were obviously unsuitable for the office, there were others who set a much higher standard than most of the rest of the population. Throughout much of their history the Justices of the Peace probably provided the most efficient system of local government and administration of justice to be found in any contemporary country.

Until now little attention has been paid to Justices of the Peace beyond England and Wales, yet there are many territories within the British Isles and further afield where they were introduced and where they survived at least for a time, in each case with interesting variations, though never as successfully as in the country of their origin. I have tried in vol. III to deal at some length with the history of the office in these other countries, though it has often proved difficult to find reliable sources. In Ireland, for example, there are few records of the earlier periods, but in the United States on the other hand, where remarkably little attention seems to have been given by

American scholars to the justices in their own country, a wealth of material awaits attention. It was not my original intention to trace the history of the Justices of the Peace beyond Britain, but I was soon convinced that the story would be incomplete if I did not record and comment upon the varied incarnations which appeared in other parts of the world from the Atlantic seaboards to the islands of the Pacific. This became particularly apparent to me when attending legal conferences in Commonwealth countries and the United States, when I had occasion to discuss the subject with practitioners, academic lawyers and members of the judiciary. I therefore spent as much time as I could researching in those countries which seemed to have the richest material. I would have made little progress had it not been for the help and massive encouragement I received from the citizens of each territory. The JPs who are to be found in parts of the world outside the British Isles are often thought to be fossilized replicas of those operating in England at the time when the system was exported, but by no means is this invariably the case, and in some instances the intervening history of the justices presents an interesting picture of developing nations.

In England itself little has been done to describe the peculiar facets of the magistracy in the boroughs and in the counties palatine. Attention has been focused almost entirely upon the justices in the ordinary counties and it is only in the local histories of London, Lancaster and some other areas that one finds any reference to the divergent systems which developed elsewhere. Yet there have been people performing the duties of justices in boroughs for almost as long as they have done in the counties, and by the eighteenth century they outnumbered the county magistrates. I have therefore sought to give due weight to these heterogeneous siblings by describing them in separate chapters.

The picture which now emerges differs markedly from that which was presented to historians even at the beginning of the present century, and still more enlightenment may follow with further research. Perhaps some aspects of the earlier history which remain clouded by legend will be clarified, but it seems probable that, whatever else emerges, it will relate only to detail and will not affect the overall concept as it now appears to have been established.

A conspicuous feature of the magistracy in England and Wales today is that it is composed almost entirely of men and women with no legal qualification. They also act part-time and without remuneration. One tends therefore to think of Justices of the Peace purely as amateurs, but this has been far from apt since the introduction of modern compulsory training, and although it might have been applied with justification to their predecessors during the previous two centuries, the earlier justices were probably rather more professional than we tend to think. Certainly a far greater number of justices in Tudor and Stuart times had studied law than is the case now.

I have been greatly encouraged by the large number of today's justices who have expressed a keen desire for a work embracing all aspects of their long and fascinating history, and it is my hope that many of them, both in the United Kingdom and in other countries, will read this work with interest, pleasure and perhaps some benefit. The peculiar system which operates today is part of a continuing process and, if they are to understand it fully, those who are responsible for its operation should know why and how it was introduced and later developed along its own unique lines, how it worked throughout the centuries and how all this led to the office and functions of Justices of the Peace as these exist at present. Previous history also emphasizes the need for the present system to move with the times and to contend with the problems of the modern world. With this in mind I have tried to minimize technical legal discussion - though this is unavoidable at certain crucial points - and to make the work readable to lay magistrates, while at the same time providing useful material for the scholar and for the authors of cognate studies. Intrinsic to this collimation has been an attempt to provide a consummate, encyclopaedic fund of referential material for those engaged in further research.

I have made a few adjustments to satisfy potential readers in other countries. It is for this reason that I have cited enactments in regnal years to a greater extent than I would otherwise have done, because I was told in some countries that the modern practice of referring to calendar years, short titles and chapters would present difficulties. Overseas friends also drew my attention to a number of other ways in which I could make the work more comprehensible to their compatriots than is usually the case with authors in England. I have endeavoured to meet these points, and it is for this reason that I have included some explanatory comments which may seem superfluous to English readers.

Apart from the first Commissions of the Peace, I have used English translations of most early documents instead of the original Latin or French. In the case of statutes the translation is that given in *Statutes of the Realm*. Quotations from English documents of later periods are in the contemporary spelling. A number of the words I have used may be spelt in different ways. This applies particularly to the names of persons and places. In these cases I have adopted the spelling which appears to be in most general use at the present time. My use of capital letters is unlikely to meet with wide approval. In earlier times it was customary to begin almost all nouns with a capital whereas it is now fashionable to use lower case even for the names of courts. I have attempted to follow the modern trend but have digressed where this seemed desirable. My reasons for my choice of capitals as well as of words and spelling may seem unconvincing, but I have tried, after consultation with a number of authorities, to adopt a practice which is likely to be acceptable to the majority of readers. I have also endeavoured to be consistent, though this is not always easy as T.E. Lawrence showed in his preface to *Seven Pillars of Wisdom.* It may be recalled that he tells how, when he wrote *Revolt in the Desert,* his publisher pointed out that he had spelt the name of his camel differently throughout the book, to which he replied simply "She was a splendid beast."

Although history deals with generalizations I have, with a view to bringing the story to life, included details of some personalities, and I have also illustrated major developments by citing specific instances.

I have been most fortunate in the help I have received from a large number of people including many eminent scholars in various parts of the world. Without their generous and often enthusiastic assistance and guidance this work would have been impossible. I express my gratitude, albeit inadequately, in my Acknowledgements.

Blockley, Gloucestershire,
December, 1990.

ACKNOWLEDGEMENTS

I HAVE BEEN EXTREMELY fortunate in the vast number of persons and institutions in the United Kingdom and in other countries who have helped me in this work. Available space allows me to mention only a few.

Among those in England I am deeply grateful to the staff of the Public Record Office, especially to Dr Roy Hunnisett, Dr John Post and Dr David Crook whose advice, particularly on the medieval period, was invaluable. I am also grateful to the long-suffering staffs of a number of libraries and of almost all County Record Offices, especially to Mr K. Hall, County Archivist of Lancashire, Mr David Smith, Archivist of my own county of Gloucester and Mrs Christine Woodland, Assistant Archivist of Warwickshire, and also Mrs Juliet Banks of the City of London Record Office. I owe a great deal to many English scholars, notably Professor John Baker of St Catherine's College, Cambridge, who took the risk of entrusting me with the original lists which he had compiled of justices serving between 1450 and 1509. I received much guidance on the peculiarities of the county palatine of Durham from Dr Constance Fraser who is the leading expert on the courts in that area. Professor Alan Harding of Liverpool University has kindly allowed me to quote from his works on the Keepers of the Peace and the law courts of medieval England. In studying the Lancastrian justices I have been greatly assisted by my old friend and former colleague, Sir Robert Somerville, the distinguished historian of the Duchy. I am also grateful to Mr Roger Morgan and Dr David Menhennet, Librarians of the House of Lords and House of Commons libraries, where I continued to spend much time after leaving my office in the Houses of Parliament. I also thank Mr Richard Grobler, Deputy Secretary of Commissions for England and Wales, and Mr. Geoffrey Norman, the Lord Chancellor's Training Officer, for enabling me to have access to current documents in the Lord Chancellor's Department, particularly the detailed lists of justices on each commission. To Mr Stephen Pyke of Blockley, Gloucestershire, I owe thanks for devoting much of his time to assisting me in reading proofs.

When I embarked upon this work I did not appreciate the amount of research that would be required in order to do justice to the history of the magistrates in the other countries of the British Isles beyond the boundaries of England. I encountered a formidable task, not least in discovering original sources, and I could not possibly have covered the ground without the assistance and support of a host of helpers. I must mention in particular Professor Beverley Smith of the University College of Wales, and also Dr Dafydd Jenkins and Mrs Auriol Watkin.

In Scotland I was extremely fortunate to be advised by Professor Sir Thomas Smith until his recent death, and I also received guidance from Dr Athol Murray, Keeper of the Scottish Record Office, while Mr Ian Wilson, Secretary of Commissions for Scotland, kindly supplied me with essential statistics. A study of the Irish justices proved to be a particularly formidable task which I could not have accomplished without the most able help, notably from Professor R.B. MacDowell and from Professor W.N. Osborough of the University of Dublin. I also received much useful advice from Professor Geoffrey Hand, at present Barber Professor of Jurisprudence at the University of Birmingham but an eminent authority on the courts of Ireland. From Northern Ireland I was given valuable guidance by Professor Desmond Greer of the Queen's University, Belfast. Apart from the Manuals, very little work seems to have been done previously on the justices in Ireland and it was necessary to research numbers of archives and to peruse reports of Parliamentary committees and debates and other documents. Much valuable research was carried out for me by Mr Tomás Clancy of the Irish Bar.

One of my most moving experiences has been to witness the enormous interest that has been shown in my work by many distinguished scholars in other countries. I was overwhelmed by the response I received to my inquiries in the United States. I am especially grateful to Professor Janelle Greenerg of the University of Pittsburgh, to Professors Charles Donahue and Terry Fisher of Harvard and to Arthur Simpson from Oxford who is now Professor of Law at the University of Michigan. By far the greatest help of all came from Professor David Condon of George Mason University in Virginia. No words can adequately express my thanks to him for the enormous amount of research he has been good enough to do on my behalf in the former British colonies in both the United States and Canada. The enjoyment of my visits to the New England states was greatly enhanced by the hospitality and help I received from my niece, Dr Jennifer Leaning, who introduced me to many of her erudite friends.

In Canada, I received generous help from Judge Sandra Oxner who, among her many activities, has spent some time in researching the early history of the courts in her country. She is also one of my colleagues on the Council of the Commonwealth Magistrates and Judges Association. I was also fortunate to receive valuable information on the Justices of the Peace in various Canadian provinces from Chief Judge S.D. Turner of Ontario and Judge J.J. Flynn of Saskatchewan, and in Nova Scotia from Judge Angus Macdonald and Mr Ronald A. Macdonald who allowed me to read proofs of his study, *The Squires of Antigonish.*

Those to whom I owe a special debt of gratitude in Australia are Professor Alex Castles, Professor of Law at the University of Adelaide, Justice Roma Mitchell of the Supreme Court of South Australia, Professor Guy Powels of Monash University and Mr R.A. Horne of the Australian Council of Justice Associations.

I am particularly grateful to Judge P.J. Trapski and to Mr G.L. Osborne, Registrar of the Royal Federation of New Zealand Justices Associations, for helping me in my inquiries into the New Zealand courts.

I am also indebted to another New Zealander, Guy Powles, for his advice regarding the territories in the Pacific - those thousands of islands scattered over millions of square miles but with certain distinct similarities.

Africa, which at first sight seemed to have nothing that was relevant to the history of lay magistrates, proved to possess forensic and social features which were of comparative interest. These were kindly brought to my notice by two friends and colleagues, Sir Bryan Roberts and Professor Anthony Allott.

The West Indies also proved to be particularly difficult for research as there were no centralized archives for the numerous island territories, but I received valuable help from the University of the West Indies, particularly from Mrs Velma Newton of the Faculty of Law library. I am also grateful to Elizabeth W. Davies of the Cayman Islands Law School for allowing me to see the outcome of her study of the legal system in the Cayman Islands and Jamaica prior to publication.

To all of these, and to the many others who have given me help, encouragement and sometimes hospitality during my travels, I offer my warmest thanks.

xxxviii

ABBREVIATIONS

AN.HIB	Analecta Hibernica
AOI	Acts and Ordinances of the Interregnum
APC	Acts of the Privy Council
APS	Acts of the Parliaments of Scotland
BIHR	Bulletin of the Institute of Historical Research
BL	British Library
Bodl.	Bodleian Library
Cal.Doc.Ire.	Calendar of Documents of Ireland
CJ	Journals of the House of Commons
CPR	Calendar of Patent Rolls
CR	County Records
CSP Dom	Calendar of State Papers, Domestic
DNB	Dictionary of National Biography
EHR	English Historical Review
ELG	English Local Government from the Revolution to the Municipal Corporation Act (*Sidney and Beatrice Webb*)
HEL	History of English Law
HMC	Historical Manuscripts Commission Reports
HLJ	Journals of the House of Lords
HLRO	House of Lords Record Office
ILTJ	Irish Law Times and Solicitors Journal
PR	Patent Roll
PRO	Public Record Office
QS	Quarter Sessions
RO	County Record Office. *Preceded by name of County*
RP	Rolls of Parliament
RPCS	Register of the Privy Council of Scotland
SRO	Scottish Record Office
SP	State Papers
TRHS	Transactions of the Royal Historical Society
VCH	Victoria History of the Counties of England

CHAPTER I

ORIGINS

*Saxon and Norman influence - Appointment of Keepers of the Peace in
times of crisis - Edict of 1195 - Development of the keepers*

Saxon and Norman influence

THERE IS NO PRECISE TIME which can be designated as the
moment when the office of Justice of the Peace first made its
appearance. The term "Justice of the Peace" began to emerge during
the first half of the fourteenth century, but this was only a stage in the
gradual evolution of an office whose origins can be traced at least as
far back as the twelfth century and whose characteristics reflect
influences from a still earlier era. Some writers have regarded the
justices as a legacy from ancient civilizations and in particular have
pointed to the classical *Eirenarcha*.[1] There is, however, no evidence to
suggest that the establishment and subsequent development of the
office in England, and subsequently in Wales, Scotland and elsewhere,
was in any way influenced by these early examples of part-time, unpaid
magistrates. The justices emerged gradually, and in a haphazard
manner, in response to a fluctuating need to deal with abnormal
conditions which prevailed in England at intervals throughout the later
Middle Ages. Their development was influenced by many factors
pertaining to this country, particularly by the Saxon tradition whereby
the principal inhabitants in each area were directly involved in the
machinery of local administration and law enforcement.

What is clear is that the justices were a natural development from
the Keepers of the Peace who preceded them. The origins of the
keepers are to' be found in the successive periods of turbulence and
unrest which occurred throughout England during the reigns of
Richard I, John and Henry III, and which led to experiments in new
methods of restoring and maintaining peace at a time when there was
increasing dissatisfaction with the existing means of dealing with
violence and lawlessness.

It is obvious from the county records of cases presented that only a
very small proportion of those who committed murder or robbery or
less serious crimes were apprehended. In the absence of any police
force, the arrest of criminals depended in most cases upon a system
whose origins are to be found before the Norman Conquest. All

1. This was the view of early Scottish writers. See William Forbes, *The Duty and Powers of the
Justices of the Peace in this Part of Great Britain called Scotland,* Edinburgh, 1707; and
Gilbert Hutcheson, *Treatise on the Offices of Justices of the Peace ... in Scotland,* Edinburgh,
1815.

persons over the age of 12 were made mutually responsible for each other's behaviour. They were formed into groups of 10 or 12, sometimes more, called tithings, and were required to take an oath which came to be known in Norman times as *Frankpledge*. Under this oath they undertook that if one of their group was suspected of having committed an offence the rest would produce him in court. If he fled, they must raise the hue and cry and capture him, under pain of a fine. The constitution of the tithings and the taking of the oaths was carried out twice a year at a meeting of the hundred court[2] presided over by the sheriff, which came to be known as the sheriff's tourn. This system, which was unimpressive even when dealing with individual malefactors, was quite unsuited to the handling of widespread outbreaks of unrest.

The officer who might have been thought to be best able to deal with these wider problems was the sheriff, the holder of an ancient office which was descended from that of the Saxon shire reeve. His position was greatly strengthened after the Conquest when the functions of the shire reeve were combined with those of the Norman *vice comtes* whose powers were considerable. The sheriff became the King's representative in the shire, responsible for collecting the royal revenue, administering the local courts, other than the feudal courts, and maintaining the peace. In 1166, Henry II's Assize of Clarendon placed responsibility for law and order in each shire squarely upon the sheriff, subject only to periodical visits by royal justices who travelled throughout the country on the King's behalf.[3] As G.M. Trevelyan observes, the sheriff was "the chief pillar of the medieval monarchy."[4] This applied only to England and there was no officer in a similar position in any other European country. The Normans did not allow feudalism to interfere with their own channels of government to the extent that occurred elsewhere.

The sheriff's normal powers and resources were not, however, sufficient to enable him to deal with widespread unrest and insurrection on a substantial scale. He might, as sometimes happened, be given a special military command with authority to deal with a particular crisis, but usually sheriffs had more than enough to occupy their time without these extra assignments. Moreover, by the twelfth century the sheriffs were falling into disfavour both with the people and with the King. The sheriff's powers of arrest and imprisonment provided him with a ready means of extortion and before the end of the century instances of false imprisonment were becoming frequent. In 1170 there was an extensive inquiry into the malpractices of sheriffs

2.   See pp. 25-6, *post*.
3.   In spite of the term "justice," these persons were at first concerned more with administration than with judicial matters.
4.   *History of England*, 1929, p. 104.

and other officials. At the same time, the King became increasingly aware that the sheriffs could not always be relied upon to further the royal interest.

The shortcomings of the existing system at a time of increasing turbulence called for new methods of maintaining order, and experiments in this direction were made at varying intervals from the latter part of the twelfth century to the beginning of the fourteenth. It should be noted, however, that although these ventures sometimes curtailed the sheriff's authority, at no time were the sheriffs supplanted. *Ad hoc* commissions *ad pacem conservandam* were issued to one or more individuals directing them to take steps to meet the current crises. These did not replace the sheriffs but supplemented them in policing the countryside. There were even occasions when a commission was directed to the sheriff himself extending his normal authority.[5]

The early commissions were issued *ad pacem conservandam* or *de custodibus pacis*, but those to whom they were directed were not given any specific title and it was not until later that they came to be known as *Custodes Pacis*. Lambard, one of the earliest writers of textbooks for justices, referred to them as "Custodians", whom he divided into two categories. In his *Eirenarcha,* first published in 1581, he commented:

"The Sheriffs I call ordinary Conservators of the Peace, because their authority was then ordinary, always one, and the same well enough knowen: But the extraordinary Conservator, as he was endowed with an higher power, so was he not ordinarily appointed, but in times of great trouble only ... And he had charge to defend the coasts and country, both from foreign and inward enemies, and might command the sheriff and all the shire to aid and assist him."[6]

Some authorities have been inclined to dismiss the "extraordinary" conservators as irrelevant to the evolution of the Justices of the Peace because they were transitory appointments with no continuing validity. They cannot, however, be ignored for they were a constituent part of the atmosphere in which the *Custodes Pacis* and later the Justices of the Peace came to life. The great troubles to which Lambard refers became so frequent that those appointed in these circumstances gradually became less extraordinary and, by the beginning of the fourteenth century, they were virtually permanent officials. The special and the ordinary commissions were analogous in many respects and they had similar objectives; indeed, the individuals to whom they were directed were sometimes the same. Reference has already been made

---

5. It was not uncommon for him to be given the additional responsibility of defending the coasts or the Marches with Scotland and Wales from invasion.
6. Lambard, *Eirenarcha,* London, 1610, pp. 16-18.

to certain sheriffs whose authority was extended by a special commission to defend a strip of coast or border area and there were instances of knights of the shire being charged with local peace-keeping operations and at the same time serving under a Commission of Gaol Delivery.

At the beginning of the period of major unrest which began soon after the death of Henry II in 1189, commissions were usually addressed to prominent individuals who were the immediate servants of the King and most of whom had already demonstrated their loyalty in some other capacity.[7] Apart from the terms of the commission, these persons often had no particular interests in the areas to which they were assigned; but a change of far-reaching significance was about to take place. Soon the pattern of government came to be based upon the services of a new class of men who had close personal ties with the areas in which they operated. These were the knights of the shire and the leading citizens in the townships. The new class of knights, who were replacing the earlier warrior knights of the Norman period, constituted a body of landed gentry who increased steadily in numbers, wealth and influence. Meanwhile the towns, most of which were only just progressing beyond the state of villages, began to contain a body of tradesmen and merchants whose rapidly increasing wealth, derived particularly through the wool trade, brought them a hitherto unknown influence upon the affairs of the land.[8] These affluent citizens were soon to constitute a new urban middle class whose leading members would follow the knights of the shire into the national arena.

William the Conqueror had ensured that England enjoyed a strong central government and the Plantagenets continued his centralizing policy. William had not allowed feudalism to establish a stranglehold on the channels of administration as happened in contemporary France. On the other hand, he and his successors did not attempt to establish royal authority through a paid bureaucracy. As J.R. Strayer comments:

"Unlike France, England had a centralized Government before she had a bureaucracy, and the English centralized Government had always depended on the unpaid services of the knights and law-abiding men of the shires and hundreds. This tradition could not be reversed without wrecking the whole structure of English Government."[9]

---

7. An appreciable number had held posts in the Royal Household. See, for example, CPR, 123-47, p. 21.
8. The development of the borough magistrate was distinct from that of the shire justices and is traced in ch. X, *post*.
9. Introduction by J.R. Strayer to *The English Government at Work, 1327-1336*.

In the course of time, the strength of the central government came to be built, not upon a continental type of bureaucracy, but upon the unpaid services of the landed gentry. The role of the gentry in local administration and the enforcement of the law has been of cardinal importance in the history of the Justices of the Peace and indeed in the history of the English nation. The strong, prosperous, influential and largely independent middle class became the core of the system of unpaid, lay magistrates, responsible both for administering justice in the local courts and, until the nineteenth century, for local government, and this accounts to some extent for the robust growth of the system and for its durability in the face of numerous eroding influences up to the present day.

This rising section of the population played an increasingly prominent part in the life of the country and soon extended its influence into many aspects of government, central as well as local. Representatives from the shires and the townships were summoned to meet the King in the *curia regis*, a practice which developed into their presence being required in the early medieval Parliaments. Although they seem at first to have been expected to do little more than listen to the proceedings, they soon began to assert themselves and, by the fourteenth century, were usually, though not always, able to make a significant impact upon national affairs. In the realm of peace-keeping, the office of *Custos Pacis* came to be conferred to an increasing extent upon the knights of the shires.

Appointment of Keepers of the Peace in times of crisis

The dawn of this long saga might be said to have begun even before the Norman Conquest. This is particularly so in regard to the judicial duties placed upon the early justices which are described in the next chapter, but the situation which led to the establishment of the forerunners of the Justices of the Peace began to develop on the accession of Richard I in 1189. The outbreaks of violence and unrest which began to occur soon after the beginning of the reign called for drastic action by the central government, and in 1195 an edict was proclaimed which introduced a novel method of handling disturbances. This edict may be regarded as the *fons et origo* of the office which was to become known as that of the Justice of the Peace.

The occasion for the edict was the state of civil war created by the treasonable activities of John, the future King, while his brother, Richard I, was abroad. Richard spent little of his reign in England and, although his knight-errant image was generally popular with his people, they had little for which to thank him, save for one blessing which he, no doubt unwittingly, bestowed upon them. He chose a man of outstanding ability and foresight to govern the country in his absence abroad. Hubert Walter, Archbishop of Canterbury, who was appointed justiciar, had served his apprenticeship in statecraft under his uncle, Henry II, and under Henry's able chief minister, Ranulf Glanvill, and he ruled England far more effectively than Richard himself would probably have done had he remained at home. Walter was faced with an almost insuperable task in being required to raise the huge sums of money required by Richard for the pursuit of his overseas ventures and for his ransom from captivity after the Third Crusade. He achieved this in the 1190s by perfecting a centralized administrative machine which operated through the itinerant Justices in Eyre[10] who were sent periodically throughout the country and were given political and tax-collecting functions in addition to the duty of enforcing the criminal law. To add to his burdens, Walter was also faced, in 1194, with rebellion led by the King's brother John, who became King in 1199. With the help of the majority of the barons and of other classes in the community, Walter succeeded in suppressing the insurrection and in establishing order throughout the realm. A significant element in this operation was a new experiment in maintaining order on a local basis which was introduced in the edict[11] proclaimed in 1195. Four knights in every hundred were to summon before them all men of 15 years of age and over and to take from each of them an oath that they would not be outlaws, robbers, thieves or abettors of such persons. They were also required to swear that whenever hue and cry was raised they would pursue the offenders, apprehend them and deliver them to the knights, who were to hand them over to the sheriff.[12]

Hubert Walter's success in suppressing the revolt was due partly to the strength of the English monarchy, but it also owed something to his initiative in placing his trust in the local gentry and in bringing them into the administrative framework. It is not surprising that such a course should have entered his thoughts. The taking of oaths for various purposes, including oaths of fealty to the King, was a well-known custom, while at the same time the possibility of making some use of the knights of the shire was not likely to escape his attention having regard to the various roles which they had already begun to

10. See pp. 28-30, *post.*
11. William Stubbs, Select Charters, *Edictum Regium.*
12. *Ibid.*, 264.

play.[13] What is important is that, instead of discarding them in favour of the traditional royal officials sent down by the central government on behalf of the Crown - a course which the King himself would probably have adopted - Walter recognized the local gentry as an effective means of establishing the authority of the government and, at a moment of peril, envisaged a further extension of their role by entrusting them to a significant extent with the safety of the realm.

Although this new experiment was temporary, it provided an important precedent for the future and may be regarded as the germ of the office of Justice of the Peace.[14] The most important feature of the innovation, which was to become a fundamental characteristic of the justices and was to endure to the twentieth century, was that, although the knights were mobilized as direct representatives of the Crown, they were local men, with their own independent interests firmly established in the areas in which they were required to function, and with a personal concern in the lives of the other inhabitants of the neighbourhood.

The precedent of 1195 was not followed immediately in the same pattern. There were still many occasions when magnates were appointed from outside the county to establish order, sometimes in an area covering several counties. Outstanding examples of this were the wardens appointed for coastal areas, particularly the Cinque Ports, and for the Marches with Scotland and Wales. These were the extraordinary custodians referred to by Lambard and a number of examples are to be found in Professor Harding's valuable work on the early history of the keepers.[15] As the thirteenth century progressed, however, there was increasing evidence of the Crown's inability to act effectively without the co-operation of the local gentry and the King found himself obliged to rely more and more upon the leading members of the community in each area.

In 1204 the loss of Normandy led to fear of attacks on the coast and in 1205, to meet this situation, a new officer in addition to the sheriff was appointed in each county to maintain order by force of arms. His title was *Capitalis Constabularius* and he was required to appoint under

13. From the time of the Conquest novel functions began to be given to local knights and to others of similar degree. To give but a few examples, in the procedure of *tolt*, dating from soon after the Conquest, a claimant demonstrated to four knights that there had been a default of right which justified the shire court in assuming jurisdiction. Again, in the procedure of *ession*, a person who was unable to travel to court was, in certain circumstances, visited by four knights who, if satisfied that he was too ill to attend, assigned him a day a year later on which to appear at the Tower of London (see Hall, *Glanvill*, pp. 7-17). In the year before the 1195 Edict the Eyre (see p. 28, *post*) was ordered to arrange for the election in each county of three knights and a clerk as keepers of the Crown pleas and there had been occasions before then when knights were appointed under Commissions of Gaol Delivery.
14. Stubbs, *Constitutional History of England*, i, 546, "The record thus forms an interesting link of connection between Anglo-Saxon jurisprudence and modern usage."
15. Alan Harding, The Origins and Early History of the Keepers of the Peace. *TRHS*, 5th ser., vol. 10, 1960, pp. 88-90.

constables for each hundred and township, one of whose duties was to receive indictments. The system of head constables lasted for only a short time and the whole of the peace-keeping responsibility in the counties soon reverted to the sheriffs, but the under constables, who were sometimes referred to as *Custodes Pacis*,[16] remained.

An indication of the growing importance attached to the new class was given in 1215 when Magna Carta provided for four knights to sit with two royal justices to take the Possessory Assizes[17] and, immediately after the signing of the Charter, all sheriffs and royal officers were ordered to choose 12 knights in each shire to inquire into "evil customs." Some of the knights and the Mayor of London were also present at the signing of the Charter.

The greatest advance came at the time of the civil war in the 1260s, when both the King and the barons relied upon the support of the local gentry, but before then there were various illustrations of the growing importance of this section of the population. In 1230, knights, together with the sheriffs, were ordered to take the Assize of arms. In 1252, writs required the sheriff and two knights to travel round each county and to compel all persons above the age of 15 to take an oath that they would arm themselves according to the amount of their lands and chattels.[18] The increasing independence of the knights became evident in 1254 when the barons refused to answer for them in consenting to grant aid and the knights had to be dealt with separately. In 1258 the King was forced to accept the Provisions of Oxford under which he agreed to important constitutional changes and it was decreed that four discreet knights be chosen in each county to hear complaints of wrong-doing on the part of the sheriffs and their bailiffs.[19]

It was Henry III's constant disregard of the Provisions of Oxford which finally drove many of the barons, under Simon de Montfort, Earl of Leicester, into open revolt. The conflict between King and barons came to a head in the 1260s. During these years both sides sought the support of the knights to an ever-increasing extent and the period marks the beginning of the gentry's successful struggle to gain recognition and to establish themselves as a major element in the political sphere. In 1261 de Montfort, together with the Earl of Gloucester and the Bishop of Winchester, issued a summons in their own name for three knights from each shire to come to St Albans to confer upon the needs of the realm. Henry countered by ordering the sheriffs to direct the knights to assemble at Windsor. Most of the knights, faced with these conflicting orders, responded to neither.

By 1263 the country was in a state of general upheaval, augmented

16.   See H.M. Cam, *The Hundred and the Hundred Rolls*, London, 1930, p. 190.
17.   Magna Carta (1215), 18.
18.   Select Charters, 363.
19.   Select Charters, 387.

by an invasion by the Welsh under Llewellyn. Immediate action was necessary, including special provisions for maintaining order in every area. The baronial party were particularly concerned to counter the authority of the sheriffs, who were royal officials, and it was they who took the initiative in the appointment of *Custodes Pacis*. In 1263 the barons appointed a *Custos* for each county who was responsible for policing his area independently of the sheriff, although he was restricted from interfering with the sheriff's fiscal and administrative functions. The King countered by appointing keepers of his own,[20] often several of them for a county or group of counties; but after de Montfort's victory at Lewes in 1264, his baronial party established the system of one *Custos* in each county to serve "until the King and barons should determine otherwise." These keepers could lead the *posse comitatus* even into another county. They were to suppress all offences against the peace and to arrest all malefactors and keep them in custody to await instructions from the Crown. In addition to their policing functions, they also led the local opposition to the King's faction and were particularly concerned to counter the authority of the sheriffs. Furthermore, they arranged for the election of knights and burgesses to Parliament.[21] The term *Custos Pacis*, which had been applied spasmodically from the early years of the century, had now become of general use and a feature of these appointments was that they were based on the same concept of local administration by local men which had characterized the appointment of the four knights in each shire in 1195.

The landed gentry and burgesses were becoming more predominant in the newly developing Parliaments. Four knights from each shire were required to attend in 1264, while two from each shire and two burgesses from each borough were summoned to the 1265 Parliament where they outnumbered the earls and barons, though this was due partly to the fact that only those barons who supported de Montfort attended. This newly emerging group, who came to be referred to as *la commune*,[22] soon sensed their increasing power and began to support one side or the other according to what seemed to suit their own interest.

In May 1265 Prince Edward, the heir to the throne, escaped from the barons' "open custody" and, to meet the ensuing uprising, de

20. These officers were not referred to as "*Custodes Pacis*" in the commission, but the latter was headed *De Custodia Pacis*. CPR, 1258-66, p. 357.
21. Rymer, O., i, 792. Select Charters, 411.
22. When the King summoned a Parliament, writs were addressed to the sheriffs directing them to arrange for the election of two knights from every shire, two citizens from every city and two burgesses from every borough from among "the most discreet and able for the work", and cause them to come to Parliament. These were *la commune*. It appears that they were not always knights but were all men of substance. They were a fairly heterogeneous body which included younger sons of noblemen and prosperous yeomen whose ancestors may have been serfs.

Montfort issued writs in the King's name ordering the keepers to suppress the revolt.[23] After de Montfort's defeat and death at Evesham in 1265, the King gained the ascendancy, but he and his followers had come to recognize the value of the gentry, especially as a means of transmitting the Crown's authority directly and effectively to local levels. Parts of the country were devastated, food prices soared and trade was almost at a standstill. In restoring order, the King made extensive use of officers, often called *Custodes Pacis*, who were usually recruited from among the knights of the shire.[24] These differed, however, from the baronial keepers in that they were not appointed on a regular basis but only to deal with emergencies and, instead of a single *Custos* for each county, several were appointed in areas where a crisis had arisen. Their functions, like those of their predecessors, were almost entirely military. These were sometimes very wide, embracing responsibility for defending the coasts and even involving authority over the King's fleets. It was their duty to raise forces, to direct the militia and to collect taxes to support the levies and they were often involved in commanding large-scale military operations in addition to local police duties. The military nature of the office is shown by the fact that sometimes sheriffs, or others who held office under the Crown in a local area, were also appointed *Custodes Pacis*, probably because this gave them the additional power to deploy the militia.

Although the keepers were still the holders of predominantly military appointments, it should be noted that the class of person who occupied these posts had begun also to undertake judicial functions, albeit in a different capacity. Early in Henry III's reign the Possessory Assizes of *novel disseisin* and *mort d'ancestor*[25] were often entrusted to four knights of the shire, though at a later date the knights were usually associated in this work with one of the King's justices. In the latter part of the reign, the knights were also frequently involved in administering criminal justice when three or four in each shire were given the task of gaol delivery. The local gentry were therefore becoming accustomed to judicial duties a century before they were established as Justices of the Peace.

Development of the keepers

When Edward I came to the throne in 1272, the office of Keeper of the Peace had still not been confirmed as a regular feature of government

---

23.   Rymer, O., i, 792. Select Charters, 411.
24.   Rymer, O., i, 814, and see RP, Henry III, i, 326.
25.   These were civil proceedings to determine the title to land where a claimant maintained that he had been wrongly dispossessed or that he was entitled to land on the death of his ancestor. The procedure was a development of the much older inquest whereby a number of reliable persons in an area were required to provide the King with certain information, Domesday being an early example.

and for a time various methods continued to be employed for preserving the peace. The King was primarily concerned with the appointment of eminent men of proved dedication to the Crown, who might or might not have personal ties with the area they were to govern, but who could be relied upon to represent the royal interest. King Edward, however, recognized the importance of middle-class support and he made use of it to an increasing degree, both in maintaining order and in the tendering of advice in Parliament. In 1275, shortly after his first Parliament, writs were sent to every county ordering the observance of recent statutes whose provisions were to be written down and shown to the inhabitants by the bailiffs, after which they were to be handed to two knights for safe keeping. In 1277, when Edward embarked upon his wars in Wales, writs were issued to the sheriffs in all English counties instructing them to arrange for the election in the county court of reliable men to maintain order.[26] The principal function of these conservators was to assist the sheriff in intercepting and apprehending malefactors during the King's absence, and they were clearly intended to devote their time to keeping the peace in their respective areas for they were to be chosen from knights who were not accompanying the army to Wales.

The class from which the keepers were drawn was widened in 1278 when it was ordained that every freeman whose revenue amounted to more than £20 should be subject to the military obligations of knighthood. As values rose, larger numbers of men found themselves in this category of respected local citizens who took an increasing interest in public affairs.

Public pressure played a leading part in developments which took place between 1285 and the early years of the fourteenth century. The Statute of Winchester of 1285,[27] which came to be cited in later years as a principal source of the people's rights, was enforced by conservators specially appointed for the purpose.[28] Their duties included a twice-yearly "view of arms" to ensure that every man between the age of 15 and 60 had arms with which to maintain the peace according to the amount of his lands and chattels.[29] Later, two knights were assigned in each shire to inquire, with the assistance of the sheriff, why the provisions of the statute had not been strictly carried out. This was followed in 1287 by the appointment of between two and six keepers in each shire with the express duty of enforcing the

26.   Patent Rolls, Edw. I, 1272-1281, p. 218.
27.   13 Edw. I, 1285.
28.   The original intention was that the statute should be enforced by the constables of hundreds and by the Justices of Assize but from 1287, as explained *post*, knights, soon referred to as *Custodes Pacis*, were specifically assigned to keep the peace in accordance with the statute.
29.   Select Charters, 468 and 473.

statute's provisions,[30] but with an important difference; their duties became less military and began to be inclined more towards the administration of justice. The keepers who were now appointed were no longer given military commands although they remained responsible for local policing and for ensuring that all men were properly armed and ready to fight. On the other hand, they assumed those duties created by the Statute of Winchester which had previously been discharged by the King's Justices of Assize who, overwhelmed by the increasing mass of suits of trespass, were unable to cope with the work.

Many of the early keepers had had the duty of assisting the sheriffs in the execution of their peace-keeping functions, but towards the end of Edward I's reign the position was reversed and writs were issued to the sheriffs ordering them to assist and obey the keepers. The sheriffs were also required to summon juries of presentment to appear before the keepers.

An important milestone was reached in the Westminster Parliament of 1300 when, in response to popular pressure, an article *super cardas* sought to enforce the Royal Charters of the previous century. In each county three knights or other suitable persons were to be elected by the community to hear and determine pleas and complaints of infringements of the charters by royal officials or others. As Professor Harding observes,[31] these were the first of the primarily judicial *Custodes Pacis*. They acted solely on the authority of their warrant and virtually became local justices. They may therefore be looked upon as the first "Justices of the Peace," although it would be a further half century before the term came into general use, and before then there were to be periods when the *Custodes* lost their judicial functions entirely.

A year later there was a foretaste of the partnership between the gentry and the lawyers which became established 60 years later. In 1301 Edward issued commissions to a lawyer and a knight in each county to hear and determine all manner of wrongs done to his people in his name because of the war.

Notwithstanding this acceleration in the employment of trusted local men to maintain the peace and to administer justice, the office of keeper cannot yet be regarded as having assumed a permanent status. It is significant in this context that, although the knights and burgesses had been present at most Parliaments during this period, they had not quite reached the stage where they were an essential element, invariably heard and listened to during the discussion of national affairs. A factor which increased their effectiveness at the beginning of

30.   CPR, 1281-92, pp. 264-5.
31.   "The Origins and Early History of the Keepers of the Peace," *TRHS,* 5th ser., vol. 10, 1960, p. 100.

the fourteenth century was that the sheriffs were ordered to see that the knights and burgesses who had been present at the last Parliament should continue to attend future meetings unless death or incapacity prevented them. The same individuals therefore began to appear at each session and thus acquired experience in procedure and an ability to face up to the King, the nobles and the prelates. Their impact became increasingly apparent throughout most of the century. They repeatedly petitioned on a variety of matters, usually, though not invariably, with success and the statutes and commissions of this period were frequently the outcome of requests of *la commune* in Parliament. As their authority grew in Parliament they also consolidated their position as local administrators and ultimately as royal justices. Through Parliament they gained for themselves recognition as the rightful appointees to certain public offices including that of keeper, which came to be established on a permanent basis.

From the beginning of the reign of Edward II in 1307, commissions were issued almost continuously. There were still occasions when special writs dealt with particular circumstances, as when keepers were appointed in northern counties to meet the threat from Robert the Bruce, and in these cases the men who received the commissions were usually prominent magnates; but the pattern was becoming established of issuing regular commissions to less eminent individuals in all counties, with the principal object of enforcing the Statute of Winchester. Edward's weakness led to a renewal of conflict between King and barons with outbreaks of disorder and, as in the time of Henry III, there was growing interest in the use of the gentry to maintain the peace of local areas.

Almost from the beginning of the reign, the keepers were empowered, with the assistance if necessary of the *posse comitatus*, to arrest people on suspicion and to place them in custody to await the King's orders. Soon they also acquired administrative duties which included supervising weights and measures and the standard of the coinage and ensuring that prices did not rise above those of Edward I's reign.[32] By 1316 they had power to inquire into felonies as well as trespasses. In that year an important step was taken when a commission for Kent gave the keepers powers of gaol delivery and they could therefore try and sentence those whom they had arrested. Later, they were given general powers to fine, or punish in any other manner they thought fit, all those who disobeyed them.[33] They were required to reside within the county and to visit all parts as the need

---

32. Parl. Writs, II, ii, 2, pp. 8, 9.
33. Parl. Writs, II, ii, 2, p. 282 "*omnes illos qui vobis inobedientes aut contrarios ... per gravia amerciamenta aut alios modo juxta discrecionem vostram castegandi et puniendi.*"

arose.

During this time one begins to see indications of the close interest which the King's Council was to take in the activities of the keepers and which was to develop into the supervision of the Justices of the Peace by the Privy Council and the Star Chamber under the Tudors. An example of this was the requirement that the keepers should make monthly returns of their proceedings to the Council at Westminster and give the names of all malefactors.[34]

By the end of Edward II's reign in 1327, the keepers had become a normal part of the machinery of government, while the men who usually held these posts were well established at national level where their influence was invariably felt when matters of state were being debated. When, in the following reign, the country was faced with unprecedented and unforeseen problems, these men and the offices they held could not be overlooked in the establishment of new machinery to meet the situation.

34.   Parl. Writs, II, ii, 2, pp. 74, 75.

CHAPTER II

TRANSFORMATION OF KEEPERS
INTO JUSTICES 1327-61

Statute of Westminster 1327 - Fluctuating fortunes of the keepers - War with France - The manner of appointment of the keepers - Establishment of the Quorum - Justices of Assize - The plague: labour and financial crisis - Deficiencies of earlier courts - Establishment of keepers or justices on permanent basis

The Statute of Westminster, 1327

THE STATUTE OF WESTMINSTER 1327[1] has often been regarded as marking the beginning of the history of the Justices of the Peace. In fact, it was but one of the many milestones, and by no means the first, in the long journey. As has been shown in the previous chapter, the process had already been under way for a considerable time. The importance of the 1327 statute lies, however, in the fact that it was the first piece of legislation which provided for the appointment of Keepers of the Peace. Until then, these appointments had been a matter of royal pleasure, entirely at the will of the King; thereafter, commissions followed the lines set out in successive statutes, though there were instances when a commission, in an attempt to try a new experiment, did not conform precisely with the statutes then in force.

The exceptional circumstances which led to the statute were the deposing of Edward II and the accession of his 14-year-old son as Edward III in his place. Steps had to be taken to ensure that supporters of the old King did not raise rebellion or cause disturbances in local areas. Soon after Edward III's accession, Parliament was asked to suggest methods for dealing with the dangerous situation. *La commune,* who had long been demanding stronger action to deal with the outbreaks of disorder which had characterized the previous reign, petitioned for the appointment of gentry to keep the peace in each county, on the lines developed under Edward II, with the power to arrest suspects (which had been included in the commissions of 1316 and 1326). In the light of the current crisis, the proposal to make use of the local gentry, who had had long experience of peace-keeping duties, probably met with a more favourable reception than it would otherwise have done. Nevertheless, those in whom power rested at the time - Roger Mortimer, Queen Isabella's lover, who had been instrumental in

---

1.   1 Edw. III, st. 2, c. 16.

deposing her husband, and particularly Geoffrey Scrope, Chief Justice of the King's Bench - were sceptical of the keepers and were determined to thwart their aspirations. Scrope was resolved to increase the use of the general Eyre[2] which was, in his view, the most effective means of restoring order and also the most profitable. In the event the statute provided:

> "For the better keeping and maintenance of the peace the King will that in every county good men and lawful,[3] which be no maintainers or barators in the country, shall be assigned to keep the peace."

The commissions, which were issued immediately afterwards, did not include authority to arrest. Apart therefore from the fact that the keepers had now been recognized in a statute, the events of 1327 could be seen as a step backwards. Far from marking the beginning of a period of continuous progress, it was the start of some 30 years of rapid fluctuation in the fortunes of the keepers. The haphazard pattern which had been followed during the previous century, when various alternative schemes were tried out, was also apparent under Edward III. His reign witnessed a long struggle between the gentry, represented in Parliament by *la commune*, who strove to extend the keepers' powers so as to include arrest and the hearing and determining of felonies and trespasses, and a group comprising the Judges, lawyers and some magnates close to the King, who favoured the issue of commissions solely to lawyers, or at most to a combination of lawyers and magnates, with very extensive powers to deal with all offences committed by officials or by other persons. The future of the keepers was often in the balance and there were times when it looked as if they would not survive. In the end, a series of unforeseen events, added to the King's increasing awareness of the usefulness of the knights and burgesses, led to a compromise which became the foundation of the office of Justice of the Peace in succeeding centuries.

Fluctuations in the fortunes of the keepers

In the meantime, the events of 1327 were followed by a series of swift changes, each one reflecting a temporary success by the gentry in advancing the cause of the keepers or by the lawyers and others in opposing them. Complaints soon began to be heard that the keepers

---

2.   See pp. 28-30, *post*.
3.   "Lawful" (*legales homines*) meant those whose oath would be accepted and who had never committed perjury. It also meant persons not outlawed, at a time when outlawry was quite common, for a variety of reasons - not all of them criminal, but some connected with technical non-appearance in civil suits. Finding that a litigant or legal official had been outlawed (or arranging for him to be outlawed) in some trifling case in a distant county was a well-tried ruse for avoiding legal proceedings.

were failing to achieve even their limited purpose and these were answered almost immediately by the reintroduction of the system previously adopted under Edward II, namely the appointment of prominent magnates to supervise the keepers. This also reflected the intense resentment shown by the magnates at the increased powers given by the Crown to the gentry. In most cases several great lords (the *Grantz*) were appointed to oversee a group of counties while the scope of the keepers' powers was reduced. Under the Statute of Northampton in 1328,4 they were merely entrusted, together with other local officials, with the enforcement of new provisions on the bearing of arms. This was followed immediately by two further swings of the pendulum. First, the tide changed dramatically in favour of the keepers. Commissions issued in May 1329 contained the additional authority for them to determine felonies and trespasses and, as Miss Bertha Putnam was the first to point out, this gave rise to the early use of the phrase *justices de la pees.*5 The triumph was short lived. In 1330 the policy was reversed by the statute 4 Edw. III, c. 2, which directed the keepers to send all indictments to the Justices of Assize; the Commissions of the Peace which followed omitted the authority to determine, and once again the powers of the keepers became negligible. The same pattern was to be seen throughout the following 30 years when the speed and frequency of the fluctuations in the authority of the keepers must at times have been bewildering to all those affected by them.6 It may be added that some of the extant records suggest that the practice in sessions did not invariably reflect the latest version of the commission (although, equally, cases can be found where defective commissions were correctly interpreted by punctilious clerks). In addition to changes of policy covering the country as a whole there were also occasions when exceptional powers were given to the keepers in a particular area where disorder was prevalent. In some cases the term "justice" was used instead of keeper, but there was no consistency in the choice of title and the two appear to have been interchangeable until the latter half of the century when "justice" gradually replaced the older term of the office became clearly identified with judicial and administrative work to a greater extent than with pure peace-keeping.

War with France

In 1337 the war in France began, though it was virtually a continuation of hostilities begun under Edward I. The cost was considerable from

4.   2 Edw. III, cc. 1-7.
5.   B.H. Putnam, "The Transformation of the Keepers of the Peace into the Justices of the Peace 1327-1380, *TRHS,* 4th ser., xii, 1929, p. 27.
6.   Professor Putnam gives a detailed account of the oscillations throughout this period, *ibid.*, pp. 28 *ff.*

the beginning and the financial burden became intolerable as the military situation deteriorated after the successes at Crécy and Poitiers. At the same time the lawlessness which had already given cause for alarm during the previous reign was increased by the return to England of large numbers of soldiers who, well versed in violence and pillage, were not prepared to engage in peaceful pursuits but, forming themselves into criminal gangs, became predators in their own land. The problem created by marauding gangs was exacerbated by the presence of numerous private armies raised by members of the nobility. Formed initially with the King's approval for service in campaigns on the Continent, these forces on their return were soon making war on each other and on the rest of the community. Patent Rolls throughout the 30 years from 1327 show an overwhelming preoccupation of the King and Council with lawlessness and the need to maintain the peace.[7] Here again, the keepers, with many years of peace-keeping experience behind them, were among the obvious objects for experiment, but there was more to it than that. The war led not only to an escalation of lawlessness, which placed more burdens upon the peace-keeping forces, but also to an increasing need for troops· and money. The King therefore required the support of the knights both to keep the peace at home during his absence and also to fight the war abroad. Furthermore, the class of knights, well placed in Parliament and representing local interests, were a potent factor in raising revenue. It was probably for this reason more than any other that, as the war proceeded, there was evidence of a greater willingness on the part of the Crown to accede to the requests of *la commune.*

The appointment of the keepers

During this period the gentry made several attempts to gain control of the selection and appointment of the keepers. There had been occasions previously when keepers were chosen locally, though in most of these cases the King made the final appointment from lists submitted to his Council.[8] We have seen that in 1277 keepers were elected in the shire court on the King's instructions.[9] There is also evidence, especially in the thirteenth century, of replacements being elected in the shire court to fill vacancies caused by a keeper

7.   See *eg* RP II, 64. 165. It is possible that the apparent increase in lawlessness during this period may have been deceptive. The available evidence supports the view that there was a substantial rise in lawlessness at this time, but this is not certain. The existence of a strong and administrative-minded government may have provided more symptoms of lawlessness which could have peaked in the early years of the century. Nevertheless, lawlessness on a large scale was indubitably rife in the middle of the century and there was justification for the firm measure taken by the government.
8.   The subject is discussed in B.H. Putnam, *The Transformation of the Keepers of the Peace into the Justices of the Peace 1327-1380,* pp. 36-38.
9.   See p. 11, *ante.* PRO, Edw. I, 1272-1281, 218.

relinquishing office during his term of service.[10] There is further evidence suggesting that some persons assumed office as keeper without any direct authority from the Crown. In 1312 a writ issued by the King confirmed that the appointment of all conservators of the peace belonged to him and it directed the sheriffs to inquire concerning those who asserted themselves to be keepers.[11] Most evidence, however, points to the appointments being made by the King, either on his own knowledge or that of persons close to the throne or on the recommendation of trusted magnates in the area. The Public Record Office contains numerous commissions which were issued to the keepers, all of which were addressed to specific individuals. At the same time, there is a large number of contemporary writs issued to the sheriffs ordering them to arrange for the election in the shire court of such persons as Members of Parliament, coroners, escheators, verderers and others, but no mention is made of Keepers or Justices of the Peace. These writs were returned by the sheriffs backed with the names of those who had been duly elected, and again no reference is made to keepers or justices. It is reasonable to infer from this, and from anecdotal evidence that, apart from exceptional cases like that of 1277, keepers were not elected but were chosen and appointed by the King, either on the recommendation of trusted persons in the area or on the personal knowledge of courtiers or of the King himself who came to know many local knights during his frequent excursions throughout the country and when they accompanied him to war. There seems generally to have been a reasonably well-defined but informal community of the shire which kept these and similar appointments within a recognized and predictable grouping, though it was fluid with the course of time.

The gentry seem to have been concerned that the keepers should be both acceptable to them as individuals and should also be drawn from the areas in which they had to operate so as to have local knowledge.[12] In view of the existing court-holding interests of the gentry, the motive for this is likely to have been exclusive - not wanting intrusive outsiders to get involved. In 1342 the gentry, with the support of the barons, petitioned that the keepers should be elected and sworn in Parliament,[13] and in 1347 a further petition asked that the choice should rest with the *gentz des contes*.[14] These proposals were not accepted and it was finally established beyond question that the power to choose and appoint rested exclusively with the King though, as will be seen later,

10. Examples are cited by Beard in *The Office of Justice of the Peace in England,* 23-28.
11. RP, II, 136.
12. RP, II, 128-30.
13. RP, II, 136.
14. RP, II, 1746. In the years 1362 and 1363, *la commune* were successful in having names of the JPs submitted to Parliament (CPR, 1361-4, 291. RP, II, 277).

he would act on advice. Had this not been so, and had the justices of the future not been appointed by the Crown as were all other members of the judiciary, it is questionable whether they could have assumed the extraordinarily extensive powers which they were ultimately allowed to acquire.

Establishment of the *Quorum*

The gentry's efforts to gain control of local affairs also involved a struggle against the domination of the magnates. On several occasions they attempted to discredit the latter by claiming that they added to the confusion and did far more harm than good. This met with some sympathy from the King, who saw the local gentry as a means of establishing royal authority without having to rely upon the great lords, who were often the most unreliable and disruptive elements in the country. There was the further advantage of providing a strong, on-the-spot counter-balance to the sheriffs who, though they too were royal appointees and were drawn from the gentry class, were showing signs of corruption and undue independence. When, however, the King was faced in 1344 with a petition that inquiries by the *grantz* should be replaced by proceedings conducted by six *Custodes Pacis* in each county, who should punish offenders reasonably according to their guilt, he agreed but subject to severe restrictions on their judicial functions unless they had persons learned in the law sitting with them. Commissions were to be issued to two or three of those of the best reputation in the county who were to keep the peace and, together with *autres sages et apris de la leye*, were to hear and determine felonies and trespasses and to punish reasonably, according to law and the nature of the offence.[15] The landed gentry and their Parliamentary allies the burgesses seem to have been principally concerned in getting the magnates off their backs and if an obligation to sit with lawyers was the price they had to pay, this was acceptable, especially if it led to an extension of their judicial powers. In fact local gentry who fulfilled the legal qualifications were already to be found on the commissions, and a year earlier *la commune* had themselves suggested that if the keepers were not sufficient for the task assigned to them they should be "afforced" by others more sufficient, while in the Parliament of 1344 itself they put forward a proposal very similar to the procedure actually adopted.[16] The gentry therefore achieved their objective of escaping from the supervising authority of the magnates. The latter continued to be appointed from time to time to perform specific tasks under special commissions but, as far as the Commissions of the Peace were

15.   18 Edw. III, st. 2, c. 2.
16.   RP, II, pp. 148-9.

concerned, they could serve on these only with powers equal to those of the gentry by whom they were outnumbered.[17] Meanwhile, the professional lawyers and particularly the Judges of the King's Bench and Common Pleas who advised the King had not succeeded in ousting the layman entirely from judicial office, but they had ensured that for some time to come he should not exercise any appreciable jurisdiction unless accompanied by a member of the legal profession. In these early years it was only the Justices of Assize who were appointed to the commissions in addition to the ordinary Justices of the Peace, each one being placed on the commissions within his circuit. It was not until 1389 that other lawyers began to be added. This arrangement was soon referred to as the "*Quorum*" because the commission which implemented this and subsequent statutes, after appointing the justices, added: "*quorum aliquem vestrum* (followed by the names of those '*apris de la leye*') *unum esse volumus.*"[18]

Justices of Assize

The antagonism of the lawyers towards the Justices of the Peace has led most historians to assume that all justices of the royal courts were competitors of the JPs in a struggle to acquire jurisdiction over felony and trespass at local level. The exhaustive research of Miss Putnam suggested that the Justices of the Peace, during their formative years in the second half of the fourteenth century, had been in competition, not only with the Justices in Eyre and other royal justices and commissioners, but also with the Justices of Assize. Edward Powell, however, in a thesis written in 1985,[19] has shown that, instead of being competitors, the Assize Justices and the Keepers and later Justices of the Peace were in practice complementary to one another within a coherent judicial structure. This is based partly upon the discovery that Assize Justices were appointed to the peace commissions much earlier than Miss Putnam believed. The 1344 Statute gave the Keepers of the Peace power of oyer and terminer but only when they had men of law with them. What Miss Putnam did not appreciate was that these lawyers were invariably the Assize Justices of the circuit, and she

---

17. As will be seen later, this did not prevent some great lords from completely dominating a commission.
18. This restriction was gradually allowed to lapse (vol. II, ch. I, *post*), but it was in a sense revived in 1938 when Quarter Sessions were granted extended jurisdiction if presided over by a legally qualified chairman (vol. II, ch. IX, *post*). The earliest known example of the *Quorum* clause was in 1343. Putnam, *Proceedings before the Justices of the Peace*, 1938, xli.
19. *The Administration of Criminal Justice in Late Medieval England: Peace Sessions and Assizes. The Political Context of the Law:* Proceedings of Seventh British Legal History Conf., Canterbury, 1985. Edward Powell compares the 1350 and 1351 peace commissions with Commissions of Assize and Gaol Delivery and shows that the Assize Justices were appointed to all the county Commissions of the Peace in their circuits and that they invariably made up the *Quorum*.

concluded that the latter were not regularly appointed to the Commissions of the Peace until the early fifteenth century. In fact, the Assize Justices were included in the commissions on their circuits at all times when the commissions included power to hear and determine felonies (apart from the unique period from 1361 to 1364 when the JPs exercised the full power alone). Conversely, Assize Justices were omitted from commissions which did not confer these powers, such as those issued between 1364 and 1368 and the Commissions of Labourers between 1352 and 1359. In 1368 the Justices of the Peace regained their power to determine and the Assize Justices were appointed to all the counties on their circuit. It was therefore only through a combination of the Assize Justices and the Justices of the Peace that the more serious criminal cases were disposed of in the local courts.

For a time, the Assize Justices were the only members of the *Quorum*, but this could result in considerable delay in delivering gaols owing to their frequent and prolonged absence from the counties. It was therefore enacted in 1394 that the *Quorum* should include not only the Assize Justices but also two or more local lawyers who were to deliver thieves and felons as often as may be necessary. Later, the Assize courts themselves were able to undertake more work and by the sixteenth and seventeenth centuries were trying the more serious cases previously dealt with at Quarter Sessions. The date of this transition is very problematic. Although the surviving peace sessions' records tend to show only business left unfinished at the end of sessions, and thus may not show the extent to which felony jurisdiction was actually exercised, it seems likely that the balance of Assizes for serious business and Quarter Sessions for misdemeanours was struck quite early. In the last decades of the fourteenth century it is possible to find cases remitted to Assizes (properly speaking Commissions of Gaol Delivery) by peace sessions' benches competent to hear and determine them.

The Plague: labour and financial crisis

The new system of associating lawyers with laymen as Keepers of the Peace had hardly begun to operate when the entire life of the country was shattered by a totally unforeseeable disaster: the first visit of the plague to England in the summer of 1348. The Black Death, as it was called, has been described as the most terrifying catastrophe in the history of Britain. The records of the time do not provide a precise picture of the extent of the disaster nor of its effect on the country but, although estimates have probably been exaggerated, there is no doubt that this and the three subsequent outbreaks of the disease which occurred during the following 40 years destroyed the social structure of the land as it had existed previously. The population, which probably numbered a little over four million at the beginning of 1348, was reduced to about two-and-a-half million in less than two years. The remaining workforce took every advantage of the situation. Ignoring the law[20] which bound them to the soil, they moved to wherever the highest pay could be obtained, while employers competed with one another to obtain their services.[21] Wages which had been stable soared, fields were left untilled, cattle died and there was an acute shortage of food. The ruling classes, both nobles and gentry, combined in an attempt to counter the threatened anarchy and to preserve the old system. With the King's approval the first Ordinance of Labourers was promulgated in 1349. This sought to peg both prices and wages at the rates current before the "great pestilence" and to restrict all movement of labour. It was an early forerunner of the legislation of modern times which set out to create prices and incomes boards and industrial tribunals but with far less drastic powers than those conferred six centuries earlier. Under the ordinance the keepers were empowered to fix the wages of servants and of almost all manual workers, including masons, carpenters and tilers, and not just those of farm labourers. As to precisely who qualified for this treatment might depend upon the keepers' interpretation. It was generally provided that the statutes did not apply to those who owned land or property from which they could live, but otherwise virtually everyone might be subject to the regulations and those who were "strong in body" and under 60 years of age, and were not already employed or engaged in a trade, were to be bound to serve anyone who required their services in work suitable to their status. After 1349 workers could be fined and imprisoned, and in some circumstances branded, for breaches of the ordinance, and employers could be fined for offering more than the fixed rates of pay.[22] The keepers also fixed the prices charged by sellers of victuals and by those who carried by land or water.

The duty of enforcing the statute was placed firmly upon the keepers who, being composed almost entirely of landowners with a strong personal interest in forcing a return to the previous position, threw themselves wholeheartedly into the task, but with little success, though the inflation which ensued might have been worse had it not been for their efforts. The keepers themselves were faced, as

20. The law on this subject was largely custom, supported in part by statute.
21. The workforce had been based on a system of villein tenure, but in the thirteenth century a movement began to replace this with hired labour, and serfdom had already declined considerably by 1348.
22. *Eg*, the daily pay of a labourer for hay-making was one penny. The authoritative study of the enforcement of the Statutes of Labourers remains B.H. Putnam's *The Enforcement of the Statutes of Labourers during the First Decade after the Black Death*, Columbia, New York, 1908.

landowners, with the problem of securing labourers, and some were convicted of paying more than the fixed rate of wages. In spite of the penalties, the peasants were forced to seek higher wages because they could not live on the old rates, while the landlord was obliged to offer more pay in order to get anyone to work for him at all. Many of the peasants moved to the towns where they were warmly welcomed by the merchants and where they swelled the ranks of urban workers. Others joined the existing bands of vagrants and robbers. Some attempted to form unions to further their interests, but these were rigidly suppressed by the keepers. The latter were faced, however, with an impossible task and the measures they took merely increased discontent among the workforce, which was ready to explode into the Peasants' Revolt in 1381 with Wat Tyler as their leader and spokesman. In the meantime, further Statutes of Labourers, the outcome of renewed demands by the landed gentry, had little effect.

In 1352 a new experiment was introduced. Separate commissions were issued to Justices of Labourers, instead of to the keepers, who were given jurisdiction over a number of additional matters such as weights and measures and the activities of victuallers and hostlers. In practice what happened was that Commissions of the Peace and Commissions of Labourers were addressed to the same persons except that the latter commissions did not include the Justices of Assize. For seven years the Commissions of the Peace did not include the labour laws, but the labour commissions seem to have been no more successful and in 1359 the latter were combined with those of the peace. At the same time the array of arms was finally removed from the duties of the keepers, except for a temporary reinstatement in 1362. (Array had been included in the peace commissions since 1338). Although they still exercised police duties, they were moving ever further away from strictly military affairs and instead were becoming more closely associated with judicial work.

The combined effect of the plague and the interminable war was to create inflation, labour shortage and high taxes on an unprecedented scale as well as lawlessness, all of which aroused fresh demands for an effective system of administration for local affairs and for maintaining order. They also led to the appearance of another unforeseen factor. This was the inability of the existing machinery to deal with the crushing new burdens which were placed upon it.

The earlier courts

At the beginning of the fourteenth century the government of the country, both national and local, was conducted through a complex conglomeration of courts which were concerned as much with fiscal and administrative matters as with dispensing justice; indeed the latter sometimes occupied a subordinate position, of interest principally as a source of revenue. Some courts operated directly in the name of the King, some were ecclesiastical, some feudal and some were the old customary courts of shire and hundred.

The system which operated in Anglo-Saxon times is highly controversial and is not susceptible to general analysis but, broadly speaking, almost all local administration had been in the hands of the shire and hundred courts. The Conqueror generally accepted the institutions which he found in England and he expressly decreed that these courts should continue to function as of old; but soon their scope was somewhat reduced by two new court systems, feudal and ecclesiastical, which arrived in the train of the invader.

In early Saxon times the shire court was probably composed of all the freemen in the shire, but in the latter part of the thirteenth century its membership came to be limited to those who held a parcel of land and who were under an obligation to do "suit of court." They met once a month and were presided over by the sheriff, who was a royal representative, but decisions were generally taken by the freeholders, known as "doomsmen." It was mostly a civil court but also dealt with some minor criminal proceedings and, in addition, it could be required to try with a jury[23] cases sent down to it by the King's court. The shire court, however, was by no means a court only in the judicial sense. It was a gathering of the leading men in the county (as the shire came to be known under the Normans) at which all matters concerning local affairs were discussed and resolved. The greater part of the time was devoted to administration and it was there that decisions were taken as to who should fill various public positions, such as coroner,[24] and which of the gentry should be chosen to represent the county in Parliament.

Counties were divided into hundreds and hundreds into vills or townships. Each hundred, sometimes called a wapentake, especially in the north, had a court which, like the shire court, was a representative gathering of the people in the area. The vill had no court of its own but was represented in the hundred court and in some cases it coincided with a feudal manor which had a court.

The hundred court was held every three weeks. Its functions were very similar to those of the shire court but on a smaller scale and

23. Jury trial at the shire court was a complicated matter and was probably not "jury trial" as understood at Assizes and elsewhere. (Various books and articles by Robert C. Palmer are the authority here, if used with caution).
24. Coroners were first established in 1194, primarily as a check on the powers of the sheriff. Their functions were to keep rolls of inquisitions into sudden deaths, indictments of felonies and concealment of treasure trove. They were from the same class as the keepers, being knights or considerable landowners. They were elected by the freeholders of the county until 1888 when the Local Government Act provided for their appointment by the county council. For a full description of the duties and the early history of coroners see R.F. Hunnisett: *The Medieval Coroner*, Cambridge Studies in Legal History, 1961.

restricted to its geographical boundaries. It dealt with minor criminal matters such as brawls and thieves caught in the act.[25] It was usually presided over by a bailiff, but twice a year the sheriff visited each hundred in his area, other than those in which a lord had exclusive jurisdiction, for the sheriff's tourn (sometimes there was one tourn for a group of hundreds) when the court heard presentments of robberies and serious assaults for which the Eyre could not spare the time. The time factor was crucial. With a tourn every six months, and an Eyre every seven years, the latter was likely to pick up only unfinished or contentious business. The tourn was also the occasion for the view of *frankpledge*.[26]

Ecclesiastical matters also fell within the jurisdiction of the customary courts before the Conquest, but in an ordinance of 1072 William I, under the influence of Archbishop Lanfranc, established ecclesiastical courts within the exclusive authority of the church. Apart from administering ecclesiastical law, however, the church was also involved as a landlord in administering justice generally for the inhabitants of the land which they owned. For this purpose, prelates, monastic houses and other church establishments held local courts which were virtually the same as the feudal courts which are about to be described.

The Normans also introduced feudalism into England (though much ink has been spilled on the question of its evolution long before that) and with it feudal courts. Every feudal overlord had a right to hold a court for his tenants. At the bottom of the scale a lord of the manor held a court at which all his tenants were obliged to attend and over which he or his steward presided.[27] These courts were the central institution of village life at which local administration was conducted and where in many cases decisions were reached by the freeholders. Their judicial functions were largely confined to civil matters concerning tenure and the relationship between lord and peasant. In theory feudal courts had no criminal jurisdiction but they usually dealt with minor nuisances and sometimes more serious offences. They were sources of revenue and regarded as perquisites by the lords, who therefore sought to extend their jurisdiction by express grants from the King. In addition, therefore, to the courts which belonged to a lord merely because he had tenants, there were franchise courts with wider

25.   It is probable that only those courts which had "*infangenthief*" jurisdiction could deal with thieves in these circumstances.
26.   See p. 2, *ante*.
27.   The manor court which was held purely on the lord's own authority was called a "court baron." The term "court leet" was generally applied to those manor courts whose jurisdiction was extended by royal franchise and whose authority was, at least in theory, delegated by the Crown. "Court leet" came to be applied to a court exercising the jurisdiction of the sheriff's tourn and sometimes included a borough court. Maitland pointed out that "leet" was the word a fourteenth-century lawyer would have used to translate *visus franciplegii, ie,* "view of *frankpledge*" (Selden Society, vol. 2, 1888, p. lxxiii).

jurisdiction depending upon the terms of the grant.

All the customary, feudal and ecclesiastical courts referred to above were deployed throughout England. In addition, there was a wide variety of special courts, some attached to fairs and markets, like the on-the-spot courts of "pie powder" where the parties still had the "dust on their feet" from the street, while some were to be found only in a particular locality. There was a more or less concordant evolution of customary courts, some very different from others for reasons of regional variation (eg, the descendants of Danish courts in the older Danelaw), all of which had been fitted into a more centralized scheme of common-law administration. The grant of powers by the Crown helped this process considerably, but the *quo warranto* proceedings under Edward I showed how multifarious and in some cases how autonomous these local courts could be even as late as the last quarter of the thirteenth century. These courts are too numerous to set out here but, like the others, they are relevant to the history of the Justices of the Peace. Firstly, because all the older courts involved a considerable degree of popular participation and through them, and through the jury of presentment[28] and later the trial jury, members of the community had long been identified with local administration and the enforcement of law. Contemporary eyes would probably have seen little that was incongruous in the prospect of similar functions being performed by the landed gentry, albeit through the medium of yet another type of tribunal. Furthermore, the jurisdiction of the justices was more popular than that of the older local courts. The new procedure, based upon presentment and trial by jury and with its comparatively speedy and more effective results, was more attractive than the old, cumbersome appeals and compurgation; though it should be added that the manorial and hundred courts did not necessarily proceed in cumbersome fashion - these strictures apply only to the more powerful of the older courts. The justices also had the advantage of operating directly in the name of the King with more satisfactory powers of enforcement than those enjoyed by the other courts. Another reason why the latter are relevant to the development of the justices is because they proved to be incapable of meeting the challenge of the new situation which developed in the fourteenth century. Their organization and procedure were antiquated and could

---

28.   The prosecution of suspected offenders had been initiated from early times by a jury of presentment which was required to present on oath to the shire court, and later to the King's itinerant justices, all crimes of which they had personal knowledge or which were reputed in their neighbourhood. Under the Assize of Clarendon in 1164 and of Northampton in 1176 these juries consisted of twelve *legales homines* from every hundred and four from every township; but much earlier, under the Danelaw, 12 leading theigns in each wapentake instituted prosecutions of suspected persons in the court of the wapentake. The jury of presentment ultimately became the grand jury of later times which was not abolished until 1933. The country gentry formed an essential element in most of the early juries, both of presentment and trial.

not adjust to the volume, complexity and novel features of the work which faced them. In consequence, after a long period of gradual eclipse, most of their functions were assumed by the courts of the justices.

The office of Justice of the Peace as it emerged in the mid-fourteenth century had therefore some appeal to the community at large. It perpetuated the tradition of popular involvement in local affairs and it provided a more effective means of obtaining justice. As we have seen, it was also attractive to the King because it finally developed as a royal appointment after several attempts by *la commune* to make it an elective office. This was of particular importance because the transition from Keeper to Justice of the Peace coincided with a campaign by the King and his Judges to replace all other courts with royal courts.[29]

The general Eyre

In the reign of William I there appear to have been no royal courts other than the *curia regis* which operated close to the King's person, and all local administration was therefore left to the courts of the shire and the hundred. William did make use of commissions sent out for specific purposes - the best-known example being the compiling of Domesday - but for a long time these rarely had any judicial functions because the King was far more concerned with government and taxation than with judicial matters. Not until it became apparent that the latter could be a source of revenue did the King take an active interest in providing judicial services for all his subjects. Under Henry I justices were sometimes sent out to take criminal pleas and under Henry II the country was divided into circuits which were regularly visited by the King's itinerant justices acting under various commissions. The widest of these in the mid to late thirteenth century was the general Eyre, composed of a small number of professional justices sent from Westminster who were mostly concerned with ensuring that the country was properly governed, but they also administered criminal justice. The Eyre's visits were infrequent, but they imposed a severe strain on the area and were intensely unpopular. All other courts in the county were suspended during the visit and everyone of any consequence was obliged to attend and to give an account of themselves. The outcome was invariably the

29.   Various devices were employed to attract cases into the courts of the King's justices which enjoyed the great advantage over their competitors of being able to compel attendance and of having ample power to enforce execution. In fact the process lasted for a very long time; there were still local courts of various kinds, functioning (though not in criminal justice) under customary rather than royal authority, into the eighteenth century and after, and some clung on until the Courts Act 1971.

imposition of heavy amerciaments on the population and fierce punishments on individuals. One positive outcome of the Eyre, and subsequently of Assizes, was that the meetings of the local population which took place on these occasions contributed to the development of a county community with a voice in Parliament and which provided a foundation for the office of Justice of the Peace.30

Meanwhile other commissions, which were more popular with the local inhabitants (at least with the landowners), began to be issued to itinerant justices from time to time. These were the Commissions of Assize, Oyer and Terminer and Gaol Delivery31 which dealt with criminal cases. In the course of time these commissions were issued not only to royal Judges and lawyers but also to trusted members of the local gentry.

The general Eyre was at its height in the reign of Edward I and then gradually faded. It became clogged with the weight of the further tasks placed upon it, especially as a result of increasing lawlessness and of the demands made by the wars. It also began to fail to achieve one of its main objects, which was the collection of money and which became more trouble than it was worth. The last of the regular county visitations was in 1294; only a very few took place under Edward II. Edward III's reign saw only an artificial, partial, and unsuccessful revival in 1328-31, after which the Eyre was used mainly as a threat to the community of Kent, who normally bought off the threat before anything materialized. As early as 1287 commissions were issued to between two and six landowners in each county to administer the Statute of Winchester of two years earlier because the justices appointed to take the Assizes did not "go every year as often as was ordained."32 The abandonment of the Eyre was due to its own unpopularity and to the greater efficiency of the new system which replaced it. The need for the Eyre also decreased with the development of Parliament because it was no longer essential for the maintenance of close contact with local areas. The same fate did not befall the other itinerant commissions and most of them survived until modern times, but they were not capable of absorbing all the additional business, administrative and judicial, which was left over from the Eyre. This was particularly so after the civil jurisdiction of Assizes was greatly increased by the Statute of Nisi Prius in 1285.

30.   J.D. Maddicott: "The County Community and the Making of Public Opinion in Fourteenth-Century England," *TRHS*, 5th ser., XXVIII, 1978.
31.   Another commission known as "Trailbaston" was also issued from 1305, but unlike the other three it did not survive the fourteenth century. It was mostly concerned with abuses of justice and administration and with hearing and determining felonies and trespasses. It was really a type of "oyer and terminer" and was originally introduced to deal with the armed bands who infested the countryside (Trailbastons) and could not be dealt with effectively by the Eyre.
32.   CPR, 1281-92, pp. 264-5.

Furthermore, the itinerant courts could not deal swiftly with the numerous cases of lawlessness which engulfed the kingdom. There was therefore an urgent need to relieve the pressure, and the remedy, which was applied gradually, was the extension of the authority of the keepers. One may conclude that the decay of the Eyre and the inability of the other commissions to absorb the whole of the residual work, combined with the determination of the Crown to establish royal courts in place of all other jurisdictions, were the immediate causes of the development of the Justices of the Peace as judicial officers.

The Eyre's departure also left a void in the supervision of administration at local level generally, at a time when there was a growing need to meet the problems thrown up by the wars and the labour shortage. This gap too was filled by extending the administrative authority of the Justices of the Peace in preference to other possible contenders, none of whom seemed as well placed as the local gentry to handle and to hold in check the increasing militancy of the peasants and labouring classes. The result was that the keepers, in addition to acquiring an established judicial status, also became responsible for almost the whole of the local government of England. The decease of the Eyre led to a reversion to the earlier tradition of government by local men of influence in each locality.

By 1360, therefore, the Keepers or Justices of the Peace had finally managed to establish themselves as a permanent and seemingly indispensable institution. They were at last recognized as the authority on which local administration, the maintenance of law and order and the dispensing of justice at local level must be based. The process of transforming the Keepers into Justices of the Peace was now virtually complete. It merely remained for the position to be confirmed by legislation.

x

CHAPTER III

THE FIRST JUSTICES

Statute of Westminster 1361 - Beginning of Quarter Sessions - Procedure - Commission of the Peace - Officers of Quarter Sessions - Peasants' Revolt 1381 - Consolidation of justices' position

The Statute of Westminster, 1361

THE STATUTE OF WESTMINSTER 1361[1] completed the transformation from Keepers to Justices of the Peace. The latter are therefore the earliest of surviving public institutions in England to have received statutory recognition, but they are by no means merely creatures of statute. Contrary to a widely held view, their origin rested, as we have seen, not upon legislation but upon the earlier exercise of the royal prerogative. During the previous two reigns the conservators were appointed under writs issued by the Crown without any statutory authority, while the earlier statutes of Edward III assumed a pre-existing power in the King to make the appointments. The same has continued to the present day when the appointments are still made through a commission under the Great Seal which confers upon the justices their authority to act; although virtually all the powers they now exercise are derived from Acts of Parliament.

The first official use of the term "Justice of the Peace" appears in the preamble to the statute which begins: "What sort of Persons shall be Justices of the Peace, and what Authority shall they have." It then goes on to state that the King, prelates, lords and commons in Parliament have ordained:

"That in every shire of England shall be assigned for the keeping of the peace one lord, and with him three or four of the most worthy in the shire, with some learned in the law; and they shall have power to restrain the offenders, rioters, and all other barrators, and to pursue, take, and chastise them according to their trespass or offence; and to cause them to be imprisoned and duly punished according to the laws and customs of the realm, and according to what shall seem best to them to do by their discretions and good deliberation; and also to inform themselves and to inquire of all those who have been pillagers and robbers in the parts beyond the sea, and have now returned and go wandering and will not labour as they were wont to do in times past; and to take and arrest all those that they may find by indictment or by suspicion and to put them in

1. 34 Edw. III, c. 1.

prison; and to take of those who are [not] of good fame, wherever they shall be found, sufficient surety and mainprise for their good behaviour towards the king and his people; and they are to punish the others duly, to the intent that the people may not be troubled or injured by such rioters or rebels, nor the peace be endangered, nor merchants or others passing on the king's highway, be disturbed ...

"And they are also to hear and determine at the king's suit all manner of felonies and trespass done in that shire, according to the laws and customs; and that writs of oyer and terminer shall be granted according to the statutes made with regard to them, but the justices who shall be assigned thereto shall be named by the court and not by the party.

"And the king wills that all general inquiries granted before this time in any lordship whatsoever shall cease utterly and be repealed, on account of the mischiefs and oppressions which have been done to the people by such inquiries. And that fines which are to be made before the justices for trespasses done by any person shall be reasonable and just, having regard to the quantity of the trespass and the cause for which they are made."

Controversy has raged around the word "not" before "of good fame" (*"totz ceux qui ne sont de bone fame"*). It does not appear in the original Norman-French, but has been inserted in all translations which have been generally supported on the ground that it would be inconceivable that Parliament would think it necessary to legislate for the taking of surety from persons of good fame, but rather from those who might be regarded as threats to the peace although they have not yet committed an offence. This view, however, is open to question. The edict of Hubert de Walter in 1195 required the four knights in every shire to take an oath from every male inhabitant irrespective of his reputation, so that good and bad alike were bound to keep the peace. When one turns to the statute of 1361 it is clear that the justices are empowered to deal with troublemakers without the need first to take any surety from them, and indeed they seem to have been able to arrest a person simply on the ground of his bad reputation, for the statute says that they may "take and arrest all those that they may find by indictment or *suspicion*" and put them in prison. It has been argued that the clause was directed towards a temporary emergency and soon fell into disuse, but was revived about the middle of the fifteenth century when an Exchequer clerk in transcribing a volume of statutes inserted a *"ne"* before *"sont de bone fame"* which was copied thereafter in printed editions and translations.[2] Professor Putman, however, while accepting that *"ne"* was definitely not in the original statute, suggests that in

2.   C.G. Crump and C. Johnson, "The Powers of Justices of the Peace," *EHR,* xxvii, 1912, 226-38.

practice many justices may have felt that it was unsuitable to take any action in respect of persons who were of good fame and soon adopted the practice of proceeding only against those who were not of good fame. As a result of this practice a number of scribes may have thought it prudent to insert the "*ne*" in their transcripts.[3] There is reason to think that this hypothesis comes nearest to the truth. The later insertion of "not" was probably done advisedly to reflect current practice and was not due to a lapse by one careless scribe.

The origin of the practice of binding persons over to be of good behaviour and to keep the peace is obscure. Sir Carlton Allen[4] distinguishes between the historical origins of sureties of the peace and those of sureties of good behaviour. He ascribes the latter to the 1361 statute but suggests (following Blackstone) that the former may be traceable to Anglo-Saxon institutions or to the powers of the "conservators, wardens and keepers of the peace" from the twelfth century onwards. It seems probable from an examination of the proceedings of the earlier courts that the concept of providing sureties to keep the peace is an ancient one which was reflected, but did not originate in, the edict of 1195. Thereafter, the keepers and early justices, whether singly or in a group, acted under the authority conferred upon them by their commissions. The Judges have always held that the power to bind over to be of good behaviour also originated long before 1361 and is independent of it. In any event, this provision of the 1361 statute has never been repealed and the power continues to the present day. It may be exercised by any court of record with criminal jurisdiction and not only by justices, but until the Justices of the Peace Act 1968 it is probable that the Judges in other courts acted by virtue of being *ex officio* on the Commission of the Peace.[5]

The statute of 1361 established the justices as an integral part of the machinery of justice. It was a compromise between the conflicting aspirations of the gentry and the King. The justices were to be appointed by the Crown, which they represented, but they were drawn from local men of substance and considerable independence whose personal interest lay in the areas in which they were to perform their duties. The importance, however, of 1361 in the calendar of the justices' development has sometimes been exaggerated. Like 1327 it was not followed by a continuous surge forward. The success was temporary and did not indicate that the justices had at last gained general approval, for they still had many enemies. They were hated by

3. B.H. Putman, "Early Treatise on the Practice of the Justices of the Peace in the Fifteenth and Sixteenth Centuries," Sir Paul Vinogradoff ed., *Oxford Studies in Social and Legal History*, vol. VII, XIII, pp. 204-6.
4. *The Queen's Peace*, 1953.
5. See vol. II, *post*.

the lower classes because of their administration of the labour laws, but for a time their main opponents were still the professional Judges and some of the leading nobles and clergy,[6] whose opposition resulted in a number of set-backs, though mostly of a temporary nature. They suffered a severe reverse in 1364 when the commissions, in defiance of the statute, excluded the power to determine felonies and to administer the labour laws. This continued until 1369 when a statute[7] expressly restored the powers. It was assumed by Professor Putnam that they were withdrawn again between 1382 and 1389, but it seems more likely that they continued to exercise their determining powers during this period, though this was done largely under powers conferred upon some of the justices by separate commissions. From 1389 the peace commissions restored the powers of the Justices of the Peace to determine all offences. When determining felonies they were required to sit with an Assize Justice, but they could take all other offences if they sat with other lawyers who were local men named in the commission as members of the *Quorum.* Thereafter the justices' powers always included the determination of felonies when sitting with members of the *Quorum.*[8]

Apart from these temporary reverses, the years following 1361 saw the start of a long period of expansion of the justices' duties and functions which was to take them to the extraordinary position they were to occupy two or more centuries later.

Beginning of Quarter Sessions

In 1362 a statute[9] directed that all commissions were to require the justices to hold their sessions four times a year. These were to be during the week after Epiphany, the week of Mid-Lent, between Pentecost and the Feast of St John the Baptist and within the eight days of Michaelmas. This was the beginning of Quarter Sessions which

6.   The prelates were especially vehement in opposing the extension of the justices' jurisdiction and in the Parliament of 1380 they strove unsuccessfully to prevent the justices being empowered to deal with extortions, which included extortions by the clergy. (RP, iii, 836). This was part of a very general opposition by the clergy to anything which suggested either encroachment upon ecclesiastical jurisdictions or attempts to extend lay jurisdiction over the clergy. Matters had come to a head in the days of Thomas à Beckett and the criminous clerks issue, but the nagging conflict was still in evidence two and three hundred years later.

7.   42 Edw. III, c. 6. Under this statute the justices were empowered to hear and determine all cases under the labour laws and to award damages.

8.   It is debated whether or not the alleged suspension of determining powers took place between 1382 and 1389. Dr John Post concludes (*EHR*, 1976, vol. XCI, no. CCCLVIII) that it did not, and that there are inconsistencies in the commissions of 1382 which suggest faulty drafting rather than policy. But see Edward Powell, "The Administration of Criminal Justice in Late-Medieval England: Peace Sessions and Assizes. The Political Content of the Law." Proceedings of the Seventh British Legal History Conf., Canterbury, 1985, which suggests that this was deliberate policy. In fact there must be doubts that the JPs used these determining powers even when they had them, save on special occasions.

9.   36 Edw. III, st. 1, c. 12.

were to be held regularly in every county, save for a few brief
interruptions caused by civil war, for more than 600 years.[10] In fact
both the regularity and the frequency of sessions were often erratic in
at least the early decades. In addition to these sessions on specified
dates, the justices could also sit at other times as often as they were
needed and, as the work increased, these "general sessions" became
more frequent. There were some instances when, in a time of crisis,
more than 20 sessions were held in a county in the course of a year.
Usually they took place in the county town but sometimes elsewhere.

The sessions could deal with all types of criminal case except
treason, though as time passed, murder trials tended to be sent to the
Assizes and the commissions directed that any case involving difficulty
should also go to those courts. This was in accordance with the
tendency, which had long prevailed, to regard the criminal jurisdiction
of the Justices of the Peace as being primarily for the purpose of
assisting the Commissions of Oyer and Terminer and Gaol Delivery
(and for a time of Trailbaston). As the courts manned by the
professional Judges became more effective they gradually
appropriated, at the expense of the justices, the most important of the
criminal work, though this made little difference to the increasing
volume of criminal cases of a less serious nature which soon fell to be
dealt with by the justices at their sessions. Furthermore, they became
solely responsible for administrative and economic matters where, at
least at the outset, their function was largely supervisory. In this sphere
their field of responsibility was expanded to an astonishing extent
during the following two centuries.

As we have seen, the early justices were involved in administrative
duties before 1361, as they were already responsible for enforcing the
labour laws. An additional economic function was entrusted to them
under the 1361 legislation itself when weights and measures were
placed under their authority. It was decreed that:

> "They which shall be assigned to keep the peace shall have Power
> to inquire of Measures, and also of Weights ... Every Person do
> sell by the Balance, so that the Balance be even ... and that the
> Beam of the Balance do not bow more to one Part than to the
> other; and that the Weight be according to the Standard of the
> Exchequer ..."[11]

Other detailed instructions followed, and anyone who contravened the
provisions was to be "grievously punished, as well at the Suit of the
Party as at the Suit of our Lord The King." The justices could make

10.　Courts of Quarter Sessions were abolished by the Courts Act, 1971; vol. II, ch. IX, *post*.
11.　34 Edw. III, c. 5.

preliminary inquiries and could hear and determine alleged offences. Further legislation ensured uniformity of weights and measures throughout the country.[12] A statute of Richard II[13] declared that there should be "one Measure and one Weight throughout all the Realm of England, as in the Great Charter and other Statutes and Ordinances thereof made." On conviction for using other weights or measures the offender was to be sentenced to imprisonment for half a year and forced to "make Recompense to the Party grieved to double that of his loss."

Procedure

The statutes of this period did not contain a clear definition of the powers which they conferred upon the justices and they were virtually silent on the procedure which was to be followed in performing the various functions. It was left largely to the initiative of the justices to decide how to implement the statutes' provisions. In the circumstances it was not surprising that they followed the procedure which already applied in the Eyre and the tourn, and they therefore adopted the system of presentment and indictment which they applied to the whole machinery of local government as well as to the trial of criminal cases. The older courts had themselves followed the same practice when dealing with either criminal justice or economic affairs. Both were conducted through machinery which was of a judicial nature, the essence being the punishment either of persons who had committed a criminal offence or of those individuals or groups who had failed to fulfil their legal obligations. "The remarkable thing was that so much government could be carried on through the forms of a criminal trial."[14]

The proceedings on all occasions began with the empanelling of a jury of presentment. A general charge was then given to them by one of the justices setting out at considerable length what was to be done. The idea of the charge was to instruct the jurors precisely as to the matters into which they were to inquire and then present. It referred to the administrative as well as the criminal responsibilities of the justices, and it concluded with a summary of the formal documents used by the court, such as writs and forms of indictment.[15] The jury were told of the matters into which they were to inquire and they

---

12. Some weights and measures jurisdiction had been exercised (and continued to be exercised) by the customary courts, especially those claiming the Assize of bread and ale, from the thirteenth century if not before.
13. 13 Rich. II, st. 1, c. 9. Further statutes on the subject were: 3 Hen. VI, c. 1 and 11 Hen. VI, c. 8.
14. John P. Dawson, *A History of Lay Judges.* Harvard UP (1960).
15. For examples of the justices' charge to jurors see Public Proceedings, List III, pp. 10-24. The first printed charge it to be found in the *Boke of Justices of Peas* of 1506.

heard reports from the constables and others on the state of law and order in the county. It was then for the jury to say whether offences had been committed, be they criminal, such as robbery, or administrative, such as failure to maintain a bridge. They then made their presentment,[16] endorsing it where appropriate with the words *"billa vera,"* (otherwise with *ignoramus"*)[17] and where this pointed to a specific person or group an indictment was drawn up and those concerned were then tried before another jury - a petty jury of trial.[18] At the close of the proceedings the sessions imposed what they considered to be a suitable punishment. This might involve the amerciament of a group of persons who had failed to discharge some administrative responsibility.

Even the most trivial breaches of the law had to be tried with a jury at the sessions if the accused pleaded not guilty, though in many cases at gaol delivery the Judges intervened and stopped the trial without putting the issue to a jury, unless an accuser objected. This was especially so where the basis for the not-guilty plea was a denial that goods had been stolen at all. It is quite likely (but the evidence is wanting either way) that similar judicial discretion was exercised at peace sessions. Courts of summary jurisdiction did not appear until much later, and any possibility of doubt about the invariable necessity for a jury was removed in 1368 when it was proclaimed by statute[19] that: "No man shall be called upon to answer without Presentment."

Apart from trials an individual justice could exercise certain functions on his own. His role was primarily to investigate complaints and, where necessary, to arrest an accused person and ensure that he appeared at the sessions. He could commit to prison pending trial and could take security to keep the peace and, at his discretion, could release the security. He could bail persons imprisoned on suspicion of felony. In certain circumstances he could impose a fine. It was also his duty to stop any riot or affray which, with his other executive duties, was a reflection of the fact that the justices were still responsible for keeping the peace as police authorities as well as acting judicially and as administrators. It was generally assumed that judicial duties were reserved for all the justices assembled at the sessions and that a single justice had no authority to hear and determine felonies, although the statutes of this period were silent on the point. They merely imposed a

16. The presentment was more than a statement of offences and often included the opinions of the jurymen as to what was wrong in the area.
17. It seems likely that originally *billa vera* was an endorsement of a bill of accusation presented to the grand jury (whether by justices, constables, or others) and reviewed by them, as distinct from their own presentments made spontaneously or upon informally obtained evidence.
18. The existence of two juries - the grand or accusing jury and the petty or trial jury - was unique to England. It was unknown on the Continent.
19. 42 Edw. III, c. 3

general duty on the justices to try offenders and to punish them, without specifying whether this had to be done by all the justices in a county or could be discharged by a limited number. During the following 200 years many statutes were to give one, two or three justices the duty of imposing punishment on those guilty of breaches of the statute.

Commission of the Peace

As already explained, the justices' authority to act has always been derived from the commission. Even though in the course of time most of the powers they exercised were acquired under statutes and were not mentioned in the commission, they could not exercise such powers unless they had been appointed under a commission. The latter was, and still is, issued under the Great Seal, whose impression is attached to the parchment scroll on which the commission is inscribed. At first, commissions were issued annually, thus providing an opportunity for both the personnel and the powers of the justices to be changed. The greatest variation was in respect of their powers which depended largely upon the whim of the Crown and to a lesser extent upon the contents of statutes.

The form of the commission in the 1360s was the same as it had been for the keepers in the previous century and it continued with no appreciable change until 1590 when a new form was introduced. It was the content rather than the form which varied from one commission to another, adding or omitting various functions which the justices were to perform. These changes did not necessarily implement the statutes currently in force. Sometimes a commission omitted a power which had been clearly conferred by statute while another included one for which there was no statutory authority. In view of the overriding authority of modern Acts of Parliament one is inclined to overestimate the importance of early statutes. In the fourteenth century the Crown obviously did not regard itself as being bound strictly by the terms of Parliamentary legislation to which it had agreed, and the fluctuating powers conferred by successive commissions, often at variance with the statutes then in force, reflected the government's uncertainty as to the efficacy of expanding the justices' authority.

The early commissions began by referring to current disorders and specifically mentioned the statutes which the Crown wished the keepers or justices to enforce.[20] In the 1360s these were the Statutes of Winchester (1285), Northampton (1328) and Westminster (1361). This

20. For a detailed account of the commissions from 1327 to the sixteenth century with a description of the charges given during this period see B.H. Putnam, *Proceedings before the Justices of the Peace in the Fourteenth and Fifteenth Centuries* Ames Foundation, 1938, pp. XX-XXIX.

was the peace clause which authorized the justices to enforce the peace, with power to punish offenders and to take security. This provision was followed by the requirement to hold sworn inquests. Next came oyer and terminer; the power to hear and determine felonies and other offences with a *Quorum*. The commission also set out the justices' other duties which included the enforcement of the laws on labourers and on weights and measures, forestalling, engrossing and regrating21 and the fixing of days and places for the return of juries. There were also various instructions, one (from 1380) being to reserve difficult cases of extortion for trial at Assizes or when a Judge of one of the benches was present at the sessions. Another directed the sheriff to assist by empanelling jurors and arresting delinquents, and yet another required one of the justices to keep the writs and indictments. The latter was the beginning of the office of *Custos Rotulorum*, though the term was not recognized officially until the middle of the following century.22 The commissions also, of course, contained the names of the justices together with those of any of the Judges of the King's Bench or Common Pleas who were included. The commissions were also addressed to the great officers of state but they were not expected to perform any of the duties. In 1378 the Commons complained that commissions were often addressed to lords who were unable to attend to the business, and in response to this it was promised that the Chancellor and Treasurer and others of the King's Council would ensure that sufficient justices in each county were placed on the commissions.23

There were complaints that the requirement of the 1361 statute that some justices in each county should be learned in the law was not always observed, and that this led to delay in disposing of important business and to offenders being released before trial and so escaping justice. As mentioned earlier, the commissions issued from November 1389 provided for two sections of the *Quorum*, one for the determination of felonies and consisting of the Assize Justice alone, while the second, covering all other offences, was composed of local lawyers in addition to the Assize Justices. This was not, however, a solution to delays in the disposal of felonies and in 1394, a return was made to a single *Quorum*, but one composed of Assize Justices and two or more local lawyers, and it was decreed by statute24 that two men

21. A forestaller was one who bought up a commodity, usually corn, on the way to a market, an engrosser bought standing crops from a grower, a regrater bought at a market for resale. In each case the object was to resell at a profit. The first two often created monopolies.
22. See p. 119-120, *post.*
23. RP iii, 44a.
24. 17 Rich. II, c. 10. "Forasmuch as Thieves, notoriously defamed, and others taken with the Manner, by their long Abiding in Prison, after that they be arrested, be delivered by Charters, and favourable Inquests, procured to the great Hinderance of the People: It is accorded and assented, that in every Commission of the Peace throughout the Realm, where Need shall be, two Men of Law of the same County where such Commission shall be made, shall be assigned to go and proceed to the Deliverance of such Thieves and Felons as often as they shall think it expedient."

of law should be assigned to deliver gaols when the need arose. By the end of the fourteenth century the lawyer justices in some counties were the best attenders at sessions.

Each justice continued to serve until a new commission was issued. This usually occurred annually, but not invariably so. In the later fourteenth century gaps of several years sometimes elapsed between general issues, with *ad hoc* afforcing commissions to remedy excessive depletions in the meantime. There were always, however, new commissions on the accession of a new monarch. Names were not removed from an operative commission as was done later. Before he could act, a justice had to pay a fee and take an oath[25] under a writ of *Dedimus Potestatem* addressed to one of the senior justices, usually a Justice of Assize who was himself on the same and on neighbouring commissions, directing him to receive oaths from all the Justices of the Peace in the area.

Executive officers of Quarter Sessions

The executive officers of Quarter Sessions were the old officials of the county and hundred - the sheriff, bailiffs and constables. Before the end of the fourteenth century the justices rivalled the sheriff in importance and they soon established a lead. The position where the keepers had held military posts in support of the sheriffs had been reversed and it had become the sheriff's duty to attend upon the justices and to comply with their directions. The sheriff, however, although deprived of most of his former judicial functions, was still an indispensable element in keeping the peace and in the machinery of justice. He had extensive powers of arrest which he might exercise through the bailiffs, who were subordinate officials whom he could authorize to make arrests, take distraints and summon persons to court. As we have seen, the commission required him to summon panels of jurors for both the jury of presentment and that of trial, although throughout the fourteenth century there were complaints against sheriffs that they indulged in corrupt practices by empanelling packed juries to suit one of the parties. Earlier commissions had sometimes appointed a sheriff as *Custos*, but under Edward III he was precluded from the office of justice. In 1445 the justices were given statutory power to punish sheriffs for negligence and for violation of statutes, and in 1461 their judicial supremacy over the sheriffs was finally confirmed when, under a statute[26] passed in response to much

---

25.   14 Rich. II, c. 7, directed that justices should be "sworn truly to execute their office."
26.   1 Edw. IV, c. 2.

pressure by the Commons, all presentments and indictments normally taken at the sheriff's tourn had to be taken before the justices.[27] It would be wrong, however, to regard the sheriff's functions thereafter as being confined mainly to empanelling juries, serving writs and enforcing judgments. He still had an important part to play, especially as a representative of the central government, and it was through him that the courts of King's Bench and Common Pleas continued to operate.

At the bottom of the hierarchy the man of all work was the constable, who was to be found in each hundred and township. He was an unpaid official, elected annually in the local customary and feudal courts, and he was responsible for maintaining order within his area. All complaints were made to him and it was his duty to pursue and arrest suspects and, as there were usually no available gaols, to detain them in some other way until they could be brought before the sessions. It is often assumed that he almost invariably did so in his own house, but this is uncertain. Early stocks and shackles and small lock-ups survive in sufficient quantities to suggest that most jurisdictions had at least some crude means of personal restraint and temporary detention to make it unnecessary to resort to overnight imprisonment in a private house.

At the sessions the constable had to give a report to the jury of presentment. It was his duty to stop brawling and illegal games and he commanded the forces of the hundred or township which made up the *posse comitatus* under the command of the sheriff. He also bore the brunt of the enforcement of the labour laws and was therefore intensely unpopular with many of the local population who sometimes subjected him to physical violence. As might be expected, the office was undertaken with the utmost reluctance and during Jack Cade's rebellion in 1450 many constables were among the rebels. During the following centuries some additional officials were appointed for specific purposes, as will be seen later, but at this time the constable was the only officer normally available in every local area to execute the instructions of the justices and, although he was by custom appointed in the old local courts, the justices, without statutory authority, quickly adopted him and made him their servant. Later he was to become the principal officer of the parish when it replaced the hundred and township as the lowest tier of local government.

The Clerk of the Peace

It cannot have been easy for the justices to know precisely what their

---

27.   This statute did not apply to private leets and some continued sporadically to hear felony at first instance.

duties were supposed to be, especially when commissions began to omit any reference to statutes currently in force, but assistance was probably forthcoming from an official who began to appear in the 1350s. This was the Clerk of the Peace who, from early times, was a lawyer. In the fourteenth and fifteenth centuries some Clerks of the Peace were clerks from the Westminster courts. The first official mention of a clerk was in 1380 when the justices were directed to administer an oath to their clerk "to conceal the Counsel of the King and to perform his Duties loyally."[28] Before then there had been a reference to a clerk in the Statute of Labourers 1351, but that related solely to the work of the Justices of Labourers. It seems probable that the office, in the form in which it came to be known as that of Clerk of the Peace, first appeared immediately after the statute of 1361. This was the view expressed by a Judge, Sir John Vaughan, in 1829 in the case of *Harding* v. *Pollock.*[29] He had no doubt that after 1361, the sessions being a court of record, the justices would have had the right to appoint a clerk "to assist them in drawing their indictments, in arraigning their prisoners, in joining issues for the Crown, in entering their judgments, in awarding their process, and in making up and keeping their records." The title "Clerk of the Peace," however, was adopted only gradually and for a long time various other expressions such as "Clerk of the Justices" and "Clerk of the Keepers of the Peace" were applied to the post. In the fifteenth century the patents of appointment referred to "Clerk of the Peace," but this title does not appear in the pipe rolls until the sixteenth century.[30]

The main function of the clerk was to keep the records but, being a lawyer, the justices came to rely upon him for guidance in the law. An important function of the clerk was to draft the charge to the jury, although this was sometimes done by one of the justices who was a lawyer or who had had long experience of the procedure. No guidance on the wording of the charge was given from above and it was left entirely to the individual sessions to compile what they thought fit. Sometimes they copied the charge of a neighbouring county, but in the early years many sessions produced versions which were original and unique.

The Peasants' Revolt, 1381

The peasants' hatred of the labour laws and of those who enforced

28. RP III, 85.
29. 6 Bingham's Reports, 25.
30. In 1404 Letters Patent were issued by the Crown for the appointment of an individual as "Clerk and King's Attorney" before the Justices of the Peace in Essex, Hertfordshire and Suffolk (CPR 1401-1405, p. 373), and there is reference to a "Clerk of the Sessions of the Peace" in a patent of appointment in 1412. For further references to the office see vol. II, chs. VI and IX, *post.*

them, which had been manifest for some time in sporadic outbreaks of violence, erupted into open rebellion under Wat Tyler's leadership in June, 1381.[31] The Justices of the Peace were regarded as an obvious target. They had applied the labour legislation rigorously and often ruthlessly. They had done so under pressure from the government, but the policy also seemed to be in their own interests as landowners. The number of labour cases dealt with during the 10 years or so before the revolt had increased significantly, especially in the counties of South East England where the outbreak was most violent. The behaviour of the justices was undoubtedly a factor in causing the uprising, but the animosity of the insurgents was also directed against the lawyers, with a certain amount of justification.[32] Even three Chief Justices of the King's Bench (Richard Willoughby in 1340, William Thorpe in 1350 and Henry Green in 1365) had proved to be corrupt, and lawyers in general had given the impression that they were the cause of much of the current troubles. One of Wat Tyler's first demands was that "all lawyers should be hung," and this was soon extended to "all justices," meaning initially the lawyer Judges but tending to embrace the Justices of the Peace as well. Pursuant to this theme, the rioters put to death the Chancellor, Archbishop Sudbury, followed by the Chief Justice of the King's Bench, John de Cavendish (who was himself on the Commissions of the Peace for Bedfordshire, Buckinghamshire, Cambridgeshire and Norfolk) and others, including a number of Justices of the Peace. Some of the justices, however, were themselves involved on the side of the insurgents, at least at the outset, and there were instances of a few of them inciting the mob with a view to working off old grudges.

A recent thesis by Dr David Crook of the Public Record Office,[33] describing attacks on John of Gaunt's estates in Derbyshire, not only reveals that the violence was more widespread throughout the country than is generally supposed, but that members of the gentry class were not slow to seize the opportunity provided by the revolt to try to further their own interests. This also applied to some leading burgesses. Any appearance of an alliance between the peasantry and the Commons in opposition to oppression was, however, short-lived

31. Although labour legislation was one of the underlying causes of discontent, the precipitant of the revolt in both the primary areas (Essex and Kent) was undoubtedly resistance to the attempted enforcement of the 1380 poll tax. Special commissions for enforcement were issued, including some JPs, and it was against these commissioners that the first risings occurred.

32. One of the objections to lawyers and laws (apart from the obvious and sempiternal complaints) was the adherence to customary, ie, villein, tenure as a means of landholding. Many rebels thought that the lawyers, especially those who acted as stewards for estates, perpetuated this, and the widespread destruction of manorial court records (in which this copyhold tenure was recorded) illustrates this element in the grievances. This objection clearly links closely with the aim of a deregulated market for labour.

33. "Derbyshire and the English Rising of 1381." *Historical Research*, vol. 60, no. 141.

and never widespread. The interests of the gentry in their opposition to the influence of the great lords and the oppression of the royal justices were far from those of the peasants. In fact, current trends were bringing together the gentry and the magnates, sometimes connected already by family ties, and were, if anything, increasing the gap between them and the labouring class. As Professor Harding has commented:[34]

> "When the gentry who protested against the maintenance of the great lords and the punitive exercise of royal justice were given jurisdiction of their own, they used it to mark themselves off from the common people by a line far more enduring and difficult to cross than that between gentry and *grantz*. The major factor of the development of fourteenth-century society was the growth of an aristocratic county community embracing both magnates and gentry, which formed in the indictments brought before sessions of oyer and terminer and of the peace its own image of a rebellious servant class."

At first, both central and local government were taken by surprise by the revolt and seemed for a time to be paralysed with fright. When they began to recover, the government, although demanding the support of the justices, did not rely upon them in the first instance to restore order. Instead, they issued special Commissions of a Trailbaston type with full powers to hear and determine and, although in some instances these included existing justices, in every case they were led by a magnate who was primarily responsible for restoring order. This was a temporary measure which seems to have been directed at augmenting the authority of the local justices and, as the crisis passed, the latter resumed their position as the principal authority for keeping the peace. This was, however, a sign that the justices were still regarded as an expedient for normal times. In moments of exceptional crisis such as the Lollards' rising in 1414 and Jack Cade's rebellion in 1450, special commissions were again issued to magnates.

The readiness of some of the justices to take advantage of the lawlessness which followed the 1381 rebellion was a manifestation of the violent nature of society in general which characterized the Middle Ages and was the subject of constant complaints in Parliament. At all levels, from the Royal Family downwards, feuds could erupt into open warfare, and it was only natural that similar situations should arise among the justices themselves. As the number of justices in each county increased, they sometimes became divided into rival groups

---

34.   A.H. Harding, "The Revolt against the Justices," *TRHS*, 5th Series, vol. 10, 1960, p. 180.

which on occasion resorted to physical violence against each other. Justices often arrived at sessions fully armed, sometimes backed by retinues of supporters, and there are records of magnates attending with bands of retainers when one of their henchmen had been charged and demanding his release. It was not uncommon for acts of violence to occur during church services and it would have been surprising if similar events had not also taken place at the justices' sessions.

On occasions, sessions were attacked and disrupted by outsiders. A not untypical example appears in the Patent Rolls some 10 years before the 1361 statute. It is recorded that Commissions of Oyer and Terminer were issued to certain persons to deal with events in Oxfordshire. They were to inquire:

"... touching the Persons who, when the King by Letters Patent lately appointed Thomas de Langele [and others] to be Keepers of the Peace and Justices of Oyer and Terminer touching divers Trespasses in the County of Oxford, and they made their Session at Eynesham for the Execution of the Appointment ..., like Madmen and Men possessed by an evil Spirit, usurping to themselves Power above the royal Power, came in large Numbers to that Town in manner of War and assaulted the said Thomas and chased him into a Chamber in the Abbey of Eynesham, besieged him therein, threatened to burn him in it if he did not deliver to them all the Indictments and Accusations against them ... which he had in his Custody, and prevented him and his Fellows from holding their Sessions according to their Office. Such great Rebellion and Misdeeds, so dishonouring to the King and especially as having been done when He is about to go forth from England for the Defence of the Realm and to repel His enemies therefrom, greatly move Him, and it is His Will that they shall meet with speedy Punishment."[35]

Many of those who perpetrated these outrages came from the same social background as the gentry who served as justices. Even a sitting of oyer and terminer was broken up by a knight invading the hall with a drawn sword and seizing one of the commissioners by the throat.[36] Among the most notorious robbers of the fourteenth century were the Folvilles, a knightly family of six brothers, one a priest, who terrorized Leicestershire in the early part of Edward III's reign. Among their associates was the constable of Rockingham Castle and their exploits included the murder of a Baron of the Exchequer and the holding to ransom of a justice of the King's Bench.[37] The situation was

35.   CPR, 1348-50, 594.
36.   *Select Cases before the King's Council,* 1390, p. 79.
37.   E.L.G. Stones, "The Folvilles of Ashby-Folville, Leicestershire, and their Associates in Crime," *TRHS,* 5th ser. vii, 1957, 117-36.

exacerbated by the fact that every male of fighting age, criminals as well as law-abiding citizens, other than the clergy, was obliged to possess arms and to be trained in their use. However, the occasions when the justices failed to carry out their duties for one reason or another were the exception rather than the rule. In spite of the difficulties, they acquired a reputation for dealing with the problems of the day more effectively than any alternative system which could be contemplated at the time.

Remuneration of justices and clerks

The justices had not yet come to appreciate the advantages of being on the commission. Later generations recognized that the rewards in terms of influence and prestige could be so great that, for many, appointment to the bench was a prize that was worth every effort to attain. In the fourteenth century, however, the perquisites of the office were not immediately apparent whereas the disadvantages were obvious. The post was time-consuming, often involving hazardous journeys over almost non-existent roadways to reach sessions where one's life might be at risk. Yet failure to attend sessions could result in a fine imposed by the Council, and further fines were incurred if the justice did not comply with the provisions of an ever-increasing number of statutes. As some inducement to attending sessions the Statute of Cambridge of 1388[38] directed that justices should receive four shillings and their clerks two shillings for each day on which they attended Quarter Sessions, though there was no payment for performing other duties. The clerks also came to be entitled to various fees. The four shillings was equivalent to 16 times the daily wage of an agricultural labourer for normal work. As an incentive to the imposition of heavy fines, the payments to the justices and clerks were to be made by the sheriffs out of the fines and amerciaments which were imposed. Lords of franchises were to contribute to the pay, "after the Rate of their Part of Fine and Amerciaments aforesaid." In 1390, lords who were on the commissions were disentitled to receive any wage.[39]

The 1388 statute fixed the number of justices in each county at six (increased to eight by the 1390 statute), in addition to Judges of

38. 12 Rich. II, c. 10. The payment of wages to justices gradually fell into disuse and was finally abolished by an Act of 1854.
39. 14 Rich. II, c. 7: *Et que null Duc, Count, Baron ou Baneret ... ne preignent gages purle dit office.* According to the statute therefore only those below the degree of Baneret qualified for payment. A Baneret was a knight who was entitled to bring vassals onto the field of battle under his banner. He is not to be confused with Baronets who were introduced by James I at the beginning of the seventeenth century.

Assize. It has already been observed that the medieval Kings did not regard themselves as being bound rigidly by the provisions of a statute and they seem to have disregarded them with impunity whenever it suited their purpose to do so. It is not surprising therefore that the number of persons on the Commission of the Peace for a county frequently exceeded the statutory maximum. Justices were required by the 1388 statute to attend sessions on at least three days each quarter. This did not apply to the Judges but only to commissioners "the which be continually dwelling in the county."

The year 1390 saw the last occasion when the Commons secured the appointment of justices by having them named and assigned (*assignez et nomez*) in Parliament. This was short-lived, and thereafter appointments were exclusively in the hands of the Council with responsibility being primarily with the Chancellor and the Treasurer. The latter officers did not, of course, rely solely upon their own knowledge of potential candidates. Recommendations were received from many quarters, as they would continue to be up to the present day, but at that time they arrived most frequently in the form of petitions from groups within the local community, though the Chancellor and his colleagues were also influenced to a considerable extent by pressure from the leading magnates and the church.

The justices were now well established as criminal Judges and as administrators, while they still maintained their traditional role of police authorities. The next chapter will show how an ever-increasing flow of legislation added to their duties, especially in the economic field where their authority grew in the wake of expanding trade and industry. They still constituted only one among a number of different authorities concerned in local government and the administration of the law, but they were establishing their supremacy over all their rivals whom they would ultimately replace. During the turmoil and the weakness of central government which marked much of the next hundred years, the justices consolidated their position as the undisputed instrument of effective local government upon which the strong Tudor monarchy was able to build.

CHAPTER IV

THE FIFTEENTH CENTURY
CONSOLIDATION AND EXPANSION

*Consolidation notwithstanding troublous times - Trade and industry -
Prices - Wages and labour - Class distinctions - Roads, waterways and
bridges - Criminal jurisdiction - Work of justices out of sessions -
Supervision by superior courts - Savagery of the times - The Wars of the
Roses - The country under the Yorkists 1461-1485 - Language used in
legal documents - Establishment of the Tudor monarchy - Recognition
of the justices as men of all work*

THE DEVELOPMENT OF THE OFFICE of Justice of the Peace
throughout its earlier history was largely fortuitous. Until the
nineteenth century any progress was unsystematic and was the chance
outcome of fluctuating circumstances arising from the political, social
and economic climate prevailing at the time. Like many achievements
by members of the human race, the justices' advance was coincidental
and was the result of being in the right place at the right time and of
being able to take advantage of an opportunity when it was offered. In
the fourteenth century they, or their predecessors, the keepers, were
on the scene when the country was overwhelmed by unprecedented
lawlessness which the existing institutions were manifestly unable to
handle. Again, when a catastrophic economic and labour crisis
developed in the aftermath of the plague and called once more for a
novel method of solution, the justices presented a ready-made piece of
machinery which could be adapted to meet the new problems, and
which had certain clear advantages such as intimate knowledge and
experience of people and conditions in their respective areas and an
obvious personal interest in implementing the new laws. The fact that
they were able to seize these opportunities when offered was due again
to chance, in that at each crucial stage they had champions who were
in the ascendant in Parliament and were in a position to press their
claims and to secure their adoption in preference to other contenders.
For nearly 200 years the Commons struggled to advance the cause of
the justices. They frequently failed to achieve their objective and as
Professor Putnam[1] has shown they sometimes suffered severe reverses,
but with remarkable perseverance coupled with their rising influence
in Parliament they ultimately triumphed, in some instances after

---

1.   B.H. Putnam, *Proceedings before the Justices of the Peace in the Fourteenth and Fifteenth
     Centuries*, Ames Foundation, 1938, p. xli.

striving for several generations.

The same phenomenon occurred again in the fifteenth century which, though an era of violence and disruption, at times on an even greater scale than in the previous century, was also a period of change and transition which was not without some positive development and significant achievement. New situations arose which the justices were able to exploit. Their ability to do so was enhanced by the increasing importance of the gentry as a class both in and out of Parliament. It was a class that now extended beyond the knights of the shire and included a growing number of leading citizens in the boroughs, though the two groups, while presenting a united front to the rest of the community, were to remain separate entities in the social order.

The fourteenth century closed with the usurpation of the throne by Henry Bolingbroke, son of John of Gaunt, who succeeded as Henry IV. Richard II had sought to meet the crisis by calling upon the justices to maintain the peace according to the statutes, but the gentry were angered by his forced loans and heavy taxes and by his adoption of the role of an absolute despot, and their response was unenthusiastic and ineffective. When Henry succeeded to the throne his position was at first precarious and he seems at an early stage to have recognized the advantage of gaining the justices' support in establishing his authority. The justices were therefore poised to take advantage of any new development which might occur.

Trade and industry

One of the most notable features of the fifteenth century was the development of trade and industry especially in the towns on a scale which had never before been contemplated, and which was surprising having regard to the unsettled state of the country at the time. With it came the need to regulate standards and to suppress graft and dishonesty, for which there were unparalleled opportunities. How was the country to deal with the novel problems created by the new trading institutions? This time there was little hesitation in reaching a conclusion. Although there were always other contenders, no one seemed to be in a position to meet the challenge as effectively as the justices who had already shown themselves to be the best potential means of keeping the peace. As each trade or industry developed, with its accompanying corruption, the Commons usually had little difficulty in persuading the government that the best means of control would be provided through a further extension of the justices' authority.

An interesting feature of this development, which will become apparent in the following pages, was that the legislators in the Middle Ages were not concerned with the elimination of corrupt practices in general but only in so far as they affected a particular trade or industry. With few exceptions, each statute was designed to deal solely with the production and marketing of a specific type of commodity - food, drink, clothing and other items considered to be essential or of sufficient importance to require special protection, such as silverware. Although the field covered by these laws was extensive, a person could still produce and sell faulty goods with impunity provided that they were not among those named in a statute.

Two other differences which distinguish the legal system administered by the fifteenth century justices from that of their successors today were, first, that the mediaeval justices not only tried the offences presented at their sessions, but in many cases were required also to carry out inquiries and to pursue and apprehend suspected offenders. Secondly, although some statutes specified the penalties which were to be imposed on conviction, others stated that the punishment was to be left to the discretion of the justices without prescribing a maximum or giving any guidance as to what might be considered appropriate.

In the fourteenth century the principal trade of the country was in wool and the early justices were responsible for enforcing regulations governing its preparation and sale. A statute of 1389[2] provided "that none buy or sell Wools at more Weight than at Fourteen Pounds the Stone, upon Pain to pay the Double to him that feeleth himself grieved and to make Fine and Ransom to the King after the Quantity of the Trespass." For a long time, much of the wool produced in England had been exported to the Continent where clothmaking was centered, especially in Flanders. By the end of the century, however, many foreign weavers had been induced by persecution at home and encouragement from the English Crown to emigrate to England, notwithstanding the ingrained hostility of the English people whose xenophobia led to the slaughter of large numbers of Continental craftsmen by the mob in London during the Peasants' Revolt in 1381.

By the beginning of the fifteenth century, cloth had outstripped wool as the major national produce, for both home consumption and export, and it was now manufactured in country districts as well as in the towns. The most noticeable change in the character of English trade during the fifteenth century was the growth in the export of cloth and miscellaneous merchandise in contrast to the earlier export of wool. This was naturally accompanied by a number of statutes containing detailed regulations for the manufacture and sale of cloth, which were enforceable by the justices at their county sessions or by the mayors and bailiffs who constituted a growing body of justices *ex officio* in the boroughs. In Richard II's reign there had been enactments governing

2.   13 Rich. II, c. 9.

the types of cloth, which varied in different counties,[3] and under Henry IV[4] it was decreed that "every Cloth made within the Realm should contain by Assize the Length of Eight and Twenty Yards by the Crest, and every Dozen of Cloth of Fourteen Yards by the Crest ..." Failure to comply entailed a fine of £10 for a first offence, £20 for a second, and on a third conviction the offender had all his goods and chattels seized and held "at the King's Will." A comprehensive piece of legislation on the cloth trade was enacted in 1464.[5] After referring to the "deceitful" making of cloth whereby purchasers were defrauded, the statute contained extensive provisions governing the length and breadth of various types of cloth and the manner in which they should be marked. It then went on to deal with the internal management of the cloth trade and ordered all clothmakers to pay their workers in "lawful money," commenting that previously the workers had been forced to take "a great Part to their Wages in Pins, Girdles and other unprofitable Wares ..." Justices of the Peace were specifically empowered to hear and determine complaints, and the statute also stipulated that a single justice might deal with breaches of the work regulations. Arrangements had to be made, of course, to ensure that infringements of the statutes' provisions were brought to the attention of the justices. This was done by "searchers" who were appointed by the justices in the counties and by the borough authorities in the towns. It was their duty to supervise the functioning of the trade and to report breaches of the regulations to the sessions.

Searchers were used in the control of a number of trades, with some variation in their functions. In the case of tilemaking they exercised the role of expert witnesses who might be ordered to carry out an examination *in situ*. Provisions to this effect were contained in a statute of 1477,[6] which also provided a good example of the careful detail in which legislation on trade and industry at this time defined its regulations and the procedure whereby the justices were to enforce them. The statute also made it clear that most of the duties which it placed on the justices could be performed by a single justice. It decreed that the justices, or anyone of them, "shall have full Power to inquire, hear, and determine by their Discretions, as well as by Examination or otherwise, the Defaults, Offences, and Trespasses which shall happen to be committed contrary to this Ordinance," and to fine the offenders. It then went on to give the justices or justice power to "call before them, or any of them, ... Persons as by their Discretion have or shall have best Experience or Knowledge in the Occupation of making of Tile, to search and examine the digging, casting, turning, parting,

3.   13 Rich. II, cc. 10 and 11.
4.   11 Hen. IV, c. 6.
5.   4 Edw. IV, c. 1.
6.   17 Edw. IV, c. 4.

making, whitening, and anealing aforesaid." These persons were again called searchers and no tile might be sold until it had been examined by them. If the searchers found anyone offending against the ordinance they should present them "before the Justices of the Peace at their next Sessions."

The earliest crafts to be covered by legislation were those concerned in the production of what were regarded as essential items. Thus in 1389 regulations were introduced governing the tanning of leather: "For as much as divers Shoemakers and Cordwainers use to tan their Leather, and sell the same falsely tanned, also make Shoes and Boots of such leather not well tanned, and sell them as dear as they will, to the great Deceit of the poor Commons,"[7] it was decreed that shoemakers and cordwainers should cease to "use the Craft of Tanning" and tanners the craft of shoemaking. The penalty for failing to comply was forfeiture of all the offending boots, shoes and leather to the King. The cordwainers, however, continued to be in trouble and in 1423 a further statute[8] proclaimed that:

"The Leather tanned by Cordwainers, using the Mystery of Tanners, ... is so deceitfully tanned, that the Boots, Shoes and other Necessaries thereof made, be in small Season wasted and destroyed, ... to the great Deceit, and Loss of the Commonalty of the Realm."

The justices were again ordered to investigate and punish.

As might be expected, one of the early manufacturing industries to be considered of national importance was the making of arrows. There seems to have been scope for corrupt practice in finishing the arrowheads, and a statute of 1406,[9] after beginning with a statement of the cause of the trouble, as was the usual practice, went on to define precisely how the arrowheads were to be made, and then empowered the justices to investigate and punish:

"Because the Arrow-Smiths do make many faulty Heads for Arrows and Quarels defective, not well, nor lawfully, nor defensibly, to the great Jeopardy and Deceit of the People, and of the whole Realm; it is ordained and established, That all the Heads of Arrows and Quarels hereafter to be made, shall be well boiled or brased, and hardened at the Point with Steel; ... And the Justices of the Peace ... shall have Power to inquire of all such deceitful Makers of Heads and Quarels, and to punish them."

A weighty problem, which has always needed to be solved in the

7.   13 Rich. II, c. 12.
8.   2 Hen. VI, c. 7.
9.   7 Hen. IV, c. 7.

process of trade, has been the identification of the standard of quality of goods sold. From early times this was done in respect of some items of merchandise by marks applied by state officials, and the justices were soon charged with the supervision of this process. A statute of 1423,[10] which was directed primarily at silver merchants in the City of London but was extended to other parts of the country, decreed that no one might sell any work of silver unless it was as fine as Sterling and that before sale it must be "touched with the Touch of the Leopard's Head, if it may reasonably bear the same Touch." Penalties were to be imposed upon those who infringed these provisions and also upon the Keeper of the Touch if he touched anything "except it be as fine in Allay as the Sterling." This passage in the statute concludes with the words: "The Justices of the Peace, Mayors and Bailiffs, and all other having Power as Justices of the Peace, shall hear, inquire and determine, by Bill, Plaint, or in other Manner, of all that do contrary to the Ordinances, and thereof to make due Execution by their Discretions."

Some statutes throw light on the amount of profit which unscrupulous traders might make at this time. In 11 Hen. VI, c. 12, it is announced:

"Our Lord the King hath conceived by the Complaint of the said Commons, that the Waxchandlers in divers Parts of England, sell Candles, Images and Figures, and other Works of Wax made for Offerings, after the Rate of a Pound of Wax for two Shillings and more, where one Pound of Wax is no more worth than six Pence, whereby they gain in every Pound of Wax so wrought 18 Pence and more."

The statute laid down that in future the waxchandlers were to take only three pence in the pound beyond the price of plain wax, subject to forfeiture and a fine, and added: "The Justices of the Peace in every County ... shall have Power to inquire, hear and determine all Things done against this statute." It concludes with a brief exclusion clause which reflects the class distinctions of the age. The provisions are not to apply to funeral lights "made for Nobles that do die." Further reference will be made later to the class consciousness which dominated the social life of these and subsequent times, but first it is necessary to turn to other aspects of trade and commerce.

10.   2 Hen. VI, c. 17.

Early use of money

Expanding trade was accompanied by a greater use of money. Coins were in general use in the reign of Richard II and by the beginning of the fifteenth century counterfeiting had become an industry in itself. Statutes of 1421 made clipping and counterfeiting of coin an offence to be investigated by the justices.

Prices

The fixing of prices for victuals and essential commodities had been part of the duties of the Justices of Labourers under the early labour legislation of 1349 and subsequent years, and price regulation continued to be the subject of statutes until the Elizabethan era. Justices were responsible for seeing that prices did not get out of hand, a task in which they did not always meet with conspicuous success. Sometimes there were complaints by suppliers that they could not make sufficient profit to keep themselves alive. In 1390 a statute[11] declared that:

"In the Right of Victuallers, it is accorded, that they shall have reasonable Gains, according to the Discretion and Limitation of the same Justices, and no more, upon Pain to be grievously punished according to the Discretion of the said Justices."

Wages and labour

Wages as well as prices were fixed by the justices at their sessions. There was to be no question of any bargaining or agreement between the workforce and the employers, and any attempt to do this was punished severely. Servants and labourers had to be kept in their place, and employers must not do anything to encourage them to have ideas above their station. In 1388 a statute of Richard II[12] began with the complaint that:

"Servants and Labourers will not, nor by a long Season would, serve and labour without outrageous and excessive Hire, and much more than hath been given to such Servants and Labourers in any Time past, so that for Scarcity of the said Servants and Labourers, the Husbands and Landtenants may not pay their Rents."

The statute went on to specify how much each servant and labourer was to receive by the year and laid down penalties for both "Givers" and "Takers," varying from a fine of the amount of the excess for first

11.   13 Rich. II, st. 1, c. 8. Confirmed by 6 Hen. VI, c. 3.
12.   12 Rich. II, c. 4.

conviction to three times the excess or 40 days' imprisonment in default for a third conviction.

In the following year the statute mentioned above which allowed victuallers to make reasonable profits but no more, also provided that the daily wages in both money and kind payable to various craftsmen and workmen should be decided by the justices in the light of current conditions,[13] and that the justices should then proclaim the amounts due in each case at their sessions twice a year:

> "Forasmuch as a Man cannot put the Price of Corn and other Victuals in certain, it is accorded and assented, that the Justices of the Peace in every County, in two of their Sessions to be holden betwixt the Feast of Easter and St. Michael, shall make Proclamation by their Discretion according to the Dearth of Victuals, how much every Mason, Carpenter, Tiler and other Craftsmen, Workmen and other Labourers by the Day, as well in Harvest as in other Times of the Year, after their Degree, shall take by the Day with Meat and Drink, or without Meat and Drink, between the two Sessions beforesaid."

Those who infringed these provisions were to be "grievously punished according to the Discretion of the said Justices" in cases where the penalty had not been previously defined.

The level of wages remained a crucial issue in the fifteenth century and the key role of the justices in enforcing the regulations was confirmed by further statutes. In 1423,[14] it was decreed that if justices found that masters were giving more than what had been laid down "each of them that giveth more, shall pay to the King, for every Salary paid to any Servant, contrary to the same Ordinance, the Excess; and that the same Servants so taking, ... have Imprisonment of a Month, without Bail or Mainprize." If any sheriff, bailiff or gaoler allowed the prisoner bail "he shall lose to the King for every such Man ... 20 Shillings." The statute also gave the justices power to call before them artificers, victuallers and others and to inquire into wages and prices and to punish those infringing the regulations. This they could do without indictment so that if they were satisfied from their examination that a person was in breach of the statute they could proceed immediately to sentence.

For a time the justices were accused of neglecting their duty to fix and enforce wage rates. The task was by no means straightforward, and in tackling it they were sometimes faced with a dilemma; although low wages could be an advantage to an employer in keeping down his

---

13.   There was as yet no statutory maximum rate of wage apart from the yearly amount laid down for agricultural workers by 12 Rich. II, c. 4. See Miss McArthur, *EHR*, ix. 310-14.
14.   2 Hen. VI, c. 18.

costs it could also make it difficult for him to retain staff who were underpaid. This was particularly so where the rate of wage was fixed at a low level by statute. The strict laws against the movement of labour did not stop many workmen seeking employment elsewhere, especially in the towns where they were welcomed, and as far as possible protected, by the trading community.

Although the shortage of labour was no longer as acute as it had been immediately after the Black Death, it remained serious for more than a century, especially on the land, and the justices and their associates as landowners and major employers of agricultural labour had a close personal interest in the issue. There were times therefore when they did not apply the wages regulations strictly in accordance with what the Crown intended when passing the legislation. This was made easier for them by the fact that the statute of 1390 did not lay down any penalty for non-observance. There was no suggestion, however, that responsibility should be transferred to any other authority, and statutes continued to place the burden firmly upon the magistrates. Their position was confirmed by a statute of 1427,[15] giving them power to proclaim rates of wages for servants, artificers and others, a power which was extended to mayors and bailiffs in cities and towns who, like the county justices, were also empowered to examine and to hear and determine any offences that might have been committed. In 1444, however, a further statute[16] limited their discretion by stipulating the amount of the wages which might be paid to various workers and which varied according to the time of year. The statute ordered the justices to enforce its provisions and a single justice was empowered to arrest and examine a labourer and to commit him to prison.

As we shall see in a later chapter,[17] the story of fixed wages continued into the Stuart era, but for the time being we must turn to other aspects of the labour laws which added appreciably to the work of the justices in the fifteenth century. Much of this arose from the labour shortage already mentioned, with the associated tendency of workers to seek new forms of employment. Any movement of labour which was not officially authorized was severely punished, as it had been since the 1350s. Labourers and servants could not leave the area of their communities unless they were accompanying their masters or had a permit to do so. A statute of Edward III[18] had declared that no servant or labourer could leave his hundred unless he had a note explaining the reason "under the King's Seal, after the Discretion of the Justices of the Peace." The Seal itself was kept under the

15.   6 Hen. VI, c. 3.
16.   23 Hen. VI, c. 12.
17.   See p. 244-6, *post.*
18.   34 Edw. III, c. 11.

supervision of the justices. The latter could issue writs to sheriffs ordering the arrest of fugitive servants and labourers who could be imprisoned and branded on the forehead with the letter "F" for falsity (a second offence could bring the death penalty, but in view of the labour shortage this may not have been applied very strictly). A servant's master had suit before the justices, and if the servant went to a city or borough the "party plaintiff" could require the mayor or bailiffs to deliver him back without delay. If they failed to do so they could be suited before the justices and made to pay £10 to the King and 100 shillings to the master.[19]

Under Richard II a statute[20] decreed that if any servant or labourer was found wandering in any city, borough or other place outside his own territory without a "Letter Patent," he was to be put in the stocks where he was to be kept "till he hath found Surety to return to his Service." As a further gesture towards increasing the workforce on the land when it was most needed, the same statute decreed that artificers must work on the land in harvest time. In the same year the justices were empowered to investigate and punish, with fines of 100 shillings, all mayors, bailiffs, stewards, constables and gaolers who failed to enforce the ordinances and statutes relating to servants and labourers and also to beggars and vagabonds.[21] Vagabonds had always been regarded as a potential source of trouble, and the first Commission of the Peace of March 20, 1361, warned the justices to beware of vagabonds who congregate "in huge, evil Multitudes and become Disturbers of Our Peace." Subsequently, justices were able to arrest, examine and imprison wandering vagabonds and compel them to find surety until the next session of gaol delivery.[22]

The importance attached to keeping labourers on the land is illustrated by a statute of 1406[23] which was aimed at preventing even the children of the lower social orders being apprenticed to a trade:

"No Man nor Woman, of whatever Estate or Condition they be, shall put their Son or Daughter, of whatsoever Age he or she be, to serve as Apprentice ... except he have Land or Rent to the Value of 20 Shillings by the Year at the least."

Instead they must be:

"put to other Labours as their Estate doth require, upon Pain of

---

19.   A similar liability had been imposed previously on mayors and bailiffs by the Statutes of Labourers.
20.   12 Rich. II, c. 3.
21.   12 Rich. II, c. 10.
22.   7 Rich. II, c. 5. Under 12 Rich. II, c. 7, travelling beggars were required to carry testimonials.
23.   7 Hen. IV, c. 17.

One Year's Imprisonment, and to make Fine and Ransom at the King's Will."

Even where the parents did possess the required property qualification, the child needed a certificate from two justices before it could be apprenticed in a town:

"Every Person that will make his Son or Daughter Apprentice to any Craft within City or Borough, that he bring to the Mayor or Bailiffs ... a Bill sealed under the Seals of Two Justices of the Peace of the County where such Infant is born, testifying the Valor of the Lands or Rents of his said Father and Mother."

The penalty for an employer taking an apprentice contrary to these provisions was 100 shillings to be dealt with before the justices "as in any other Court of the King."

Restrictions on wages and movements were by no means the only legal limitations placed on the lives of medieval servants and labourers. Under Richard II[24] they, together with artificers and victuallers, were forbidden to carry a buckler, sword or dagger "upon Forfeiture of the Same," except in time of war or array or when accompanying their masters. On the other hand, in the interest of national defence, "such Servants and Labourers shall have Bows and Arrows and use the Same on Sundays and Holydays." In order to ensure that as much time as possible was spent at archery, they were not allowed to waste their time in any other sporting activity. In particular, they were not to indulge in such "idle" games as tennis, football, coits and dice. Anyone contravening these provisions was to be arrested by the sheriffs, mayors, bailiffs or constables who were to confiscate the weapons, etc, and bring the culprits before the justices for punishment.

The obsession of the authorities with the suppression of all games and pastimes other than archery continued throughout the fifteenth century. Under Henry IV a statute[25] described the forbidden games as "unthrifty" and added that each offender should be imprisoned for six days. Sheriffs, mayors, bailiffs and constables who failed to execute the statute were to pay the King 20 shillings. By the latter part of the century virtually all games played at that time were included in the ban and a statute of Edward IV,[26] which on this occasion described them as "unprofitable," imposed heavy penalties on both the players and the owners and occupiers of the premises where they were played. The latter could be sentenced to three years' imprisonment and fined £20

24.   12 Rich. II, c. 6.
25.   11 Hen. IV, c. 4.
26.   17 Edw. IV, c. 3.

for each offence, and the players imprisoned for two years and fined £10.

Class distinctions

Reference has already been made to the predominance of class distinctions in the Middle Ages. To some extent this was evident in the restrictions on the carrying of arms and the playing of games, and the same two-tier system operated in respect of hunting which might be enjoyed by the gentry and the nobles but not by the lower orders. Ostensibly this was because Parliament had observed that "when good Christian People be at Church hearing Divine Service," servants and labourers were often out hunting and indulging in various mischiefs at the same time.[27] Accordingly, it was decreed that no layman who did not have tenements to the value of 40 shillings a year, and no priest who had less than £10 a year, could keep a hunting dog or use a ferret, net or other "engine" to take deer, rabbits, hares or other "Gentlemen's Game."[28] A previous statute had forbidden anyone to keep a hawk unless he was "of Estate to have a Hawk."[29] This was the beginning of the game laws which were to play a prominent part in the lives of the justices in later centuries.

·In the instances of class distinction mentioned so far, the nobles and gentry, from whom those on the Commissions of the Peace were drawn, were together in the same privileged class to which the restrictions did not apply. This two-tier system was not, however, applied invariably, and in some instances distinctions were made at a number of points in the social ladder. The most striking exhibition of class consciousness was to be seen in the law governing apparel. One of the earliest statutes to be promulgated after the justices were established in 1361 began with the preamble: "For the Outrageous and Excessive Apparel of divers People, against their Estate Degree ... It is ordained." It went on somewhat incongruously to prescribe the food and drink which might be taken each day by "Grooms as well as Servants of Lords ... according to their Estate," and it then stated: "And that they have Clothes for their Vesture, or Hosing, whereof the whole Cloth shall not exceed two Marks," and they must wear nothing made of gold, silver, silk, nor embroidered. The same applied to their families. Next came the yeomen whose clothing was limited to 40 shillings in value. Esquires and gentlemen below the "Estate of Knight" who did not have land to the value of £100 a year were limited to cloth priced at four-and-half marks. This applied also to "Merchants,

27.   RP, iv, 24a.
28.   13 Rich. II, st. 1, c. 13.
29.   37 Edw. III, c. 19.

Citizens and Burgesses in London and elsewhere." Knights were in two classes: those with land worth less than 400 marks a year and those above. The latter "shall wear at their Pleasure, except Ermins and Lutuses, and Apparel of Pearls and Stone." Explicit provisions were also made for the clergy. At the very bottom of the scale, apparently below the grooms and servants of the Lords, came carters, ploughmen, cowherds and shepherds who were not allowed to wear cloth at all but only "Blanket and Russet [Wool] of 12 Pence." Breaches of the law resulted in forfeiture of the offending garment to the King.

Roads, waterways and bridges

In Tudor times an appreciable amount of the justices' work was to be concerned with what might be described as public services, including the maintenance of roads, waterways and bridges. They were already involved in these matters to a small degree by the end of the fourteenth century, mainly because the enforcement of the common law liability to maintain thoroughfares was enforceable at Quarter Sessions. At common law, responsibility for maintaining highways, most of which were little more than mud tracks, fell upon the inhabitants of the villages through which they passed. The Statute of Westminster 1285, also made provision for keeping open, and where necessary enlarging, highways between market towns, with liability falling upon the manor. Breaches of these provisions seem to have been dealt with in the court leet but by the end of the fourteenth century, the enforcement of the laws on highways in general had been assumed by Assizes or by Quarter Sessions, the failure to maintain a highway being a common law nuisance which was indictable before one or other of these courts. The most frequent practice was for a presentment, usually by a single justice, to be made at Quarter Sessions, who would impose a fine on defaulting parties. In the fifteenth century the roads were used less extensively than they had been previously, and their maintenance, although occupying some of the time of Quarter Sessions, did not figure as prominently in the proceedings as many other matters. The picture was to change significantly under the Tudors, as will be seen in chapter VII.

Bridges were for practical purposes merely parts of the highway. In ancient times no one was under an obligation to erect a bridge, and consequently they were few in number, but once built there was an immediate obligation on someone to maintain the bridge and keep it in repair. This obligation might fall upon the original builder, but in the course of time it came to devolve upon the owners of neighbouring estates or, more often, upon a hundred, a municipal authority or the county as a whole. Whoever it might be, failure to keep a bridge in good repair had from earliest times been a common-law nuisance because it interfered with the use of the highway and it was presentable at the court leet. In time it became an offence which was indictable before the itinerant Justices in Eyre or of Assize, and subsequently before the Justices of the Peace at Quarter Sessions when, on conviction, they usually imposed a substantial fine.

The waters which flowed under the bridges were not the concern of the justices at common law but several statutes made it an offence to obstruct a waterway, particularly by the construction of a weir.[30] Various other statutes which were concerned primarily with the protection of fishing also brought rivers within the justices' jurisdiction. The Statute of Westminster of 1285[31] had forbidden the taking of young salmon "by nets nor by other Engines, at Mill Dams, from the midst of April till the Nativity of St John the Baptist." This was confirmed in a statute of 1389[32] which extended the restriction to all places on all rivers and included salmon fry, lampreys "or any other Fish." It also provided for the appointment of conservators who were to punish offenders. Four years later, a further statute[33] proclaimed that Justices of the Peace of all counties were to be conservators of these statutes with power to punish those who contravened the provisions. They were to survey and search the weirs and were to appoint under-conservators who attended to most of the practical work on the spot and then reported to the justices at sessions. Offenders might be imprisoned and fined at the discretion of the justices and the under-conservators were to receive half the fine. Thus the justices began a long period of responsibility for river conservancy.

Criminal jurisdiction

The justices' functions which have been referred to so far in this chapter relate mainly to social and economic matters which they controlled, as previously, through judicial procedures. At the same time they continued to exercise the criminal jurisdiction which had become established by the end of the fourteenth century. In the field of criminal law, as distinct from the enforcement of economic legislation, they had virtually reached their zenith, although there were a few further advances during the ensuing 100 years. The most noteworthy of these occurred in 1461 when their superiority over the sheriffs was finally confirmed by a statute[34] which laid down that all indictments

---

30. 25 Edw. III, st. 3, c. 4; 45 Edw. III, c. 2; 1 Hen. IV, c. 12; 4 Hen. IV, c. 11; 9 Hen. VI, c. 9; 12 Edw. IV, c.7.
31. 13 Edw. I, st. 1, c. 47.
32. 13 Rich. II, st. 1, c. 19.
33. 17 Rich. II, c. 9. This statute also empowered them to enforce the laws governing watches on the sea coast.
34. 1 Edw. IV, c. 2.

and presentments which were taken at the tourn should in future be taken before the justices at their sessions. Failure by a sheriff to comply involved a penalty of £40. This virtually completed the replacement by the justices of the old communal and feudal courts, although some of them were to continue to function in a minor way for a long time. This usurpation by the justices of the older jurisdictions had the important result of substituting common law with its newer forms of procedure for the old local customary law. The 1461 statute was also a triumph for the Commons in Parliament, but even at this stage they were not invariably successful in pressing the claims of the justices. For example, they were still striving unsuccessfully to secure the right for justices to assign a coroner to take approvements.[35]

A remarkable example of the Commons' perseverance was seen in 1441[36] when the justices were finally granted authority to deal with purveyancing (the right of the Crown to provisions or the use of horses at fixed prices). The Commons had petitioned repeatedly since Edward III's reign for this power to be conferred upon the justices but it was nearly 80 years before they were successful. Another milestone was reached when the justices' power to bail was finally confirmed. There had been previous instances of justices granting bail or mainprize in certain cases, but the position was not clear until a statute of 1483[37] gave them power in general terms to bail persons arrested by the sheriffs on suspicion of felony.

There appears to have been an increase in the volume of criminal work handled by the justices during the fifteenth century, but this coincided with an encroachment by the Justices of Assize who, as the century progressed, took over most of the more serious cases. These justices were not only the Royal Judges but also senior legal practitioners, especially Serjeants-at-Law who were becoming prominent in the profession and who, by reinforcing the small number of whole-time Judges, made it possible for Assizes to visit all parts of the country at frequent intervals. The result of this was that the spectacular expansion of the role of the Justices of the Peace in the administration of the new economic legislation was not paralleled in the criminal judicial field and, on the contrary, this section of the justices' work became in practice less extensive in range though not in volume.

Court records show that in the fifteenth century, although the Justices of Assize were taking many of the more serious cases, the Justices of the Peace were exercising a wide jurisdiction over felonies. The number of cases with which they had to deal increased throughout

---

35.   An approver was an informer; one who proved, or offered to prove another guilty. The term is now obsolete but was similar to the modern Queen's evidence.
36.   20 Hen. VI, c. 8; confirmed by 23 Hen. VI, c. 1.
37.   1 Rich. III, c. 3.

most of the period and included murder, assault, robbery, theft, rape, arson and also witchcraft and numerous trespasses. The most frequent to appear were homicide, housebreaking and trespass - both to the person and to land. Assaults on the person were extremely common and included many against officials as well as private individuals. As already mentioned, constables were particularly prone to attack, but bailiffs, jurors and others all came in for a share of violent treatment. At the same time, the officials themselves were not infrequently charged with these offences. Forcible entry on to land was a common subject of complaint. Where this occurred, one or more justices had authority to take with them the county posse and to go to the place in question, and if they found anyone holding it by force he was to be arrested and put "in the next gaol, there to remain convict by the Record of the same Justice or Justices until they have made Fine and Ransom to the King."[38] As will be seen later, this was easier said than done when the culprits were powerful men with many retainers.

The definitions of some of the offences which came before the justices were not precisely the same as those of today. For example, malice aforethought was not an essential element in murder, nor had breaking into a dwelling-house by night with intent to commit a felony developed into the distinct crime of burglary. A case of this kind would seem to have been dealt with as felonious housebreaking.

Work of justices out of sessions

There was a considerable amount of activity by individual justices out of sessions. We have already seen that a single justice was given power to enforce the statutes regulating the manufacture of cloth, tiles and other commodities. Records suggest that at least half the cases of binding over to keep the peace were conducted before a single justice. They also acted singly on a considerable scale in the exercise of their original police powers of pursuit, arrest and imprisonment pending trial.[39] One aspect of this was to be seen in the cases of forcible entry mentioned above. These powers were sometimes abused, however, when the justice happened to be the constable of a castle. Such justices seem to have made a practice of arresting and imprisoning innocent persons in order to extort fines and ransoms from them.[40] To prevent this, justices were ordered to imprison only in the "common gaol."[41] In fact, the common gaol itself was often situated in a castle at this time, but it was under the supervision of a gaoler to whose custody the

38. 2 Hen. V, st. 2, c. 1.
39. A statute, 5 Hen. IV, c. 3, directed that the commissions for coastal counties were to include authority for keeping watch, together with others, on the coasts.
40. RP, iii, 540a.
41. 5 Hen. IV, c. 10.

prisoner would have had to be committed and who was responsible for producing him at the sessions.

Sometimes at least two justices had to be present. In cases of riot, "the Justices, Three or Two of them at the Least, and the Sheriff or Under Sheriff of the County," were to make arrests and record what they found to have been done against the law. The statute[42] containing these provisions also sets out what was to be done if the truth could not be established at the outset, and it finished by making all justices and sheriffs and also Justices of Assize liable to a fine of £100 if they failed to execute the statute.

Supervision by superior courts

Up to the end of the fourteenth century it had been the peripatetic justices of the King's Bench, Common Pleas and Exchequer rather than those of Assize who had hampered the justices' sessions. In the judicial heirarchy these three courts came immediately below the King and his Council and when they visited an area all local courts were suspended, as had been the case during visitations of the Eyre. At a time when the Justices of the Peace were no longer meeting opposition at their own level from the local courts these three higher courts began to exercise control from above. The Common Pleas heard cases between subject and subject and the Exchequer has been described as the "Local Government Board of medieval England,"[43] but it was the King's Bench with its unlimited criminal jurisdiction which was the principal restraint on the justices' exercise of judicial powers. After the Eyre fell into disuse the King's Bench continued in full strength but early in the fifteenth century it and the other higher courts became stationed permanently at Westminster. They therefore ceased to cause any interruption to the justices' sessions and the King's Bench no longer delivered the prisoners who had been indicted in the sessions, but it continued to have a considerable impact on their work. In particular, it kept the cases of felony and disorder in the counties under constant review. This was done by having the cases removed to it at Westminster by *certiorari, mandamus* or writ of error. Professor Putnam estimates that by the middle of the fifteenth century nine-tenths of the *Rex Roll* in a normal year was filled with cases from the Sessions of the Peace.[44] In this way the King's Bench exercised control of all aspects of the justices' criminal work, both in and out of sessions, and could quash what they had done on the ground that they had

---

42.   13 Hen. IV, c. 7.
43.   H.M. Cam, *Shire Officials: Coroners, Constables and Bailiffs, on English Government at Work,* 1327-1336.
44.   B.H. Putnam, *Proceedings before the Justices of the Peace,* Ames Foundation, p. lxiv.

exceeded their powers.

Savagery of the times

A common feature of the times was the ruthlessness with which the powerful oppressed the weak and their ability to influence the course of justice in their favour. Some families, like the Folvilles mentioned earlier, behaved as if the law did not apply to them, and it was pointless to attempt to bring them to justice in any of the courts in the county. These situations arose particularly where there had been forceable entry on land involving violence, and the complainant was prevented from obtaining redress against a powerful opponent through any of the common-law courts owing to intimidation of jurors, witnesses, bailiffs and others. In these circumstances the only course was to resort to the King in Chancery. This was done by petitioning the Chancellor to inquire into the matter. He would do so by removing the case to the Chancery by writ of *terminariari* and by applying an equity jurisdiction which was not subject to rules of common law. The parties were summoned to attend by subpoena. After examination, a decision would be reached and, where appropriate, specific restitution of goods and chattels might be ordered, a remedy that was not always forthcoming in the common-law courts. By the middle of the fifteenth century this procedure seems to have been operating effectively on a wide scale.

It was not only the lower orders who required such protection and indeed it was more often members of the gentry and the upper classes who resorted to this procedure. The Justices of the Peace were sometimes in the thick of the fray themselves. An example of this, described by R.L. Storey,[45] involved one Robert Crakenthorp, a Westmorland justice, who complained that there had been many breaches of the peace by large assemblies of armed men. The local justices at Appleby inquired into the complaint, but the jurors were so threatened by some of those involved in the disturbances, who included a knight of the shire and several others who had previously been on the Commission of the Peace and had sat in Parliament, that they dared not speak the truth, and Crakenthorp himself was also threatened. Resort was therefore had to the Chancellor.

It is clear from the records of proceedings that the life-style of the population was no less savage than it had been under the Plantagenets and that this extended to all sections of the community from peasants to the highest of the nobility. In 1428, the Duke of Norfolk and the Earl of Huntingdon engaged in a violent feud and both were removed

45. R.L. Storey, "Disorders in Lancastrian Westmorland: some early Chancery Proceedings," Cumberland and Westmorland Arch. Soc. Transactions, New Ser. iii, 1954, p. 75.

from the Bedfordshire Commission of the Peace. The notorious case of the Duke of Clarence, though exceptional, was by no means out of place in the current climate. A lady named Ankerrette Twynyho, who does not appear to have committed any offence apart from incurring the displeasure of the Duke, was seized by his followers at her manor at Crayford and carried off to Warwick where, without any apparent justification, she was indicted on a trumped-up charge, convicted and hanged at the direction of the county sessions which were dominated by the Duke, himself a justice for the county. Afterwards, the other justices and the jury were exonerated on the ground that they were in fear of the Duke.[46]

There must have been an element of chivalry in the social structure, as described by Froissart, but there is little indication of it in the records of the courts or in the writing of some contemporaries. There are numerous references to outbreaks of violence at sessions, with physical attacks on jurors, witnesses and justices and sometimes the proceedings broke up with the justices divided among themselves. Some idea of the atmosphere of the times can be gained from *The Paston Letters*[47], which are private correspondence between members of a family who took their name from the village of Paston in Norfolk. The Letters cover all but the first 20 years of the century and give a vivid picture of the feuding which was commonplace throughout the period and the difficulties faced by those seeking justice. John Paston was in dispute with Lord Moleyns over the manor of Gresham which had been bought by Paston's father, who had been a justice. Moleyns had Paston's wife ejected by force from her house. The letters describe the frustrated attempts of Paston to obtain justice. His efforts met with violence and were also sometimes thwarted by Moleyns getting a letter of support from the King; whereupon Paston, who was obviously an able and persevering man not without influence himself, set about obtaining a similar letter from the King on his own behalf. The *Letters* give many other glimpses of these harsh times in which no person and no property was immune from violence. They contain instances of churches being ransacked and the clergy assaulted.

The Wars of the Roses

Feuding and violence did not stop short of the Royal Family and open conflict between the rival houses of York and Lancaster broke out in 1455. Special commissions to deal with the anarchy were not issued on

---

46.   RP, VI, 173-5.
47.   *The Paston Letters, 1422-1509* ed., by James Gairdner.

a wide scale as had been done on previous occasions of great crisis,[48] and the burden of keeping order remained with the justices who at times found the task impossible. They did, however, function more effectively than is sometimes supposed. Unlike the Civil War two centuries later, the Wars of the Roses, which lasted intermittently until 1485, were largely the concern of only one section of society, and the majority of the population, who did their best to keep out of the struggle, were unaffected save in the areas where hostilities were taking place. The battles were on a limited scale and of short duration, and they affected only small areas of the countryside. Only to an inconsiderable extent was there interference in the ordinary life of the people and in their trade with one another. There was surprisingly little interruption of the holding of Quarter Sessions. In some counties the justices delivered the gaols, though in others indictments were sent to the Justices of Gaol Delivery. In general, the Justices of the Peace carried on effectively in governing the lower classes, the largest part of their work being concerned with minor offences and with enforcing the labour laws. It was a different matter where the nobles and gentry were concerned. Many were involved directly or indirectly in the dynastic struggle, most of them motivated solely by the prospect of personal profit. At this level, the life of the community was often disrupted and sometimes members of the same family fought one another. *The Paston Letters* mention the Tunstale brothers of whom Sir William was given custody of Bamborough Castle by the Yorkists but was ousted and executed by his brother, Sir Richard, on behalf of the Lancastrians. It was natural that in this disturbed state of society the conduct of the justices themselves, which was already far from perfect, should have deteriorated, and some were among the lawbreakers. There were occasions when the same individual who sat at sessions dispensing justice was shortly afterwards indicted for robbery or other offences. The magnates were among the worst offenders and did their best to intimidate their fellow justices if they showed any independence. In particular, they frequently obtained acquittals of their followers who had committed offences. Maitland rightly expresses the view that more injustice was done during this period by wrongful acquittals than by wrongful convictions.

One new development in the history of the justices which does seem to have occurred in consequence of these turbulent conditions was that meetings of justices took place on an appreciable scale out of sessions. Contemporary documents relating to this period are so sparse that it is

48. The last occasion on which special commissioners were appointed to deal with a national crisis instead of relying upon the Justices of the Peace was at the time of Jack Cade's rebellion in 1450. These commissions were similar to those issued to quell the Peasants' Revolt in 1381, although the circumstances were somewhat different. Jack Cade had substantial middle-class support and the rebellion was aimed at oppressive magnates and officials and also at ecclesiastics rather than at the landed gentry.

impossible to draw any firm conclusions, but such evidence as there is certainly points to these meetings taking place more frequently than they had done previously. Two or three justices would gather together in some convenient place - an inn or a private house - where, so far as one is able to discover, they were concerned mostly with the various functions they could perform out of sessions; and no doubt they also discussed the political situation. There is no evidence that these gatherings attempted to conduct judicial trials and they did not therefore resemble the Petty Sessions of later years. On the other hand, the idea was obviously gaining ground that there could be a useful intermediate stage between the formal assemblies of all the justices and officials in sessions and the sitting of a single justice to bind over, or the gallop across country of one or two justices at the head of the posse in pursuit of offenders or to quell a riot. Informal meetings of small groups of justices, especially those resident in the same area, had practical advantages which would lead to the statutory recognition of such gatherings a century later and their ultimate conversion into courts of summary jurisdiction.

The country under the Yorkists, 1461-1485

In 1461 there was a change of dynasty when the battle of Towton put the Yorkist Edward IV on the throne but, although one of the first things he did on arrival in York after the battle was to issue Commissions of the Peace, he was too lazy to establish a firm government. An able soldier, full of vigour while the fighting lasted, Edward chose to sit back and relax once he was on the throne, and local affairs continued to be conducted in the disorganized manner of the previous reign with periodical interruptions by feuding factions. This state of affairs continued until Edward's brother, Richard III, was defeated at Bosworth in 1485 and the strong Tudor dynasty was established by Henry VII. The only new developments of interest to the justices during this period were further extensions of control over trade.[49]

Commissions of the Peace

The Commissions of the Peace increased in size throughout the century from the eight justices stipulated in the statute of 1390 to more than 30 in some counties. There is no obvious reason for the considerable differences between counties. Gloucestershire, for

---

49. This was effected by various statutes, two of which have already been mentioned: 4 Edw. IV, c. 1 (Cloth trade) and 17 Edw. IV, c. 4 (Tilers). Others were: 4 Edw. IV, c. 8 (Horners), 12 Edw. IV, c. 1 (Bowyers) and 22 Edw. IV, c. 5 (Fullers).

instance, usually had more justices than any other county except Kent whereas the Middlesex commission was among the smallest. The position in Middlesex may perhaps be accounted for by the fact that its sessions were well served by professional Judges. Between 1450 and 1509 the total number of appointments made to all commissions (excluding those of the palatinates of Lancaster and Chester and of franchise owners such as Peterborough) was 2,933 apart from nobles and Assize Judges.[50] Usually an individual was appointed to serve only in the county in which he had his principal property, but some appeared in more than one commission simultaneously. This was usually because they were members of the King's Council or were regarded as dependable government men. For example, Sir Walter Blount (later Lord Mountjoy) was included in the commissions for Essex, Kent, Derbyshire and Devon, but whereas he was a justice for his home county of Derbyshire from 1449 to 1473, it was not until he had been Lord Treasurer (1464-66) that he was appointed to the other three.

The quality of those appointed to the commissions was long the subject of complaint. Before the end of the previous century some steps had been taken to disqualify those who were not thought to be of sufficient stature or who might be prejudiced. One of the statutes of Richard II mentioned above (12 Rich. II, c. 10) had decreed that no "Lord's Steward shall be a Justice of the Peace." Early in Richard III's reign the Commons had complained that, as many of those appointed to the commissions were too busy to attend to their duties, the work was left to *"les plus povres et nient suffisantsz."*[51] Several statutes repeated the wording of that of 1361 and required "the most worthy" in each county to be assigned to keep the peace. In 1414 it was laid down that:

> "The justices from henceforth to be made within the Counties of England, shall be made of the most sufficient Persons dwelling in the same Counties, by the Advice of the Chancellor and of the King's Council, without taking other Persons dwelling in Foreign Counties to execute such Office, except the Lords and the Justices of Assizes now named and to be named by the King and his Council."[52]

A further enactment of 1439,[53] emphasized the importance of having men of standing to discharge the functions of Justices of the

---

50. This figure is taken from a list of justices appointed between 1450 and 1509 (when the printed Calendar of Patent Rolls ended) compiled by Professor J.H. Baker of St. Catherine's College, Cambridge.
51. RP, iii, 44.
52. 2 Hen. V, st. 2, c. 1.
53. 18 Hen. VI, c. 11.

Peace, and the need for them to be recognized as such. It also showed clearly that the justices were regarded as governors of their respective areas. After referring to previous statutes on the calibre of individual justices, it proclaimed:

"Which statutes notwithstanding, now of late in many Counties of England ... some be of small Behaviour, by whom the People will not be governed nor ruled, and some for their Necessity to great Extortion and Oppression upon the People."

Henceforth no one was to be a justice unless he had land to the value of £20 a year.[54] Anyone who was appointed without having this qualification was to give notice within one month. Failure to do so involved expulsion from the commission and a fine of £20. The property qualification did not apply to lawyer members of the commission nor to justices in cities, boroughs or towns, and there was also a proviso that if there were not sufficient qualified persons in the county the Chancellor should appoint other "discreet Persons" although they did not have the land qualification.

The importance attached to wealth as a qualification for public office at this time was also illustrated by the removal in 1430 of the county franchise from the whole body of freemen. Until then, all freemen who were suitors in the shire court had the right to vote for the election of knights to represent the county in Parliament, but a statute[55] of that year limited the franchise to freeholders of land valued at 40 shillings, so that only the more prosperous landowner had a voice. The Commons continued to be drawn from the same section of the community as the justices but this section was drawing closer to the nobility and further from the other classes of the population.

Once appointed, a justice could not decline to act, and the only means of escaping service was to obtain a royal patent of dispensation.[56] In spite, however, of the increasing onerousness of the office in the fifteenth century, few sought to be relieved of their post; a fact which was probably due to growing awareness of the political and social advantages which could be derived from membership of the commission.

The majority of those appointed to the commissions continued to be recruited from the landed gentry but there was a fair proportion of

54. This was raised to £100 in 1732. The property qualification was abolished in 1906.
55. 8 Hen. VI, c. 7.
56. See CPR, 1476-1485, 53.

lawyers who were almost all men of substance[57] and who seem to have been the most regular attenders at sessions. They included Judges of the royal courts whose names appeared on the commissions for a number of counties and were usually added to the *Quorum*. They sat at some of the sessions, though of course they did not have time to do so in every county and there seems to have been a tendency for them to confine their sittings to their own counties.

As in the earlier commissions, one of the justices was designated by the Crown to keep the rolls of the peace. The commission contained the words "*assignavismus denique* ..." followed by the name. The *Custos Rotulorum* was chief magistrate and one of the functions he assumed was the appointment of the Clerk of the Peace. His position became more clearly defined under the Tudors when it was confirmed by statute, as will be seen in ch. VI.

There were also several members of the local nobility on most commissions, in addition to the great officers of state, and not only the "one lord" of the 1361 statute. The replacement of the older feudal courts by those of the Justices of the Peace may have been made slightly more acceptable to the feudal lords by the fact that their appointment to the commission enabled them at least to continue to exercise jurisdiction over the neighbourhood.

The most marked difference from the earlier commissions was the inclusion of ecclesiastics from 1424. Until then the prelates had been among the justices' principal opponents in Parliament but after that year it became the practice to include archbishops, bishops and abbots in the commissions. One often finds several of the higher clergy on the same commission and the same individuals were appointed for a number of counties. Some of them were not mere figureheads and they took an active part in the proceedings of sessions, but they were excluded from dealing with certain types of cases, notably those involving the shedding of blood, counterfeiting, Lollards and heresy. In the course of time all justices were given a number of duties relating to church affairs. The earliest statutory instance was in 1414[58] when they were made responsible for suppressing the followers of the ecclesiastical reformer, John Wycliffe. The Lollards, as they were called, had been persecuted since the beginning of the century and they were now indicted frequently at Quarter Sessions. The justices were required to take a special oath to do all in their power to destroy "all manner of Heresies and Errors, commonly called Lollardries," and

---

57. In the 1460s, Sir John Fortescue wrote in his *De laudibus legum Angliae,* "there is scarcely a man learned in the laws to be found in the realm who is not noble or sprung of noble lineage." It seems that this was because others could not afford the cost of joining an Inn of Court. Sir John served on the commissions for 17 counties at different times and became Chief Justice of the King's Bench in 1442.
58. 2 Hen. V, St. 1, c. 7; RP., iv, 24a.

they were also given power to inquire about all those who held "Errors or Heresies, as Lollards, and which be their Maintainers, Receivers, Favorers, and Sustainers, common Writers of such Books as well as of the Sermons as of their Schools, Conventicles, Congregations, and Confederacies."

Language used in legal documents

Wycliffe himself had another claim to fame in that he was responsible for the first full English translation of the Bible. The birth of the English language in the fourteenth and fifteenth centuries was a phenomenon not without significance for the Justice of the Peace. Chaucer, himself a justice for Kent, who died in 1400, wrote his *Canterbury Tales* in early English and gave an interesting character sketch of a fourteenth century justice in his references to the Franklin. Described as a "landowner," and indeed "a model, among landed gentry," the Franklin was an epicurean and a generous host. In addition to being a justice, "as justice at the Sessions none stood higher," he had often represented the county in Parliament and also held the office of sheriff (he would soon have become disqualified from holding both offices at the same time). Chaucer, together with Wycliffe and their contemporary William Langland, whose *Vision of Piers Plowman* described scenes in fourteenth century life, were in the forefront of the establishment of English as the national language. The courts took a little time to respond. At the beginning of the fifteenth century they were still confronted with forms which were either in Norman French, like the statutes, or in Latin, like the commissions, and it would be some time before they were issued in English - the statutes in 1487[59] - and the commissions continued to be in Latin until the 1730s (except during the Commonwealth when they were in English). Gradually English was becoming the universal language of all classes and when Caxton introduced the printing press in the 1470s the way was opened for the profusion of manuals in English which were to guide the justices under the Tudors.

Establishment of the Tudor monarchy

With the death of Richard III at Bosworth in 1485 and the accession of Henry VII, the internecine strife of the previous epoch was replaced by sound government firmly established under the Tudors. An important outcome of the Wars of the Roses was the elimination of most of the greatest magnates and their families who had long dominated the land.

59.   3 Hen. VII, c. 16.

Most of them and their heirs were dead and their estates confiscated, and those who remained no longer enjoyed virtually unfettered power. This made it easier for the new monarchy to establish direct control of all areas, and it left the way open to the Justices of the Peace to govern the country on behalf of the King but with a considerable degree of independence.

It was in 1485 that Chief Justice Husey of the King's Bench made his famous comment, quoted by Lambard,[60] about the number of additional duties placed upon the justices since the mid-fourteenth century:

"How many Justices think you, may now suffice, without breaking their backs, to beare so many, not loades, but stacks of statutes that have since that time been laid upon them."

The number of statutes affecting the justices was to increase still further on a considerable scale during the following centuries, but Husey's remark was significant in that it reflected the fact that by 1485 the justices were recognized as the men of all work. They had become established as the principal administrators and supervisors of local affairs, just as their judicial functions had been confirmed a hundred years earlier. Consequently, the Tudors had merely to adopt a system which they found ready to hand. They added further to the justices' duties but did little to alter the structure. They introduced a strong and stable government, but there was no need for them to develop a system of centralized bureaucracy in order to achieve this. They were able to rule England, and later Wales, almost entirely through the Justices of the Peace, an expedient which proved to be eminently effective. Once again, the justices were in the right place at the right time and were ready to provide what came to be accepted as the right answer.

60. Lambard, *Eirenarcha*, Bk. 1, c. 7, 1581.

CHAPTER V

THE COUNTIES PALATINE

Exceptional positions of Chester - Durham - The Duchy of Lancaster

FROM THE FIRST APPEARANCE OF Justices of the Peace in the fourteenth century they were appointed by being named in Commissions of the Peace which were issued to the various counties and liberties as shown in Appendix II. At an early stage, however, certain areas had the status of counties palatine, the precedent for which was to be found in the territories of the *comes palatinus* of the Frankish empire, and in some of these the selection and appointment of justices was effected in a somewhat different manner from that in the rest of the country. There were six regions which at one time or another were described as counties palatine: Chester, Durham, Lancaster, the Isle of Ely, Hexhamshire and Pembrokeshire. In the last three of these areas justices were appointed in much the same way as elsewhere, save for the fact that in the Isle of Ely the Lord Palatine issued his own Commissions of the Peace until the eighteenth century. Thereafter the justices for this area were appointed by the Lord Chancellor in the name of the King. In 1888 the Isle of Ely was made a separate administrative county with its own Commission of the Peace. The counties palatine of Chester, Durham and Lancaster need to be considered at greater length for they differed in several respects from other parts of England and Wales, especially in their early history, in addition to the fact that the Lord Palatine appointed his own justices as an exception to the statute 27 Hen. VIII, c. 24, which confirmed that all appointments must be made in the name of the King.

By the sixteenth century Chester, Durham and Lancaster were permanently annexed to the Crown but all three still held positions essentially different from that of other counties and liberties, and in the case of Durham and Lancaster the Lords Palatine continued to play a prominent part in the appointment of their own Justices of the Peace. Only the Duchy of Lancaster, however, retains distinctive features to the present day.

The fundamental difference between the palatinates and other areas of England and Wales, in so far as Justices of the Peace were concerned, was that the selection of candidates and their inclusion in the commissions were in the hands of local magnates and officers instead of being handled directly on behalf of the King by officers in Westminster. Once the justices had been appointed they continued in early times to operate in the name of their Lord Palatine, but in other respects there was no difference between them and the justices for other areas. The law they administered was the common law and that enacted by the national Parliament, which was the same for the country as a whole. The procedure followed by these justices was also the same as elsewhere, and so too were their courts, save for differences in nomenclature and variations in the extent of their jurisdiction which arose largely from geographical circumstances.

In the palatinate areas there were differences in the composition of the benches and in the attitudes adopted by the justices as compared with other counties and boroughs, but these were no greater than the idiosyncracies to be found among the different counties where magistrates were appointed in the name of the King, and they had only a limited effect on the administration of justice.

The counties palatine are of interest because they reflect the piecemeal development of the country in early times which involved the creation of exceptional institutions to meet various peculiar needs. In the course of time, as the abnormal circumstances vanished and as centralized government became more powerful and effective, they were gradually assimilated and were absorbed into the national structure. From the point of view of the Justices of the Peace they are of interest as showing how the system could thrive under varying conditions, and how, in practice, it always operated in an almost identical manner in every part of the kingdom, even where there were marked differences in local circumstances and in the higher levels of regional government.

The creation of the counties palatine was not the product of any definite policy. Like the Justices of the Peace themselves they emerged in a haphazard manner to meet varying circumstances. In both Chester and Durham the confirmation and development of the palatinates, if not their initial creation, was probably due to a large extent to the need for buffer states on the borders with Wales and Scotland. There was clearly an intention to create a strong local government in an area which was difficult to administer directly by the central government. Lancaster, on the other hand, was more a device to honour the son of the King, though its military potential was not without significance.

Chester

In Chester, the differences between the Justices of the Peace system and that in most other counties were fewer than in Durham and Lancaster. Such dissimilarities as are to be found lie largely in the social and political background, in the structure of the higher courts and of the older customary courts and in the lateness of the arrival of the justices in the palatinate.

It has been claimed that Chester was a county palatine with its own Parliaments and system of administering justice from before the Norman Conquest. At an early stage it was conferred as a feudal honour upon the Earls of Chester. In 1301 Edward, the son of Edward I, was created Prince of Wales and Earl of Chester, and during the following centuries it became usual for the King's heir to receive these titles, though from time to time the earldom reverted to the Crown, as happened in 1376 when it was resumed by Edward III on the death of the Black Prince.

In the fourteenth and fifteenth centuries the history of the county palatine of Chester was more closely intertwined with Wales than with England, and the system of Justices of the Peace which, as we have seen, was introduced into all English counties in 1361, was not extended to Chester until 1536 when it was also introduced into the Welsh counties. Before then various *ad hoc* commissions for conserving the peace had been issued in the palatinate to meet local or temporary needs, as they had been much earlier in England. Under Edward IV and the first two Tudors Chester began to be assimilated to the normal English counties.

The city of Chester acquired its own magistrates under Royal Charters, and the office of Conservator of the Peace appeared somewhat earlier than in the county. Various officers of the Earl of Chester, including sheriffs, coroners and justiciars, exercised jurisdiction within the city until the end of the thirteenth century, and the justiciar presided at the trial of both county and city pleas. In 1300 Edward I empowered the mayor and bailiffs of the city to try cases and to appoint their own coroners. In 1506 a charter of 21 Henry VII was granted to Chester confirming the *de facto* position of the city magnates as being virtually that of Justices of the Peace. The city was constituted a county by the charter which expressly provided that the mayor, recorder and the aldermen who had served as mayor were to be *Custodes Pacis* and *Justiciari ad Pacem.* They were to keep all statutes for the preservation of the peace and those relating to labourers and the sumptuary laws, and they were to perform the duties exercised by Justices of the Peace in other shires of the realm. They were to have power to appoint under-sheriffs, clerks and bailiffs as freely as was then done in the City of London.

In spite of these developments in Chester it was not until 1536 that Justices of the Peace were introduced into the county. This was effected by the same statute[1] which also introduced the system into the Welsh "shired" counties as we shall see in a later chapter. Fines and amerciaments from the justices' sessions were to be estreated into the

---

1.   27 Hen. VIII, c. 5. The Act provided for the appointment under the Great Seal of Justices of the Peace, Justices of the *Quorum* and Justices of Gaol Delivery.

Chester Exchequer. From then onwards justices were appointed to serve in the palatinate for both the maintenance of law and order and for the administration of local affairs in the same manner as in the English counties.

The palatinate was then vested in the Crown, and appointments to the commission were made in the King's name. Under a further Act of 1536 original and judicial writs were also to run henceforth in the name of the King alone. Justices of the Peace were appointed under commissions issued by the Lord Chancellor or the Lord Keeper who also usually issued Commissions of Gaol Delivery to the same individuals. For all practical purposes therefore the position of the Chester palatinate justices was from the beginning the same as that in the ordinary counties of Wales.

There was considerable delay in preparing the first commission for Cheshire and this was probably not issued until 1539, the earliest surviving commission being dated July of that year. A *Custos Rotulorum* was also appointed, the first being Bishop Rowland Lee, the president of the Council in the Marches, who was one of the justices named in the 1539 commission. A commission issued in 1544 contained the names of 38 justices of whom 20 were of the *Quorum*.[2]

One difference between the courts of the palatinate and those in England was that in Chester the County Court was nominally held before the justiciar of Chester and not before the sheriff. In 1540 it was said that the additional sessions of the Justices of the Peace imposed a heavy burden upon the freeholders, who also owed suit at the County Court, and it was therefore enacted that the criminal jurisdiction of the County Court should be curtailed and that it should be held only twice a year, though its sittings might be extended as long as necessary.[3] This, however, had the unintended result of limiting the occasions on which proclamations of outlawries could be made and therefore an act of the following year[4] authorized the sheriff of Cheshire to hold a monthly court for this purpose, at which he might also hear civil plaints for claims under 40 shillings. The effect of these enactments was to throw more work upon the Justices of the Peace and to strengthen their jurisdiction.

At first, there was no suitable accommodation for the justices' courts, but in 1545 a new hall was built in Chester in which both the city and the county justices sat, the courts being held every six weeks.

2.   See Appendix II for comparison with other commissions issued in the same year and in a number of subsequent years.
3.   32 Hen. VIII, c. 43. The Act explained the difficulty in attending so many sessions by saying that the "appearance and attendance cometh so often times and so thick together that at many times they cannot depart from the one court and attend another business scarcely one day and sometimes less but they must again ride to serve the other court, which is too painful, changeable, intolerable and importune for any man to sustaine and abide."
4.   33 Hen. VIII, c. 13.

Appointments to and removals from the Cheshire commissions were made in the same way as in other counties and lists of justices reflected political and social changes as elsewhere. One exceptional event which resulted in the replacement of Cheshire justices was the spectacular progress of the Duke of Monmouth through the county in 1682 when he was entertained by various local personages. Some of these were justices and they were removed from the commission, including the *Custos*, Henry Booth, later Earl of Warrington.

The commission usually included the élite of the county, but whereas most of the local knights and baronets were named, there were few peers because no members of the peerage were regularly resident in Cheshire. There were also few professional lawyers though many of the justices on the commission had attended the Inns of Court. The earlier commission included Judges of the Great Sessions (described later) and some members of the Council in the Marches of Wales, most of whom took little or no part in the work, though there were a few notable exceptions. Members of the Council continued to serve on the commission after Cheshire had been excluded from the Council's jurisdiction. The Bishop of Chester was normally on the commission and occasionally attended Quarter Sessions. In the nineteenth century a large number of successful business men were included but the lead at Quarter Sessions was still taken by the large landowners.

From the reign of Elizabeth, Cheshire had a Lord Lieutenant as well as a *Custos*. Often, until the seventeenth century, the two offices were held by different individuals. For most of the time between the Restoration in 1660 and the Revolution of 1689 the Earls of Derby were Lords Lieutenant of both Cheshire and Lancashire. From the end of the seventeenth century, however, these two offices were never held jointly and the Lord Lieutenant of Cheshire, who was invariably a leading member of the peerage,[5] was also *Custos* for the county.

In 1542 Henry VIII established an independent system of law courts in Wales and Chester. The highest of these courts were the Exchequer and the Great Sessions. The latter took the place of the English Assizes but, like the Assizes, the Great Sessions were organized on a circuit basis, those of the Cheshire palatinate being one of the four circuits into which Wales was formally divided. The sessions, which had exclusive jurisdiction except in treason, error, foreign plea and foreign voucher, were held twice yearly for six days. They were presided over by a legally qualified Judge, who became the Chief Justice of Cheshire when a second Judge was appointed in 1575. All

---

5.   During most of the eighteenth century the offices of Lord Lieutenant and *Custos* were held by the Earls of Cholmondeley and between 1783 and 1845 by the Earls of Stangford and Warrington. Thereafter the holders were; the Marquess of Westminster (1845-67), Lord Egerton (1867-83) and the first Duke of Westminster (1883-1900).

the Judges were included in the Commission of the Peace for the county.

Below the Great Sessions the Chester courts, like those in the Welsh counties, were modelled on the English courts of Justices of the Peace. Between 1559, when continuous records begin, and 1660 the general or Quarter Sessions were with one exception held in five towns: Chester, Knutsford, Middlewich, Nantwich and Northwich, generally successively, according to a set routine. They usually lasted for one day only. Attendances varied from time to time and according to the place in which the sessions were held. In view of the fact that the number of justices in the county was supposed to be limited to eight by the Act of 1535 (although this limit does not seem to have been always observed) it is not surprising to find that attendances until 1580 were usually about seven. For the next 20 years they were around nine and then rose to 10 before falling back to eight after 1630. (Details of attendances of justices at Quarter Sessions between 1665 and 1795 are given in VCH Cheshire, p. 62). Although the number of justices on the commission was significantly larger in the eighteenth century than it had been in the seventeenth, the number of those attending Quarter Sessions did not increase proportionately because many of them failed to take the oath.

After the Restoration, Quarter Sessions continued to be held in the five towns for a further century, but after 1760 they took place only in Chester itself (in January and April) and in Knutsford (in July and October). In the nineteenth century the Quarter Sessions of Cheshire were among the busiest in the country, and when all Quarter Sessions were abolished by the Courts Act 1971 the Act recognized that the chairman and deputy chairman of the sessions should rank as full-time judicial officers and be converted into Circuit Judges.[6] All the boroughs and towns in Cheshire were under the jurisdiction of the county justices with the sole exception of Chester city itself, which became a county borough and which had its own Quarter Sessions presided over by a recorder appointed under the Municipal Corporations Act 1835. The city Quarter Sessions, like all others in the country, were merged in the new Crown Court under the Act of 1971. The city also lost its separate Commission of the Peace in 1973 when all borough commissions except that of the City of London were merged in those for the counties by the Administration of Justice Act.

The Cheshire justices operated out of sessions in the same manner as they did in the rest of the country, and Petty Sessions developed from monthly meetings begun in Chester from the late sixteenth century.

6.   Schedule 2, Pt. I, 7(2).

Cheshire Quarter Sessions resolutely refused to adopt the County Police Act of 1839[7] and the county had no general police force until 1857. In the meantime Quarter Sessions employed a large force of assistant petty constables to keep the peace.

Durham

In 1302 the then Bishop of Durham, Antony Bek, proclaimed:

> "There are two kings in England, namely the Lord King of England wearing a crown in sign of his regality, and the Lord Bishop of Durham wearing a mitre in place of a crown in sign of his regality in the diocese of Durham."

Although an overstatement, this presumptuous claim was based on what was undoubtedly a unique authority enjoyed by the Bishops of Durham as Lords Palatine at that time. They certainly behaved as if they were kings.

The county palatine of Durham covered an area which lay mainly between the rivers Tyne, Derwent and Tees but also included certain other territories, notably Islandshire and Norhamshire lying along the Scottish border in north Northumberland, Bedlingstonshire (also in Northumberland) and a very small area north of York.

Durham was never expressly created a palatinate. Its peculiar position can be traced to the grants made to St Aidan of Lindisfarne and his successors, particularly St Cuthbert and his monks, and its recognition as a county palatine began in the thirteenth century. Its development was probably encouraged by the need for a strongly administered area on the Scottish border. By the time that the Justices of the Peace appeared on the scene it was vested in the bishop whose position was unique. From the fifteenth century he was the only lord of a palatinate which was not under the direct control of the monarch. He exercised the same spiritual jurisdiction as other bishops, but he also had his own temporal courts whose jurisdiction was as extensive as that of the King's courts at Westminster. Actions in these courts were commenced by writs issued in his name. The courts' records were dated in pontifical years of the bishop and not in the regnal years of the King. Fines were paid into the funds of the county and the property of persons convicted of felony were forfeited to the bishop and not to the King. In fact, the bishop claimed all forfeitures, deodands and fines save only those which had been annexed to the

---

7.   In 1839, 1840 and 1841 Quarter Sessions refused to adopt the Act (Cheshire RO. QJB 6/1 March 25, 1839, March 23, 1840, January 4, 1841).

Crown by Henry VIII and Elizabeth.

The procedure of the Durham courts was, however, the same as that in the royal courts and they operated in accordance with laws passed by the King and Parliament. From the fourteenth century those suspected of felony were usually tried before a court of gaol delivery (under a commission issued by the bishop) having been first charged either before the Justices of the Peace or at a coroner's inquest.

Among the many general statutes which applied to Durham were those relating to Keepers and subsequently to Justices of the Peace of 1327, 1344 and 1361. Early material is scarce and it is difficult to find instances of the appointment of Keepers of the Peace before the fourteenth century. In January 1312, however, when the north-east of England was disrupted by Scottish raiders and by civil unrest, Edward II appointed Ralph Fitz-William to be a Conservator of the Peace and later in the same year Robert Hylton was also appointed *Custos Pacis* to act in accordance with the customs of the kingdom and of the Royal Liberty of Durham.[8] His position was enhanced by the issue of a writ requiring general obedience to his authority. The need for this appointment was said to be because of the "great number of vagabonds and disturbers of the peace." In 1345 Bishop Hatfield issued a commission to nine persons to serve as Conservators of the Peace to execute the statutes of Winchester, Northampton and Westminster within Durham and Sadberge.[9] As was the case in commissions issued in other parts of the country at this time, the conservators were directed to punish all the offenders against the statutes or take from them security to be of good behaviour and to maintain the peace. The conservators were also appointed to be Justices of Oyer and Terminer within the same area. When, in 1369, the King appointed *Custodes Pacis* to act as Commissioners of Array to raise the militia and to correct the Judges who failed to enforce the Statute of Labourers, a special royal writ was addressed to Bishop Hatfield directing him to appoint similar officers in the county palatine.

Justices of the Peace as such were not appointed quite as early in the county palatine as they were elsewhere, the first recorded appointment being that of six men who were made justices under a commission issued by the bishop in 1375. They were directed to inquire into offences under the same three statutes as the conservators 30 years earlier. Until 1536 the palatine commissions were issued by the Durham Chancery in the name of the bishop (as were Commissions of Oyer and Terminer, Gaol Delivery and others) and the justices were required to maintain the bishop's peace instead of

8.   CPR, 1307-13, 428.
9.   The wapentake of Sadberge was not originally part of the county palatine of Durham but was bought in 1189 from Richard I by Bishop Hugh du Puiset.

that of the King.

During this period the bishop's commissions included local magnates together with senior officers of the palatinate and some of the Royal Judges and Serjeants-at-Law. They did not include many national figures like the Lord Keeper, as did those of other counties, but in 1477 the commission contained the name of Richard, Duke of Gloucester, the future King Richard III, who was connected with the county through his marriage into the Neville family of Durham. Among the bishop's officers who were usually placed on the commission were his steward and sometimes the spiritual Chancellor (as well as the temporal Chancellor who was always included). The bishop's Attorney General and Solicitor General were invariably in the commission. These two posts were peculiar to Durham and, although they held office as justices, they were responsible for prosecutions. It was not uncommon for the Solicitor General to serve as chairman of Quarter Sessions, especially in the early part of the eighteenth century. The fact that the bishop himself or one of his officers usually presided and that there was also a large proportion of his officers on the bench meant that he personally maintained a tight control over the sessions which could not be equalled by an individual, however eminent, in any other county.

A substantial proportion of the Durham justices were men who held other offices in the palatinate and, as might be expected, the Durham commission included a larger proportion of clerics than did those of other counties, though the number was not always as great as is generally supposed. It was claimed in the House of Commons in 1621 that nearly all the Durham justices were clergymen, but this was not true. At the beginning of the seventeenth century about one in seven of the total number of justices on the Durham commission were in the church, while a 100 years later, when the clergy figured prominently on most commissions, the proportion had increased to about one in four (in the year 1800, out of a total of 196 justices, 44 were from the church). As in other counties, however, clerics were usually among the most assiduous in their attendances and the majority had had a legal training; they therefore tended to dominate sessions and it is true to say that, although in a minority, they had a greater influence than most of the lay justices.

In 1535, the Act of Resumption (27 Henry VIII, c. 24) empowered the King to assume the criminal jurisdiction of the bishop and of other magnates. Durham was the only palatinate to be affected by this statute because Chester and Lancaster were already in the King's hands. The bishop, however, retained his regality until 1835 and he continued to exercise civil jurisdiction and administrative power. From 1536 onwards Durham sessions were dated in regnal years but for a time they were also recorded in the years of the bishop. The bishop could no longer appoint Justices of the Peace in his own name but he continued to nominate all those included in the Durham commissions. New commissions for Durham were issued once every year, and this practice continued long after commissions for other counties were sealed at far greater intervals. In practice, the Lord Chancellor accepted without question the lists of nominations prepared by the bishop but, once appointed, the Durham justices from 1536 acted in the name of the King and enforced his peace. On taking the oath, which was required before they could act, the new justices swore "to well and truly serve our sovereign Lord King in the office of Justice of the Peace within the County Palatine of Durham and Sadberge." It would seem that when submitting names for inclusion in new commissions the bishop was not entitled to omit any of those who had served previously. In 1810 Bishop Shute Barrington did not include the names of two of the existing justices in the list which he submitted to the Lord Chancellor and they were not appointed. The reason for the omission was that the two, one of whom was a clergyman, had granted an alehouse licence out of Brewster Sessions. The omission attracted strong criticism from both clerics and laymen and the two were restored to office when the next commission was issued the following year.

The 1535 Act also declared the bishop and his temporal Chancellor to be justices *ex officio* and the bishop or his representative was to be *Custos Rotulorum*. The right to appoint a *Custos* in the county was transferred to the Crown by the Durham (County Palatine) Act 1836 (s. 6). The bishop himself was also on the commission for Northumberland which was in his diocese. As already mentioned he often presided in person at Durham Quarter Sessions, and he did so at least once a year from the end of the sixteenth century to the beginning of the eighteenth. In some instances the bishop was already a justice before becoming incumbent, as for example William James who, as Dean of Durham, was on the commission for several years before being installed.

After 1536 the Durham commissions resembled more closely those for other counties. In addition to being addressed to the local élite they now for the first time began with the Lord Chancellor, Lord Treasurer and members of the Privy Council. They also included the President of the Council of the North. The Council was similar to the Council of Wales described in vol. III. It was reconstituted in 1522 by Henry VIII to handle the peculiar problems of a frontier region and it provided, *inter alia,* for the defence of the border with Scotland and generally maintained law and order in the area. As such it supervised the proceedings of the Justices of the Peace in the county palatine and in adjoining areas and, to this extent, it overshadowed the jurisdiction of the bishop. Like the Council of Wales and the Star Chamber, the

Council of the North was a prerogative body with extensive judicial powers which was biased towards the Crown and it was therefore abolished during the Interregnum. Unlike the Council of Wales it was never restored.

There were several boroughs in the county which acquired their own courts and magistrates by charter, but in every case, including the city of Durham itself, the bishop's courts retained some jurisdiction, the extent of which varied from time to time. During the 55 years before the Municipal Corporations Act 1835 Durham city had no borough court of its own, but from 1856 the earliest surviving Petty Sessions' books in the county are those of the city. The city never had its own court of Quarter Sessions and it always lay within the jurisdiction of the county sessions which sat in Durham. In the nineteenth century there were four other boroughs in the county which had much larger populations than Durham itself but only one of those, Sunderland, had its own court of Quarter Sessions which it acquired in 1907, together with a statutory recorder, after a successful petition under the Municipal Corporations Act 1882. Three other boroughs - Darlington, Stockton-on-Tees and West Hartlepool - were granted their own Commissions of the Peace and became county boroughs but they had no separate Quarter Sessions. Durham city and Hartlepool had recorders, but these posts were honorary and neither had separate sessions of their own. When, however, the new type of county court for the hearing of limited civil actions was created in 1846 the recorder of Durham, Henry Stapleton, became the first County Court Judge in the city. Durham and Hartlepool, as well as Darlington, Stockton-on-Tees and West Hartlepool, were granted their own Commissions of the Peace under the Municipal Corporations Act 1835. This remained the position until all borough commissions were merged in those of the counties in 1973.

Quarter Sessions, and later Petty Sessions throughout the county, operated in much the same way as in other parts of the country, and work conducted in these courts was similar. The earliest surviving records, dating from the fifteenth century,[10] show that, when exercising criminal jurisdiction, Durham Quarter Sessions dealt with numerous cases of assault and affray[11] and also with theft, especially of horses and cattle. There was also an increasing number of cases under the game laws.[12] Murder figured prominently until these cases were

10.   There is an almost continuous series of Durham Quarter Sessions records from January, 1598.
11.   K. Emsley and C.M. Fraser, in an article in the *Justice of the Peace and Local Government Review* of May 1, 1971, p. 301, give examples of affray cases tried at Durham sessions and state that between August 12, 1555 and August 3, 1556, no fewer than 765 persons were involved in such cases at the sessions.
12.   One of the early surviving rolls of presentments, of January 1511, records action taken against several yeomen for being in possession of hunting dogs when they did not have the statutory requirement of lands to the value of 40 shillings.

normally taken before Assizes from the seventeenth century onwards. In the administrative sphere much time was spent on dealing with vagrancy, the Poor Law, the maintenance of roads and bridges and, from the end of the seventeenth century, with licensing. As a large part of the territory was maritime the justices also had to deal with customs offences, port regulations, quarantine, the maintenance of beacons and coast and ship watching. As in other parts of the country, a substantial number of matters were brought before Quarter Sessions by presentment of single justices. This was especially so in respect of bridge and highway repairs.

Decisions of the Durham justices were subject to scrutiny in that proceedings could be removed by prerogative writs to the Court of Pleas or of gaol delivery within the county or to the King's Bench at Westminster. Writs of *certiorari* were issued for this purpose from the Court of Chancery and not infrequently indictments were removed in this way from Quarter Sessions to the Durham gaol delivery or Assize courts.

Lords Lieutenant began to be appointed by the King in the county palatine from the end of the sixteenth century but they played no part in the appointment of justices. The bishop continued to be *Custos Rotulorum*.

As elsewhere, there was a Clerk of the Peace for Durham Quarter Sessions. He was appointed by the bishop until 1836; thereafter the appointment was made by the sessions. The clerk was usually a local man who also held other offices in the palatinate such as Clerk of Assize. Sometimes he was a member of a bishop's family. John Barnes, whose father was bishop from 1575 to 1587, served as clerk from 1610 until his death in 1613, and he was also steward of the bishop's forest and halemote courts. By the seventeenth century Durham had a county treasurer, and two were appointed at the same time in 1618.

In the Civil War, Durham Quarter Sessions continued to operate save for a short interruption in 1644 when the Scots invaded the country. From 1649 the composition of the Durham commission varied according to political fluctuations, but no more so than in other counties. In James II's reign many of the Durham justices were opposed to the King's proposals (described in ch. IX) to relax the laws against dissidents of any persuasion. In 1688 six were removed from the commission because of their hostility and were replaced by others who were expected to be more amenable.

Under an Act of 1836 the temporal power of the bishops was entirely annexed to the Crown and the county palatine was absorbed into the legal system of the rest of the country, though, as explained below, its courts were allowed to remain as separate parts of the national system and its Court of Chancery retained a unique identity. Nevertheless, the term "county palatine" continued to be used.

After 1836 the nomination of persons for inclusion in the commission was made by the Lord Lieutenant, though the bishop continued to exert some influence over the choice. From 1910 advisory committees for the selection of justices were established for the county and for the city of Durham and the other boroughs with separate commissions on the same lines as in all other commission areas, as described in a later chapter.

Petty Sessions were reorganized throughout the county between 1848 and 1849, and at the time of the Courts Act 1971 the county was divided into 11 divisions. Under the Local Government Act of the following year some of these were transferred to other local authority areas, particularly to the newly created metropolitan county of Tyne and Wear. Considering the heavy pressure of work which came before the summary courts in the county boroughs within the Durham area it is curious that none of them had applied for the appointment of a stipendiary magistrate. This is one of the few heavily industrialized areas where no stipendiary has been introduced.

The Act of 1836 had no effect upon Quarter Sessions, and both those of the county and of Sunderland continued as before. The work of the county sessions increased dramatically as they absorbed the business of the many rapidly growing boroughs which had no Quarter Sessions of their own. In 1971, when all Quarter Sessions courts were abolished and merged with Assizes to form the Crown Court, the work of the chairman and deputy chairman of Durham sessions like those for Chester and Lancaster had become recognized as of sufficient weight to warrant the appointment of full-time officers, and they were converted by schedule 2 to the Courts Act into Circuit Judges. As such they sat in the Crown Court at Durham.

As regards the higher palatinate courts, proposals were put forward in 1836 for their abolition, but these were strenuously opposed. During a heated debate in the House of Lords it was argued that the courts saved the inhabitants of the county considerable expense and also the time and trouble of having to travel to Westminster. In the event the courts were allowed to remain for a time as separate parts of the judicial system. The Court of Pleas was reorganized in 1839 and again in 1852, 1854 and 1860, but finally under the Judicature Act 1873 it was absorbed into the High Court at Westminster and ceased to exist as a separate entity. The Durham Chancery Court survived for another 100 years. Its jurisdiction was strengthened by the Palatine Court of Durham Act of 1889, and in 1952 the Evershed Committee recommended that it should be extended further to include additional areas to the north and south, but this was only partly implemented.

The final act in the saga was in 1971 when, following the recommendations of the Royal Commission on Assizes and Quarter Sessions, the Courts Act abolished the Durham Chancery Court, and since then the Vice-Chancellor of the Duchy of Lancaster has heard Chancery cases at Newcastle and Leeds, both outside Durham county, and so the last vestige of the Durham palatinate courts vanished from January 1, 1972.

The Duchy of Lancaster

The county palatine of Lancaster was the last of the palatinates to be established in England, and it is the only one which still survives. It was created, following the model of Chester, by Royal Charter in 1351 to honour Henry, Earl of Lancaster,[13] grandson of Henry III. He was then made a Duke - following the precedent of the Black Prince who was created Duke of Cornwall in 1337. At the same time Lancashire was transformed into a county palatine with Henry as Lord Palatine having authority to appoint his own Chancellor and to issue and execute his own writs as well as to appoint justices of the higher courts; though prerogative writs still ran in the palatinate and the King's courts retained the power to scrutinize decisions of these courts and to correct them for error. The King also reserved the power to pardon life and limb. At that time the county palatine covered roughly the area of what is now embraced by the counties of Greater Manchester and Merseyside as well as of Lancashire. Henry of Lancaster was a distinguished leader and it was reasonable that Edward III should confer upon him the second dukedom in the history of the country, but a mark of greater favour was the transformation of the Lancastrian estates into a county palatine.

The powers granted to Henry lapsed on his death in 1361, but they were revived in 1377 in favour of his son-in-law, John of Gaunt, fourth son of Edward III, who had inherited the Lancastrian estates when he married Henry's daughter Blanche. The grant was for his life only, but in 1390 the authority was made permanent in him and his successors and it became part of the Duke's wider possessions. In 1399, Henry Bolingbroke, John of Gaunt's son, ascended the throne as Henry IV after ousting Richard II and, on John of Gaunt's death in the same year, the county palatine and its special jurisdictions were attached to the Crown and remain so to the present time. It has always been administered quite separately, however, as part of what is known as the Duchy of Lancaster.[14]

Judges and officials, including the Chancellor, were appointed in the

---

13.   The first Earl of Lancaster was Henry's father Edmund Plantagenet, second son of Henry III, to whom the King transferred various lands in 1265. These became the nucleus of the Duchy estate. The effect of the charter was to give Henry the *jura regalia* and liberties of a county palatine. See *Charter of the Duchy of Lancaster*, ed., W. Hardy, London, 1845, 9.

14.   A full account is given by Sir Robert Somerville in *History of the Duchy of Lancaster*, London, 1953, pp. 56-57, 64.

name of the Duke and were paid by the Duchy, but Justices of the Peace were always appointed in the name of the King even before the Dukedom was merged in the monarchy in 1399. The commissions were always issued in the name of the King, although they were passed under the Duchy seal (which was a Great Seal distinct from the Duke's privy or personal seal) and the procedure was in the hands of the Chancellor of the Duchy and was never under the authority of the Lord Chancellor.15 There was therefore a curious difference in the fifteenth century between the practice followed at Lancaster and that at Durham where the appointment of justices and their subsequent service was in the name of the bishop. Before the establishment of Justices of the Peace in 1361, Justices for Weights and Measures were appointed in the county palatine in 1354 and 135516 and Justices of Labourers in 1359.17

The first commissions to Justices of the Peace in most counties of England were issued on March 20, 1361, but that for the Duchy of Lancaster is dated May 13. It was the first to be issued after the bulk of the commissions for the rest of the country were sealed. It was in the King's name (and stated that it was sealed *"coram Regis apud Westmonasterium")*18. It was addressed to seven justices with no mention of the Earl or Duke of Lancaster. The reason for this omission is no doubt that Duke Henry died of the plague in March 1361 and there was a short delay before the Dukedom was revived in his son-in-law; this was confirmed when John of Gaunt was summoned to Parliament as Duke of Lancaster on August 14, 1361. There was therefore no Duke when the first Lancaster commission was issued. One might have expected that thereafter, on the analogy of Durham, Lancastrian commissions would have been issued in the name of the Duke until his death in 1399, but this was not so. The first commission issued after John of Gaunt's creation as Duke was dated May 12, 1363.19 John's name headed the list of eight commissioners, of whom four were the same individuals as in the previous commission, but the commission was still issued in the name of the King.

The form of the 1363 commission was the same as that for other counties, and for the earlier commissions of 1361. It empowered the justices to keep the peace within the county of Lancaster pursuant to the statutes of Winchester, Northampton and Westminster, to compel all those who had made threats against any of the King's people of

15. For the wording of a Duchy commission see Appendix IB.
16. Deputy Keeper's 32nd Report, Appx. I, pp. 334 (No. 8) and 344 (No. 19). The unique character of the Duchy is illustrated by the statement in early enactments that there was to be one measure or weight throughout the realm except in Lancashire "because in that county it hath always been used to have greater Measure than in any other part of the Realm."
17. *Ibid.,* pp. 334, (No. 10) and 345 (No. 38); *cf.,* 40th Report p. 523.
18. PRO, c 66/263, m. 32d. CPR, 1361-4, p. 66.
19. *Ibid.,* c. 66/267, m. 15d. CPR, 1361-4, p. 366.

bodily injury or of firing of their houses to find security for their good behaviour, to hear and determine the accounts of the receivers of fines, amerciaments and profits levied of labourers, to correct weights and measures according to the statutes and ordinances, and to inspect and determine all indictments begun before Justices of Oyer and Terminer "in time passed and not yet determined."

A further commission for Lancaster was issued on October 30, 1370. This seems to have remained in force for the remaining 29 years of John of Gaunt's life and no commission was issued during the short period between his death and the usurpation by his son as Henry IV. However, whenever new appointments were required additional justices were brought into the Lancaster commission by means of an association which was recorded on the back of the Patent Roll. Thus on October 8, 1370[20] William de Nessefeld was associated "in the Commission of the Peace and of Oyer and Terminer in the county of Lancaster to John Duke of Lancaster" and the five other existing justices.

Provision was also made in 1374 and 1375 for occasions when not all the justices could be present. Thus it was directed on December 1, 1374 that:

"Whereas the King lately associated Roger de Kirketon, Thomas de Sandford and John de Dent in the commission of the peace and of oyer and terminer in the county of Lancaster to John Duke of Lancaster and his fellows, he now orders that, if all the said commissioners cannot be present, then six, five, four, three or two, of whom the duke, Roger de Kirketon and Geoffrey de Foljeambe shall be one, may proceed to the business."[21]

There was a further direction on November 29, 1374 to the effect that the Duke and the other two should not wait for any of the remaining justices to appear before they proceeded to business:[22] and on January 1, 1375 a mandate was addressed to five of those named in the commission ordering them not to proceed to take indictments or do other business unless the Duke or one of the two other named justices was present.[23] This and the other measures mentioned above was in accordance with the formula employed by the royal chancery for the rest of the country.

As elsewhere, additional commissions were sometimes addressed to Lancastrian justices for specific purposes. One of these is of particular interest as it shows the Crown's increasing dissatisfaction with the

20.   *Ibid.,* c. 66/281, m. 36d. CPR, 1367-70, p. 428.
21.   *Ibid.,* c. 66/291, m. 10d. CPR, 1374-77, p. 59.
22.   *Ibid.,* c. 66/291, m. 3d. CPR, 1374-77, p. 64.
23.   *Ibid.,* c. 66/291, m. 4d. CPR, 1374-77, p. 63.

sheriffs. It is dated January 28, 1371 and is addressed to two of those who are on the Commission of the Peace. They are ordered:

"to make inquisition in the said county touching all trespasses, conspiracies, extortions, oppressions, champerties, maintenances, damages, grievances, falsities and excesses committed by Richard de Radeclyve, sheriff of the said county, William de Chorle, his under-sheriff, ... and others of their confederacy" against the abbot of Evesham and the prior of Penwortham and others "of the King's people by colour of the said office of sheriff."

The coroners of the county were to send jurors before the commissioners.[24]

During the period that John of Gaunt held the Dukedom fewer commissions were issued for Lancaster than for most other counties, but this probably amounted to no more than a bureaucratic accident. After John's son Henry took the throne the commissions for Lancaster were issued in his name as King and they were no longer addressed to the Duke. Most of the original Lancastrian commissions survive only from the sixteenth century and are preserved in the Quarter Sessions records at the Lancaster Record Office, but there are a few survivals from earlier times in addition to the ones between 1361 and 1399. In February 1402 a commission was issued to eight persons and in August 1426 to 13.[25] In November 1473 a commission was issued to 17 people as Justices of the Peace and under diverse statutes. They were headed by Richard, Duke of Gloucester (at that time the Duchy's Chief Steward in the county) but all the rest appear to be Lancashire men.[26]

In addition to these commissions there are a few early references to the work carried out by the justices. In February 1432, justices were ordered to arrest named disturbers of the peace and to hold them until the coming of the Lancashire Justices of Assize, etc, and other members of the Council of the Duchy.[27]

As in the other palatinates, the Duchy justices were entitled under the statute of 1388 to receive a daily fee for their attendance at Quarter Sessions at the same rate as in other counties, and payments were made by the Duchy out of county funds into which fines collected by the courts were paid. As we have seen, the payment of justices' daily fees in all counties was dependent upon their raising sufficient "profits"

24.   *Ibid.,* c. 66/284, m. 38d. CPR, 1370-74, p. 100. Sometimes the King granted a pardon to a person convicted by what were described as the Duke's justices. On October 28, 1386, a pardon was granted "at the supplication of Robert Ursuryk, knight, to Amice Barnes of Preston, co. Lancaster, of the execution of a judgment against her for divers felonies, whereof she is convicted in that county before the justices of the King's uncle John, Duke of Lancaster, and of any consequent waivers." (*Ibid.,* c. 66/322, m. 16. CPR, 1386-89, p. 233).
25.   Deputy Keeper's 40th Report, Appx. 4, p. 530; PL3/3/22 (PRQ).
26.   DL 37/42, rot. 4 no. 22.
27.   February 9, 1432. DL 42/18 f. 15.

from fines and amerciaments to cover the cost and this point was made on a number of occasions in Lancashire when the justices did not appear to have been sufficiently severe in imposing fines. Thus, in May 1493, it is confirmed that the justices should get four shillings for their attendances at sessions, but it is said that they "be very negligent to see to our profits such as should rise before them." No payment was therefore to be made unless it could be met from the profits of the sessions.[28] Records exist from fairly early times of the dates and places where sessions were held and of the names of the justices (usually two per session) and of the clerk to whom payment was made. As elsewhere, the Clerk of the Peace was paid two shillings a day for attending and for writing the rolls.[29] Not only did the same individual appear as clerk on each occasion but often the same two justices were paid at successive sessions. Thus in 1438-39, Robert Brockholes appears in all seven sessions' lists,[30] and William Ambrose was paid for attending all the five sessions in 1455-56.[31] There is a record of 1375 showing that the sheriff was ordered also to pay the Justices of Labourers and Artificers at their sessions in Lancaster provided that the Duke had a profit from their sessions.[32]

The Duchy had its own superior courts. Under the original charter Duke Henry was able to have his own chancellery with its Chancellor and with its courts and writs, and also to appoint justices to hold pleas. These powers were revived in John of Gaunt after Henry's death. In addition to the Chancery Court there were two other courts in the palatinate, the Crown Court and the Court of Common Pleas. As already stated, the power to pardon life and limb and to correct error in the Duchy courts was reserved to the King. Writs from the courts at Westminster, however, usually did not run directly in the Duchy but were sent to the chancellery or to the Chancellor himself who caused appropriate writs to be issued under the palatinate seal.

The work of the Lancastrian justices, judicial, administrative and executive was the same as that performed by justices in other counties, though they were not always among the foremost in introducing reforms. This was especially evident in their failure to establish houses of correction in which the able-bodied poor were to be put to work. As we shall see, all counties were required to introduce these establishments by an Act of 1576, but it was not until 1619 that Lancashire Quarter Sessions finally erected a building for this purpose, and even then action seems to have been taken only in response to a direction delivered by the Assize Judges that it was "His Majesties

28.   May 13, 1493. DL 37/62 m. 17.
29.   DL 29/1932.
30.   DL 29/1930. Lists give the names of the justices who received payment (usually two per session) with dates and places.
31.   DL 29/1945 [1441/2].
32.   Camden 3rd series, vol. 21, No. 1697. October 12, 1375.

pleasure and expres charge and comande of the better ordering, governing and punishing malefactors and the meaner sort of people" that a house of correction should be set up. Again, whereas an Act of 1597 decreed that every parish should levy a compulsory rate for poor relief, Lancashire was slow to respond, and as late as 1637 it was found that the parish of Middleton still had no poor rate.

The Duchy has never been much involved in the actual work of its justices which was left to Quarter Sessions, but in the fifteenth and sixteenth centuries it laid down the arrangements for holding sessions and it stipulated the towns where they were to sit. Thus, rules were made by the Justices of Assize at Lancaster from April 5 to 10, 1546, in the presence of most of the Justices of the Peace and with their assent, for the fixing of days and places for keeping the General Quarter Sessions in Lancashire, and these rules were approved by the Chancellor and Council of the Duchy on June 6.[33] Initially, Quarter Sessions were held in Lancaster, but as there were other towns of importance and the distance between them was considerable, the practice was adopted of opening the sessions at Lancaster, where matters arising in the Lonsdale hundred were dealt with (there were six hundreds in the county) and then adjourning them to a number of other centres. In this way sessions were held at Preston for the hundreds of Amounderness, Blackburn and Leyland, alternately, at Ormskirk and Wigan for West Derby hundred and at Salford for the Salford hundred. Later, the Ormskirk and Wigan sessions were held in Liverpool and the Salford sessions in Manchester as these industrial centres became more populous and important. These arrangements did not always work smoothly and there was opposition from the older sessions towns, especially Lancaster. The justices from any part of the county were entitled to attend all the sessions, but few sat outside the court for their own hundred. Only the *Custos* and Clerk of the Peace attended regularly in each centre. Consequently there were seldom more than 12 justices present at any one session, and sometimes only three or four attended. The majority of the county justices therefore were never together at any one time and, whereas matters concerning limited areas were dealt with in detail, little attention was paid to those which concerned the county as a whole. There was, however, an opportunity for all justices to meet together during Assizes. Until the eighteenth century they were all required to attend the Assize Judge, and in Tudor times the Judge imposed fines on those who failed to appear. At that time the Privy Council sought to promulgate its directions through the Assize Judges, who also addressed the local justices on various aspects of their work. This was therefore an opportunity for the county justices to hold formal meetings of their

33.   DL 42/45, fs. 167 v., 168; *cf.* DL 42/96, f. 147 v.

own, and in the sixteenth century they adopted the practice of having annual meetings at which they dealt with administrative matters. These meetings were held in Lancaster and coincided with Lancaster Assizes. This practice, which grew up on the initiative of the justices themselves with the support of the Judges, was unique to Lancashire and is not to be found in other parts of England and Wales. The gatherings came to be known as Meetings at the Sheriff's Table.[34] The first known record of a meeting of this kind dates from March, 1578.

The scope of Meetings at the Sheriff's Table became more clearly defined in the early seventeenth century. They were firmly supported by the Assize Judges who exercised a considerable influence over the proceedings throughout this period. It was at one of these meetings, held in 1618, that the resolution was passed to erect a house of correction after the justices had been ordered to do so by the Judge, as mentioned above.

As the seventeenth century progressed the Privy Council became preoccupied with political matters and foreign policy and the Judges showed less interest in the justices' meetings, while the latter established themselves as county sessions from which the administration of county affairs was controlled, leaving it to Quarter Sessions to deal with the detailed problems arising in the hundreds and parishes (though the justices at the Table appointed the high constables of the hundreds). The Table became the forum for discussion of all aspects of county administration. There is little evidence of the Table's activities during the Civil War, but after the Restoration it became clearly established as the centre of county government, while at the same time the Judges ceased to use it to any great extent as a channel for the dissemination of national government policy. The attention of the Table was focused on matters which concerned the county generally, especially those involving the expenditure of county funds and the appointment of county officers. A subject which occupied a great deal of time at the Table was the repair of bridges, particularly those at Lancaster, Crosford and across the Ribble near Preston. The maintenance of bridges was of vital importance to communications throughout Lancashire, and the cost was by custom borne by the county. Those present at the Table were usually members of the *Quorum* but some of the other justices also attended. It would seem that the Assize Judges were not normally present at meetings at the end of the seventeenth century but there is no clear evidence of this.

As county business increased it became more and more difficult to deal with this at the same time as Assizes, and attendances at the Table fell away during the eighteenth century until it became virtually

34. Described fully in *Proceedings of the Lancashire Justices of the Peace at the Sheriff's Table during Assize Week, 1578-1694*, ed. B.W. Quintrell.

impossible to continue the meetings at all. There was, however, an even greater need for a central body which could effectively deal with the affairs of the county. In 1789 it was proposed that the justices' meetings should no longer coincide with Lancaster Assizes but that general sessions should be held annually in Preston for the purpose of transacting business relating to the county as a whole. Preston was chosen as being in a central position which would make it easier for the justices from all parts of the county to attend. This proposal, however, was strenuously resisted by Lancaster. There followed several years of wrangling. In 1795 the justices of the Lonsdale hundred who met in Lancaster arrogated authority to act for the county at large and, having dismissed the county treasurer, appointed a successor without reference to the justices in the other divisions. The justices meeting at Preston immediately declared this to be "highly improper and its legality also questionable."[35] The Lancaster justices, on the other hand, remained adamant, refusing to meet anywhere other than in Lancaster and claiming that any general sessions held elsewhere than in their city were invalid. The only way in which the rest of the county could overcome this obstruction was by means of an Act of Parliament and they therefore applied for a statute to establish annual general sessions at Preston at which certain county business had to be transacted. The Lancaster justices opposed the Bill vigorously, and the county incurred considerable expenditure in securing its passage. It was finally passed in 1798,[36] thus establishing general sessions for the county at large to be held annually at Preston. Thereafter decisions taken at these sessions were binding throughout the county area, whereas previously decisions taken at the Table had had no binding legal authority. They had merely been promulgated to the justices throughout the county with requests that they should be accepted and followed, which they usually were.

Since 1399 the reigning Sovereign has always been Duke of Lancaster but the Duchy has been administered by its Chancellor who has exercised delegated power. At first, he was a prominent figure in attendance on the Sovereign, and from the early days of parliamentary government he was a Minister. For some time he was in the House of Commons, but throughout the eighteenth and much of the nineteenth centuries he was usually a peer. From the mid-eighteenth century the Chancellor has been a member of the Cabinet and in the twentieth century two Chancellors - Clement Attlee and Winston Churchill - subsequently became Prime Minister. It was not, however, until the end of the seventeenth century that the Chancellor of the Duchy played an active part in the selection of Justices of the Peace, and it

35.   Lancashire QS Minutes, May 18, 1795.
36.   38 Geo. III, c. 58.

was not uncommon for the King to order the Vice-Chancellor to seal a commission without any reference to the Chancellor. This practice, which continued into the seventeenth century, was effected either by warrant of the King himself or by a direction from the Secretary of State.

In the Civil War the Chancellor, on orders from Parliament, dismissed a number of justices with Royalist sympathies and replaced them with others favourable to Parliament. This sometimes placed the Chancellor in an awkward position because until the Interregnum the statute 27 Hen. VIII, c. 24, which declared that only the King could make justices, remained in force. Thus, in 1642, the Chancellor appointed a number of justices on a warrant he received from the King. Parliament then ordered him to issue a commission to 14 new justices and to remove 10 Royalists, whereupon the King sent the Chancellor another warrant directing him to renew the earlier commission.[37]

The last document issued under the Duchy seal before the King's death was dated January 4, 1649. After some delay an Act was passed on April 26, 1649 for constituting Justices of the Peace in Lancashire, and later the Commissioners of the Great Seal were empowered to appoint the justices. At the beginning of the Interregnum in 1649, the Chancellor, John Bradshaw, was continued in office and appointed justices from time to time until October 1653 when the Duchy jurisdiction ceased. It was revived in 1655 when Thomas Fell was made Chancellor but lapsed again later in the same year and was not restored until the return of Charles II in 1660. Under the Protectorate of Richard Cromwell Parliament ordered the Great Seal Commissioners to issue Commissions of the Peace for Lancashire as in other counties.

By the eighteenth century the Chancellor had become actively involved in the appointment of justices and has continued to be so up to the present day. In the early years he received recommendations from a number of sources. Some came from the justices themselves who were often consulted on proposed candidates. As the chancellorship was a political appointment and was often filled by someone who had no great knowledge of the county and who spent much of his time at Westminster, it was necessary for him to seek local advice to a much greater extent than would have been the case with a resident Lord Lieutenant. In selecting candidates the Chancellor came to be guided by the Duchy officers, particularly by the county palatine seal-keeper who relied to some extent upon his local contacts for names and advice. Considerable weight was placed on political views and many names were submitted by Members of Parliament. The Lord

37.   HMC, Le Fleming, p. 202.

Lieutenant of the county, who was appointed by the King, does not seem to have played as significant a part in the selection of justices as he did in other counties and he was not even consulted on every occasion. The procedure for the appointment and removal of justices was conducted entirely in the Duchy office. The Chancellor's secretary would prepare a list of names which the Chancellor endorsed and he then issued a fiat directing the Duchy seal-keeper to insert the names in a commission and, having done so, the seal-keeper filed the fiat in his office. As in the other counties palatine, the early commissions for the Duchy were issued more frequently than in the rest of the country, and even in the first part of the eighteenth century they appeared about every two years, but the commissions and lists were not kept in the Chancellor's office at the Savoy in London until the nineteenth century.

The Clerk of the Peace for Lancashire was also appointed by the Chancellor under the Duchy seal in the same way as the justices. The procedure therefore differed from that in other counties where the clerk was appointed by the *Custos*. Between 1780 and 1879 the work of the Clerk of the Peace was done by deputies and the office itself was a sinecure, as was the case in many other counties.

The personnel of the commissions was similar to that elsewhere save that, as in Durham, the members of the Privy Council were not automatically included in the earlier commissions. From 1687, however, they were named at the head of each Duchy commission following immediately after the Chancellor of the Duchy. The Lord Chancellor, Lord Treasurer and Lord Keeper of England were not included in the Duchy commissions. The proportion of justices in the *Quorum* followed the same pattern as elsewhere. Thus, in 1675 there were 71 "working" justices of whom 48 were of the *Quorum*, while by 1720 only four out of a total of 95 were not of the *Quorum*.

Lancashire contained a large Roman Catholic population and this accounted for some extensive changes in the composition of the commission under James II[38], who adopted a policy of removing Anglican justices and replacing them with those who had Catholic connections. The greatest number of Catholic justices were placed in the Lancashire commission in 1687 and 1688 when some 50 Catholics were appointed. One of these, Viscount Molyneux, was made Lord Lieutenant in 1687 in place of the Earl of Derby. The new Catholic justices were mostly men of standing and ability, who should have been well able to administer the county, but they were prevented from doing

38.   Previously, those who were then serving on the commission were critical of Charles II's Declaration of Indulgence, issued in 1672, in which he expressed his wish that all penal laws against nonconformists and recusants should be suspended, and that all Judges and Justices of the Peace should act accordingly. The Lancashire justices reacted by questioning the validity of the King's action in a letter to the Council from whom they received a severe rebuke. HMC, Kenyon, p. 33.

so by the antagonism of the rest of the population. It was not long before James, alarmed at the effect his policy was having throughout the country, reversed it and restored a number of Anglican justices. Molyneux was dismissed and Derby reappointed both to the commission and as Lord Lieutenant.

As in other counties, politics played a prominent part in the Lancashire commissions after the Revolution.[39] Derby resigned in 1688 and was succeeded as Lord Lieutenant by the Whig, Lord Brandon (later Earl of Macclesfield), while the Tory, Lord Willoughby d'Eresby (later Duke of Ancaster), became Chancellor. A conflict developed between the two, in the course of which candidates for the commission put forward by Brandon were turned down by the Chancellor, who appointed candidates of his own. Brandon, who was also *Custos*, complained to the Privy Council but does not seem to have received any support from that quarter. From 1694, however, he was successful in securing the appointment of a number of Whigs while some Tories were omitted from new commissions. In the following years more Whigs were appointed to the Lancaster commission and many of them were alleged by opponents to be of low quality. Some were certainly drawn from trade and industry and their origins were far removed from those of the traditional gentry. Most of them were soon dismissed after vehement protests from the Tories and the old established families. In 1702 Lord Derby again became Lord Lieutenant and *Custos* while the Tory, Sir John Leveson Gower (later Lord Gower), was made Chancellor, and there followed a revival of the Tory element on the commission. This in turn was succeeded by a mild swing back to the Whigs when there was a change of government in London. At the same time Derby died and was succeeded in the Earldom by his brother who supported the Whigs and who became Chancellor, and also Lord Lieutenant and *Custos*, in 1706. During the latter part of this Chancellorship which ended in 1710 no substantial changes were made in the commission, and there were also no marked alterations in the balance under Derby's Whig successor, Lord Aylesford. When, however, the Tory justices showed sympathy for the rioting which broke out in the south of the county in 1715 the King was persuaded by the Privy Council to take the exceptional step of ordering Aylesford to issue a new commission which was predominantly Whig and was composed of names prepared by the Council. This brought the Lancashire commission more or less into line with those in other counties and thereafter the political pattern

39. A detailed account of the Lancastrian commissions between 1675 and 1720 is given by Lionel Glassey in *Politics and the Appointment of Justices of the Peace, 1675-1720*, pp. 270-296. Glassey also points out that the Lancaster commission still contained many justices who were not of the *Quorum*. Thirty-three of the 87 county justices in 1701 were not accorded this distinction.

was similar to that in the rest of the country as described in a later chapter. As in other counties, clerical justices were appointed to the Lancashire commission and their numbers became substantial at the end of the eighteenth century.

The Industrial Revolution probably affected Lancashire more than any other county. It was accompanied by a vast increase in population in the southern part which was remote from the traditional centres of justice at Lancaster and Preston. This area came to be dominated by the cotton industry and considerable fortunes were amassed by the leading manufacturers. Successive Chancellors, however, as well as the Lancaster gentry, were strongly prejudiced against the appointment of such persons as justices and for a long time there was a rigid rule that no one of this kind should be placed on the commission. When the rule was discussed in Parliament in 1813[40] it was explained that it was necessitated by the fact that disputes between manufacturers and their workmen frequently came before the magistrates' courts.

This was the view of the then Chancellor, Lord Bathurst. A later Chancellor, Lord Bexley, defined the qualification for the office of Justice of the Peace as being that of a true gentleman - intelligent, socially acceptable in the eyes of his fellow magistrates, the owner of property and having no connection with trade.[41] Under the Reform Government of the 1830s, however, there was an indication that the Chancellor's rigid ban on cotton manufacturers might be alleviated to some degree. In 1833 Lord Holland commented that "the rule against persons in trade neither is nor ought to be invariable," though he himself did not seem inclined to make exceptions.[42] It was accepted, however, that exceptions could be made to the established rule, and from then onwards a number of cotton manufacturers were appointed. This was done partly in recognition of their services to the party and partly because of the need to provide justices resident in those areas where it proved impossible to find candidates from among the old landed gentry.

By the 1840s the exclusive monopoly of the Lancashire benches by the established landowners had been broken, but this was not followed by a domination of the courts by the manufacturers. David Foster[43] has shown that power still rested in the members of the old regime and that the new manufacturing class was apparently content to leave it to them to play the leading role, at least at Quarter Sessions and especially at the general county sessions at Preston. Foster gives a

40.   *Hansard*, 3rd Series, May 12, 1813.
41.   Duchy of Lancaster Office, County Bundles, Bexley to G. Harrison, August 1, 1826.
42.   *Ibid.*, Holland to F.D. Francis, August 5, 1833.
43.   *Class and County Government in Early-Nineteenth-Century Lancashire.* Northern History, Univ. of Leeds, vol. IX, 1974.

table showing that only a small proportion of the justices who attended the general sessions were cotton magistrates. The only years in which they appeared in appreciable numbers were 1841 and 1842 when their presence was explained by their close interest in the police system. (For several years from 1840 the sessions debated the establishment of the Lancashire constabulary under the Rural Constabulary Act of 1839). Foster concludes that:

"The extent of the power which the cotton magistrates assumed was closely delineated by their industrial region. In these areas, and particularly in the Salon hundred, landed society appears to have yielded to the new leaders in much the same way as they took little or no interest in the Parliamentary constituencies created there in 1832. The rural areas of the county remained firmly under traditional influence, as did the principal organ of county government, the annual general sessions ... The Lancashire cotton manufacturers gained admission to the county commission by a mixture of necessity and ambition but, since their principal aim was to join rather than to transform an èlite group, the system of county government survived their onslaught."

One finds a similar process in other parts of the country, but the phenomenon appeared earlier and on a larger scale in Lancashire than in most other areas.

By the end of the eighteenth century it had already become very difficult to maintain a ban on the appointment of trading justices in those areas where the vast increase in the working population led to a serious escalation in crime and outbreaks of rioting and where magistrates were needed at short notice. It was on the occasion of one of these riots in the Manchester area in 1819 that the reading of the Riot Act by the justices who were present led to what came to be referred to as the "massacre of Peterloo" which is described in a later chapter. The landed gentry in these areas were comparatively few in number and many of them were reluctant to serve as justices in the adverse conditions. Robert Peel was to comment later that the great increase in the working population around industrial centres not only encouraged crime but diminished the number of magistrates because it drove away the country gentlemen.[44] In the circumstances, the narrow restrictions on membership of the bench were modified and in addition to the cotton magistrates a certain number of men of lower degree were appointed, although even then it became customary for

44.   *Hansard,* vol. XVIII, 1828, pp. 893-4.

appointments to be made on the recommendation of existing justices.[45] The change of policy, however, did not meet with great success, as many of the new appointees in the worst-affected areas proved to be ineffective and some behaved like the trading justices of Middlesex who will be described in a later chapter. In some respects the situation in south Lancashire, especially in the Manchester area, resembled that in Middlesex, although it never became as serious. At the end of the eighteenth century the Chancellor of the Duchy had difficulty in finding justices to sit in Manchester and a similar situation soon arose in Wigan. There were a few outstanding individuals who went some way towards making up for the shortage of efficient justices. Such a one was Thomas Butterworth Bayley who became chairman of Quarter Sessions and, among other achievements, secured the erection of a new prison at Salford. Bayley, however, was exceptional, at least in the Salford hundred which included Manchester, and in the 1790s there was a serious shortage of justices in the area and many of those who did serve were corrupt.

The work in this part of the county was clearly beyond the capacity of the existing system and the only alternative was the establishment of a full-time stipendiary magistrate. An Act of Parliament was therefore sought to authorize such an appointment, and the task of initiating the legislation was entrusted to the Reverend W.R. Wray, one of the many prominent clerical justices of this era. In addition to being a diligent justice, Wray, like many of his clerical brethren, had studied law and had been called to the Bar, and he was not only successful in securing the passage of the necessary Bill in 1805[46] but he himself was then chosen to be the first stipendiary for the area. He held this post until 1823, and during this time he does not appear to have drawn the salary authorized by the Act, though he continued to take a comfortable clerical stipend. This was the first stipendiary magistracy to be created outside the London area. After the passing of the Municipal Corporations Act in 1835 it was open to the council of a borough to petition for the appointment of a stipendiary magistrate (s. 99) and in accordance with these provisions three such appointments were made within the county palatine. All of these magistracies were still operating busily in 1989, their courts being established in Liverpool, Manchester and Salford.

The later history of the Lancastrian Justices of the Peace followed the same pattern as that of the justices in the rest of the country. They were subjected to the sweeping reforms of the nineteenth century,

45. The Liverpool papers in the British Library contain a few references to this practice in the eighteenth century. In 1786 three JPs were appointed on the recommendation of three existing JPs. Add. MS. 38446, p. 98, *cf.*, p. 140; and Add. MS. 38447, pp. 43, 231, 339.
46. 45 Geo. III, c. 59.

mentioned later. The position of the justices in the boroughs was revolutionized in 1835 by the Municipal Corporations Act, and the county justices lost their remaining administrative functions in 1888. Some of the higher courts were also affected. Under the Judicature Act 1873 the Lancashire Court of Common Pleas became part of the new High Court of Justice, and Lancashire, like Durham, ceased to be a county palatine as regards Commissions of Assize. The Duchy, however, remained unique in having its own justices appointed in the name of the King by its Chancellor and not by the Lord Chancellor of Great Britain. This did not apply to the stipendiary magistrates who, until 1949, were appointed by the Crown on the recommendation of the Home Secretary. This function was transferred to the Lord Chancellor by the Justices of the Peace Act 1949 which made no exception in respect of stipendiaries in the Duchy.

We shall see later that in the nineteenth century it became well established that, in the appointment of Justices of the Peace throughout the rest of England and Wales, the Lord Chancellor was not obliged to accept recommendations made by the Lord Lieutenant, though in the majority of cases he did so. In Lancashire, however, the practice was not so clear and towards the end of the century there were several oscillations in policy. Until 1870 the Lord Lieutenant played little part in the selection of candidates for appointment to the bench, but in that year the Chancellor of the Duchy, Lord Dufferin, decided to change the procedure and, with the approval of the Prime Minister (Gladstone) and the Cabinet, directed that in future all appointments should be made only on the nomination of the Lord Lieutenant. The reason given for this change was that there had been considerable dissatisfaction with the previous arrangements because they had resulted in an unnecessarily large number of justices being placed on the county commission, chiefly as a reward for political services. Accordingly, for some 20 years thereafter the choice of candidates was left largely in the hands of the Lord Lieutenant, but this procedure also proved to be unsatisfactory and the Chancellor, after consultation with the Lord Lieutenant and with Queen Victoria's approval, reverted to the former practice, under which the Chancellor of the Duchy received recommendations from various quarters, and himself selected persons to be appointed magistrates for the county palatine. Two years later, on a change of government, there was yet another *volte-face*. In a minute dated January 27, 1896 the Chancellor recorded that the arrangements under which the magistrates had been appointed since 1893 had "produced results very injurious to the public service." He had accordingly decided, with the approval of the Queen, to revert to the practice established in 1870 under which justices "for the county palatine were appointed by the Chancellor of the Duchy upon the recommendation of the Lord Lieutenant ...". This practice has remained basically the same to the present day, but there was a modification in 1906 when the then Chancellor, Lord Wolverhampton, made it clear that he was prepared to receive recommendations from other sources which, if he thought fit, he would refer to the Lord Lieutenant who would be expected to nominate them if he saw no reason to the contrary. This in turn was varied in 1908 when Lord Wolverhampton agreed to revert to the practice whereby all recommendations should in the first instance be made by the Lord Lieutenant. This remained the position until advisory committees were appointed for each commission area following the recommendations of the Royal Commission of 1910,[47] after which appointments were normally made on the advice of the committees but the Chancellor, like the Lord Chancellor, reserved the right to make appointments on his own initiative if he thought fit. Unlike advisory committees throughout the rest of Great Britain, which were appointed by the Lord Chancellor, those in the Duchy were appointed by the Chancellor of the Duchy and were responsible to him. The Lord Lieutenant has always been chairman of the Lancashire county advisory committee while each of the boroughs having separate commissions has had its own committee presided over by a person appointed for the purpose by the Chancellor.

The 1910 Royal Commission had been appointed to consider "what steps should be taken to facilitate the selection of the most suitable persons to be Justices of the Peace." They recommended that the Lord Chancellor should remain responsible for the selection and appointment of justices in all parts of Great Britain other than the Duchy of Lancaster and, in doing so, they gave as some of their reasons that he was head of the judiciary and also responsible for advising on the appointment of Judges, and that "in giving such advice he did not act as a politician." These considerations did not, of course, apply to the Chancellor of the Duchy; nevertheless the commission proceeded to recommend that he should "continue to discharge the duty of advising the Crown in regard to the appointment of justices within the county." They gave no reasons nor made any comment beyond observing that "in the County Palatine of Lancaster the Chancellor of the Duchy occupies a position in relation to the appointment of Justices of the Peace similar to that which the Lord Chancellor holds in the rest of England and Wales."

The subject of responsibility for appointments was not raised again until 1946 when the second Royal Commission on Justices of the Peace was appointed to review afresh the arrangements for selecting and removing justices. The Lord Chancellor of the day, Lord Jowitt,

47.   Cd. 5250.

felt that the time had come to end the peculiar system which still pertained in Lancashire and to bring the appointment and removal and conditions of service of the Duchy justices into line with that of lay magistrates in all other parts of the country where responsibility rested solely with him. He took this view, not only because of the Lord Chancellor's position as head of the judiciary and as Minister responsible for advising the Crown on other judicial appointments, including those of all stipendiary magistrates, but also because proposals were being advanced for making the Lord Chancellor accountable for a number of other matters concerning JPs. These proposals, which were subsequently implemented, were that the Lord Chancellor should be required to make rules governing the size and chairmanship of magistrates' benches and the procedure of their courts, and that he should also supervise schemes of training which were to be introduced by statute for the first time. Lord Jowitt felt that these two functions could be performed more efficiently if all justices to whom they were to apply were to be appointed by the Minister who was responsible for their operation. He did not express his views in his evidence to the Commission, but it was generally known that he favoured the transfer of responsibility on the grounds of expediency. The Commission, however, were conscious of the deep resentment that such a change would cause in the Duchy and, after some hesitation, unanimously agreed to maintain the *status quo*. Their recommendations are set out in para. 43 of their Report:[48]

"The Lord Chancellor as head of the judiciary and at the same time a Minister of the Crown is eminently qualified for the exercise of the power of appointment of justices, and in broad outline our recommendations depend upon his continuing to exercise his present powers. The Chancellor of the Duchy of Lancaster is a Minister of the Crown, but he is never a Judge and has not the special qualifications of the Lord Chancellor for this particular duty. We have carefully considered whether his duties in respect of justices should be transferred to the Lord Chancellor. The evidence has satisfied us that the duties in respect of justices are performed in the Duchy at least as well as in the rest of the country, and that opinion in Lancashire favours the retention of the existing system and would indeed resent any change in it. The argument for transfer to the Lord Chancellor rests on the desire for the removal of what appears to be an anomaly in order to secure a logical system. Against this must be set the long tradition which has resulted in these duties of the Chancellor of the Duchy being performed with care and in a judicial manner. In practice, he is advised by

48.   1948, Cmd. 7463.

competent officials who act on principles which closely correspond to those which guide the Lord Chancellor and his Department. We recommend that the Chancellor of the Duchy should continue to be the Minister responsible for justices in Lancashire."

This was confirmed in the Justices of the Peace Act 1949 which implemented the Commission's proposals. As we shall see in another chapter this Act conferred a number of new duties upon the Lord Chancellor and it expressly provided that two of these should be exercised by the Chancellor of the Duchy in respect of justices within the county palatine. The first was contained in s. 1 which empowered the Chancellor to make exceptions to rules governing the residential qualification of a justice. The second was in s. 4 which enabled him to operate the supplemental list to which justices were to be retired on reaching a certain age. On the other hand, the Lord Chancellor alone was made responsible for rules governing the size and chairmanship of benches and for rules of procedure (to be made on the advice of a Rule Committee appointed by the Lord Chancellor).[49] He and he alone was also empowered to reprieve boroughs which were liable to lose their separate commissions or Quarter Sessions under the Act, even if the borough were within the county palatine.[50] As regards training, s. 17 of the Act required every magistrates' courts committee to make and administer schemes providing for courses of instruction for justices in their area and for these to be approved by the Lord Chancellor even within the county palatine. Under s. 29 stipendiary magistrates, including those in the county palatine, were to be appointed by the King on the recommendation of the Lord Chancellor, and similar provisions were applied to recorders and assistant recorders by s. 39.

These arrangements operated satisfactorily in practice. The Duchy and the Lord Chancellor's Office worked closely together on matters concerning JPs, and the policy applied by the two Ministers was almost invariably identical.

Twenty-two years after the 1949 Act the last of the higher courts of the county palatine were abolished. The Courts Act 1971 replaced all Quarter Sessions with the Crown Court and it merged the Lancaster Court of Chancery with the High Court. A salaried chairman of Lancashire Quarter Sessions had been appointed under the Administration of Justice (Miscellaneous Provisions) Act 1938 and, after the War, the work of the sessions increased to such an extent that the post was regarded as a full-time office. The 1971 Act transformed the chairman into a Judge of the Crown Court. The same Act (s. 43)

49.   Sections 13 and 15.
50.   Section 10.

also abolished the Liverpool Court of Passage and the Court of Record for the hundred of Salford, both of which exercised civil jurisdiction. The only vestiges of earlier times which remained among the higher judiciary were the Vice-Chancellor of the county palatine and the Recorders of Liverpool and Manchester, all of whom became Circuit Judges in the Crown Court. On the creation subsequently of the grade of senior Circuit Judge all three were promoted to this level.

In 1972 the Duchy's area of responsibility had to be redefined in consequence of the recommendations of the Boundary Commission, and thereafter it comprised the three new counties of Greater Manchester, Merseyside and Lancashire. In 1973 the Administration of Justice Act abolished all Commissions of the Peace except for those of counties and the ones in the London area, and accordingly the only commissions within the county palatine were those for the three county areas. At that time, 30 of the boroughs in the county palatine had separate Commissions of the Peace, all of which were abolished. The Act expressly confirmed, however, in s. 1, that the Chancellor of the Duchy should continue to be responsible for the appointment on behalf and in the name of the Queen of all justices within these areas and also for their removal. The same section also provided that the Chancellor of the Duchy and not the Lord Chancellor should have authority to enter in or remove from the supplemental list the name of any person who was a justice for any of those counties and for no other. Further, the Chancellor of the Duchy was authorized to designate one of the justices for each of these three counties to be Keeper of the Rolls - the term which had now formally replaced that of *Custos Rotulorum*.

In 1989 the three offices of Vice-Chancellor and Recorder of Liverpool and of Manchester still remain, at least in name, but they are part of the judicial hierarchy of the country as a whole, and the only courts which could be said to be wholly within the Duchy are those of the Justices of the Peace.

It is easy to point to the advantages of a unified system, but even the critics of the peculiar position in the Duchy have to admit that the magisterial arrangements seem to work as well there as they do in the rest of the country. The Lord Chancellor has the advantage that a specialist section of his staff is concerned exclusively with magisterial affairs whereas in the Duchy the officials are engaged also in numerous other matters, but this seems to be outweighed by the intimate local knowledge and experience of the Duchy officials and by the close personal touch which they are able to maintain, without exercising any undue influence, with the personnel of every bench. So long as the responsible officials answerable to the Lord Chancellor and to the Chancellor of the Duchy respectively continue to work in unison, and so long as the judicial administration of the Duchy's Chancellor continues to be segregated from his political and other functions, there is no convincing reason for a change in the present scenario and the Lancastrians may continue to take a justifiable pride in their special privileges.

CHAPTER VI

THE EARLY TUDORS 1485-1558
I - THE NEW SYSTEM OF GOVERNMENT

The new regime - Supervision by the higher courts and by the Council - The Commission of the Peace - Custos Rotulorum - Lord Lieutenant - Deputy Lieutenant - Clerk of the Peace - Other officers - The constable - The parish

The new regime

AT HENRY VII's ACCESSION, the country was in a state of disorder and his own position was precarious. It was imperative that he should restore order and establish a firm and effective government as quickly as possible. He had the advantage that the power of the leading nobles, who had been the cause of much of the trouble in the past, had been broken; and there was the additional advantage that their confiscated estates had augmented the royal wealth, enabling the thrifty King to operate without having to rely to any great extent on Parliament. On the other hand, it was essential that he should have the support of the population at large, and it was soon apparent that the most effective way of achieving this was through the gentry, including the leading burgesses of the boroughs, who managed the local government of the country as Justices of the Peace. These people had greater ability to get to the root of things and at the same time to secure the support of the native population than did state officials sent down by the central government. The justices, as we have seen, had certain other characteristics which were attractive to the Crown. They were appointed by the Sovereign and acted in his name; they were far cheaper than an army of salaried bureaucrats like those employed in Continental countries; they were not dependent upon fees and therefore not open to corruption like the sheriffs and some other officials; and they were not a potential danger to the Crown as were the principal nobles who, as experience showed, were likely, sooner or later, to abuse any powers that were given to them.

The justices were an institution ready to hand and as André Maurois points out, "The natural tendency of the Tudor Sovereign was to use whatever was ready to hand and to solve new problems by referring them to the established mechanism."[1] Henry therefore turned to the justices as the appropriate vehicle for maintaining law and order

1. André Maurois, *History of England*, p. 204. As Sir Winston Churchill observed: "Henry worked almost always by adaptation, modifying old forms ever so slightly, rather than by crude innovation." *History of the English Speaking Peoples*, vol. II, p. 19.

and for conducting national administration. They were drawn from the middle classes whom he trusted far more than he did the nobility and in whom he found ready and sound support. It was upon them that he relied to defeat the backers of the Yorkist pretender, Lambert Simnel, in 1487. The Justices of the Peace and their associates, for their part, were ready to give full support to the Crown because they realized that it was only through a strong monarchy that they could be protected from the tyranny of the great nobles and could attain the peace and security they needed to develop their estates and other interests.

The term "middle class" may not be entirely apt in this context as it is usually associated with an industrialized and urbanized society which did not exist in the Tudor era. Nevertheless, "upper middle class" does describe the position in the social structure of those who were included in the Commissions of the Peace. The same group, as we have seen, were also increasing their influence in Parliament. Each of the 37 counties was represented by two knights who, since 1430, had been elected by the 40-shilling freeholders. About a third of the 224 borough members were also country gentlemen, whose stature was higher than that of the burgesses, and for this reason they were chosen by the borough electors who were usually composed of an oligarchy of merchants and traders. Many of the wealthy burgesses, however, sought to improve their standing by buying land and striving to be accepted as country gentry. In any event, the influence of the burgesses was increasing and in 1533 one of their number was elected Speaker of the Commons. During this period the association between the Commons and the justices became even closer and of greater significance than it had been before. By the reign of Elizabeth I it was usual for at least half the members of the Commons to be justices, and a large proportion of the remainder had previously served on a commission or were destined to do so later. Most of the county members were serving justices, and so too were numbers of borough members though the proportion was much smaller. In 1559, 80 per cent of the county members were justices, compared with 34 per cent of the borough members. By 1593, as many as 90 per cent of the county members and 36 per cent of the borough members were on a commission[2]. As Sir William Holdsworth remarks:

"The training in the work of government which these men got as justices made them efficient members of Parliament, and had no small influence in gaining for Parliament its supremacy in the state."[3]

2.   *History of Parliament. The Commons,* 1558-1603, vol. I, 45-58.
3.   HEL, vol. I, 292.

Holdsworth also quotes Gneist[4] in saying that these justices gave the English constitution "a foundation upon which the conduct of the highest state business could be left to changing cabinets."

Until now local affairs had been dominated by the feudal nobility, but under the Tudors the latter were replaced by the justices who became the virtual rulers of the counties and the principal organs of local government through whom the monarchs operated.

The middle-class gentry, who included the Justices of the Peace, were also replacing the nobles as the principal performers on the national stage. From the outset, Henry VII chose his leading ministers from this section of the community - men like Robert Fox, Bishop of Winchester, who became his chief minister, and lawyers like Empsom and Dudley. Henry VIII's chief minister, Cardinal Wolsey, also came from middle-class origins and so too did the Cecils, the Walsinghams and the Bacons, who took over the most prominent positions from the clerics after the Reformation. Basing their government on middle-class support, the Tudors extended their control to every aspect of public life and in so doing they laid more and more duties upon the Justices of the Peace. The most remarkable feature of the social history of the Tudor era was the variety and extent of the administrative duties placed upon them.

This chapter, and the one that follows, are concerned principally with the history of the Justices of the Peace under the first four Tudors from Henry VII to Mary I, but the developments which took place during this fertile period can sometimes be best described by drawing illustrations from the reign of the last and greatest of the Tudor monarchs, Queen Elizabeth. For this purpose we shall anticipate a little of what should properly fall within a later chapter.

Supervision by the higher courts and by the Council

As we have seen, the justices enjoyed a considerable degree of independence in the fifteenth century and there was little supervision of their work. This was consistent with the practice which had continued from Saxon times of leaving local communities to govern themselves so long as they complied with national policy. From the twelfth century, however, they had been subject to supervision by the *curia regis* through the medium of the Eyre. As the Eyre decayed and ceased to function it was necessary for the central government to resort to other devices. The solution which was adopted was to govern the country through the justices, who were supervised in two ways; by review of their work through the higher courts and by direct

4.   *History of the English Constitution*, vol. II, p. 372.

intervention of the Council. From the end of the fourteenth century the work of the justices at sessions was reviewed to an increasing extent by the Judges of Assize and by the common-law courts at Westminster, mainly through writs of *mandamus* for omissions and of *certiorari* for things alleged to have been done wrong. This trend for judicial review was accelerated under the Tudors, and at the same time the Justices of Oyer and Terminer were empowered by the terms of their commissions to determine charges of negligence and transgression and other misdemeanours by the justices. Simultaneously, a dramatic new development took place in the shape of direct surveyance of the justices by what began to be called the "Privy Council." This Tudor innovation was a select inner body of the larger Council of the King and was composed exclusively of members chosen personally by the Sovereign. They included no hereditary peers of long standing and were selected on their merits from among the new men who had risen to eminence through their own ability. This was in contrast to the earlier Council which had included almost all the leading nobles and had suffered from constant bickering between the feuding factions. The men who now formed the Privy Council were far removed from the ignorant, self-seeking and often incompetent lords who were responsible for governing the country before the arrival of the Tudors. The new, able and dedicated servants of the Crown were to turn England into a world power, while at home they governed the land through the justices, most of whom were of similar social standing to themselves. The members of the Privy Council themselves were placed on the Commissions of the Peace throughout the country, thus enabling them to keep in close personal touch with local affairs and also strengthening the authority of all the justices in the eyes of the rest of the population.

A committee of the Privy Council containing some of its leading members came to be known as the Star Chamber from the *décor* of the chamber in which it sat. This was, basically, a judicial body. It included the two Chief Justices and exercised unlimited jurisdiction on behalf of the King over all matters of state. It was not a common-law court and was not governed by any formal rules of procedure, though its proceedings, which were inquisitorial, tended to resemble those of the Roman law courts. It could summon anyone it pleased to attend, and no one, however powerful, dared to disobey. Those who appeared were interrogated, a decision was reached and an order made. This was particularly effectual in dealing with powerful magnates, who still on occasion attempted to dominate their local areas and to pack juries and intimidate justices. Anyone aggrieved by a decision of a local court could bring the matter before the Star Chamber and obtain redress. Its decisions were arbitrary and many of them were directed at the justices. The Star Chamber also became the channel through which the Council issued its instructions to the justices and to others.

Although Parliamentary influence was increasing steadily, the King and his Council still did not accept that only those measures which had the approval of Parliament enjoyed the force of law. The Tudor Council frequently issued ordinances and proclamations which the community were obliged to obey even though they had not been passed by Parliament, and no one challenged their authority. Blackstone claimed that royal proclamations had the force of law provided that they did not contradict existing laws or seek to establish new ones, but the Tudors do not seem to have regarded themselves as being under any limitation in the scope of their law-making ordinances.

The Council administered government, first by initiating policy and promulgating their directions to the justices, and secondly by keeping a check on the justices to ensure that their instructions were implemented. The Council's decrees were despatched from Westminster to the *Custos Rotulorum* in each county, but by Elizabeth's reign it was not unusual for the Queen to call all justices who happened to be in the Westminster area, together with the Judges of Assize, to meet in the Star Chamber where the Lord Chancellor would bring to their attention matters to which she wished them to direct their efforts. In addition to this, letters on a vast field of subjects passed between the Council and the justices in specific counties. The *Acts of the Privy Council*, particularly in Elizabeth's reign, are full of such letters, directed to both counties and boroughs, ordering them to take certain action. What is not apparent from these records is that many of these letters were not initiated by the Council but were in response to communications from the counties and often to complaints against the justices by some local faction. The most striking feature of the letters is the almost unlimited area which they cover. They give an interesting insight into the numerous problems arising in the lives of the people. Certain subjects occupy a great deal of attention and are continually appearing. Food shortage is a good example of this and attempts to deal with it often vary from county to county. Thus, in 1596 a letter to the Devon justices refers to the current scarcity of corn and tells them that when a supply arrives in ships for further transport to other parts, they should take some of it and arrange for it to be sold at a reasonable price to the local inhabitants.[5] At almost the same time another letter went to Nottinghamshire where, it seems, it was the practice to feed sheep on peas. The justices were told to stop this in time of scarcity and to arrange for the peas to be sent to market for

5.   APC, 1596-7, 59-60.

sale to the poor at a reasonable price. Some letters dealt with several totally unrelated subjects, and the one to Nottinghamshire also commends the justices for what they had done to raise troops for service in Ireland, and it directs them to send to the Council two men who had failed to assist in the work.[6] In the same year the Lord Lieutenant of Essex is ordered to take several justices and to examine the parson of Haydon, who was alleged to have shown sympathy with Jesuits in his sermons, and to report the outcome to the bishop of the diocese.

Ecclesiastical matters figure prominently in the letters and sometimes general instructions were issued to the justices in all counties, as in 1582 when they and the sheriffs were ordered to indict all the principal recusants within their charge who had not previously been indicted and to take bonds from those who had already been indicted to appear at the next Assizes.[7] Letters addressed to all justices throughout the country, or to those in limited groups of counties, were issued fairly frequently and, in addition to religion, dealt with a variety of subjects such as national defence, riots, sedition and vagabonds. The periodical visitations of the plague gave rise to instructions to the justices in the affected areas to take suitable precautions. In 1581, the Lord Mayor of London and the justices of the adjoining liberties and the county of Middlesex were directed to stop all plays and entertainments in their area until the end of September or until further orders, because the plague was on the increase and these might spread it further.[8] The Lord Mayor of London was the recipient of many communications from the Council. One of these, issued in 1587, concerned the justices in other areas. It required him to find out and report the names of all justices from other parts who were residing in London and to send the list to the Council, who were concerned at the large number of absentee justices who spent their time in London instead of attending to their duties. Justices throughout the country had already been told to return to their houses and "attend to the office of Justices of the Peace as well to keep house and hospitalities for their better relieving of their poor neighbours in this time of common dearth and scarcetie."[9] Usually the Council's letter did not set out in any detail the manner in which the instructions were to be carried out, but occasionally it was thought prudent to do so, particularly where the justices' excessive zeal might give rise to hostile reaction. During one of the periods of corn shortage, the Gloucestershire justices were ordered to appoint persons to search

6. APC, 1595-6, 6-7.
7. APC, 1581-2, 451.
8. APC, 1581, 128. See also DP 1598-1601, 347.
9. APC, 1586-7, 120.

houses and to arrange for any surplus grain that might be found to be put weekly on the market. It would seem that the justices had already shown too much enthusiasm for the job because the letter also contains a caution "to proceed with such good discretion as there grow no disorder and inconvenience thereby."[10] If anyone disobeyed the justices when performing these duties, they were to "take bonds with sufficient sureties for their personal appearance before their Lordships to answer their contempt." On another occasion, the Gloucestershire justices were the recipients of one of the highly critical letters which the Council despatched with great frequency. In 1596 they were accused of misconduct in carrying out their instructions, and the letter comments: "When the Justices of the Peace (and, indeed, we think divers of the Justices more in fault than any others), are themselves authors and maynteyners of the same, no marvaile though the poor people fynde no remedy, nor our orders take effect."[11]

Under all the Tudor monarchs, except Mary, the justices were subject to constant criticism and rebuke for failing to perform their duties. Usually this came from the Council in a letter addressed to all the justices in a particular county and occasionally it invited them to spy on their colleagues and to report cases of misconduct in confidence to the Judges of Assize or to the Council itself. Sometimes the rebuke was administered by the Sovereign. An oft-quoted letter of disapprobation was despatched to all justices by Henry VIII in 1539:[12]

"The King to the Justices of the Peace

"Trusty and well beloved. We greet you well, and cannot a little marvel to hear, that, notwithstanding our sundry advertisements made unto you for the doing of your duties, many things be nevertheless directed at will and pleasure than upon any just contemplation of justice ...

"Therefore, yet once again, before we shall correct the lewdness of the offenders with any extremity, we have thought meet to write here our letters unto you, and, by the same token, to desire and pray you, and yet nevertheless to charge and command you, that for the repairing of all things negligently passed you should have especial care to the following:"

There followed various instructions on a number of matters including the punishment of followers of the Pope, the spreaders of rumours about the King and the state of the realm, vagabonds and beggars; and

10.   APC, 1586-7, 71-2.
11.   APC, 1596, September 8.
12.   *Letters and Papers of Henry VIII,* vol. xvi, 945, 1541.

also on the suppression of unlawful games. The letter finished with a severe warning of what would happen to the justices if they continued to fail in their duties:

"If you shall give such diligence as may satisfy your duty, leaving all disguised corruption, we shall be content the more easily to put in oblivion all your former remissness and negligences. But if, on the other part, we shall perceive that this kind of gentle proceeding can work no kind of good in you, assure yourselves that the next advice shall be of so sharp a sort as shall bring with it a just punishment of those that have been found offenders."

These threats were not carried into effect so far as the general body of justices were concerned, but it was not uncommon for an individual to be punished by a fine or by having his name omitted from the commission.

It was not only the Council who were censorious of the justices. Notwithstanding their close affinity to the Commons, the justices were subjected to a most humiliating legislative rebuff in a statute of 1489, only four years after Henry VII's accession. They were commanded to promulgate four times a year, in four principal sessions, a proclamation which, after setting forth the disorders of the realm and the efforts of the Crown to cure them, declared that the laws had not been put into execution because of the failure of the justices. The justices were ordered to do their duty and the public were told that, if anyone was abused by a justice, he could seek a remedy from a neighbouring justice or, failing this, from a Judge of Assize, and in the last resort from the King or his Chancellor.[13] Nothing could have been more degrading nor more calculated to undermine the authority of the justices than this regular, public announcement of their shortcomings, yet there was no pause in the further extension of their statutory powers nor in the growing number of jobs they were required to undertake by the Council. The year 1495 was particularly prolific in this respect. The justices' authority was further enlarged in the economic sphere and in the suppression of riots, while they were empowered to hear and determine all statutory offences short of felony without indictment, to punish sheriffs and bailiffs found guilty of extortion and to supervise the panels of local juries.[14] Legislation of 1504 added further to their competence, especially in stressing their powers to deal with livery and retaining and in giving them the right to certify who were retainers and embracers when an intimidated or corrupted jury failed to find that there had been a riot.

13.   4 Hen. VII, c. 12.
14.   11 Hen. VII, cc. 15, 24, 25.

There was a curious antithesis between the readiness of the government to entrust justices with vast new areas of responsibility and their apparent mistrust of the same justices, which was exhibited in the contemptuous rebukes that were issued with equal readiness. The explanation probably lies in the fact that the justices were by now firmly established in the judicial and administrative systems and the government accepted that the difficulties involved in replacing them would far outweigh any advantage that might be derived from such a course. There can be no doubt that, notwithstanding the mood demonstrated in the statute of 1489, any attempt to diminish the authority of the justices would have met with the strongest opposition in the Commons. The justices also possessed certain qualities, as already mentioned, which made them preferable to alternative systems, but the Council would no doubt avoid drawing attention to these lest they gave the impression that the justices were indispensable. It was a question of making the best of what was there, and the Council rightly took the view that this could be achieved only by keeping the justices under constant pressure to ensure that they did not fail in the performance of their vital public duties. The fact that from time to time they did fail (often through the fault of subordinate officials) was not sufficient justification for transferring their duties to others who might well prove to be still less effective, and the best way to deal with the justices' lapses seemed to be to step up the pressure put upon them.

The justices did not always accept the dictates of the Council in a servile manner. They were generally loyal to the King but were not dependent upon him, and usually they did not fear to express disagreement with policies to which they were opposed. Sometimes they indicated their disapproval and sometimes merely neglected to implement the instructions. There has been much discussion on the question of the justices' independence at this time. There is no doubt that a great deal was left to their discretion and that for the most part they carried on their work without interference; but what was the position when their conduct met with the clear disapproval of the Council? On the one hand, it is claimed that they had no scope for opposition to the will of the government. If they failed to comply, their names would be omitted from the commission, which was reissued each year, and they could not afford to take this risk, which would entail the loss of their standing in the county as well as possibly incurring other penalties. On the other hand, it is pointed out that, with no standing army or national police force, the government was powerless in the last resort to compel obedience from those upon whom they had to rely for the running of the country. Close examination suggests that the answer depended upon whether, in any particular circumstance, the justices acted together as a body, in which case the Council had no effective means of securing their obedience, or whether one or two justices alone incurred the Council's displeasure, in which case they might be obliged to appear before the Star Chamber and could be subjected to severe punishment, or they might, at the Council's discretion, be tried and punished by their fellow justices. There are plenty of examples of the latter, but there are also many instances where the whole body of justices, except perhaps those who were also members of the Council, refused to implement government policy and nothing seems to have come of it. An example was in Lancashire, a predominantly Roman Catholic county, where the recusancy laws of Elizabeth were readily flouted with impunity. Another example, which applied to the whole country from 1488, arose from the legislation prohibiting the enclosure of land. The country had begun to suffer from severe inflation, due partly to the sudden growth in the population, and this led the landed gentry to enclose land on a large scale with a view to exploiting their assets. It proved to be futile for the government to enact laws prohibiting enclosures because these were against the interests of the justices who were responsible for enforcing them. Wolsey took a firm line with the justices, but in the long term it was unsuccessful and merely fuelled the unpopularity which contributed to his downfall. Whereas therefore, individual justices responded readily to the Council's orders, or were severely disciplined in default, the Council was unable to impose its will upon the mass of justices provided that they stuck together and presented a united front.

The Commission of the Peace

The Commission of the Peace from which the justices derived their authority was still basically the same as that of 1361 and it would continue in this form until 1590. Its size and composition, however, were undergoing change. From the beginning of the sixteenth century all counties far exceeded the eight justices specified in the statute of 1390. Some had more than 30, Middlesex over 40, and even the smallest, Rutland, had 15.[15]

The commissions continued to be composed principally of the landowning gentry. Some justices continued to have lands in several counties and served on more than one commission simultaneously. They were wealthy, independent of mind, well educated and usually in general accord with government policy; but they were also ambitious

---

15.   The number of justices on the commissions at various periods is given in Appendix II.

and often prejudiced. They included a growing number with legal qualifications, for it was becoming popular for young men to study at the Inns of Court, and it was the lawyer justices who provided the members of the *Quorum* and who were usually the best attenders at sessions.

In addition to the inclusion of larger numbers of landed gentry, the commissions were increased in size by the appointment of more men drawn from other sections of the community. Most commissions contained several names from the local nobility which, as a class, was also represented in the commissions by justices who were junior members of noble houses or were related to them by marriage. The proportion of clergy was also increasing, although many had a purely passive role as justices. The two archbishops were on a number of different commissions simultaneously, while most commissions contained the names of two or more bishops, and sometimes an abbot or other cleric, and many of these played an active part at the sessions for the county from which they came. Members of the church were among the earliest justices *ex officio*. A select few were given this distinction by a statute of Henry VIII[16] which provided that the Archbishop of York and his Chancellor, the Bishop of Durham and his Chancellor and the Bishop of Ely and his Steward should always be justices in their own areas. These provisions remained in force until 1949, and throughout these 400 years nothing similar applied to the Archbishop of Canterbury nor to any other bishop.

The Assize Judges for the circuit in which the county was situated were almost invariably included in the commission and the role they played in the system was of considerable importance. It was their function to scrutinize the work of the justices, to attempt to rectify their errors and to give them guidance in the performance of their judicial duties. It was also customary for the justices to attend Assizes as a body, and the Commissions of Assize were addressed not only to the Judge (who was usually one of the Judges of the courts at Westminster or a Serjeant-at-Law) but also to several of the local justices. At the opening of the Assize, the Judge would promulgate policy, refer to matters requiring attention and give general advice on how justice should be administered; all in accordance with instructions he would have received from the Chancellor before leaving Westminster.

Where applicable, commissions also contained the names of the

16.   27 Hen. VIII, c. 24, s. 22.

Vice-Chancellors of Oxford and Cambridge Universities[17] and of officers of the counties palatine and of the Duchy of Cornwall. Occasionally other local officials were included, such as the senior naval officer at Chatham, Plymouth and Portsmouth. At the head of the list one usually found the whole of the Privy Council and the Attorney General and Solicitor General, sometimes the Prince of Wales and a few court favourites. The Lord Chancellor or Lord Keeper was included in every commission, except those of the counties palatine, as explained in the last chapter, and after ceasing to occupy these high offices he usually remained on the commissions as a Privy Councillor. Sometimes these individuals spent their retirement sitting as Justices of the Peace in their own counties. Lord Rich, whose perjury had contributed to the impeachment of his predecessor Sir Thomas More, retired to Essex after ceasing to be Lord Chancellor and sat on a number of occasions as a justice for the county. It was only the middle-class gentry, however, who normally carried out the practical duties of the justices and many of them were absent from time to time. Usually their absence was justified by attendance in Parliament or by involvement in other national activities, such as the maritime exploits of Drake and Hawkins, both of whom were on the Devon commission.[18] There were many, on the other hand, who had no justification for neglecting their duties and sometimes there were barely sufficient available to form a court of Quarter Sessions. The majority of the absentees were to be found enjoying life in London, and at the beginning of Edward VI's reign they were ordered to return home at their "uttermost perils." We have already seen how in 1587 the Lord Mayor was ordered by the Council to send it a list of justices from other parts residing in London. During the following two centuries, however, the problem of absenteeism was to grow worse rather than better.

A statute of 1535[19] confirmed that "no person or persons, of whatever estate, degree or condition whosoever they be" should have any power or authority to make Justices of the Peace; but that all such appointments should be made by letters patent under the King's Great Seal in the name of the King. It has been held subsequently that this right, vested in the Crown, cannot be delegated to any other authority without legislation.[20]

---

17.   A charter of Henry VIII, confirmed by the Oxford University (Justices) Act 1886, made the Chancellor, Vice-Chancellor and Deputy Vice-Chancellor of Oxford justices *ex officio*, but there were no similar provisions for other universities, apart from s. 249 of the Municipal Corporations Act 1882, under which the Vice-Chancellor of Cambridge became a justice *ex officio*.
18.   As Treasurer of the Navy Hawkins was also on the Middlesex and Kent commission.
19.   27 Hen. VIII, c. 24.
20.   *Jones v. Williams* (1825), 3 B. & C., 762, 767; *Arnold v. Gausson* (1853), 8 Exch. 463.

Appointments to the commissions, other than those in Lancaster (and in Durham until 1536) were made in the name of the King on the advice of the Lord Chancellor and the Privy Council in accordance with 2 Hen. V, st. 2, c. 1, of 1414.

Justices were still entitled to receive four shillings for each day on which they attended Quarter Sessions, but this was usually spent on "defraying their common diet"[21] when they met together. They also received fees for performing three different statutory duties; 2s. 6d. for each enrolment of land,[22] five shillings a day (not exceeding three days) for attending sessions to enforce the labour laws, and 12 pence for taking innkeepers' recognizances.[23]

They were also entitled in certain circumstances to receive a portion of the value of goods confiscated from convicted persons - notably from "Egyptians" or gipsies about whom more will be said later. All these payments were negligible so far as the justices were concerned and they were far from being dependent upon their office for their living. Their wealth came from their estates, and in the towns from trade, and although they were servants of the Crown, they did not regard themselves as being in any way in the King's pay.

Custos Rotulorum

The most important member of the commission, as mentioned earlier, was the *Custos Rotulorum* whose duty it was to keep the rolls of the peace. He took precedence among his fellows and came to be regarded as the principal justice through whom communications should be addressed for distribution to the justices, other than those which were transmitted through the Clerk of the Peace. In time, the Lord Chancellor came to rely to a large extent upon his advice when choosing candidates for appointments to the commission. No precise date is known for the first appointment of a *Custos* but, as we have seen from the early days of the justices, it became customary for one of them to be nominated for this purpose in a clause in the commission.[24] At first this was done by the Chancellor at the instigation of the Council, but later the appointment was made at the personal direction of the King. The office was placed on a statutory basis in 1545 when an enactment[25] provided that the *Custos* should be

21.   Lambard, *Eirenarcha,* Bk. IV, c. 21.
22.   27 Hen. VIII, c. 10.
23.   5-6 Edw. VI, c. 25.
24.   For a consideration of the origins of the *Custos Rotulorum* see *Harcourt v. Fox,* (1693) 4 *Modern Reports,* 173.
25.   37 Hen. VIII, c. 1. This provided that the appointment of *Custos* be made only by "bill signed with the King's hande," which directed that in each case the appointment be passed under the Great Seal and on this authority it appeared in the commission. The Act was not finally repealed until 1968 (Justices of the Peace Act, sch. 5, pt. II).

appointed by the Crown. A few years later it was decided that the appointment of the *Custos* could be made effectively by the Lord Chancellor on the King's behalf and therefore another statute[26] provided for this to be done in the commission. These arrangements continued until the reign of William and Mary, when the position was reversed once more and the appointment was made personally by the King.[27] The *Custos* was chosen as being an outstanding member of the local community, a man "especially picked out either for wisdom, countenance or credit."[28] He was usually a knight, but seldom a lord, until a later date when most were noblemen. He was invariably a member of the *Quorum* and usually presided when present. With the Clerk of the Peace he controlled the administrative arrangements for the sessions.

Lord Lieutenant

A wholly new office-holder, who was to become of greater importance in the county than the *Custos*, began to appear in the reign of Henry VIII. He was the Lord Lieutenant, who was appointed by the Crown and was responsible for the military forces. His office was a device to deal with outbreaks of local unrest which continued during the Tudor era, particularly during the reigns of Henry's three children, and which the sheriffs proved to be incapable of handling effectively. The Lieutenant therefore took over the functions of the sheriff, whom he replaced in the command of the local levies which came to be called the militia, a force on which all able-bodied men between the ages of 16 and 60 were liable to serve. The Lieutenant's sphere of activity therefore overlapped that of the justices, who although the Commission of the Peace no longer included array, had some responsibility for the local forces; but it was made clear from the start that he was the over-all commander and that the justices must give him such assistance as he required. This was emphasized in a statute of 1549,[29] which was the first legislative recognition of the office and which stated that the justices were "bound to give attendance upon the same Lieutenant to suppress any commotion, rebellion, or unlawful assembly."

As in the case of the early justices, the development of the Lords Lieutenant was haphazard. At first they were temporary appointments made only in times of trouble when the need arose to suppress

26.   3 and 4 Edw. VI, c. 1.
27.   1 William and Mary, Sess. 1, c. 21, s. 3. For further changes in the method of appointment see *post*, p.256
28.   Lambard, *Eirenarcha*, (1602) Bk. IV, c. iii, 371.
29.   3-4 Edw. VI, c. 5, s. 13.

rebellions and uprisings. Often one individual was appointed for several counties, while other areas were left without a Lieutenant. The appointment was made by the King by letters patent under the Royal Prerogative, and the appointee was invariably a man of great eminence, almost always a member of the higher nobility. A report by the Privy Council in 1595 showed that all of the 17 Lords Lieutenant at that time, some of whom held office in several counties, were great nobles with the sole exception of Sir Walter Raleigh, Lord Lieutenant of Cornwall. Usually at least a third and sometimes half of their number were also members of the Council. It has been rightly said that the post was a typical Tudor creation, combining great panache with utility and responsibility.[30]

The office was confirmed as a permanent institution during the war with Spain after 1588, but it was not until the reign of James I that, although the climate was by then comparatively peaceful, there was a Lord Lieutenant in every county. After 1588, the Commissions of Lieutenancy did not lapse at the end of each emergency and in the majority of cases the appointment was made for life. The appointment continued to be for life for nearly four centuries, but those appointed after April 1948 have been obliged to retire on reaching the age of 75.

It will be seen later that the Lord Lieutenant was to become the dominant figure in every aspect of the justices' office, including responsibility for their appointment and conduct, and he would himself become the principal justice in the county, but this position was not fully realized until the seventeenth, and, in some counties, as late as the eighteenth century, when it became common practice for the same person to be appointed both *Custos* and Lieutenant. The joint appointment[31] was then for life and was usually made to a single county. Until the Civil War, the Lieutenant was primarily an agent of the Council, but thereafter he ceased to be answerable to them. He was the personal representative of the Sovereign in the county, and when he also held the office of *Custos,* he was the principal adviser to the Lord Chancellor on appointments to the commission. He has continued to occupy these positions to the present day, though, as we shall see, there have been some modifications in the system of appointing justices, notably with the introduction of an advisory committee system in the twentieth century.

From the end of Henry VIII's reign the Lieutenant began to assume responsibility for a wider range of matters than the purely police functions which arose from his military commitments and he was given

30.   A.L. Rowse, *The England of Elizabeth,* 1950, p. 383.
31.   The appointment of the Lord Lieutenant has always remained in the hands of the Sovereign but is now normally made on the recommendation of the Prime Minister. That of the *Custos* has always been the responsibility of the Lord Chancellor.

a number of duties which coincided with those of the justices. By the end of Elizabeth I's reign he was playing an important role in social and administrative matters in addition to his military function. Thus, although he was not supposed at that time to interfere in any way with the sessions of the justices, he was required to take an active part in dealing with recusants and with vagabonds, while to an increasing extent directions from the Council to the justices on almost every subject tended to be passed through the Lieutenant, who was expected to report back on the state of affairs in the county. He, as well as the *Custos* was also consulted by the Council on the selection of candidates for appointment to the commission.

Deputy Lieutenant

The eminence of most of the individuals who were Lords Lieutenant meant that they were often absent from their counties, attending to duties on a national level, and this problem became more acute as the appointment of Lieutenants was extended for longer periods. Moreover, the work involved in viewing and training levies and in other business could not be done without assistance. To meet this situation Deputy Lieutenants were appointed. It is not known at precisely what date these officers were first nominated, but the earliest mention of the title was in 1585 and they gained in importance steadily during the latter part of Elizabeth's reign. They were drawn from the same section of the community as the justices, and many served in both capacities. Some had also served already as Commissioners for Musters. Their duties were entirely military but, as most of them were on the Commissions of the Peace, the additional commitments added further to the burden of the busy justices. During the following centuries the symbiotic justices and Deputy Lieutenants would have a closely related history. At first there were usually two Deputies for each county, but the numbers soon increased. They were appointed under a clause of deputation in the Lord Lieutenant's commission which gave him power to confer letters of deputation on certain of the gentry nominated by the Crown within his area.

Clerk of the Peace

The statute of 1545, which established the office of *Custos Rotulorum*, also provided that he should appoint the Clerk of the Peace who was to be an "able person instructed in the laws of this Realm." Previously the clerk had been appointed sometimes by the *Custos*, sometimes by the Crown and sometimes by the justices. The decision to place the appointment exclusively in the hands of the *Custos* seems to have been taken on the ground that it would be unfair to hold him responsible for the custody of the records when these were normally in the possession of someone who might not be of his choice.[32] The preamble to the 1545 statute also stated that unsuitable persons had received life appointments as Clerks of the Peace, with the result that many indictments had "not only been frustrated and void, sometimes by negligent engrossing, and sometimes by the embezzling or razure of the indictments, but also sundry bargains and sales have been void for lack of sufficient enrolment."

We have seen in ch. III that the first statutory reference to a clerk was in 1380, and that his functions included drafting the charge to the jury and advising the justices on points of law, as well as keeping the records. He attended to all the clerical and administrative work of Quarter Sessions and also conveyed the directions of the sessions to those, such as the constables, whose duty it was to implement them. Furthermore, he kept the accounts, and it would be some time before this side of his work was relieved by the appointment of a treasurer. From 1544, however, he was allowed to appoint a deputy.[33] It has been maintained that the Clerk of the Peace was not an officer of the court but only clerk to the *Custos*,[34] but this is not borne out by the fact that proceedings were taken in his name. For example, a statute of 1586 declared that proceedings against the inhabitants of a hundred who had not followed the hue and cry were to be in his name.[35] As we have seen, the Clerk of the Peace was paid two shillings per day at Quarter Sessions under the statute of 1388 which granted four shillings a day to the justices, all of which came from the fines and amerciaments imposed at the sessions, but his principal income came from fees. In the sixteenth century these were mostly paid for indictments, recognizances and various licences, but the clerks, who had considerable expenses to pay out of their own pockets, took every opportunity to extend the range.[36] By 1545 appointments were usually for life, but under the statute of that year they were terminated when the *Custos* who made the appointment ceased to hold office. That in turn was changed by the Great Seal Act of 1699,[37] which provided that the clerk should hold office for life, though he might be removed on complaint in writing to Quarter Sessions if he misdemeaned himself in the execution of his office.

32.   See Holt C.J., obiter in *Harcourt v. Fox* (1693) 4 *Modern Reports*.
33.   37 Hen. VIII, c. 1, s. 2.
34.   Marowe's Lectures at the Inner Temple, 1503.
35.   27 Eliz., c. 13, ss. 1, 2.
36.   See vol. II, ch.IX *post*.   Fees were replaced by a salary in 1851.
37.   1 William & Mary, c. 21.

The Clerk of the Peace was usually an attorney[38] and a man of some substance. There are instances in the fifteenth century of clerks being appointed to the Commission of the Peace for their county, usually after ceasing to be clerk, and in some cases they also became Members of Parliament. John Hampton, for example, who had been attorney to the sheriff of Wiltshire, was Clerk of the Peace for the county from 1481 to 1483 and Member for Salisbury from 1483 to 1495. He was a justice for Wiltshire from 1494 to 1507.

Other officers

In addition to the Clerk of the Peace, there were signs of other clerks being engaged by the justices to assist them in their work out of Quarter Sessions. Some individual justices employed their own clerks to help them privately, and the sessions which were beginning to be held in addition to Quarter Sessions and which will be described later, also created a need for clerical assistance similar to that rendered by the Clerk of the Peace. This was sometimes supplied by one of the justices themselves, but on other occasions a clerk was appointed who at first had to be remunerated by the justices.

Apart from the Clerks of the Peace, there were no other officials attached to Quarter Sessions during this period, but the justices were still able to call upon the officers of the old communal and franchise courts, mainly the sheriffs and the high and petty constables. By the end of the sixteenth century the sheriff's only major responsibility in the judicial sphere was to preside over the County Court, whose jurisdiction was small and whose most important function was the infrequent one of organizing the election of the knights of the shire to Parliament. It was also his duty, however, to summon persons to Quarter Sessions, to collect fines and to execute writs.

The constable

The constable was a well-known figure in English society for several centuries, but one that seldom inspired much respect. The character of Dogberry, portrayed by Shakespeare in *Much Ado about Nothing*, reflected the opinion held by many in Elizabethan times of the contemporary law-enforcement officer.

We have already seen that in the fifteenth century the task of executing the justices' orders was falling largely upon the unwilling shoulders of the constable, who was an unpaid parishioner elected by his neighbours to serve for one year. The naming of the constable was

38.   See "The Attorneys and Officers of the Common Law in 1480" by J.H. Baker of St. Catherine's College, Cambridge. *Journal of Legal History*, vol. 1, No. 2, September 1980.

still the responsibility of the feudal courts, but if they failed to do so, as they often did, Quarter Sessions made the appointment, acting solely on the authority contained in their commission, on the ground that this was necessary to enable them to keep the peace. This continued to be the position under the Tudors and their successors in spite of the huge increase in the duties placed upon the justices and consequently upon the constables. The only relief came in the creation of certain additional officers to implement new statutes dealing with specific problems, such as the overseers of the poor and the surveyors of highways who will be described later, but their appointment still left a host of other duties for the untrained, uneducated, unpaid and unwilling constables, who were already overwhelmed by their duties, and when these were increased beyond recognition during the following centuries it is not surprising that many constables gave up any attempt to perform them. What seems miraculous is that the system was regarded as satisfactory, at least according to the criteria of the times.

The man-of-all-work, who operated in each parish and township, was called the petty constable, whose duties included the apprehension of suspected criminals and bringing them before the justices. To assist him he had authority to raise the hue and cry, which obliged the local inhabitants to join in the pursuit of the suspect. In so far as anyone at that time could be described as the village policeman it was he, but he had many other duties besides policing, as was clear from the "presentments" he was obliged to deliver to Quarter Sessions. These involved reporting to the sessions on the general state of affairs in his parish, including an account not only of any criminal activity but of other matters for which the justices were responsible, such as the state of the highways and bridges. The presentments supply a picture of the everyday life of local communities at the time. Unlike the constables of later days, the petty constables received no training or remuneration, which is no doubt why they failed singularly to perform many of the duties which were placed upon them. This was a fundamental weakness of the system and it was aggravated by the failure of the justices in very many instances to take any steps whatever to see that the law was obeyed.

Above the petty constable was a head, or high constable, one for each hundred which comprised 12 or more parishes. The high constables had existed from the thirteenth century and had been elected at the court leet. As the latter fell into disuse the appointment, like that of the petty constable, was taken over by the justices at Quarter Sessions. It was usually for one year but came to be extended indefinitely. The high constables supervised the work of the petty constables and also exercised some of the powers of the justices; for example they could sentence vagrants to be whipped.[39] In time, the reports of the petty constables on conditions in their respective areas - from crime and vagrancy to bridges and alehouses - came to be made to sessions through the high constable. The high constables held meetings at which every petty constable in the hundred was supposed to be present and to report on the state of his parish. These meetings came to be called Petty Sessions but were quite distinct from the later Petty Sessions held by the justices. The records of these meetings were then presented to Quarter Sessions, to which the high constable had to account for the money he had spent. Service as high constable was compulsory and unpaid, though later he could take certain fees, and indeed it often involved disbursements which could not be reclaimed. It seems surprising that the office of high constable was not even more unpopular than that of petty constable. The fact that it was not (although those who held it often complained of their lot) was probably due to its being regarded as a position of some influence and standing among the yeomen and tenant farmers in the countryside and the more prominent tradesmen in the towns who normally held the post. Having once held the office of high constable they seem to have been regarded as suitable to perform other duties of importance in the county. In the seventeenth century, when high constables in most counties were appointed for a limited period, they went on to serve on juries of presentment at both Quarter Sessions and Assizes and they were chosen to survey bridges and to perform various other duties on behalf of Quarter Sessions.

The parish

Subsequent chapters will refer to the increasing involvement of both the high constables and the petty constables in the work of the justices for some 300 years until the reforms of the eighteenth century. In the meantime, the most important development in local administration under the Tudors was the establishment of the civil parish, within which the petty constable operated, as the unit of government. Despite earlier views to the contrary, it is now generally accepted that the parish was originally a wholly ecclesiastical unit and that it only became an arm of the secular government slowly in the last half of the sixteenth century. As Holdsworth points out, the secular parish was a post-Reformation phenomenon resulting from the new relationship between church and state effected by the legislation of Henry VIII and Elizabeth.[40] No statutes of Henry VII gave any civil functions to the

39.   22 Hen. VIII, c. 12.
40.   HEL, vol. IV, p. 152.

parish, but the scene began to change dramatically under Henry VIII and the position of the parish as the basic unit of secular government was finally established under Elizabeth, largely as a result of the statutes relating to the Poor Law and, to a lesser degree, the repair of highways and other services, as will be seen in ch. VIII. It was through the parish and its officers that the justices were to govern the country, assisted by the parish vestry.

This chapter has described the structure which bore the burden of the "stacks of statutes" to which Chief Justice Husey referred in 1485. A few of the additional duties which they and orders of the Council imposed upon the justices have also been mentioned, but the bulk of the early Tudor legislation, and its effect, will be reviewed in the next chapter. This will be followed by an account of the even faster growth which characterized the reign of Elizabeth.

CHAPTER VII

THE EARLY TUDORS 1485-1558
II - FUNCTIONS, ORGANIZATION AND PROCEDURE

Powers of the justices out of sessions - Quarter Sessions and discretionary sessions - Appeal - Expansion of powers (Trade; Shipping; Agriculture; Liquor Licensing; Games; Hunting; Weights and measures; Prices; Wages; Vagrants; Poor Law; Egyptians; Religion; Bridges; Highways; Gaols; Military)

THE JUSTICES' FUNCTIONS in the sixteenth and the following two centuries continued to be threefold: police, judicial and administrative. Their original task of keeping the peace remained of prime importance, for they were still the only police authorities, supported by the sheriffs, the constables and, in exceptional circumstances, the militia. The strong Tudor rule did not bring an age of uninterrupted peace and calm. The lawlessness which reached its height under Henry VI, and was still rife under the Yorkists, was largely curbed by the Tudors through the agency of the justices, but robbery, especially on the highway, trespass and violence to the person continued on a considerable scale, while periodical riots and open rebellion led, as we have seen, to the establishment of the Lords Lieutenant. Henry VIII's extravagance emptied the Treasury and caused a high rate of inflation, and after his death the prices of essential commodities doubled. He was also responsible for the dissolution of the monasteries, thus creating unprecedented unemployment together with a drastic reduction in the relief of the poor; a situation which was exacerbated by a rise in the population. This, coupled with the uprooting of village life by the ensuing enclosure system, led to vagrancy and pauperism and ultimately to open rebellion.

This was the prospect which faced the justices throughout most of the Tudor period; yet it is also true that the English people in general began to enjoy a more peaceful existence than they had done before. The gentry, although still indulging in vitriolic disputes, abandoned the open warfare of their ancestors and usually settled their quarrels in a more civilized manner. Quarter Sessions were no longer subject to frequent disruption by violence, although there were still instances of powerful nobles exercising their influence to secure the improper release of their friends and supporters. The rest of the community, perhaps because they no longer had the example of lawlessness set by the upper classes, tended to follow suit, and it is noticeable that the courts dealt with fewer crimes of violence than previously and that the majority of offences coming before Assizes and Quarter Sessions were of a non-violent nature. Nevertheless, crime was still rife and this, added to the justices' escalating administrative work, kept them well occupied. In discharging their many duties they soon began to experience a new phenomenon in a considerable extension of their powers out of sessions.

Powers of the justices out of sessions

Reference has been made in a previous chapter to certain powers which were exercisable by a single justice and by two or three acting together. A substantial increase in this side of their work occurred throughout the Tudor reigns.

The single justice

The powers exercisable by a single justice at the beginning of Henry VII's reign were mostly related to the preservation of the peace. In addition to the purely police function of pursuing, or ordering others to pursue and arrest suspects, he could issue a summons requiring a person to appear at the next sessions; he could take security for keeping the peace and for good behaviour and could, at his discretion, release such security. In other words, he did not have to wait until an offence had been committed, but could anticipate it by binding over a person of whom he was suspicious. In the case of a breach of the peace involving affrays, assaults and violence to the person he could commit to the common gaol if he could not stop the affray.

The "reading of the Riot Act," which was to be the last surviving executive duty of the justices, extending into the twentieth century, began in the reign of Edward VI. (What is usually referred to colloquially as "The Riot Act" was passed in 1715 and is described in vol. II). When there was an unlawful assembly threatening a disturbance of the peace, a single justice could take the posse to the scene of the trouble and read the following proclamation ordering the rioters to disperse:

"The King our Sovereign Lord charges and commands all persons being assembled immediately to disperse themselves and peaceably depart to their habitations or to their lawful business upon pains contained in the Act lately made against unlawful and rebellious assemblies: God save the King."

If anyone disobeyed the order, the justice could arrest them, using such force as was necessary and, if any participant was killed in the process, neither the justice nor his posse were to be held responsible.[1]

A single justice had power to examine felons. Persons who molested priests, damaged church property or abused the sacrament were to be arrested by a constable or churchwarden and taken before a single justice who was to commit them to custody pending inquiry by the justice and one of his fellows.[2] In 1495 a single justice was empowered to inquire into alleged malpractice by sheriffs, under-sheriffs and shire clerks and if, on examination, he found "default in the said sheriffs ..." they were to be convicted "without further Inquiry or Examination" and forfeit 40 shillings. The justices making such examinations had to certify the result to the Exchequer within the quarter, or they too had to pay 40 shillings.[3] The same Act authorized a single justice to deal with irregularities in the county and hundred courts on complaint by an aggrieved party.

An appreciable amount of time was spent by a single justice in dealing with cases of disseisin, or the unlawful dispossessing of a man's house or land. Although the country became considerably more law-abiding under Henry VII and Henry VIII than it had been before, disputes over the title to land often involved one party taking the law into his own hands. With the help of neighbours and any servants he might have he would evict the occupier of property to which he laid claim. Such events were common under the early Tudors and continued to occur frequently throughout Elizabeth I's reign and beyond. Disseisin had been regarded as a serious offence at least since Magna Carta and it could involve the Justices of the Peace in both a policing operation and in a judicial trial following an inquisitorial inquiry. The offence had been defined in various statutes of Forcible Entry[4] under which a single justice could arrest the offender and reinstate the party ousted. In Tudor times it was still based on a statute of 1391 (15 Richard II, c. 2) but it was governed mainly by one of 1429 (8 Hen. VI, c. 9). The victim of the dispossession was entitled to make complaint to the nearest justice, who was then required to go without delay to the property which was alleged to be forcibly held. He would take with him the parish constables, and if he anticipated unusual difficulty he would ask one or more of his neighbouring justices to accompany him. Having arrived on the scene the justice would restore possession to the rightful owner, but if the disseisor refused to give up occupation it was the justice's duty to arrest him, confiscate any weapons he might have used and commit him to gaol pending a trial at

1.　　3 & 4 Edw. VI, c. 5. The earlier statute, 13 Hen. IV, c. 7, had empowered not less than two justices with the sheriff to arrest those involved in a riot. Further enactments covering the justices' duties in quelling riots were 1 Mary st. 2, c. 12 and 1 Eliz. c. 16.
2.　　1 Mary, st. 2, c. 3.
3.　　11 Hen. VII, c. 15.
4.　　5 Rich. II, st. 1, c. 7; 15 Rich. II, c. 2; 8 Hen. VI, c. 9; 31 Eliz. c. 11.

Quarter Sessions. If the alleged disseisor resisted arrest a jury of 24 men was summoned to consider the matter and their findings were submitted to Quarter Sessions together with a report from the justice. Almost all disseisin cases ended with the original occupier reinstated in the property and the intruder fined, with or without imprisonment.

The single justice's criminal jurisdiction was extended under Elizabeth to enable him to deal with a number of additional offences, and during the same period his administrative duties were increased, as will be seen in the next chapter.[5] He was also given a small civil jurisdiction which involved the hearing of disputes between master and servant and between master and apprentice.[6]

Two or more justices

The work done by one justice on his own could also, with few exceptions, be performed by two or more justices acting together. The single justice did much of his work in his own home, while groups of justices met either in the house of one of them or in a local inn. Records suggest that it became fairly common in the sixteenth century for justices to meet informally at regular intervals of three or four weeks. On these occasions they would carry out any inspections - of gaols, bridges, etc - which they deemed necessary, after which they would dine together and then hear reports from the high constables, settle disputes and deal with any other matters which required their attention. They had no legal assistance, but usually at least one of them was a member of the *Quorum* and was legally qualified, and gradually they began to engage a clerk at their own expense, though it is not clear what function he performed except to take care of the documents. There was no jury at these meetings and the justices were not governed by any rules of procedure. They conducted their affairs in any manner they thought fit. They were in fact policemen, prosecutors and judges, for their powers included those of arrest, followed by examination without counsel on either side and with no safeguards for the accused, and finally they gave judgment. In some cases involving a minor transgression they could impose sentence; in most they decided whether the alleged offender should be committed for trial or discharged. This system was to last until 1849 when the preliminary hearing of a criminal charge was regulated by Act of Parliament.[7]

There was no formal procedure laid down for any of the meetings of two or more justices. As yet the organization was left entirely to the discretion of the justices themselves who might summon a meeting at

---

5.   Lambard devotes one whole book to the functions of a single justice out of his four books on Justices of the Peace.
6.   5 Eliz., c. 14.
7.   11 & 12 Vict., c. 43.

any time they chose. It is, however, in these informal gatherings that one can find the origin of the Petty Sessions of modern times. The term "Petty Session" appears occasionally in Tudor legislation but not in the context of a court of summary jurisdiction of the type in operation today. The latter was not established in practice until the eighteenth century, and did not receive statutory recognition until 1849.[8]

During the sixteenth and seventeenth centuries numerous statutes, now usually referred to as Acts of Parliament, conferred additional powers, both criminal and administrative, on two, four and sometimes six justices acting together, the object being to relieve Quarter Sessions of the task of trying less serious offences. This was particularly so from the reign of Elizabeth onwards, but already under Henry VII two justices were empowered to supervise weights and measures,[9] and in the same reign they were given the task of examining the books of the sheriffs and checking the amerciaments that they imposed. The two justices who performed this function had to include a member of the *Quorum*, and they were appointed at the sessions by the *Custos* or, in his absence, by the senior member of the *Quorum*.[10] An Act of 1547[11] authorized two justices to "enslave" a vagabond who left his work without authority. The same number were enabled to exercise a limited civil jurisdiction. This involved arbitrating in disputes over the clearing of woodland and supervising partitions between landlords and commoners, if appointed for the purpose at sessions,[12] and also settling disputes between farmers and butchers over the price of bullocks.[13] In the reign of Edward VI we see the beginning of the justices' licensing functions when two were given power to deal with cases of keeping alehouses without a licence.[14]

Four justices are first mentioned in an Act of 1530 which gave them power to deal with decayed bridges,[15] and in the following year six justices were empowered to supervise gaols.[16]

Bail

An important function of justices out of sessions was the granting of bail. Their power to do so had been growing since the statute of 1444 under which sheriffs were obliged to release on bail all persons, with certain exceptions, who were in custody by reason of any personal action or of any indictment or trespass.[17] Holdsworth thought that the

8.   *Ibid.*
9.   11 Hen. VII, c. 4; 12 Hen. VII, c. 5.
10.   11 Hen. VII, c. 15.
11.   1 Edw. VI, c. 3.
12.   35 Hen. VIII, c. 17; made perpetual by 13 Eliz., c. 25.
13.   32 Hen. VIII, c. 1.
14.   5 & 6 Edw. VI, c. 25.
15.   22 Hen. VIII, c. 5.
16.   23 Hen. VIII, c. 2; extended by 13 Eliz., c. 25.
17.   23 Hen. VI, c. 9.

origin of their power to bail was to be found in the statute of Edward III[18] under which sheriffs were not to let to mainprize anyone indicted or taken by the Keepers of the Peace if not mainprizable, and the keepers might punish them if they did so. In any event, as he points out, the power was certainly conferred upon them in general terms in 1483-84, when every justice was given authority to bail prisoners arrested on suspicion of felony, in like form as if the prisoners had been indicted before the same justices.[19] Soon after the accession of Henry VII, the Act of 1487 announced that persons who were not bailable were often bailed and in consequence many murderers and felons had escaped. Accordingly, the power to bail was to be exercised by not less than two justices, one of whom must be of the *Quorum*, and the prisoners so bailed were to be certified at the next general sessions of the peace or of gaol delivery.[20] In spite of this, it was declared in a further Act of 1554[21] that some of the "greatest and notablest Offenders" had been set at large by one of the justices in the name of himself and of another justice who knew nothing of the case. Justices were therefore forbidden to bail anyone not bailable by law under the statute of 1275,[22] and where it was lawful to grant bail this could be done only if the two justices granting it were both present at the bailment where they must take statements of the accused and witnesses and bind them over to appear at the court of trial. The statement must be forwarded under the seals of both the examining justices. A justice failing to comply with the Act was to be punished at the discretion of the Judge of Gaol Delivery. In the following year this process was extended to all felons whether bailed or not. The justices had to examine all suspects before committal for trial and could bind over to appear at the trial any witnesses whose evidence they deemed to be essential.[23] The reason for these provisions seems to have been to check undue leniency by the justices rather than any concern for the interests of the accused. These two statutes may be regarded as the origin of the justices' power to hold preliminary examinations before committing accused persons for trial and binding over witnesses to attend.

Quarter Sessions and discretionary sessions

The principal powers and duties of the justices had always been centred on the courts of Quarter Sessions, and by 1485 these had

18.   4 Edw. III, c. 2; 34 Edw. III, c. 1, s. 6 gave them power to take security for good behaviour.
19.   1 Rich. III, c. 3.
20.   3 Hen. VII, c. 3.
21.   1 & 2 Philip & Mary, c. 13.
22.   3 Edw. 1, c. 15.
23.   2 & 3 Philip & Mary, c. 10.

undergone little basic change since they were instituted in 1362. Research into the work of the sessions becomes easier from the sixteenth century onwards because a number of counties possess Quarter Sessions rolls in an almost unbroken series from this time and also minute books from the early seventeenth century. They show that Quarter Sessions had become the hub of county affairs around which the whole community revolved. They were attended by everyone of any significance in the county and many more besides. Sometimes the Assize Judge was present (he was normally on the county commission) and took the opportunity to give advice and guidance on matters of law and procedure and also to proclaim national policy on which he had been briefed by the Chancellor. Quarter Sessions were a court of law with jurisdiction to try the same cases as those triable at Assizes with the exception of treason (though the more serious cases were also being transferred to Assizes with increasing frequency) and at the same time they controlled the whole civil administration of the county.

The constantly increasing work of Quarter Sessions gave rise to a need for sessions to be held more frequently than the four times a year decreed in the statute of 1362. To meet this, an Act of 1541-42[24] directed the justices in each county to divide themselves into groups of at least two for each hundred and to hold a session every quarter in addition to the regular Quarter Sessions and at least six weeks before them. At these meetings the justices were required to inquire into the working of certain statutes. This arrangement proved to be too rigid and restrictive and was repealed in 1545,[25] leaving the justices a wide discretion to organize themselves as they thought fit. The result was an increasing use of additional, discretionary sessions. They could be summoned by a writ issued by any two justices, but many of them were virtually the same as Quarter Sessions, with juries of presentment and trial, and they were attended by the *Custos*, Clerk of the Peace, sheriff, coroner, bailiffs and constables. Virtually the only difference, apart from the elasticity of the timing of sittings, was that a few offences could only be dealt with at Quarter Sessions and that the intermediate sessions sometimes sat in places other than those in which Quarter Sessions were held. Lambard explains that the custom in some counties was:

> "to summon yearely six standing Sessions of the Peace; in others 8; in others 12 or 16, and in others otherwise. All of which is done chiefly upon pretence to ease the inhabitants of the Countie, for whom it would otherwise bee verie painefull to travell so often and so farre from all the partes of the Shire to any one place of the

24.   33 Hen. VIII, c. 10, s. 1.
25.   37 Hen. VIII, c. 7.

same. And, therefore, such as do maintain 6 or 8 sessions, do use to summon all the whole Shire to a couple of them, and to the residue they call only such parts of the Shire as they doe specially appoint."

Procedure at Quarter Sessions

The system under which the justices operated remained fundamentally the same as it had been in previous reigns. Their supervision of all aspects of local government was still based, at least until Elizabeth's reign, entirely upon criminal judicial procedure, the principle being that administrative duties should be entrusted to local officers and members of the community and that the justices should punish those who failed to comply. The result was, as the Webbs observe:[26]

> "It is not too much to say that at the assizes and quarter sessions the county, the hundred, and the parish, together with most of the unpaid and compulsory serving officers, were, one or other of them, always in the dock as defendants to criminal indictments, on which they were perpetually being fined."

Holdsworth comments that "the old idea of local self-government subject to the law" was retained in the form of government through the justices which was adapted by the Tudors. The machinery by which they acted continued to operate through presentment and indictment for the non-performance or the mis-performance of legal obligations.

> "The fact that, in the sixteenth century, this idea was preserved and these self-governing judicial officers of the later mediaeval period were adopted as the basis of the scheme of English local government, is a unique phenomenon in Western Europe of the utmost significance for the future of our constitution and our law."[27]

In studying the courts of Quarter Sessions during the first four centuries of their history it is important to bear in mind that there were considerable variations in practice between the sessions in different counties. Each adopted its own procedure which, although complying in theory with the directions contained in legislation and in council directives, often digressed significantly from what was intended by Parliament and the government. However, the same basic characteristics were to be found in every county and were applied at each stage of the proceedings.

The precise time and place of each Quarter Sessions was fixed by

---

26.   "The Parish and the County", ELG., pp. 307-309.
27.   HEL, vol. IV, p. 136.

two or more justices, of whom one was a member of the *Quorum.* They issued a precept 15 days in advance to the sheriff directing him to summon the jurors and to warn all concerned to attend. The dates fixed were generally in accordance with the statute 2 Henry V, st. 1, c. 4 which directed the justices to meet four times a year in the weeks following the feasts of Epiphany, Easter, the Translation of St Thomas the Martyr and St Michael the Archangel. In practice some counties diverged from these dates, and in Middlesex there was a considerable digression due to the sittings of the court of King's Bench in the county.

On receiving the justices' precept the sheriff directed warrants to the bailiffs of hundreds and liberties ordering them to cause the high and petty constables, bailiffs, coroners and stewards of leets to attend bringing with them their records, rolls, indictments and other documents. The gaolers, and later the keepers or masters of houses of correction, were also ordered to attend bringing lists of those who had been committed to their custody.

The juries which attended Quarter Sessions were of three kinds. There were juries from each of the hundreds and liberties in the county who were drawn from the same class as the constables. It was their duty to present to the sessions all nuisances, defaults and minor offences which arose within their respective areas. (In addition to the presentments of the juries the high and petty constables also made presentments for each hundred). There was also the county jury of presentment or inquiry, which came to be known as the grand jury. It was composed of knights and other leading landowners with at least 40 shillings annual rent of lands and tenements (later raised to £10 per annum of freehold or copyhold by 4 William & Mary, c. 24). They were all men of substance and were composed of the most substantial freeholders in the county, being drawn from the same class as the Justices of the Peace. No case could be tried at the sessions unless it was presented by the grand jury who took evidence before deciding whether to endorse the bill as *billa vera,* or if they did not consider that there was a *prima facie* case to answer they would endorse it *ignoramus.* If they returned a true bill it became a formal indictment. The grand jury's presentments covered not only persons who were alleged to have committed offences against the criminal law in the usual sense but also anyone who had failed to carry out some public duty such as the repair of a highway or bridge. In the course of time they also came to express their views on any matter of importance in local and sometimes national affairs. The third type of jury was the petty or trial jury which tried on indictment all cases which had been presented by the grand jury. It was they who, like British juries of modern times, decided the guilt or innocence of those who had been indicted. Petty juries were composed of freeholders but they were generally of lesser standing than the members of the grand juries.

When the justices and all others who had been summoned to attend had assembled at the time and place fixed for the sessions, the Clerk of the Peace read the commission under which the justices were empowered to hear and determine cases and to perform the other functions set out in the commission and in statutes. The sheriff then delivered the names of the jurors and of others who had been summoned to appear. Their names were read out by the Clerk of the Peace and the crier then called upon them to answer. Any who were absent were fined unless they could prove illness or give other good reason. (Any justice who failed to attend was also fined). This was followed by reports from the justices, coroners and stewards on those whom they had bailed and from whom they had taken recognizances. The juries were then sworn and one of the justices gave the charge, which explained the duties of the juries and of all others concerned with the work of the court.

It was usually at this point that the justices dealt with administrative and executive matters such as the appointment of officers, the fixing of prices and wages, hearing petitions for the relief of those reduced to poverty by some disaster and with other financial matters. The justices would then adjourn for dinner, and when they resumed they would return to criminal judicial matters and the juries would be called upon to fulfil their duties. At the end of these proceedings the justices pronounced sentence on those who had been convicted. The justices then dispersed, leaving the Clerk of the Peace to record the proceedings and to prepare certain returns.

Under the Tudors all procedure at the sessions was therefore still by way of a charge to the jury, followed by presentment, indictment and trial before a trial jury; but certain changes soon began to take place. The first was that whereas the jury of presentment had in the past been composed of the inhabitants at large who were expected to have a personal knowledge of the events, this was no longer so and the high constables made the presentments on the strength of information collected from the petty constables. Secondly, new Acts gave the justices administrative functions which were no longer implemented through criminal judicial procedure, but instead required the justices to take independent administrative action on their own initiative. We shall see later that these were to arise particularly in respect of such matters as the Poor Law, the granting of licences, rating, prison administration and highways. These did not reach an advanced stage until the reign of Elizabeth and will be described in the next chapter.

Appeal

The decision of the justices both in and out of sessions could have momentous consequences, yet there was no system of appeal against their adjudications. An aggrieved party could not as yet appeal to Quarter Sessions from the decisions of one or more justices out of sessions, nor was there any right of appeal from Quarter Sessions to the King's Bench or other higher courts. The remedy, in so far as one was available, was to have the proceedings reviewed by prerogative writ or to have the justices tried and punished for misconduct. The concept of an appeal as it is understood today was alien to the common law under which the only means of reversing a court's decision was through the cumbrous and limited procedure of writ of error. The ingredients of an appeal procedure may be seen in the Act of 1489, already mentioned, under which redress against a justice might be sought from a neighbouring justice or from a Judge of Assize or, failing that, from the King or the Chancellor; but this seems to have been directed more towards rebuking a justice for wrong doing than towards redressing the wrong done to the complainant. A further advance was made a century later when a right of appeal to Quarter Sessions was granted to anyone with a complaint against the poor rate or any acts of the local justices.[28] It was not until 1907 that an effective system of appeal from Assizes and Quarter Sessions was introduced.[29]

Expansion of powers

We have seen that the justices' original policing powers were conferred by the Crown without any statutory backing, and subsequently a number of additional executive functions were given to them by directions of the Council, but although the Council continued to issue further instructions from time to time, the flood of extra duties both judicial and administrative which engulfed the justices during the sixteenth and subsequent centuries was almost entirely created by statute.

> "To enumerate all the powers conferred upon each individual Justice of the Peace, upon groups of justices, or upon quarter sessions would involve a summary of the greater part of the legislation of the Tudor period."[30]

At the close of the sixteenth century Lambard listed 309 statutes which related to justices. Of these, 99 were passed during the 73 years of the first four Tudors and 77 during the 45 years' reign of Elizabeth. A number of these enactments were of very limited scope or were

28.   39 Eliz., c. 3, s. 6.
29.   Below vol. II, ch. VI.
30.   Holdsworth, HEL, vol. IV, p. 137.

merely re-enactments, but others were of the foremost importance, some of them adding appreciably to certain of the duties which the justices were already performing while others opened up new vistas. The spate of legislation was symptomatic of the underlying trend in Tudor policy to transfer ultimate control of all social and economic matters from the localities to the central government. The process was, however, tempered by the principle that, subject to the overriding scrutiny of the Council, a wide discretion should be left to the justices through whom the system was to be administered. The following paragraphs give an indication of the principal directions in which the justices' functions were extended under the first Tudor monarchs and the next chapter will show how the peace accelerated under Elizabeth I.

Trade

Chapter IV described the beginning, under Richard II, of the justices' responsibility for the regulation of trade and industry and its development during the fifteenth century which was marked by growing internal trade coinciding with an advancing interest in overseas markets and increasing international rivalry. During the trade expansion of the fifteenth and the first half of the sixteenth centuries, the changing situation continued to be handled through the same system as before of judicial control by the justices. More progressive methods were to be introduced under Elizabeth.

As we have seen, by the end of the fifteenth century England, having been the main source of wool for mediaeval Europe, had become the chief supplier of cloth to the Continent. The regulation of the cloth trade therefore remained a major responsibility of the justices, and substantial legislation continued to be aimed in that direction.[31] By the end of the sixteenth century England's trade in general was assuming world-wide proportions which were beginning to embrace overseas territories - in North America and soon afterwards in the Far East. This involved control by the justices of both imports and exports. For the protection of home trade, imports had to be restricted. For example, worsteds made in Norwich had to be shielded from foreign competition,[32] and similarly home industry was protected by the prohibition of the wearing of silk on bonnets, hats, girdles and hose.[33] On the other hand, restrictions were sometimes placed on exports. This occurred most frequently in times of scarcity, as when the carrying of corn, victuals and wool overseas were prohibited,[34] but the export of gold and silver bullion and coins was banned at all times

31. A major Act on the subject was passed in 1552 (5 & 6 Edw. VI, c. 6).
32. 1 & 2 Philip & Mary, c. 14.
33. 1 & 2 Philip & Mary, c. 2.
34. 1 & 2 Philip & Mary, c. 5.

except with a royal licence.[35] Within the realm itself, the buying of corn and its transport from one port to another in England and Wales required a licence from three justices.[36]

As trade increased, demarcation disputes between craftsmen had to be resolved under legislation which was enforced by the justices. In ch. IV we saw that shoemakers and cordwainers were to cease to tan leather and that tanners had to stop shoemaking. Further instances are to be found in the sixteenth century; for example, brewers were forbidden to act as coopers who in turn were regulated as to the size and price of the barrels they supplied,[37] and an Act of 1555 defended the weavers against the sharp practices of the clothiers.[38]

Another Act of 1555[39] contained lengthy regulations governing the trade of watermen and bargemen on the River Thames. It specified the size and type of boat to be used, the number of the crew and their qualifications. The Mayor and Aldermen of the City of London, who were justices *ex officio,* were to fix the rates to be charged and were to appoint eight overseers annually to supervise the watermen and to keep order. The mayor and aldermen and the justices for the counties adjoining the river were given full power to enforce the provisions of the Act and to deal with complaints from the overseers. There were many other Acts directed at various trades, including further legislation on leather and shoe manufacturing,[40] all of which were enforced by the justices.

Shipping

Expanding foreign trade and the acquisition of overseas territories created a keen interest in shipping as England became a leading maritime power. In coastal areas the justices sometimes received orders from the Council to see that ships were built and properly manned, and even the inland areas did not necessarily escape responsibility as where the Council ordered the justices in every county to levy an additional rate of 2s. 6d. on every alehouse to assist in the construction of the harbour at Dover.[41]

Fishing was an industry of special importance, being a source both of food and of sailors for the merchant and fighting ships, and the enforcement by the justices of the obligation to eat fish on Fridays and in Lent was inspired more by a desire to foster the trade than to support religious observance.[42] To keep prices down the buying of fish

35. 17 Edw. IV, c. 1; 7 Edw. VI, c. 7.
36. 5 & 6 Edw. VI, c. 14, s. 9.
37. 23 Hen. VIII, c. 4; 35 Hen. VIII, c. 8, allowed prices to be increased and added that coopers might charge whatever they could get for barrels exported to Flanders.
38. 2 & 3 Philip & Mary, c. 11.
39. 2 & 3 Philip & Mary, c. 16.
40. 24 Hen. VIII, c. 1; 2 & 3 Edw. VI. cc. 9. 11.
41. DP 1547-1580, 649.
42. 2 & 3 Edw. VI, c. 19. There were also many directions on the subject by the Council.

for resale at a profit was prohibited, except in the case of persons living within one mile of the sea provided that they resold at a reasonable price.[43] An Act of 1495[44] contained extensive provisions governing the fishing industry, including directions as to how fish were to be packed and arrangements for the appointment by magistrates in towns of gaugers of fishing vessels, searchers and packers. To encourage the country's shipping an Act of 1485 prohibited the import of wine except in English, Welsh and Irish ships.[45]

Agriculture
Agriculture, upon which the whole population depended for their food, was in the forefront of legislative activity. It was also of major concern to the justices themselves as it was from the land that they derived their personal wealth which enabled them to maintain a high degree of independence. Soon after the accession of Henry VII, steps were taken, both by legislation[46] and directions of the council, to curb enclosures. These proved to be among the least successful measures taken by the Tudor governments because, as we have seen, they did not receive the support of the justices. In the following reign attempts were made to check the evils arising from the conversion of fields from tillage to pasture by restricting to 2,000 the number of sheep which might be owned by one farmer, under penalties to be imposed by the justices.[47] Later, each parish was required to show that it still had as much land under cultivation as at any time since 1509, and the justices had to certify to the Chancery the presentments made by each parish.[48] The government was concerned not only by the unemployment problem caused by the loss of arable land but also by the drop in milk production which resulted from the transfer to sheep farming. Accordingly, it was enacted that a farmer must keep one milch cow for every 60 sheep and must rear one calf annually for every 120 sheep.[49]

In spite of these measures, there were numerous insurrections by the peasantry, whose livelihood was threatened by the changing system of agriculture. A notable example was the rising in Norfolk under Kett in 1549, in whose suppression the justices played a prominent part.

The justices were obliged to implement a good deal of agricultural legislation aimed at other targets in addition to enclosures. In the interest of the weaving industry and to provide work for the unemployed they had to see that in every 60 acres under cultivation one-quarter acre was devoted to flax.[50] They also became responsible

43.   5 & 6 Edw. VI, c. 14, s. 12.
44.   11 Hen. VII, c. 23.
45.   1 Hen. VII, c. 8.
46.   4 Hen. VII, c. 16.
47.   25 Hen. VIII, c. 13.
48.   5 & 6 Edw. VI, c. 5.
49.   2 & 3 Philip & Mary, c. 3.
50.   24 Hen. VIII, c. 4.

for the preservation of woodland.[51] They were involved in the smallest details, such as fixing the time for killing calves,[52] or in the extermination of pests. Among the latter were rooks, crows and choughs which, it was said, "do daily breed and increase" and "do yearly devour and consume wonderful and marvellous great quantity of corn and grain of all kinds." Therefore, every town and hamlet had to provide crow-nets, and landowners were obliged to arrange for the destruction of these birds, anyone who killed them being entitled to two pence per dozen. The justices had to enforce the Act and hear complaints over payments.[53]

Corn was of particular importance as providing part of the staple diet of the population. As we have already seen, export of grain was prohibited in times of scarcity and during such periods the justices took steps to see that farmers supplied the home markets.[54]

The importance of the horse in the national economy was illustrated by an obligation placed upon the justices to take steps to deal with any deterioration in the breed of horses in a county.[55] In the case of cattle, drovers might buy and resell at reasonable prices, provided that they sold at a market at least 40 miles away and that they had a licence granted by three justices, of whom one must be of the *Quorum*. Later, in addition to drovers, all carriers, buyers and transporters of corn, grain, butter and cheese had to hold licences issued under the seal of the justices in Quarter Sessions.[56]

Liquor Licensing

Reference has already been made to the beginning of liquor licensing in 1552, when two justices could deal with infringements of the Act of that year. Long before that date, justices had been concerned with alehouses because of the conduct of those who frequented them and who committed offences which were dealt with as part of the justices' criminal jurisdiction. They also punished alehouse keepers for allowing unlawful games to be played on the premises or for creating nuisances, but alehouses as such did not figure in legislation until Acts of 1495[57] and 1503[58] authorized two justices to suppress disorderly or useless alehouses in their area. It was not, however, until 1552[59] that a system

51.   35 Hen. VIII, c. 17.
52.   24 Hen. VIII, c. 7.
53.   24 Hen. VIII, c. 10.
54.   APC, 1586-1587, 119; DP, 1547-1580, 26. Under 13 Eliz., c. 13 they were required to fix an export quota for corn.
55.   32 Hen. VIII, c. 13.
56.   5 Eliz., c. 12.
57.   11 Hen. VII, c. 2.
58.   19 Hen. VII, c. 12.
59.   5 & 6 Edw. VI, c. 25. The difficulties in enforcing this Act are set out in the preamble to 3 Charles I, c. 24.

of licensing began when two justices were required to take recognizances from alehouse keepers, who had to provide sureties for the maintenance of good order and against allowing unlawful games. The recognizances were to be certified to Quarter Sessions, "there to remain on record." The justices had complete discretion as to whether or not they should grant a licence (a discretion which was challenged in the courts from time to time but always without success).[60] An incentive to grant a licence lay in the fact that the justices were entitled to take for themselves half of the fee of one shilling for each recognizance. The legislation referred specifically to alehouses and not to inns which were quite distinct. The latter were places where travellers lodged and took refreshment, and where sometimes the justices met and held their sessions. From early times inns, like alehouses, could be controlled by indictment under the common law of nuisance, but as many also supplied ale to all-comers the justices came to treat them as alehouses subject to the licensing laws. This was the beginning of the justices' liquor licensing duties which they were to continue to exercise to the present day.

Games

Mention has already been made of various enactments prohibiting unlawful games. The object of these measures was threefold: to curb absenteeism from church, to prevent lawlessness to which the playing of games was alleged to lead, and to encourage the practice of archery. These continued to be the objectives at the beginning of the sixteenth century, but whereas the first two remained of prime concern to the authorities, the third was eliminated by the demise of the longbow. In 1503 an Act of Henry VII[61] extolled the advantages of the longbow "whereby Honour and Victorie hathe ben goten ageyne utwarde enymyes" and condemned the use of newfangled crossbows. It forbad anyone to shoot with a crossbow except to defend his house, or unless he were a lord or person having 200 marks freehold. The penalty was forfeiture of the bow and a fine of 40 shillings per day. More than four centuries later crossbows were again the subject of restrictive legislation under the Crossbows Act 1987, but the object then was to remove a danger to the public. By the end of the sixteenth century, bows and arrows had been superseded by gunpowder. Armies were making increasing use of cannon, while the militia were armed with muskets, and it was the duty of the justices and Deputy Lieutenants to see that they were equipped and trained in the use of the new weapon. On the other hand, preoccupation with the evils thought to be

60.   The courts declined to issue *mandamus* to compel the justices to grant a licence even where there was evidence that it had been maliciously or corruptly refused. See, 1 *Barnardiston*, p. 402.
61.   19 Hen. VII, c. 4. Under 6 Hen. VIII, c. 2, bows had to be made of elm and certain other woods.

associated with games lasted throughout the century. In 1555 an Act sought to close all "Bowling-Allies" and other "Houses, Gardens and Places" where unlawful games were played, the reason given being that "many unlawful Assemblies, Conventicles, Seditions and Conspiracies have been daily secretly practised by idle and misruled Persons repairing to such Places; of which, Robberies and many other Misdemeanors have ensued."[62]

It seems to have been assumed that anyone who was engaged in playing a game was necessarily plotting some more serious breach of the law, and it does not appear to have occurred to anyone that the playing of harmless games might provide the lower classes with an acceptable alternative to the commission of crime and might serve to keep them out of mischief. Virtually every game that was played in Tudor times was unlawful in so far as the great majority of the population was concerned. The games were listed in a statute of 1541 (33 Hen. VIII, c. 9) and comprised cards, dice, football, bowls, tennis, quoits, tables (backgammon), cales (ninepins), logats (also ninepins but using bones), shovegroat and casting stone. Many of these had already been named in the statute 12 Rich. II, c. 6, passed in 1388. Those who were specifically forbidden to indulge in any of these pastimes were artificers, husbandmen, labourers, mariners, fishermen, watermen, apprentices and servants. A special exception was made in 1535 by the statute 27 Hen. VIII, c. 25, s. 7, for those who played games in their homes during the 12 days of Christmastide, and servants and apprentices were permitted to play in their master's house or the house in which he was staying provided that they had his approval. The penalty for playing an unlawful game was 40 shillings, which was a considerable sum of money for a labourer. The same amount per day was imposed on those who kept a place in which the games were played. The justices were empowered to search alehouses in which they suspected that games took place, and they could require the keeper to provide sureties for the cessation of games on their premises. Those who refused were imprisoned until they produced the required sureties. Quarter Sessions were obliged to publish the statutory restrictions, and mayors and officers of boroughs had to proclaim them four times a year in the market place.

Hunting
As in the use of crossbows, the restrictions on games did not usually apply to the upper classes. The Kings themselves indulged in the older form of tennis as it was played long before the introduction of lawn tennis. Similarly, hunting, which had been reserved as a royal sport by the Norman monarchs, came to be enjoyed by the gentry, but was

62.   2 & 3 Philip & Mary, c. 9.

strenuously denied to the lower classes. Reference was made in ch. IV to the property qualification required of any priest or layman who wished to keep a hunting dog. There will be much to say on the subject of the game laws when we come to the eighteenth century, but it should be noted that, although hunting did not become the exclusive privilege of the landed gentry until 1671, several further steps were taken in this direction under the early Tudors. The justices were empowered to arrest persons accused of hunting by night and to bind them over to appear at sessions.[63] They could also hear and determine cases in breach of the Acts for the protection of game birds and their eggs and fine the culprits, and they enforced early legislation which prohibited unqualified people from hunting.[64] An Act of Henry VII[65] imposed a number of restrictions on hunting and upheld the right of a landowner to exclude anyone else from hunting in his park, chase or forest without his permission. Any two justices were given power to call before them those suspected of committing any breach of the Act and to try them summarily. Those convicted were to be committed to prison until they had paid the penalty. A tenth part of the latter was to be given to the justices "for their Labour in that behalf."

Weights and measures

The justices' responsibility for regulating weights and measures, which had begun in 1389, was continued and extended. Thus, it became their duty to fix the measures of coal and the size of pieces of wood that were sold,[66] and their authority extended to the principal officers of non-corporate towns where they could fine the mayors and bailiffs who did not comply with the Acts.[67] They could also compel the mayors, bailiffs and other officials to accept the coin of the realm.[68]

Prices

We have seen that justices had been concerned in the regulation of both prices and wages from the fourteenth century when they were given responsibility under the Statutes of Labourers, and there was further legislation under Richard II. This became of even greater importance under the Tudors. It has been estimated that between 1500 and 1650 there was general price inflation of about 500 per cent, and as much as 700 per cent in the price of foodstuffs, the greatest jumps occurring after the many bad harvests. Steps were taken to control price levels in the light both of inflation and of the conduct of unscrupulous persons who endeavoured to profit unfairly. The justices

63.   1 Hen. VII, c. 7.
64.   11 Hen. VI, c. 17; 25 Hen. VIII, c. 11.
65.   19 Hen. VII, c. 11.
66.   34 & 35 Hen. VIII, c. 3.
67.   7 Hen. VII, c. 3.
68.   11 Hen. VII, c. 4.

were required to take action against forestallers (who intercepted goods before they reached market and bought them up to enhance the price) and regrators (who bought up commodities, especially victuals, in order to resell at a profit in the same or a neighbouring market). Sometimes this was done under an Act,[69] sometimes by order of the Council.[70] The latter was quick to step in when the price of an essential commodity like grain rose too high and the justices were then ordered to take action.[71] Some trades had specific provisions directed to themselves. Butter and cheese might not be bought to be resold except by retail in open shop, fair or market,[72] on pain of forfeiture of double the value. Special exceptions applied to innholders and victuallers in respect of butter and cheese sold "Retail in any of their Houses."

Wine had to be sold at fixed prices and the justices could enter the premises of those selling it and seize any which was being sold contrary to the regulations.[73] A later Act went further in regulating the sale of wines and authorized the justices to hear and determine all matters relating thereto and to appoint retailers in all places other than corporate towns.[74] Beef, pork, mutton and veal must "be sold by Weight called *Haver-du-pois*" and at fixed prices.[75] Butchers, bakers, brewers and other tradesmen who conspired together to sell goods at unauthorized prices were tried and punished by the justices in sessions.[76]

In this context it may be relevant to mention that there was also legislation from the beginning of Henry VII's reign against usury and defrauding creditors. An Act of 1487 prohibited fraudulent deeds of gift[77] and in the same year another Act forbad usury and unlawful bargains.[78]

Wages
The control of wages by justices also dates from the labour laws of the mid-fourteenth century, and the measures already described were affirmed and extended under the Tudors. Wages of labourers and artisans were fixed under an updating enactment of Henry VII, under which anyone who refused to work for the legal rate, or who took or paid an unlawful amount, could be convicted by the justices and fined 20 shillings.[79] Under this Act the proceedings had to be in sessions, but by a subsequent Act of 1514, two justices out of sessions were

69.   5 & 6 Edw. VI, c. 14.
70.   DP 1547-1580, 26; DP 1581-1590, 328.
71.   APC, 1575-1577, 219.
72.   3 & 4 Edw. VI, c. 21.
73.   24 Hen. VIII, c. 6.
74.   7 Edw. VI. c. 5.
75.   24 Hen. VIII, c. 3.
76.   2 & 3 Edw. VI, c. 15.
77.   3 Hen. VII, c. 4.
78.   *Ibid.*, c. 5.
79.   11 Hen. VII, c. 22.

empowered to investigate all such cases.[80] Justices were often involved in settling disputes over domestic servants,[81] and special provisions sometimes applied to those employed in a particular occupation like the Thames watermen.[82] Any attempt by workmen to force employers to increase wages was punished severely, particularly so if they tried to combine together for the purpose. The latter brought a penalty at the hands of the justices of £10 or imprisonment for the first offence, £20 or pillory for the second and £40 and loss of an ear for the third.[83]

A comprehensive Act covering all aspects of the service of "Artificers, Labourers, Servants of Husbandry and Apprentices," and empowering the justices to fix wages at their discretion was passed under Elizabeth and will be described in the next chapter.

Vagrants
From early times the King and his ministers had viewed all vagrants and beggars as potential sources of crime and violence, a view which was shared by Parliament and the gentry. Vagrancy in general was therefore harshly suppressed in an unsuccessful attempt to stamp out crime and also to compel the able-bodied to return to work. At first no thought was given to the relief of the destitute, this being left entirely to the church and charitable citizens. Notwithstanding a formidable series of measures which heaped savage punishments upon the vagrant population, their numbers increased inexorably and the preamble to each succeeding statute became ever more vehement in deploring the deteriorating situation. The numbers increased substantially from the fourteenth century with the breakdown of the old feudal system whereunder the labourer was tied to the land. They became still more numerous in the sixteenth century as a result of the dissolution of the monasteries and of the enclosure system, both of which threw large numbers of people out of work. An accurate estimate of the numbers involved is impossible, but one may gain some idea of the size of the problem from an inquiry which was ordered by the worried Council in 1569. Alarmed by the growing menace of the vagrant population, it ordered a search to be made of "vagabonds" throughout the country, and this resulted in the temporary apprehension by the justices and constables of 13,000 "masterless men,"[84] out of a total population of, probably, a little over four million. Although many of the vagrants were undoubtedly bad characters, some were not, and the records of those who were arrested and the passports issued to enable them to return to their places of birth, show that large numbers were obliged to

80.   6 Hen. VIII, c. 3.
81.   APC, 1571-78, 381.
82.   6 Hen. VIII, c. 3; 2 & 3 Philip & Mary, c. 16.
83.   2 & 3 Edw. VI, c. 15.
84.   H.J. Trail, *Social England,* vol. iii, p. 550.

take to the road to seek employment. It would be surprising if many of them did not take to crime to keep themselves and their families alive. In any event, the marauding gangs who had terrorized the countryside in the past became an even greater menace, and much of the justices' time, both in and out of sessions, was given to dealing with the crimes they committed. In this task the justices were only partly successful even in the populated parts of the country where they could exercise their authority effectively. England at that time was covered with large, virtually uninhabited areas where constables and posses, who had more than enough on their hands, rarely trod, and in which robbers preyed with impunity upon travellers on the isolated highways. It was a situation which gave constant anxiety to the central government, the local administration and to Parliament, as is clear from the number of lengthy statutes and ordinances which appeared throughout the Tudor period.

It was only gradually that the authorities came to realize that a policy based solely upon the infliction of cruel punishment could not solve the problem, and that it could in itself lead through desperation to widespread revolt and violence. The appreciation of this axiom dawned only slowly upon the early Tudors, although it was beginning to be recognized on the Continent, and it was not until the reign of Elizabeth that a solution was devised in the form of the Poor Laws.

New measures against vagrancy began to appear soon after the start of Henry VII's reign,[85] but the first comprehensive Act was passed in 1503.[86] This confirmed that the justices were to inflict harsh punishments on vagabonds, and they were also to impose penalties on sheriffs and other officers who neglected to execute the Act and on anyone who housed a vagabond. For this purpose they were authorized to search houses. There were indications, however, of a more humane approach. The aged and impotent were to be sent back to the hundred where they were born, and so long as they remained there they were not to be punished and they might be allowed to beg within certain limits. If, however, they strayed outside the hundred they were to be whipped and set in the stocks. Special exceptions were also made in favour of certain other types of person. A woman with child was to be treated more leniently than other vagabonds. A student found on the road was not to be punished if he had with him a letter from the Vice-Chancellor of his university. Similarly, sailors on their way home from a voyage were not to be molested if they kept to the most direct route and were in possession of a letter from the captain of their ship or from the town where they landed. Foreigners, on the other hand, who did not have special authority to remain, were to be punished and sent

85.   3 Hen. VII, c. 9.
86.   19 Hen. VII, c. 12.

back to their country of origin, and if this involved crossing the sea they were to be put to work in the port of embarkation until they could sail. Under a later Act special treatment was accorded to lepers and "bedridden creatures" who were to be allowed to stay where they were and not returned to their places of origin.[87]

The Act of 19 Henry VII was followed by further lengthy enactments on vagrants under Henry VIII and Edward VI, and by 1550 a comprehensive code had been established. The legislators were still convinced that all vagrants were *prima facie* rogues and troublemakers and that they deserved the harshest treatment unless it could be shown beyond doubt that they merited leniency. This attitude is clear from the preamble to an Act of 1530-31[88] which proclaimed:

> "Vagabonds and Beggars have of long time increased and daily do increase in great and excessive Numbers by the Occasion of Idleness, Mother and Root of all Vices, whereby hath insurged and sprung ... continual Thefts, Murders and other heinous Offences and great Enormities to the high Displeasure of God and the Inequietation and Damage of the King's People and to the marvellous disturbance of the common Weal of this Realm."

Every vagrant who was able to work but who begged was to be whipped and then sent to his place of birth or where he had last lived for three years. In order that he should not receive punishment in every parish through which he passed on his return to his birthplace he was given a licence which he was to show to the constable, and the latter was then obliged to give him meat, drink and one night's lodging only. The length of each day's journey was to be 10 miles. If he became a vagrant again he was to be whipped, set in the pillory and have an ear cut off. For a third offence he was again to be whipped, put in the pillory and lose the other ear. Those who removed a vagabond's ear were obliged to certify his name in writing to the Clerk of the Peace at the next general sessions. The job of inflicting punishment in all these cases fell usually upon the constables but they were entitled to call upon the assistance of the "most substantial" in the parish.[89]

Any labourer who left his job, or who refused to work, was treated as a vagabond. On being apprehended by his master he could be brought before two justices who, on conviction, could order him to be branded with a "V" and adjudged a slave to such master for two years. If he ran away again, the justices could order him to be branded with an "S" and to become a slave of his master for ever.[90]

87. 27 Hen. VII, c. 25.
88. 22 Hen. VIII, c. 12.
89. 27 Hen. VIII, c. 25.
90. 1 Edw. VI, c. 3.

The Acts contained a number of special provisions regarding children. The age of criminal responsibility was seven,[91] and below that children were not supposed to be punished for vagrancy. Poor children between the ages of five and 14 could, however, be put to masters in husbandry or other crafts,[92] and under a later Act could be taken into service without the consent of their parents.[93] If they resisted or ran away they could be whipped, and any officer who failed to carry out the justices' orders to inflict this punishment could be put in the stocks. Under a more humane provision, however, the justices could discharge a child from such service on the misconduct of the master. Under an order of the justices, male beggars could be taken as apprentices up to the age of 24 and females to 20.[94]

The most lengthy of the Acts was passed in 1536.[95] It began by referring to the fact that the Act passed five years earlier made no provision for the employment of able-bodied vagrants and it went on to direct that all "sturdy and valiant beggars" should be set to work "for their maintenance." It also commented that the earlier Act had not set out the manner in which the cost was to be borne. It therefore made it clear where the burden was to fall. This was largely on the cities and parishes, and those which failed in their duty were fined 20 shillings per month. Churchwardens and other parish officers were to collect alms on Sundays and holidays for the maintenance of the impotent and the employment of sturdy beggars. Contributions were not at first obligatory, but the clergy were to exhort everyone to give alms freely and to admonish those who failed to do so. Later they became virtually compulsory.[96]

This was the beginning of the close relationship which was established between the justices and the parish when the latter became the unit for the administration of Elizabethan Poor Laws. It was made abundantly clear in the various Acts that the overall responsibility for dealing with vagrancy and its ancillary problems rested squarely upon the justices. They were to keep a constant watch on the situation and were required to carry out searches and inquiries for the purpose of identifying both the rogues and vagabonds and the aged, sick and infirm. For this purpose they were to divide their counties into districts with some justices allocated to each, so as to ensure that every part of the area was investigated thoroughly. They were given almost unlimited powers in exercising their functions. Contemporary records

---

91.   The Saxons held that a child under the age of 12 could not be guilty of crime, but this was
       reduced by the Normans to seven, where it remained until 1933 when it was raised to eight,
       and to 10 in 1963.
92.   27 Hen. VIII, c. 25.
93.   3 & 4 Edw. VI, c. 16.
94.   1 Edw. VI, c. 3.
95.   27 Hen. VIII, c. 25.
96.   2 & 3 Philip & Mary, c. 5.

suggest that a good deal of their time was devoted to these duties - perhaps more towards the employment of the able-bodied than to the relief of the impotent - but that the Council often took the view that they were not doing enough.

Poor Law

Legislation under the early Tudors laid the foundations for the comprehensive Poor Laws of the Elizabethans. As we have just seen, the earlier Acts drew a clear distinction for the first time between the treatment of the deserving poor and that of the able-bodied rogue and vagabond, but this merely allowed the aged and impotent to be dealt with more leniently than the others. It was not until the reigns of Edward VI and Mary that provision was made for the relief of the worthy poor, at first through voluntary, charitable contributions and then by the levy of what amounted to a compulsory rate. This was gathered by collectors who were elected for the job but who were punished by the justices if they neglected it.[97] In the following chapter we shall see how the process was continued under Elizabeth until it reached its culmination in the fortieth year of her reign.

Egyptians

There was a class of vagrants who were treated even more harshly than the others. These were the gipsies, always referred to by the Tudors as Egyptians. Being foreigners there was no question of returning them to the hundred of their origin, and the justices had to see that they were banished from the kingdom and that they did not return. This applied also to other foreigners, but the Egyptians were deemed to require further measures of their own. An Act of Henry VIII[98] was directed at "certain outlandish People calling themselves Egyptians" who, instead of gaining a living by a craft or trade, went about the country "in great Companies, using great, subtil and crafty Means to deceive the King's Subjects" and committing "divers great and heinous Felonies and Robberies." The Act forbad any such persons to enter the country. If they did so, they were to forfeit all their goods and chattels and be expelled within 15 days. Any who were already in the country at the time of the Act had to leave within 16 days, failure to do so involving imprisonment and forfeiture.

In spite of these provisions, numbers of Egyptians saw fit after a time to enter England, "using their old accustomed, devilish and naughty Practices ... and such abominable Living as is not in any Christian Realm to be permitted." Accordingly, another Act[99] provided

97.   *Ibid.*
98.   22 Hen. VIII, c. 10.
99.   1 & 2 Philip & Mary, c. 4.

that anyone bringing Egyptians into the country was to be fined £40 on each occasion. The Egyptians themselves were to suffer far worse. Any who remained for more than a month were to be deemed felons and therefore to suffer death and loss of all possessions, and they were deprived of benefit of clergy and sanctuary. As regards those who were already in the country, they must depart within 20 days on pain of loss of all their goods and chattels, half of which was to go to the justices involved in apprehending them. If they were not gone within 40 days they were to suffer death.

These unfortunate people could, however, escape these dire penalties by placing themselves in the "service of some honest and able Inhabitant," or if they "honestly exercise" themselves in some lawful work or occupation. Whether or not they qualified for exemption rested entirely with the justices.

Religion

Much extra work fell upon the justices in enforcing the new ecclesiastical system after the separation of the church in England from Rome. Many of their duties in this field were placed upon them by directions of the Council under Elizabeth, but from the latter part of Henry VIII's reign they were being closely involved in establishing the new order and in the repression of those who held religious views at variance with those of the government. First, they were required to assist church officers and to see that offenders against the new church laws were handed over to the ecclesiastical courts.[100] After such persons had been convicted, two justices could, at the request of the ecclesiastical Judge, commit them to prison until they had found security to comply with the sentence he had imposed.[101] A later Act provided[102] for two justices under the degree of baron to sit, if summoned, with the ecclesiastical Judge, to examine and determine offences arising from a law against Romish books, English translations of the Bible and public readings of the Scriptures. Under an Act of 1536,[103] which extinguished the Pope's authority in England, persons who upheld the jurisdiction of Rome by writing, preaching or teaching were charged by writ of *praemunire*, and by the same Act, two justices, one of whom must be of the *Quorum*, were empowered to inquire into all offences against its provisions to certify presentments to the King's Bench. Three years later, justices in sessions could inquire by jury of all heresies, felonies and contempts against a new Act and send the indictments to the ecclesiastical commissioners.[104] Later it was

100.   27 Hen. VIII, c. 20.
101.   32 Hen. VIII, c. 7.
102.   34 & 35 Hen. VIII, c. 1.
103.   28 Hen. VIII, c. 10.
104.   31 Hen. VIII, c. 14.

stipulated that on such occasions the indictment must be by a jury of 12 before at least three justices.[105]

Six Acts relating to ecclesiastical matters were passed in the first six years of Edward VI's reign. Under the first,[106] persons reviling the Sacrament were to be imprisoned and fined. Any three justices, one of whom must be of the *Quorum*, had to take information of the offenders and record the depositions of witnesses who were to be bound over to appear at Quarter Sessions. The justices were also to require the bishop of the diocese to attend the trial, either in person or by representation. The second enactment,[107] ordered the abolition of all books and missals, except those authorized by royal authority, and the defacing and destruction of all images in churches. The enforcement of this Act was in the hands of the justices.

Two years later, no less than four separate enactments dealing with ecclesiastical matters were passed within the space of 12 months. The first[108] was entitled "An Act for the Uniformity of Common Prayer, and Administration of the Sacraments." It established the Protestant Book of Common Prayer and also declared that everyone must attend their proper church on Sundays and holidays unless they had lawful excuse. Failure to do so involved punishment by the church authorities, but the Act also directed that those who attended any other service should be tried and punished at Assizes or before the Justices of the Peace at sessions. The penalty was imprisonment which, for a third offence, was to be for life. This was closely followed by another enactment[109] defining the days which were to be recognized as holidays and reinforcing the earlier prohibition of the eating of meat in Lent and on Fridays and some Saturdays. A third measure[110] laid down severe penalties for quarrelling in church. If anyone drew a weapon with intent to strike another he was to be excommunicated and one of his ears was to be cut off. If he had no ears he was to be branded on the cheek with "F" for fray-maker or fighter. Offenders were to be dealt with either at Assizes or before the justices in sessions. Finally,[111] benefit of clergy was removed from anyone found guilty of treason, murder or robbery in a church or dwelling-house.

Under Mary I the justices were naturally required to shift their stance to the support of Roman Catholicism. As soon as she was on the throne an Act[112] repealed the earlier Act of her brother which established the Book of Common Prayer, and substituted new

105. 35 Hen. VIII, c. 5.
106. 1 Edw. VI, c. 4.
107. 3 & 4 Edw. VI, c. 10.
108. 5 & 6 Edw. VI, c. 1.
109. 5 & 6 Edw. VI, c. 3.
110. *Ibid.,* c. 4.
111. *Ibid.,* c. 9.
112. 1 Mary, st. 2, c. 2.

provisions. These were directed at anyone who disturbed a priest during his sermon or the celebration of Mass or who pulled down or destroyed the altar or crucifix in a church. The offender was to be apprehended by the churchwardens and the constable and brought before a justice who could commit him to custody. Within six days, two or more justices were to examine him and, if satisfied of his guilt, bind him over to appear at Quarter Sessions. The Act also stressed the increasing significance of the parish by directing that if anyone who had committed such an offence escaped from the parish, the justices in sessions could impose a fine of £5 on the inhabitants. Shortly after Mary married Philip of Spain, a further Act[113] ordered harsh punishment to be meted out to anyone who uttered seditious words against the Queen or her husband. For the first offence it was to be the pillory in the market place where the words were spoken plus a fine of £100, and if this was not paid within a month the offender was to lose both his ears. Slanderous and seditious words written in a book or letter were to be punished by cutting off the right hand. A second offence resulted in imprisonment for life and loss of all goods and chattels. The tables were quickly turned again under Elizabeth when the second Act of her reign[114] repealed 1 Mary, st. 2, c. 2, and re-enacted 5 & 6 Edward VI, c. 1., and the justices were required to suppress all aspects of papal influence.

Bridges
We saw in ch. IV how justices came to assume responsibility for the maintenance of bridges. Failure to repair a bridge caused interference to the highway which was a common-law nuisance and therefore those responsible, usually the inhabitants of the surrounding area, could be proceeded against in the court leet, but later they became indictable before the justices at Quarter Sessions. An important development took place in 1531 when the Statute of Bridges[115] extended the justices' responsibility for the upkeep of bridges and also introduced a significant evolution in the procedure whereby they were to perform their task. At least four justices, in both counties and boroughs, were empowered to "inquire, hear and determine, in general sessions, of all manner of annoyances of bridges broken in the highways" and to take such action as they thought fit against those responsible for repairing the bridge. In addition to this, they were authorized to appoint two surveyors in each county "to see every such decayed bridge repaired and amended from time to time, as often as need shall require." Finally, the most interesting provision in the Act was the power it gave to the justices to levy a rate on the inhabitants of the area to meet the

113.   1 & 2 Philip & Mary, c. 3.
114.   1 Eliz., c. 2.
115.   22 Hen. VIII, c. 5.

costs of repair, the amount being left entirely to the justices' discretion. The enactment therefore went a stage further than the traditional process of providing a public service purely through the machinery of the criminal law, whereby those who failed in their obligation to fulfil a duty were punished, time after time, until they had completed the work to the satisfaction of the court. The justices were now given the additional task of assessing the cost and of raising the necessary funds.

This system was to be followed in other fields - gaols, highways and the relief of the poor - and it is interesting to speculate on why these new horizons should have been opened to the seemingly overworked justices rather than taking the opportunity to entrust these functions to some new authority created for the purpose. The fact that the justices already had some responsibility for ensuring the maintenance of bridges is not in itself an explanation. A new organization could well have been developed to replace at least this sector of their functions, just as the earlier feudal and communal administration was superseded by the justices themselves. No doubt the presence of the justices throughout the countryside, already in a position to supervise the needs of each locality, must have carried weight in the minds of the legislators, and it may have seemed easier, in the Tudor tradition, to extend their existing role rather than create something entirely new. Yet the old customary courts had been equally well deployed; the reason for their decay was their manifest inability to cope with changing circumstances. The thinking behind the Tudor progression is not entirely clear, but at least two conclusions may be drawn. First, there must have been continuing confidence in the justices, and second, the justices themselves must have been prepared to accept further responsibilities notwithstanding their already heavy burden. Had they wished to avoid further commitments they were in a position at least to make their views apparent in Parliament, but there is no evidence that they did so. They may have been motivated by jealousy of possible rivals in the county heirarchy if they surrendered any area of their responsibility and also by the conviction that, by proceeding down new paths, they were adding still further to their status and prestige.

Highways
It is curious that statutory provision for the maintenance of public roadways developed later than those for bridges. This may have been due, in part, to the fact that the roads were used less in the fourteenth and fifteenth centuries than they had been before, whereas merchandise was transported in considerable quantities by water during this period. It was also probably due to two other factors. The first was the need for a good deal more expertise and technical skill in the repair of bridges than in the maintenance of roads. The second was

the comparative ease with which regulations could be enforced in respect of the few existing bridges, whereas roadway ordinances had to be applied widely throughout the county, involving administrative problems on a considerable scale.

It has been explained earlier that at common law the duty to maintain public roads rested upon the inhabitants of the areas through which they passed. The first piece of legislation on the subject was the Statute of Westminster 1285, which directed that highways between market towns should be kept open and that, in the absence of some special obligation, the duty to do so fell upon the inhabitants of the manor. This was enforced in the court leet, but later in Quarter Sessions. No further measures of any importance were taken during the next two centuries, unlike the growing interest in bridge maintenance during the period, and it was not until 1555 that a major piece of legislation was passed. By then the use of the roads was increasing rapidly, especially for trade, while their condition had seriously deteriorated. The Crown and Parliament therefore set about constructing new machinery for road maintenance. Under the Act of 1555,[116] the parish and all of its inhabitants were accountable for the maintenance of public roads passing through their territory, and they were obliged to provide the labour, materials and equipment, including horses and carts, to carry out the work on four consecutive days - increased to six in 1563. In default, they were collectively liable to pay a fine, which could be repeated continuously until the work was completed satisfactorily, which normally meant to the satisfaction of the justices.

A significant innovation was the requirement in the Act that each parish should nominate one or more of its inhabitants to serve as surveyor of highways for one year. The person so nominated was then appointed surveyor by the justices. Like the constable, he was unpaid and his duties were onerous. He had to review all roads and highways in his area at least three times a year. He reported his findings to the nearest justice, to whom he also gave the names of any parishioners who had failed in their duties, so that they might be fined. He was obliged to see that the owners of adjacent land cleared away any obstructions and scoured the ditches and that users of the highway did so in accordance with the statutory regulations. He had to see that everyone in the parish contributed his share of the labour, and in some cases of horses and carts, and he fixed the dates on which they had to leave their other work and present themselves on the site to carry out the repairs. Although he had no training in road building he was in charge of the operations.

Another novel provision of considerable importance for the future

116.   2 & 3 Philip & Mary, c. 8.

was that, whereas previously any fines imposed for breaches of the highway law went to the King and were not spent on maintenance, in future they were to be assigned to the parish officers "to be bestowed on the highways." The justices could compel the high constables to account for all fines received for highway offences and to pay them over to the place where the offence was committed. A consequence of this was that paid labour could be hired as required in place of the reluctant conscript labour force. There was, however, no system of rating for highway maintenance as there was for bridges, and it would be a very long time before it was introduced.

Whereas the old system of presentment had not given the justices any strictly administrative powers they now assumed an administrative role under the 1555 Act which was the foundation on which the English highway system was based for the next three centuries. It was confirmed and extended under Elizabeth I and continued to develop in succeeding reigns and under the Commonwealth. These milestones will be mentioned as we reach them chronologically, but a comprehensive review of the justices' highway involvement will be postponed until we reach the eighteenth century when it had attained its zenith.

Gaols

The situation regarding gaols remained the same under the early Tudors as it had been in previous centuries, save that in 1504 they were placed under the control of the county sheriffs.[117] The common gaol was usually in a castle or some municipal building, and was not purpose-built as a prison. When no common gaol was readily available imprisonment might take place in a private house. This could happen when a constable made an arrest and was then obliged to take his prisoner into custody in his own home unless he could find some other secure place. In most instances detention was only temporary pending trial or until an amerciament had been paid. It was not until much later that it became a principal form of punishment in itself; the more usual types of sentence imposed in the sixteenth and seventeenth centuries will be listed in the next chapter.

The justices had a supervisory role in the prison administration and they were often required by the Council to inquire into specific instances of incarceration, whether in a gaol or elsewhere. The Essex justices, for example, were ordered to call the bailiffs of Colchester before them and to find out why certain persons were being kept imprisoned in the castle at Colchester.[118]

Changes in prison administration, in which the justices were to play

117.   19 Hen. VII, c. 10.
118.   APC, 1558-70, 26.

a prominent role, were to take place under Elizabeth as part of the Poor Law system, but a foretaste of this was provided by an Act of Henry VIII[119] which authorized justices in certain counties to decide which towns were to have gaols and to summon high constables and officers of the municipalities to discuss the question with them and to determine the amount of money required for the gaol's construction. The justices could then levy a rate on the inhabitants for the amount required to build the gaols, and could appoint collectors with authority to collect the rate from individuals and to levy distress if necessary. The justices were also empowered to appoint two surveyors to ensure that the gaols had been properly built. Both surveyors and collectors were accountable to the justices and might receive payment for their labours at the justices' discretion. If any money were left over from the rate after the work was completed the justices could distribute it as alms to the prisoners. It was the stated intention of the Act that all murderers and felons should be imprisoned only in these new gaols and nowhere else.

Military

The justices' early policing duties led in due course to their involvement in the maintenance of military forces. We have seen how they were able to make use of the *posse comitatus* to pursue and apprehend those suspected of offences against the criminal law. In time they came to be responsible for the enlisting, training and equipping of the local forces composed of all the able-bodied men below 60 in their respective areas.

In the Middle Ages the forces which served the King in his campaigns abroad were not made up of the local levies but were mainly an agglomeration of private armies raised by nobles and a few of the leading knights. These same bands of retainers tended also to be used to suppress insurrections at home, but this had obvious disadvantages in that the same forces frequently conducted minor wars against each other and sometimes, especially in Henry VI's reign, against the King himself. At the beginning of the Tudor era, private armies still dominated the military scene. They were composed of armed servants and retainers and included tenants and some members of the local gentry who enlisted for service. All wore the livery of the magnate whom they served, and it was such bodies of henchmen who intimidated juries and disrupted Quarter Sessions, as we saw earlier. Henry VII sought to reserve to the King the sole right to raise armed forces, and a number of Acts were passed to suppress livery and maintenance. In 1504, it was enacted that two justices, including one from the *Quorum*, should summon "all such persons as they shall think

119.   23 Hen. VIII, c. 7.

to be suspect," examine at their discretion and certify to the King's Bench the names of persons found to be retained. It was some time, however, before the Tudors were able to dispense entirely with forces raised by their magnates.

The institution of the office of Lord Lieutenant was an important step towards the replacement of private armies with a national force organized on a local basis. The forces at the disposal of the Lieutenant were local levies raised under Commissions of Muster, and they could be used for national defence against a foreign invader as well as for quelling internal uprisings. There were even occasions when the King, without any legal right, sent some of them overseas. The mustering, training and equipping of these forces, which came to be called the militia, was the task of the justices and the Deputy Lieutenants. They were also required from time to time to recruit soldiers for some specific undertaking and to arrange transport and supplies. Each county was told how many men it was to levy.[120]

The records of the Privy Council are full of directions to justices on military matters. The county justices of Nottingham and Derby are to muster men on behalf of the new Lord Lieutenant, the Earl of Westmorland.[121] In Rutland, they are rebuked for failing to levy men,[122] while in Sussex, where they have failed to levy and arm troops as ordered, the Lord Lieutenant, Lord Buckhurst, is commanded to tell the defaulting justices to present themselves before the Council.[123] In Hertfordshire, on the other hand, the justices must not levy tenants of Sir John Mordaunt because he has been appointed to serve with them himself.[124] In Northumberland, they are criticized for not being prepared when the Scots crossed the border and burnt and pillaged villages and houses, "which might well have been prevented if they had looked in time convenient to the same." In future they must be ready with forces under their authority fully equipped with armour and weapons.[125]

Correspondence on military and other matters did not always originate with the Council. Often it was in response to a question from the justices themselves or to a complaint from elsewhere. The Nottingham justices, for example, asked the Council whether they should serve with their forces northward under the Earl of Shrewsbury and were told to place themselves under his command and under that of no one else.[126]

Sometimes an order directed that horses as well as men and armour

120.   DP, 1581-1590, 175.
121.   APC, 1556-1588, 49.
122.   *Ibid.*, 152.
123.   APC, 1589-90, 166.
124.   APC, 1556-1558, 162.
125.   *Ibid.*, 138.
126.   *Ibid.*, 117.

should be provided,127 and, in addition to supplying armed cavalry, the justices might be required to provide horses for messengers.128 The impressing of men for service in the navy or the army overseas was often the job of officers specially appointed for the purpose by commission. On these occasions the justices were expected to give them such support as they required. Thus in 1557, the justices and sheriffs of Gloucestershire and Somerset were told to aid and assist an officer who was impressing soldiers and mariners and, when some of those impressed had escaped, they were to apprehend them and return them to service.129 Deserters were also the subject of legislation. An Act of 1511 declared that any soldiers "who depart out of the King's service without licence of the King's Lieutenant" were to be deemed felons, and the justices were to examine such cases and where appropriate punish the offenders even though the desertion had taken place outside the county.130

Impressment was used to supply men for the British army and navy only, but although no force was involved in recruiting for allied armies there were occasions when the justices were asked to encourage men to serve. In 1597 they were requested to urge volunteers to serve with the army in the United Provinces because these forces were besieging Dunkirk "which had been such ill neighbour" to the maritime parts of England.131

In addition to men and their weapons, the justices were frequently ordered to produce supplies. This applied particularly to the naval forces for whom food, timber, hemp and other requisites had to be produced.132

The organization as well as the equipping and training of the militia was in the hands of the justices and the Deputy Lieutenants. This gave rise to problems which also figured in the correspondence of the Council. For example, at the beginning of Elizabeth's reign, a letter went to Lord Wentworth and the other justices in Suffolk about one John Brown whom they had appointed as one of the captains of the county levies. Brown claimed that he was not up to the job. The Council told the justices to inquire and, if they thought fit, to appoint another in his place.133 Similarly, the Devon justices appointed Symon Worth to lead certain levies, but he said that he was over 60 and infirm, so the justices were told to inquire and if necessary appoint someone else.134

---

127.   DP, 1547-80, 343.
128.   APC, 1556-1558, 236.
129.   *Ibid.,* 141.
130.   3 Hen. VIII, c. 5.
131.   CSP Dom., 1597, 559.
132.   APC, 1556-1558, 70; 1571-1575, 124; 1575-1577, 343; 1589-1590, 390.
133.   APC, 1558-70, 124.
134.   *Ibid.,* 128.

Fortifications and signal beacons were also the responsibility of the justices. Whenever there was thought to be a threat from overseas, orders went to those in coastal counties to ensure that beacons were set up and watches kept along the shore.[135] Parliament as well as the Council took a keen interest in the matter when they thought there was danger of invasion. In 1512 the Cornwall justices were ordered by statute to "ride and view all the said South-Coast from Plymouth Westward to Lands End," and to designate such towns and parishes as they thought fit to erect bulwarks and fortifications. The mayors and constables of the areas so designated were in turn given power to employ all the inhabitants in the work. The justices in areas other than Cornwall were to take the same steps in respect of any piece of coast where they thought that a landing might be made.[136] These duties fell upon the justices particularly heavily when an attack by Spanish forces seemed imminent in 1588.

Pirates were as great a menace at sea as the gangs of robbers were on the land and sometimes special measures had to be taken. In 1564, justices, sheriffs, and mayors were ordered to assist the town of Bristowe to furnish and put to sea ships to suppress pirates operating between Bristowe and the Scilly Isles.[137] Similarly on the East coast, the justices were to assist the Vice-Admiral of Norfolk and Suffolk to suppress pirates.[138]

The use of the military in the suppression of riots has already been touched upon. Legislation against riots and unlawful assemblies was prolific under the Tudors and began soon after the accession of Henry VII.[139] It was enforced by the justices, who called upon the militia as they thought fit.

How was the cost of the military commitment defrayed? The necessary funds were raised through rates, the justices arranging for their assessment, collection and disbursement, for all of which the justices were accountable. It was rare for the Council to find it necessary to goad the justices into raising money once the expenditure had been incurred, but not uncommon for them to call for the accounts. Thus the Hertfordshire justices were required to certify their proceedings in procuring returns of the sums collected and expended on armour and munitions,[140] while the Lord Lieutenant and justices of Buckinghamshire had to account for money raised and expended on armour and weapons in certain hundreds.[141] Apart from the training of the militia, the government had long been concerned, as we have seen,

135.   DP, 1547-1587, 7, 8.
136.   4 Hen. VIII, c. 1.
137.   APC, 1558-70, 164.
138.   *Ibid.,* 244.
139.   11 Hen. VII, c. 3 and 7. 19 Hen. VII, c. 13.
140.   DP, 1547-1587, 374.
141.   *Ibid.,* 376, see also 377, and APC, 1586-1587, 388.

that every male citizen should be proficient in the use of the longbow and statutes were passed to ensure that no other sports or games should interfere. These laws continued well into the sixteenth century but, as has also been noted, the longbow was being superseded by new types of weapon. This change can be seen by comparing Acts passed under Henry VIII. Early in the century, an Act required all subjects to have bows and arrows ready in their houses and to practice using them. Judges of Assize and Justices of the Peace were to investigate all premises within their respective areas and those in default were to be fined 12 pence per month. The justices were also to appoint bowyers to make bows in every county, city and borough.[142] Twelve years later, another Act repeated the restriction, mentioned earlier, on the possession of crossbows but also attempted to discourage the use of handguns. The qualification for possessing either weapon was raised to £100 and the penalty to be imposed by the justices on offenders was £10.[143] This Act was confirmed eight years later, but with certain provisos. The authorities had begun to appreciate that there was some merit in a gun used as a personal weapon, and accordingly the Act allowed handguns to be used for practice shooting at butts within certain limits and they could also be owned and used by anyone living within five miles of the coast or within 12 miles of the border with Scotland.[144] Before the end of the century the justices' interest had shifted to that of ensuring that militiamen were proficient in handling muskets.

Wales

Before concluding our review of the position under the first four Tudors it must be noted that during this period Justices of the Peace made their first appearance in Wales. There is no evidence that either Justices or Keepers of the Peace existed in Wales until they were introduced there by Henry VIII in 1535. A full account of the establishment of the first Welsh justices and of their subsequent progress will be given in vol. III.

142.   3 Hen. VIII, c. 3.
143.   25 Hen. VIII, c. 17.
144.   33 Hen. VIII, c. 6.

CHAPTER VIII

THE ELIZABETHANS
ESTABLISHMENT OF ROYAL AUTHORITY
THROUGH THE JUSTICES OF THE PEACE

The justices become men of all work and rulers of the countryside - Government of the country by Queen and Council through the justices - Supervision and intervention by the Council - Guidance from printed textbooks - New administrative functions - Personnel of the commissions at the end of the sixteenth century

THE JUSTICES OF THE PEACE under Elizabeth I were described by Holdsworth as "men-of-all-work" and by G.M. Trevelyan and the Webbs as the "rulers of the countryside" and "of the county." By the end of the reign they were concerned in every aspect of the life of the local population and their duties had become so multifarious that, as Maitland was to write later:

"Long ago lawyers abandoned all hope of describing the duties of a justice in any methodic fashion and the alphabet became the one possible connecting thread."[1]

Sir Thomas Smith in *De Republica Anglorum* wrote of the Justices of the Peace in this period that: "There was never in any Commonwealth devised a more wise, a more dulce and gentle, nor a more Christian way to rule the people." To modern eyes this enthusiasm may seem excessive, but there is no doubt that the Justices of the Peace system was unique and that it was generally accepted as being better fitted to deal with the problems of the sixteenth century than any that had existed previously or were to be found in other lands at that time.

This remarkable situation was achieved during the last half of the century with the addition of a new class of governmental duties to the justices' existing police, judicial and administrative functions, but there was no diminution in the various fields of responsibility in which they had become involved during the previous 200 years. Under the Elizabethans the emphasis was placed upon social and economic functions in which the paternalistic government, inspired by the Queen's Secretary of State, William Cecil (later Lord Burghley), took an ever increasing interest, but at the same time the justices' peace-keeping and judicial functions continued as before.

1.   *Justice and Police,* p. 84.

Although a strong and stable government was established during Elizabeth's reign, the country was far from enjoying a long period of peace and quiet. On her accession her position was precarious, as was shown by the Northern Rebellion in 1569-70, and it was by no means certain at first that the people would accept her. Part of the unrest was due to sectarian strife which had been generated by Henry VIII and which continued throughout the reigns of his three children. There was also much disruption from the war with Spain. This did tend to unite the population in allegiance to their Sovereign, but when the foreign threat subsided it was replaced by other disruptive influences - political, social and ecclesiastical.

The justices' peace-keeping role therefore remained paramount. They, together with the sheriffs and constables, were still the only police authority. The hue and cry was still followed. A justice still spent much time taking sureties to be of good behaviour. The practice was also growing of arrest by justices on the evidence of others, whereas previously there was no legal authority to arrest save on their own personal suspicion.[2]

Similarly, the justices' judicial work in the disposal of criminal cases remained of prime importance, and even increased in volume as statutes transferred to them jurisdiction over numerous minor offences. Although Quarter Sessions remained the principal court of trial, more work of a judicial nature was being placed on justices out of sessions and in some cases it was given to a single justice.

In addition to this, the justices' administrative role, especially in the field of trade, labour and highways, was extended considerably, and on top of it all they were made to enter a new area of social economy.

The material available to the historian when researching the work of the justices in the last half of the sixteenth century is far greater in volume and extent than for earlier periods. Much of this is in the form of contemporary letters and other documents which have been preserved and which were the product of the better education and literacy of the upper classes. Even more valuable are the numerous text books for Justices of the Peace (or "JPs" as they came to be referred to) which were published during this period and which give us a clearer insight into their work and conditions of service than was possible previously.

Beginning of the justices' textbooks

Textbooks for JPs appeared with growing frequency throughout the

---

2.   *Eirenarcha,* Bk. I, c. 6.

sixteenth century in response to a demand from the increasingly literate justices and facilitated by the development of the printing trade. Sir Paul Vinogradoff and Miss Putnam[3] have identified 57 editions of treatises which were printed between 1506 and 1599. These began with the anonymous *Boke of Justyces of Peas*, first published in 1506, which contained summaries of the principal statutes relating to JPs and details of the numbers and qualifications of the justices, followed by a commentary on the charge to the jurors. There were also precedents of writs and indictments. Before the publication of the *Boke*, lectures on the peace, which were cited extensively by some, though not all, subsequent authors, were delivered by Thomas Marowe in 1503. Marowe, who must be regarded as the earliest authority on the subject, died in 1505. He was the youngest son of a wealthy grocer who was Mayor of London. He was called to the Bar by the Middle Temple, became a Serjeant-at-Law and served as a Commissioner of Assize and on the Commission of the Peace for Middlesex. Sometimes he and his friend, Chief Justice Frowyck of the Common Pleas, sat alone together as JPs in Middlesex. His lectures included a description of the distinction between conservators and Justices of the Peace and a full account of their powers in and out of sessions. As Miss Putnam points out, however, Marowe's lectures were of value to the legal justices on the *Quorum* rather than to the country gentlemen who made up the majority of the commission. The latter probably derived more benefit from the Justice of Assize who usually gave them a lengthy summary of their duties when he delivered the charge at the county Assizes which were attended by most of the Justices of the Peace twice a year. The Assize justices also gave dissertations about the JPs' work on the occasions when they attended Quarter Sessions.

The *Boke*, which appeared three years after the lectures, was better suited to serve as a manual for the general body of JPs and for the Clerk of the Peace. This was followed in 1510 by Sir Anthony Fitzherbert's well-known *L'Office et auctoryte des Justyces de peas*, of which an English translation was published in 1538. In 1583 a revised edition, which was virtually a new work, was produced by Richard Crompton.

The best-known textbook for JPs in the sixteenth century was the classic *Eirenarcha* or "The Office of Justices of the Peace," by William Lambard, which has already been mentioned. It was first published in 1581[4] and was regarded as the standard work on the subject until the

---

3.   B.H. Putnam, *Early Treatises on the Practice of Justices of the Peace in the Fifteenth and Sixteenth Centuries,* ed. Sir Paul Vinogradoff, *Oxford Studies in Social and Legal History,* vol. VII, 1924. This contains a careful study of all known treatises on the subject.

4.   This is the year printed on the title page of the first edition, but some claim that it was published in 1582.

mid-seventeenth century. Lambard, who was born in London in 1536, was a barrister and a Bencher of Lincoln's Inn. He later became a Chancery Master. In 1580 he was appointed to the Commission of the Peace for Kent where he had property. He stressed the moral and intellectual qualities required of a justice, who, he said, should "come furnished with three of the principal ornaments of a Judge, that is to say, with Justice, Wisdome, and Fortitute ... And above all, that he love and feare God aright, without whiche he can not bee accounted good at all."

Eirenarcha gives a brief historical sketch of the origins of the JPs and describes their office and its functions, citing the relevant statutes. Lambard explains how to become a JP, what are the qualifications and how many are appointed, commenting that in his day there were far too many. He writes at length about the commission and the charge to the jury. His work is divided into four books: I: "What Justices of the Peace be, and why they are called Justices of the Peace;" II: "The functions of one JP out of Sessions;" III: "Cases dealt with by 2, 3 or more justices " and IV: "Quarter Sessions." Much space is devoted to the forms to be used for indictments, presentments and other documents.

Historians are also indebted to Lambard for a book on the constables, and particularly for his diary, or *Ephemeris* as he called it, which records his service as a justice and notes the events which occurred on each occasion when he sat. This gives an intimate insight into the operation of the commission at this time. Unlike *Eirenarcha*, which was written for the benefit of his fellow magistrates, the *Ephemeris* was intended to assist him in performing his own duties.

While referring to the principal written works on JPs of the sixteenth century, it may be helpful to continue the story with a brief account of subsequent literature on the subject. In the following century the most widely read manual was Dalton's *Country Justice*, published in 1618 and re-published throughout the seventeenth and first half of the eighteenth century. Coke, in his *Institutes,* published in 1628, devotes a chapter to JPs, but this can have been of little value to those on the contemporary commissions and is of no assistance to the historian. A more useful work was *The Justice of the Peace, his calling and qualifications,* by E. Bohun, published in 1693. This stressed the need to preserve the established church and the monarchy and to enforce the laws against conventicles and recusants. It also referred to the fact that justices tended to be divided into hostile groups. Another useful work of this period was Shephard's *Sure Guide for his Majesties Justices of the Peace,* published in 1663. There was also an anonymous guide for clerks which was published in 1682 and gave a useful account of the procedure of the courts. This work, *The Office of the Clerk of the*

Assize, together with the Office of Clerk of the Peace, is an excellent authority on the procedure of the justices at Quarter Sessions under the Tudors and the Stuarts. At the beginning of the eighteenth century, W. Nelson of the Middle Temple published a substantial work on the *Justice of the Peace,* and a book on JPs in Scotland was published by William Forbes in 1707 (another on Scottish justices by Gilbert Hutcheson appeared in 1815), but one of the greatest treatises on JPs appeared in 1755 under the hand of the Reverend Richard Burn. Educated at Oxford, Burn was a lawyer and also one of the clerical justices who figured prominently on the commissions of the eighteenth century. He was a JP for both Cumberland and Westmorland and chairman of Quarter Sessions. He became Chancellor of the diocese of Carlisle in 1765. His book on the *Justice of the Peace and the Parish Officer* passed through 30 editions and was the standard work on the subject until well into the nineteenth century when the scene changed with the age of reform.

The first periodical publications, to keep the justices abreast of current developments, appeared with the advent of the reforming era. The first number of the the *Justice of the Peace* was published in January 1837 and has continued to appear regularly ever since. The opening article of the then fortnightly journal explains the reason behind the new venture:

"While the Agency of the Press is resorted to by several of the other Orders of Society, as the Clergy, the Medical, and a Branch of the Legal Profession, for protecting their interests, and supplying the information properly belonging to each of them, it is a matter of some surprise that so large and influential a part of the Community as that comprising Justices of the Peace, Clerks of the Peace, Clerks of Petty Sessions, Town Clerks, and Parochial Officers, is yet without this universal medium of Communication; especially when it is considered that to most of them, it is of primary importance to be furnished with the earliest and most correct Intelligence upon the many, and often complicated questions with which they have to deal."

At this time, Burn's work, now in three volumes, was still in demand, and there were also much shorter handbooks, such as a *Magistrates' Companion* by William Eagle, a barrister who was the first editor of the *Justice of the Peace,* and *The Practice of the Petty Sessions* by John Stone, also a barrister. In 1842, Samuel Stone, clerk to the justices for Leicester city, published *The Justices' Pocket Manual* which, as the author explained, was "intended to furnish, in a portable form, a convenient Alphabetical Reference to such Orders under the Penal

Criminal Law, as comprise the *ordinary* business of the Petty and Quarter Sessions." Since then, the *Manual,* which is published annually in three volumes and is no longer easily portable, has become the principal work of reference in all magistrates' courts in England and Wales. A comparison of the early editions with those of today gives a remarkable insight into the increasing volume and complexity of legislation relating to magistrates' courts which has been passed during the past 140 years.

When the Magistrates' Association of England and Wales was formed in 1920, they published their own journal for their members, *The Magistrate,* which appears monthly. The Commonwealth Magistrates' Association, founded in 1970, publishes the *Commonwealth Judicial Journal.*

The large amount of literature on the JPs which appeared in the sixteenth century may lead one to assume that a fundamental change occurred in the office during this period. This was not so. The many works on the subject were part of a vast quantity of law books which were printed at this time and, as already indicated, they were the product of a cultural revolution in England, involving better education and greater literacy and aided by effective methods of printing. What the books describe is a system which had been established in the two previous centuries. Under the Tudors there was very little change in the police and jurisdictional functions of the justices, and basically much of their administrative authority also remained the same, although extended by numerous additional duties. It was only near the end of the century that a new social service dimension emerged.

The books written in the sixteenth century and contemporary records show how the JPs had taken over most of the remaining business of the feudal and communal courts, although some of these continued to operate on a minor scale. (In 1589 an Act gave the court leet concurrent jurisdiction with the JPs in restricting the building of cottages).[5] The justices achieved their ascendancy through statutes which transferred to them jurisdiction over minor offences and also by attracting business through their ability to dispose of cases more quickly and effectively than the other courts.

The majority of the justices seem to have made a genuine effort to master the leading textbooks of their day and to follow the good advice which they contained. The private papers of the Elizabethan justices

---

5.   31 Eliz. c. 7.

show that most of them tried,6 though not always successfully, to base their conduct on the terms of their oath as paraphrased in verse by Lambard:

> "Doe equal right by rich and poore
>   as Wit and Law extends,
> Give none advice in any cause
>   that you before depends,
> Your Sessions hold as Statutes bid,
>   the forfeits that befall
> See entered well, and then estreat
>   them to the Chequer all
> Receive no fee but that is given
>   by King, good use, or right
> No precept send to party, self, but
>   in indifferent wight."

Quarter Sessions

A substantial amount of the justices' work was performed out of sessions mainly on peace-keeping and military duties and to a lesser extent on highways, trade and other matters. Quarter Sessions, however, continued to be the core of their judicial and administrative authority, the centre of local government and the channel through which contact was maintained with the central government. It was the meeting place for virtually all those who held positions of importance in the county. It was there that the more important criminal cases were tried, where many of the acts performed by single justices or by a limited group were ratified or disallowed, and where the constables had to make their reports.

Quarter Sessions continued to sit in various types of accommodation, often in a municipal building in a county town or in a substantial inn, but not always in the same place. In the larger counties they began to be held under a peripatetic system whereby they visited certain centres in turn on a regular basis. Thus, in Somerset they always sat successively at Wells, Ilchester, Taunton and Bridgewater; in the county palatine of Lancaster, as we have seen, at Lancaster, Preston, Ormskirk or Wigan (alternately) and Salford. In 1599 West Riding Quarter Sessions were held, with adjournments, in nine

---

6.   There were certainly some who made no effort to behave properly. In 1577 the Lord Lieutenant of Kent, Lord Abergavenny, described one of his county justices in a letter to Lord Burghley: "By the means that he is a Justice of the Peace he over beareth our men with such disordinate dealings both against law and conscience. When malefactors heare of any warrants out for them, they go straight to Sir Waler Waller's house, and are there harboured that the constables dare not come thither without danger of their lives."

different towns. In each of these cases the sessions dealt with matters arising within the hundreds adjoining the town. Where, however, a county had one predominant town, reasonably accessible from all parts, the sessions were usually held there. In Gloucestershire they almost always sat in the city of Gloucester, where 24 sessions were held during the six years 1595 to 1601, and only one elsewhere - at Cirencester in 1597. Occasionally, exceptional circumstances led to the holding of special sessions in a particular town for a specific purpose. Thus, in July 1598, sessions were held at Chipping Sodbury in Gloucestershire by three justices with a hundred jury to deal with a case of forcible entry under the statute 8 Henry VI, c. 9, which required the justices to whom complaint was made in such a case to inquire into the matter "in some good town next to the tenements so entered." Sometimes the sessions were held in different buildings in the same town on different occasions. At Southwark, the Surrey sessions were held within a short space of time at four separate inns as well as at the New Hall and the Town Hall. The York sessions were normally held in the council chamber on the Ouse bridge, but when this was damaged by floods they moved to the "closet within the Minster." There might also be separate Quarter Sessions for a borough and a county where the borough had been granted the privilege by Royal Charter. In Gloucestershire, the city of Gloucester and the liberties of Cheltenham and the Slaughters each had their own sessions distinct from those of the county.

Virtually all offences were dealt with at Quarter Sessions other than treason and murder and some relating to morals and religion which were still tried in the ecclesiastical courts. Treason and murder were tried at Assizes to which other serious felonies were also sometimes, but not always, committed. An exhaustive list of cases triable at Quarter Sessions is set out in Lambard's *Eirenarcha*. The most common were cases of general nuisance, including particularly drunkenness, common scolds and keeping disorderly alehouses. Alehouse keepers also appeared frequently on charges of selling or brewing ale on Sundays, permitting unlawful games and harbouring rogues and vagabonds. The most common of modern offences was petty larceny, but there were also many assaults, batteries, forcible entries, detainers, housebreakings, hedgebreakings, breaking into closes, unlawful assemblies, riots and routs. Nightwalkers, or suspicious persons who went about at night and had no apparent means of livelihood, often appeared before the sessions. Breaches of the game laws were not as numerous as they became later. On the other hand, there were many charges of libel, especially against the authorities, of barratry (stirring up quarrels between neighbours), extortion and fraud. Actions were often brought against officials, sometimes for neglect of their duties, sometimes for extortion, for the acceptance of bribes and for offences against individuals. Overseers of the poor and churchwardens were presented for failure to perform their duties and for not holding their monthly meetings. There were disputes between masters and servants and breaches of the wages and prices regulations. In the sphere of trade and commerce many charges were brought under various statutes against forestallers (who bought up goods on their way to fairs and markets and forced up the price), regrators (who bought grain, victuals and cattle at wholesale prices for resale) and engrossers (who bought up the whole stock of a commodity to create a monopoly), as mentioned in the last chapter.

Attendance at sessions varied greatly. Some justices were assiduous in performing their duties while others were not, and risked being dropped from the commission in consequence. There were also considerable variations in the attendance in different counties, and at different centres and times of year in the same county. These discrepancies were due largely to difficulties of travel. Some of those on the commissions were exonerated from attendance. This applied to most of the magnates at the head of each commission, many of whom do not appear to have performed any duties either in or out of sessions. There were, however, notable exceptions and a number of leading noblemen with large estates in a county took an active interest in the work. Lambard's *Ephemeris* records many occasions when he sat with Lord Cobham, the Lord Lieutenant. Most of those who were expected to undertake the main burden of the work were men of less degree, but their liability to be removed for failure to perform their duties does not seem to have had much effect on absenteeism, probably because threats of dismissal were not often carried out. Attendance depended, of course, upon the size of the commission, the difficulties of travel and the frequent periods of epidemic; but over the country as a whole a very rough average of attendances at each sitting of Quarter Sessions at the end of the century was a quarter of the total number of working justices. At some sessions only two or three justices were present, but usually there were considerably more; sometimes over 20. Lambard criticized the poor attendances and also deprecated the haste in which the business was disposed of so that sometimes the sessions dispersed after about three hours. The lawyers, like Lambard himself, though fewer in number, were usually the best attenders at sessions, but what little evidence is available suggests that the others may have spent more time on out-of-court duties.

A principal cause of absenteeism was the tendency of many JPs to spend much of their time in London whither they were lured by the attractions of the court and the theatre. As we have seen, the Council ordered them to return to their own counties and also directed the

Lord Mayor of London in 1586 to find out and report their names. There is no evidence that this had more effect on the elusive justices than previous admonishments.

The practice of transferring all the more serious and difficult cases to Assizes continued under Elizabeth, although some capital offences were still dealt with at Quarter Sessions to the end of her reign. In 1598, for example, 18 felons were hanged on the order of the Devon[7] justices at their Epiphany sessions, followed by a further 12 after the Easter sessions. During this time the Queen's Bench Judges were clearly endeavouring to limit the justices' criminal jurisdiction. Lambard was probably right in suggesting that the justices themselves were not unduly perturbed by this because it relieved them of some of the extra pressure to which they were subjected by the new administrative legislation.

Work out of sessions

The acquisition of powers by justices acting out of sessions has been described in previous chapters, and we have seen that these increased considerably under the early Tudors. The process continued under Elizabeth, and some of this development was mentioned in the last chapter. One whole book of *Eirenarcha,* which accounted for nearly a third of the 634 pages of Lambard's work, was devoted to the duties of a single justice, and there was more relating to two or more justices. Much of this described their increased administrative work, which is mentioned later in this chapter, but they also acquired certain additional judicial functions during Elizabeth's reign.

The powers of a single justice were confirmed and extended by a number of Elizabethan statutes. He was given further authority to enforce the law relating to the preservation of game (23 Eliz., c. 10), rogues and vagabonds (39 Eliz., c. 4), thefts of horses (31 Eliz., c. 12), and from gardens and orchards (43 Eliz., c. 7). His powers to order rioters to disperse and to arrest those who disobeyed were confirmed by 1 Eliz., c. 16, and a further statute of forcible entry (31 Eliz., c. 11) empowered him to arrest an offender and to reinstate the ousted party.

When committing a person to gaol for any reason the single justice had to send the gaoler a *mittimus* giving the name of the offender, a description of the offence and a statement of the period for which he was to be kept in custody. The justice also had to send a record to the Exchequer so that, in Lambard's words, "the Barons may cause the King's dutie to be levied to his use."

7.   Devon RO, QSO/I (QS Order Bk., 1592-1600).

As mentioned earlier, the single justice's civil jurisdiction was limited to the settlement of disputes between masters and servants and between masters and apprentices (5 Eliz., c. 14). In the sphere of trade his powers of supervision were extended by several statutes (27 Eliz., c. 14; 39 Eliz., c. 16 and c. 20), and he could also issue a certificate, which in certain circumstances could be produced in defence of a charge of forestalling of corn (13 Eliz., c. 25).

Among the new duties assumed by a single justice during the reign were several relating to religion. He could fine for non-attendance at church (1 Eliz., c. 2) and certify to the King's Bench non-attendance for a period of 12 months (23 Eliz., c. 1). He could also move Quarter Sessions to make an order that any seditious sectaries, who obstinately refused to attend church should adjure the realm (35 Eliz., c. 1).

The powers of two or more justices were also extended under Elizabeth. Under 5 Eliz., c. 4, they could deal with offences against the Statute of Labourers; under 39 Eliz., c. 4, they could levy forfeitures incurred on the conviction of rogues and vagabonds; and under 18 Eliz., c. 3, they could make orders in respect of bastard children. Other new administrative and governmental duties are described below.

Sentencing

Until the advent of houses of correction, described *post*, no thought was given to the rehabilitation of offenders, and sentences were designed to be punitive, retributive and deterrent. Lambard drew attention to the range of punishments available to the JPs, commenting: "A JP is superior to the old Conservators of the Peace who had only Coertion or Prehension in a few cases, and no Jurisdiction in any Cause. The justices have both Jurisdiction and also power of Execution and Punishment." He divided the punishments into three categories: corporal, pecuniary or infamous.

Corporal punishment according to Lambard might be capital or non-capital. A very large number of offences were capital for which the penalty in most cases was hanging. Death was the sentence for all felonies, which also entailed (until 1870) forfeiture of the offender's property. Even some minor offences carried the death penalty, the most notorious being to be found without any means of livelihood. The most frequent offences in this category were what came to be called "grand larceny," which was the theft of anything worth more than one shilling (below that amount it was petty larceny, a non-capital offence). The harshness of this law led to cases where an article was deliberately undervalued by the jury or the justices to save the offender from the gallows; but there were many cases where he or she was not so fortunate even as late as the nineteenth century. In *Barnaby Rudge*,

Charles Dickens tells the story, which is believed to be true, of Mary Jones, a mother aged 19, who stole a piece of cloth worth more than a shilling for her two children. She was convicted and hanged. Court records contain many references to cases of this kind. A form of capital punishment which was confined to offences against religion was burning at the stake. This was mainly imposed in Mary I's reign when several hundred heretics were burned, but numbers of Roman Catholics were also sentenced to death for treason under Elizabeth and many were hanged, drawn and quartered.

Able-bodied prisoners who had been sentenced to death might escape this penalty by being sent to serve in the galleys, but not many were treated in this way, largely, it seems, because the justices were unwilling to involve the county in the payment of the £3 per annum required for their upkeep. It was for this reason that in James I's reign the justices exercised their power to conscript numbers of lesser offenders into the army and navy where they might render profitable service instead of being a burden on the county.

The non-capital punishments involved a wide range of sentences, most of which have already been mentioned. Whipping was the universal treatment for minor offences. It was usually inflicted in an ostentatious manner so as to be a deterrent to others as well as to the offender. Statutes which created an offence sometimes stipulated that the whipping was to be carried out in the market place, sometimes on several consecutive occasions, and it was not uncommon for an offender to be whipped continuously from one part of a town to another, both men and women being stripped to the waist. Both parents of a bastard child were usually ordered to be whipped together, either in the market place or in the churchyard after evening prayer.

The cutting-off of ears was a penalty for persistent vagrancy, and of hands for a variety of deeds, including the writing of seditious books. Branding the hands, face and shoulder were probably intended as a means of identifying recidivists as well as a punishment.

Other forms of punishment designed to humiliate the offender and to deter others were the stocks, pillory and tumbrel or hurdle. From 1405 every parish was required to provide and maintain stocks and it usually had a pillory and whipping post as well. Like the pillory, the stocks laid the offender open to public ridicule, but they could also cause considerable physical suffering. The records of the King's Bench sitting at Westminster in 1384 mention that two men indicted for felony had not appeared for trial because the gaoler had put them in the stocks in winter-time and left them there so long that their feet rotted and they died. (The gaoler himself was tried *coram Rege* for having caused their deaths). Sometimes, however, the offender's plight was alleviated by his friends. Pepys, in his diary, records an occasion when a number of apprentices were rescued from the pillory by other apprentices, and Daniel Defoe, author of *Robinson Crusoe*, was sentenced to the pillory because of a book he wrote about dissenters, but he was protected by his friends who draped the pillory in flowers.

The tumbrel was usually used to take a convicted person to execution, but sometimes also to exhibit him to public gaze. Whipping might be carried out while the offender was tied to the back of a moving cart. The hurdle was also used to focus attention on a culprit. For example, a baker who baked defective bread might be drawn through a town on a hurdle where he was a target for missiles thrown by bystanders. It was often claimed, though usually without any supporting evidence, that the sight of the gallows, stocks, pillory and whipping post in public places deterred many a would-be criminal from persisting in his ways.

No mention is made by Lambard of the ducking-stool, perhaps because it was not as widely used as the other punishments. It was mostly applied to scolding women, but sometimes also to men, such as brewers of faulty ale or those who beat their wives unduly. It usually amounted to being tied to a seat on the end of a pole and immersed in a nearby pond or river. Whereas the immersion was supposed to deliver a short, sharp shock, it was often prolonged and the offender drowned.

Lambard also included imprisonment in his list of non-capital corporal punishments but, as we have seen, it was exceptional until the nineteenth century for imprisonment to be used as a punitive measure. On the other hand transportation of criminals to penal colonies overseas, which was introduced in 1598 (by the Act 39 Eliz., c. 4), came to be used extensively during the following two centuries. A principal aim of transportation was to put criminals to useful employment.

Pecuniary punishments were, of course, fines, amerciaments and confiscation which might be imposed in a number of different circumstances. The proceeds did not always go to the Crown. As we have seen, those incurred in respect of highway offences were spent on road repair. It was also common for a statute, when creating a new offence, to encourage prosecution by providing for part of the fine to be paid to the informer or prosecutor. A fine was the most likely penalty to be incurred by the justices themselves who were liable to be amerced for failure to perform their duties.

The "infamous punishments" to which Lambard referred arose largely in cases of conspiracy, involving forfeiture of land, and the removal of legal rights and outlawry.

There was a class distinction in the type of punishment which was inflicted on persons in different sections of the population. Whipping, branding and most other forms of corporal punishment were reserved for the lower classes, while those in the upper levels were subjected only to fines, forfeiture, outlawry, imprisonment and death. Even the latter had an element of class distinction in that those at the top end of the social scale were executed with an axe while the others were hanged.

Assizes

The Elizabethan Justices of the Peace were obliged to attend Assizes, and failure to do so incurred a fine. Such fines were ordered frequently but were not always estreated. One reason for requiring the justices' attendance was to instruct them in law and procedure and to enable them to discuss points of difficulty with the Judges, for, although most commissions contained a proportion of lawyer JPs, there was often a need to obtain authoritative interpretation. The Assize Judges therefore ensured that the JPs throughout the country operated within the common law in a reasonably uniform manner. The Judges' charges to the juries at Assizes often castigated the justices for failure to discharge their duties and sometimes accused them of corruption. The comments of the Judges show that justices were sometimes responsible for creating lawlessness instead of suppressing it. In 1561 the Judges were required to reduce the excessive size of the commissions by advising on the removal of those justices who were the retainers of other men. The numbers removed in this way were small and most of them were suspect Roman Catholics.

The Justices of the Peace for their part generally found it useful to be present at Assizes, partly because almost everyone of importance in the county attended Assizes in Elizabethan times and partly because they recognized the value of the instructions they received from the Judges. Many of them kept books in which they entered Assize orders. On the other hand they were not generally overawed by the Judges and did not hesitate to criticize them in communications with higher authority. The Judges were not superior to them in the social scale and some of the county magnates who were JPs clearly assumed that they were in a higher social position than many of the puisne Judges. Such men could well jeopardize a Judge's career by submitting an adverse report to the Council. An example of this is to be found in a letter from an Essex justice, Sir John Smythe, to Lord Burghley in 1589 which contains caustic criticism of the leniency of certain Assize Judges.

The rulers of the counties

Before the end of the sixteenth century the JPs as a body had replaced the feudal magnates and the principal churchmen as the most influential body in each locality. In counties they comprised almost all of the nobility, most of the prelates and a large proportion of the leading gentry. From the early years of Elizabeth's reign every secular peer, with only one or two exceptions, and about three-fifths of the spiritual peers were on the commissions. In the cities the office was automatically tied to that of mayor and of the principal officers. All justices were men of wealth. The combined class from which they were appointed accounted for only about two per cent of the population.

The list of justices in each commission began with the names of a number of exalted persons, starting always with the Lord Chancellor or Lord Keeper and the Lord Treasurer. These were usually followed by one or more bishops and possibly one or two court favourites. Also included were members of the Privy Council and certain Judges of the King's courts at Westminster and of Assize, together with the Lord Lieutenant and most, if not all, of the secular peers owning estates in the county. This group at the head of the commission formed, on average, about a quarter of the total. Only a small proportion of them took an active part in the work which was performed mostly by the remaining "working" justices. One of the latter was named in the commission as *Custos Rotulorum*. It was still unusual for the same person to hold office as *Custos* and Lord Lieutenant, though there were exceptions, such as the Earl of Pembroke who was Chancellor of the Household and also both Lieutenant and *Custos* of Kent.

An analysis of the composition of the Elizabethan and Stuart commissions is to be found in an erudite study by J.H. Gleason[8] which contains a careful and detailed examination of the JPs and their personal backgrounds in five representative English counties between 1558 and 1640. This shows that, whereas membership of the commission varied noticeably from county to county, there was an overall pattern which was common to them all.

Gleason's precise figures show that the working justices were composed almost entirely of landed gentry and lawyers, the latter being only about a quarter as numerous as the gentry who accounted for more than half the total on the commission. In addition to these, however, there were often one or two justices drawn from commerce and the junior clergy. The proportion of justices who were also on the *Quorum* increased throughout the reigns of Elizabeth and the first Stuarts, and consequently the majority were no longer legally qualified, although a substantial number had been educated at the Inns of Court.

8.   J.H. Gleason, *The Justices of the Peace in England, 1558 to 1640,* Oxford, 1969.

By 1630 almost all those on each of the five commissions examined by Gleason were on the *Quorum*.

He also examines the educational background of the justices, a matter which had considerable bearing on the work they performed. Prior to the Tudor period, the upper classes had received singularly little education in academic subjects and it was rare for them to attend a seat of learning, though from the early part of the fifteenth century some were attending one of the Inns of Court without becoming qualified lawyers. Under the Tudors, however, the sons of the nobility and the leading gentry attended the universities of Oxford and Cambridge or the Inns of Court, particularly the latter (the universities were still mainly concerned to provide clergy). As Gleason says, this cultural revolution transformed "the usual experience of the English gentry and aristocracy. From a group which received its training primarily in the skills of a feudalistic society, and its literary education largely at an elementary level and perhaps at home, it became one whose members commonly enrolled for study at the universities or the Inns of Court and not infrequently both."[9]

Gleason shows that, whereas very few of the justices at the beginning of Elizabeth's reign had been educated at any of these institutions, by 1584 nearly a half of the working justices had studied at one of the Inns (though by no means all were called to the Bar), and a quarter at Oxford or Cambridge, and one in seven had done both. The proportions continued to increase during the ensuing 50 years. At all these institutions they met young men from other parts of the kingdom and other sections of the community. In addition therefore to improving the intellectual standard of the justices, this experience broadened their outlook on a national and classless basis whereas previously it had been parochial and limited to their own social group.

The character which probably occurs to most people in the context of the Elizabethan JP is Shakespeare's Justice Shallow who, in spite of his manifest shortcomings, held the elevated position of a member of *Quorum* because he had read for the Bar. Although there may have been some justices of very inferior quality at this time there can be little doubt that Shallow was in no way typical of the men on the Elizabethan commissions. The question arises as to why Shakespeare, whose father[10] had been a magistrate in Stratford-on-Avon while serving for a year as bailiff, should have ridiculed the office by portraying such a miserable and contemptible country bumpkin. The answer could be simply that Shallow and his associates create an entertaining farce, but there is probably more in it than that.

9.   *Ibid.,* p. 85.
10.   The father, John Shakespeare, later fell into decline as a result of persecution by the bishop because of his Puritanism, and he ceased to be a magistrate.

According to tradition, young William was addicted to poaching deer in the park of Sir Thomas Lucy, a JP, who lived at Charlecote Park near Stratford, and Lucy's assiduous prosecution of Shakespeare in 1585 resulted in his being whipped and imprisoned and finally driven to flee to London.

Some dismiss this story as fiction, and it has been said that there were no deer at Charlecote, but there is sufficient circumstantial evidence to suggest that there may be some truth in it. It is quite possible that Justice Shallow was a caricature of Lucy who, like Shallow, was also a Commissioner of Musters. There can also be no doubt that there were some examples of Shallows and Silences in the contemporary commissions, and Shakespeare was justified in lampooning them, but it is clear from even a cursory study of sessions' records and other documents that the proceedings could not have been conducted by inept oafs. Had there been many such persons among the justices it is inconceivable that they would have discharged their multifarious duties as satisfactorily as they obviously did. Many of them were arrogant and determined to advance their own interests but they were also reasonably competent and possessed a fairly high sense of responsibility. There is plenty of evidence that most of those who formed the nucleus of magistrates in each county were upright, vigorous and efficient.

A number of justices of this period left diaries, letters and other papers which show that they were honest, dedicated and conscientious, and which also give an interesting picture of their daily lives and of the work which they performed during Elizabeth's reign and later. They show the multitude of onerous problems in which the JP was involved, some of which arose from other commissions, in addition to those of the peace, to which it was customary for the justices to be appointed. One of many such examples which can be found in local records was that of Sir Nathaniel Bacon,[11] of Stiffkey in Norfolk. In addition to the routine administration of the criminal law involving thefts, assaults, bastardies, witchcraft and other minor offences, Sir Nathaniel was also concerned regularly with vagrants, disputes over boundaries and commons, licensing alehouses and supervising high and petty constables. As well as performing these duties he had to direct his attention from time to time to regulating the export of grain, wool and leather, assessing and collecting subsidies and loans, detecting recusants and reporting the unseemly behaviour of incumbents to the bishop, and on one occasion dealing with the rebuilding of the pier at Cromer.

11.   A selection from Sir Nathaniel Bacon's papers was published by the Camden Society in 1915.

If Shakespeare did have a vendetta against Sir Thomas Lucy it did not taint all his references to justices, and a more accurate description of those who held office in his day is probably that given in *As You Like It*:

> "And then the justice,
> In fair round belly with good capon lined,
> With eyes severe and beard of formal cut,
> Full of wise saws and modern instances."

Appointment

Appointment to the commissions continued to be in the hands of the Lord Chancellor, often advised by the Judges of Assize and leading nobles in the county, who were expected to recommend on their own personal knowledge of the candidate. Such recommendations, however, did not necessarily secure appointment. There was careful scrutiny of the lists by the Chancellor and by other members of the Council, and particularly by Lord Burghley, who became Lord Treasurer and was himself included in every commission. This is clear from the detailed marginal notes made by Burghley in copies of the *libri pacis*[12] which were lists of the justices in each county. The lists were prepared from time to time and provide the most valuable source of information on the individuals who comprised the commissions. They were lists of existing justices, and Burghley's comments related to their suitability for retention. In 1587 the bishops were asked to report secretly on the conduct of the Justices of the Peace, and this seems to have been used by Burghley as a check on the information he had received from the Assize Judges.[13] There can be no doubt that there was equally careful scrutiny before anyone was appointed in the first place. Many names were added to or deleted from the list after it reached the Council and before it passed the Great Seal, the number of changes being far greater in the counties with which members of the Council were best acquainted. Under Elizabeth, influence at court became of greater importance than it had been before in securing appointment or in holding one's place on the commission, and a friend at court, or personal attendance there by the aspirant, was often necessary.[14] The group from which appointments were made, however,

---

12.   Lansdowne MS, 1218, British Museum. Gleason examines the significance of the annotations in *The Justices of the Peace in England*, p. 62 and ch. V.
13.   *Ibid.*, 103 ff. 85-86 v.
14.   Lawrence Stone, *The Crisis of the Aristocracy*, 1558-1641, p. 210. A.H. Smith, *The Elizabethan Gentry in Norfolk*, London Ph.D. thesis 1959, pp. 38-47 gives an account of court influence in the appointment of JPs.

was always small, and it would have taken a very powerful friend at court to ensure the selection of someone from outside that select body. There was a very clear distinction between the class of nobles, knights and esquires who were regarded as eligible to serve on a commission and other members of the population, though it was not impossible to cross the barrier.

Removal

JPs held office during the Sovereign's pleasure, as in theory they still do, and therefore the appointment could be determined at any time without showing cause. For the same reason it also ceased on the demise of the Crown, until this was altered partially by an Act of 1702,[15] and wholly by the Demise of the Crown Act 1901.[16] The power of the Crown to remove JPs throughout the United Kingdom is explained, *post.*[17]

Under Elizabeth, justices were removed from office for a variety of reasons, the most frequent being failure to perform their duties or not complying with religious requirements; and occasionally for political motives. There were, however, many threats of dismissal which were not carried out, probably because the men concerned were able to secure support at court and because the number of those regarded as suitable for appointment was so small that it was not easy to find acceptable replacements.

Conduct of the Justices of the Peace

Removal from the commission for any reason had come to be regarded as a serious disgrace. An example of this is to be found in the Council records of 1577. One Richard Shelley had been removed because he was "backward in religion." This proved to be a mistake and he was restored, but because of the stigma attaching to removal he was given special compensation by being also appointed to the *Quorum.*[18]

The conduct of JPs and other members of the upper classes had improved greatly since the previous century, yet the justices and their associates continued to behave in a manner which would have been considered highly unfitting by later generations. There were innumerable examples of justices who were quarrelsome and quick to engage in disputes with their neighbours, including fellow-justices. There were still some knights as well as nobles who appeared at

---

15.   1 Anne c. 2.
16.   1 Edw. VII, c. 5.
17.   Appendix VI, which discusses the power to remove justices from office.
18.   APC, February 19, 1577.

sessions and Assizes with armed retainers and disrupted the proceedings. There were also instances, even at the end of the century, of magnates intimidating justices and juries and shielding their servants from the law, though their ability to do so had been significantly curtailed by the end of Elizabeth's reign.

Livery was still an important issue notwithstanding Acts forbidding the giving of livery to other than household servants. The livery of a powerful magnate could enable the wearer to exercise influence which he would not otherwise enjoy. During the conflict between Lord Burghley and the Earl of Leicester it was said that many JPs openly wore Leicester's livery. Throughout the Tudor period there were constant struggles for position among the upper classes which often led to violence. Members of society were quick-tempered and fiercely dedicated to the acquisition of prestige, and appointment to the Commission of the Peace was an indication of success in achieving their aspirations.

There were also cases of venality but these were probably confined to a small proportion of the justices, though examples were also to be found among the higher, professional Judges. The subject was raised in Parliament in December 1601,[19] during debates on two Bills, the first against cursing and swearing for which a single JP was to impose fines on the evidence of two witnesses, and the second on compulsory attendance in church. One Member, Mr Glascock, was opposed to giving justices any more responsibility because, he said, they already did their work so badly and were open to bribery. "A Justice of the Peace is a living creature that for half a dozen chickens will dispense with a whole dozen of penal statutes." He was taken to task by other Members. Sir Francis Hastings said: "I never, in my life, heard Justices of the Peace taxed before in this sort. For ought I know, Justices of the Peace be men of quality, honesty, experience and justice." The Comptroller said: "I much marvel that men will, or dare, accuse Justices of the Peace, ministers to her Majesty without whom the Commonwealth cannot be." In response, Glascock qualified his remark by explaining: "I spoke only of the inferior sort of justices, commonly called basket justices." This did not satisfy all his critics, Sir Robert Worth commenting that the office of JP was too good for the likes of Glascock who would obviously never receive such an appointment himself.

The same debate also contained some informative comments on the work of the contemporary justices. Robert Owen, another Member, opposed the first Bill on the ground that justices already had too much to do. "I think it too great a trouble, and they are ever laden with a

19.   Corbett's *Parliamentary History*, vol. I, p. 994.

number of penal statutes, yea, a whole alphabet, as appears by Hussey in the time of Henry VII. And this is so obvious that a Justice of the Peace's house will be like a Quarter Sessions, with the multitude of these complaints."

Whatever may have been the views of Members of Parliament, the majority of whom were either JPs themselves or closely associated with them, there was plenty of critical comment from the Council. In a speech at the closing of the session of Parliament on May 29, 1571,[20] Lord Keeper Sir Nicholas Bacon said, in the presence of the Queen, that Her Majesty "granteth out her commission into every of her shires to men which are or should be of greatest consideration within the limits of their charge," but in fact many of these JPs "are yearly once at least called into Her Highness's Star Chamber; and there in her Majesty's name exhorted, admonished and commanded to see the due execution of their charges." He pointed out that JPs had been specifically chosen from among many throughout the realm and entrusted by their Sovereign with a specific charge, yet many of them failed in the duty placed upon them for the good of the state. A justice "should by his oath and duty set forth justice and right" yet against his oath he offered "injury and wrong." Having been "specially chosen amongst a number by a prince to appease all hardship and controversies," he became "a sower and maintainer of strife and sedition, by swaying and leading of juries according to his will, acquitting some for gain, indicting others for malice," befriending some who were his servants or in his livery and overthrowing others as enemies. "His winks, frownings and countenances may direct all inquests." The Lord Keeper went on to say that the remedy lay in greater care in the choice of candidates for appointment and in "sharp corrections" imposed on offenders who should be removed from office "to their perpetual ignominy." He proposed that there should be visits of special commissioners to each county every two or three years to check the justices' performance, but this suggestion does not seem to have been followed.

Nicholas Bacon's rebuke appears to have had little effect as it was felt necessary to deliver a further speech on very similar lines at the end of the sessions four years later.[21] The JPs were again criticized severely for failing to implement the laws and the Lord Keeper observed that not to execute the laws "is to breed a contempt of laws and law-makers, and of all magistrates." He concluded that the serious problems which had arisen had been due to the justices' failure to perform their duties. Then came a most interesting comment which forecast the possible replacement of JPs with paid, professional

20.   *Ibid.,* p. 770.
21.   *Ibid.,* p. 807.

magistrates. Unless the justices mended their ways, "Her Majesty shall then be driven, clean contrary to her most gracious nature and inclination, to appoint and assign private men for profit and gain sake, to see her penal laws to be executed." Up until now the Queen had relied upon "having her laws executed by men of credit and estimation for the love of justice, uprightly and indifferently," but if this failed then she would be compelled "to commit the execution of them to those who in respect of profit and gain will see them executed with all extremity." It was implied that the Queen would much prefer the JPs whom she regarded as of superior quality to the possible alternatives, but it were better to have the job done by inferior bureaucrats than not to have it done at all under the gentry.

In 1795 Lord Keeper Puckering referred to the excessive number of ineffective justices in his address at the first sitting of the Star Chamber. As usual the JPs living in or near London were ordered to attend. After commenting that the number of JPs "are growne almoste infinite to the hinderance of justice," so that there were "more justices than justice," he added that many of them were "insufficiente, unlearned, negligente and undiscrete," and continued:

"Her Majesty therefore, like a good huswyfe looking unto her household stuffe, took the booke in her handes, and in the sight of us, the Ld Keeper and Treasurer, wente through and noted those justices she would have continue in Commission, and whom she thought not meete."22

The Lord Keeper went on to say that the Queen had ordered that all those who were unsuitable should be removed from the commissions, including those who did not live in their respective counties. In fact, the number of those removed was still not very great, and even blatant acts of misbehaviour did not always result in dismissal. Physical disability, on the other hand, if brought to the attention of the Council, would result in removal. In 1595 John Burgoine of Bedfordshire, aged 60 and blind, was exempted by patent from holding the office of JP and from payment of any fines for non-performance of his duties.23

The available evidence leads one to conclude that many of the justices failed to attend to their duties and were guilty of the other forms of misconduct with which they were charged. These phenomena, however, were common to society at all levels and were to be found among some of the higher judiciary and officials. Whereas by modern standards a substantial number of Elizabethan justices and their successors should have been removed from office, there were probably

22.   John Hawarde, *Les Reportes des Cases in Camera Stellata,* 1593-1609, pp. 19-21.
23.   CSP Dom., 1595, 48.

few men among the rest of the population who would have behaved impeccably. Graft and corruption were regular features of everyday life, and violent enmities were common both at court and throughout the rest of society.

A new commission

The Commissions of the Peace continued to be similar to those which had been issued since they were first introduced in the fourteenth century. They were very explicit and detailed, mentioning all the statutes which the justices were required to enforce and dealing minutely with the method, though not the procedure, for enforcing them.[24] Sometimes commissions included statutes which had been repealed or at least superseded by later legislation. They had therefore become very lengthy and cumbersome. Lambard complained of the confusion which this caused and urged that the form of the commission be revised. He observed in 1581 that:

"By the number of statutes in charge of justices, and by much vain repetition and other corruption, and by the huddling of things together, it hath become so foully blemished that of necessity it ought to be redressed."

This was achieved in 1590 when the Judges of the King's Bench, Common Pleas and Exchequer, headed by Sir Christopher Wray, Chief Justice of the King's Bench, Sir Edmund Anderson, Chief Justice of Common Pleas, and Sir Roger Manwood, Chief Baron of the Exchequer, drafted a revised and much shorter version which was approved by the Lord Chancellor, Sir Christopher Hatton, and adopted for all commissions thereafter until 1878.

A certain amount of obsolete matter of a general nature was omitted, but the language was not modernized and continued to be Latin for a further 33 years. The most noticeable change was the omission of all references to specific statutes. Instead, there was a comprehensive reference to any legislation which the justices might be required to enforce: *"omnia Ordinationes et Statuta pro bono pacis nostrae, ac pro conservatione ejusdem."*

The new commission began, as previously, with a salutation to those who were to be justices and whose names were set out, the *Custos* and members of the *Quorum* being specifically designated. There followed a description of their powers and duties. A second clause set out in

24.   Commissions are set out in Prothero's *Statutes and Constitutional Documents*, pp. 144-149 and in Appendix I, *post.*

general terms the procedure to be followed at the sessions. This contained a list of the offences to be inquired into by two or more justices (one to be of the *Quorum*). A third clause directed that in case of doubt or difficulty the justices must not proceed unless a justice of the King's Bench or of Assize were present. A fourth clause charged the justices to carry out their functions diligently. The fifth and final clause ordered the sheriff to return juries at the times and places designated by the justices.[25]

New developments in administration and social service in an era of expanding industry and colonization

As has been noted, the outstanding feature of the Elizabethan era was that, while the justices were faced with an increasing volume of criminal work and were also obliged to accept a substantial extension of their administrative duties, they were now required to embark upon a wholly new social and economic function.

Poor Law

The sixteenth century saw the beginning of the social services and in England it was the JPs who were to play the leading part in administering the system. The most important and effective development concerning JPs under Elizabeth was what came to be known collectively as the Poor Law, which was designed for the dual purpose of providing work for the able-bodied and relief for the destitute.

Like the office of JP itself, the Poor Law system was a response to current needs. The policy of rigorous repression of vagrancy had proved unsuccessful, and the removal of many of the old sources of charitable help, coinciding with a rapidly growing population and with exceptional economic stress, posed a danger from the vagabond class which was seen to be more ominous than ever before. The mastermind behind the new scheme was probably Lord Burghley, but the system which finally emerged from numerous Acts and edicts of the Council was not entirely the outcome of original thought. The concept of the relief of the impotent poor had appeared before the Elizabethans came on the scene and, as we shall see, was already being put into practice on the Continent and in the English municipalities. Burghley and some prominent Members of Parliament created a system which could be applied to England and Wales but was based on existing institutions. The JPs were again ready at hand and, although we see a new development away from the old legalistic procedure towards a

25.   For the form and wording of the 1590 and other commissions see Appendix I.

genuinely administrative function, the latter was still based on the prevailing court system. Quarter Sessions remained the governing body. One of the principal innovations was the creation of an infrastructure with new officials to operate the scheme in the parish, which was now firmly established as the unit of local government.

The relief of the poor in earlier centuries was the concern, not of the state, but of the church and particularly the monastic foundations, augmented by the charity of individuals. In addition, destitution in the fourteenth and fifteenth centuries was relieved to some extent by municipal corporations and by merchant and craft guilds in the towns and by fraternities and religious guilds in the rural villages. As the Webbs have shown,[26] the latter two provided a kind of mutual insurance for members of the community in addition to the spontaneous acts for relief of the poor. The municipal corporations gave help both by administering institutional relief and also by providing direct aid in money and kind out of their own resources. It was those persons who exercised magisterial functions - the mayors and other officials and the JPs where they existed - who were principally involved in this work.

The central government on the other hand, far from sharing this charitable approach, adopted an increasingly uncaring policy aimed at the repression of beggars and vagrants who were assumed to be the cause of most crime and unrest. The need to keep the peace was regarded as being of paramount importance in securing stable and effective government. The measures taken by the Crown and statutes passed by Parliament were all directed towards this end and took no heed of the plight of the sick and aged poor, nor of those who were out of work through no fault of their own.

There is evidence that not all landowners, even if they were JPs, applied the regulations rigidly. Workers on the land were in short supply and some employers, largely in their own interest, welcomed wandering labourers and induced them to stay by paying wages above the fixed rate. Generally, however, the county justices, as agents of national policy, were concerned in implementing the harsh laws and were not interested in the administration of more humane measures.

In the end, repression failed totally to achieve its aims. Notwithstanding the risk of incurring harsh punishment, the ever-increasing mass of labourers abandoned the rural areas and sought a livelihood elsewhere. From the beginning of the sixteenth century, experiments were made in several parts of Western Europe and in the English municipalities in the relief of the sick and aged and in the provision of remunerated work for those who were able and willing to

---

26.   *ELG, English Poor Law History,* Part I. "The Old Poor Law," pp. 21-22.

undertake it.[27] These sentiments were shared by some of the more influential men in England. In 1516, Sir Thomas More, in his *Utopia* said of the destitute unemployed: "neither is there anything so horrible that it can keep them from stealing which have no other craft whereby to get their living." At last, the manifest failure of the old system and the example provided by the Continent and the municipalities persuaded the government and Parliament to adopt a similar approach for the whole of England and Wales.

We have seen that the first attempts to draw a distinction between able-bodied vagrants and aged and impotent poor were made under Henry VII and Henry VIII and that during the following reigns steps were taken to relieve the worthy poor. The Act, 27 Hen. VIII, c. 25, had placed responsibility for succouring the "impotent, lame, feeble, sick and diseased" upon the officers of boroughs and parishes, but funds to support these measures were collected by voluntary alms. In 1562, the first of the Elizabethan Acts[28] relating to Poor Law imposed a compulsory levy on all those with ability to pay. Anyone who "obstinately" refused to give a weekly sum to the poor "according to his or their abilities" was to be bound by the bishop of the diocese to appear before the next sessions of the justices, and if they refused to be bound he could commit them to prison. At the sessions, the justices were to "charitably and gently persuade ... the said obstinate person" to give to the relief of the poor, and if he still refused they were to order him to pay an amount at their discretion, and he could be committed to prison in default.

This was followed in 1572 by a long enactment[29] entitled "An Act for the Punishment of Vagabonds, and for the Relief of the Poor and Impotent," which codified and extended the system. It began with the customary recital of the evils caused by vagrancy: all parts of England and Wales were infested with vagabonds and sturdy beggars who were daily responsible for "horrible Murders, Thefts and other great Outrages." It went on to replace previous Acts with provisions for seizing and punishing every person above the age of 14 who was a rogue, vagabond or sturdy beggar and who was found begging or wandering. The Act defined those who were to be classed in this category which included fortune-tellers and even players and minstrels, jugglers and pedlars unless they held a licence from two justices, including one of the *Quorum*. In the first instance they were to be brought before a single justice, or the mayor or chief officer of a town, who should commit them to prison pending the next sessions of the peace or gaol delivery. If convicted at the sessions they were to be

27. An account of this movement is given by the Webbs, *ibid.,* pp. 29-41.
28. 5 Eliz. c. 3.
29. 14 Eliz. c. 5.

whipped and "burnt through the right ear" to manifest "his or her roguish kind of life," and the conviction was to be recorded by the Clerk of the Peace. If, however, "some honest Person" who had goods to the value of £5 or 20 shillings in land, was prepared to take the offender into his service for one year, subject to a £5 bond, then the justices might at their discretion suspend sentence and it was not to be imposed unless the offender left the service within a year. If, on the other hand, the punishment of whipping and burning was duly inflicted, the individual concerned was to receive a licence from two justices which protected him from further prosecution for 40 days. Should he thereafter "fall again to any kind of roguish or vagabondish trade of life" he was to be adjudged a felon and punished accordingly with death and forfeiture, unless, again, some "honest Person" was prepared to take him into service, but this time the employer must be worth £10 in goods or 40 shillings in land and agree to take him for two years.

The Act re-enacted provisions of earlier statutes, such as the special exceptions for soldiers and sailors returning home, the liability of constables and tythingmen to apprehend offenders and the penalties for harbouring vagabonds, and it added a ban on the bringing of vagabonds into England and Wales by ships from Ireland or the Isle of Man.

Having dealt with the vagabonds, the Act proceeded to make provision for the deserving poor and impotent. The justices were to divide themselves into divisions and to "make diligent Search and Inquiry of all aged, poor, impotent and decayed Persons" born within the division or who had resided there for three years. A record was to be kept of their names and they were to be settled in "meet and convenient places," which were to be selected by the justices at their discretion. The justices were further required to calculate the weekly charge needed to maintain them and to assess and tax the local inhabitants with a weekly tax. Persons failing to pay were to be brought before two justices (one to be of the *Quorum*) and if they failed to comply with the justices' orders they were to be imprisoned. The tax was to be collected by collectors appointed by the justices. Collectors were to serve for one year and to pay the proceeds of the tax to the poor at the discretion of the justices. Every half-year the collectors had to render an account to two justices living next to the places in which the paupers "abided." It was recognized that in some areas it might not be practicable to raise the necessary funds, and it was therefore provided that in such circumstances the justices of the division might issue licences allowing certain poor persons to beg. The grouping of justices into divisions for Poor Law purposes was the origin of the Petty Sessional divisions which exist today.

The Act also created overseers of the poor who were to supervise the work and see that it was properly carried out according to the justices' orders. They, like the collectors, were appointed annually by the justices at the Easter sessions. In 1597 the two offices were combined and the overseers assumed responsibility for collecting and distributing the tax as well as supervising the work of the able-bodied and relieving the impotent poor.

Children of beggars between the ages of five and 14 could be taken into service under an order of the justices in sessions. Male children were obliged to remain in service until the age of 24 and females until 18.

The justices were also empowered to levy a rate, not exceeding eight pence a week, in each parish to provide sustenance for prisoners in the common gaol (who risked starvation unless they paid the gaoler to give them food or persuaded others to supply it). The rate was collected by the churchwardens and paid over to the high constables who in turn gave it for distribution to persons living near the gaols and nominated by the justices.

The Act went so far as to make provision for poor persons who needed to visit a spa for their health. In order to protect the citizens of Bath and Buckstone from having to support the large numbers of poor who came to the towns to be cured of their ailments, it was provided that in future "no diseased or impotent poor Person, living on Alms" should visit either town "to the Baths there for Ease of their Grief," unless they were licensed to do so by two justices of the county where they lived, and unless the cost of their travel and maintenance was born by their parish.

An interesting feature of the Act was that in spite of the severe measures which it contained against able-bodied vagrants and beggars, it also empowered three justices (one to be of the *Quorum*) to "settle to work Rogues and Vagabonds that shall be disposed to work," so that they might earn a living through their labours. Such an arrangement, which would be supervised by the overseers, was at the discretion of the justices who could introduce it only if there were sufficient funds available in their area after they had met the needs of the poor and impotent. Four years later, an Act of 1576[30] directed the justices to arrange for a stock of wool, hemp, flax, iron "and other stuff" to be provided from the rates and given to such persons as the justices might decide who would see that every poor and needy person who was able and willing to work had work to do and did not have to rely on begging or stealing. Those in charge were to pay for the work done, sell the products and replenish the stock.

---

30.   18 Eliz. c. 3. This and the Act of 1572, were temporary but were continued in force by 27 Eliz. c. 29, 29 Eliz. c. 5, 31 Eliz. c. 10 and later replaced by 39 Eliz. c. 2 and 43 Eliz. c. 3.

The Act of 1576, which amended and extended the long and comprehensive enactment of 1572, was entitled: "for Setting of the Poor on Work, and for the avoiding of Idleness." Its main feature was the establishment of houses of correction in which the inmates were made to do profitable work and were also subjected to what was hoped to be a reforming influence. These institutions will be described later. The same Act also dealt with illegitimate children who were a burden on the parish. Two justices (one from the *Quorum*) could order the mother or the reputed father to pay for the child's upkeep and imprison them in default.

Further legislation on the Poor Law was passed under Elizabeth culminating in Acts of 1597 and 1601 which finally established the system which was to survive for the following three centuries, and in which can be found the basis of the twentieth century rating law. There were two Acts on the subject in 1597 which clearly marked the classes into which the poor were to be divided. One was for the "Relief of the Poor" and referred to those who were poor through no fault of their own. They were to be given relief in the form of pensions, food or clothing and also housing.[31] The other adopted the old harsh approach towards those who were considered to be poor because they were idle.[32] It repealed and partly re-enacted the previous Acts on "Rogues, Vagabonds and Sturdy Beggars" and directed that particularly brutal punishment should be inflicted upon such people. "Every Rogue, Vagabond or Sturdy Beggar which shall be at any time ... taken begging, vagrant, wandering or misordering themselves" was to be "stripped naked from the Middle upwards, and shall be openly whipped until his or her Body be Bloody."

The Act of 1601[33] consolidated the position and imposed a fine of £5 on every justice who failed in his duty to appoint overseers. Under the system which was then established, two or more justices (one from the *Quorum*) living in or near each parish were to nominate the churchwardens and two, three or four "substantial Householders" (the number depended upon the size of the parish) to serve as overseers for one year. It was the job of the overseers, subject to the approval of the justices, to set to work all persons who had no trade or means of support and to provide housing for them. They were also to provide work for children whose parents could not maintain them and to apprentice them. Parents were, however, liable to maintain their children and the children to support their parents and grandparents. The cost of the scheme was defrayed by a rate on all householders and landowners within each parish according to their ability to pay. This

31. 39 Eliz. c. 2.
32. 39 Eliz. c. 3.
33. 43 Eliz. c. 2.

was collected by the overseers who were to use it in providing work for the able-bodied and for the relief of the old and disabled. The overseers were accountable to the justices.

The parish was therefore established as the unit for relief under the supervision of the local justices acting through subordinate officials. The people to whom the new laws applied were divided into three categories: (1) Those willing and able to work but unable to obtain it. These were given paid work and the parish provided them with tools and materials. Children too were given work and apprenticed. (2) Aged and infirm who were unable to work. They were supported by outdoor relief in their own homes. (3) Those able but unwilling to work. As in the past, they were whipped, branded and either returned to their parish of origin or sent to a house of correction where they were forced to work.

The spirit of care which characterized much of the Poor Law legislation was apparent in other related measures. Another Act of 1601[34] provided for weekly pensions to be paid to soldiers and sailors disabled in the Queen's service. The system was placed under the supervision of the justices who decided the validity of claims and also imposed a rate on the parish householders. This was collected by the churchwardens and paid over to treasurers, appointed by the justices, who were responsible for distribution. Householders dissatisfied with their rate assessment could appeal to the justices and one may see in this the beginning of a right of appeal to Quarter Sessions.

Further examples of a humanitarian trend were the issue of appeals by justices to collect funds for those who suffered loss at sea or by fire.[35]

The administration of poor relief as well as of the vagrancy law arose not infrequently in the case of servants who had been dismissed and turned out to fend for themselves. This was almost invariably the fate of maidservants who got into trouble over some sexual affair. They, like all others accused of fornication and adultery, would usually be dealt with in the first instance by the archdeacon's court (though they were sometimes brought before the justices, depending upon the whim of the constable), but more often than not, having been punished and made to do penance, they would become the responsibility of the justices as burdens on the parish and vagrants.

The Elizabethan justices varied in the enthusiasm with which they entered into their new obligations. In some areas years passed before the new system was brought into operation. In general there was a tendency to concentrate upon keeping down the cost of relief and sending paupers away into other areas, after due punishment, rather

34.   43 Eliz. c. 3. Earlier enactments for the relief of wounded soldiers and sailors were 35 Eliz., c. 4 and 39 Eliz., cc. 17, 21.
35.   DP, 1591-94, 128, 144, 187. See also Appendix IV.

than providing help to the needy. This problem of "settlement" was to bedevil the Poor Law administration throughout its existence. As the parish was obliged to provide only for its own poor, any claimant who could be said to belong elsewhere was despatched to his place of origin, a course which often resulted in great hardship to the individual and bitter disputes between parishes. One may, indeed, take a cynical view of the whole development. The strongest incentive for the legislation was the necessity to remove a pressing danger to society rather than a spirit of charity, or to ensure an adequate supply of food for the whole population rather than to see that the poor were properly fed. Even the Act of 1601 for the relief of wounded soldiers and sailors declared that one of the principal objects was to encourage others to join the forces. There are, however, clear indications of a genuine spirit of compassion both in documents of the Privy Council and in reports to the Council from the justices in some counties. County records show that whereas some justices were callous and concerned only with keeping down the rates, others exhibited clear feelings of humanity, and in some places they themselves bore the loss on resale of corn at below market price "for the relief of our poore neighbours."[36]

The Poor Law legislation introduced a number of provisions which were of the greatest importance to the future of the justices and of local administration. Those which were of special significance were: the grouping of justices into divisions, the justices' power to levy rates, and the appointment of paid officials as permanent staff.

The Elizabethan Poor Law machinery was well in advance of any system in other parts of Europe and gave England a social stability which was not enjoyed elsewhere. It was the greatest social achievement of the age and a landmark in the history of the JPs. It confirmed them as the focal point for local administration in a system of government which was to last until the nineteenth century.

Houses of correction
The Act of 1576[37] directed that a house of correction should be established by the justices in each district. These were modelled on the Bridewell which had been set up in the City of London in the 1550s and which was intended to be a place in which the poor could find work rather than a prison in the usual sense. Following this example, the houses of correction were places in which able-bodied vagrants and local unemployed could be compelled to work; the principal object being to make the idle earn their keep and to reform criminals, but

36.   CSP Dom., vol. 189, 50.
37.   18 Eliz. c. 3.

they were also places where any poor person might find employment, and in time all the inmates in some areas were paid for the work they did at rates fixed by the justices.

It was the duty of the JPs to erect, maintain and staff the houses. As with other branches of the Poor Law, the justices in some districts were more conscientious than in others, and it was many years before all areas were provided with institutions. In many counties on the other hand a principal house was built for the whole county with several subsidiaries. The justices owned the property and were entirely responsible for the upkeep and management, including the appointment of staff and the feeding and working arrangements of the inmates.

Although the inmates might be detained against their will and subjected to compulsory labour, the idea of punishment was alien to the houses of correction, at least in their earlier years. Imprisonment continued to be a concept applied to the common gaols which remained quite separate from the houses. Most of those in the gaols were awaiting trial or had failed to pay a fine. Only a small proportion had been sentenced to imprisonment for some offence. It was not until the nineteenth century that imprisonment in itself became a major form of penal treatment and until then most of the sentences imposed by the courts were ones of capital or corporal punishment.

Gaols
The gaols were owned by various authorities, including feudal manors, and ranged from a "cage" provided by a parish for the use of the constable to a castle or municipal building. County gaols were under the control of the sheriff. The gaols were run mainly on a profit-making basis, the gaoler charging fees from the prisoners. The JPs could make contributions towards the relief of prisoners (as we have seen, the 1572 statute enabled them to levy a rate to provide them with food) but otherwise had little to do with the management and were only concerned with committing persons into custody and securing their subsequent appearance at sessions.

Highways and bridges
The new system of local services, based on the secular parish and administered by local officers appointed and controlled by the JPs, was not confined to vagrancy and the relief of the poor and disabled. It extended to such divergent matters as the destruction of vermin and the maintenance of highways.

We have seen that at common law liability to repair public highways rested upon adjoining landowners, but that under an Act of 1555 the parish became responsible for maintaining roadways within its territory and the justices were to appoint surveyors of highways to supervise the work. The justices could also compel the high constable to account for fines collected for highway offences and to pay them over to the constables and churchwardens in the place where the offence had been committed. An early Act of Elizabeth ordered surveyors to present offenders to the nearest JP who had to certify the offence to the next general sessions.[38] This Act also extended from four days to six the time which the local inhabitants could be obliged to work annually on repairing highways and ditches. A further Act of 1576[39] enabled two justices to compel the surveyors, petty constables and churchwardens to account for all moneys they had received.

There was no further legislation of any significance on highways for the next 100 years. In the meantime, however, an increase in the use of the roads for trade and military purposes as well as private travel obliged the justices to spend an appreciable amount of time on this part of their work, although the interest they showed in it varied greatly between counties and especially between individuals.

Sometimes the Privy Council was obliged to rebuke county justices for the state of the highway in their area. On the other hand, there were numbers of individual justices who took an almost obsessive interest in inspecting roadways in their neighbourhood and presenting all and sundry who, in their opinion, had caused damage or failed in their duty to maintain. Highway inspections provided the busy-body justice with an unrivalled opportunity to throw his weight about.

An Act of Henry VIII made general provision for the maintenance of bridges some 20 years earlier than the corresponding legislation for highways. This included authority for the justices to appoint bridge surveyors and to levy a rate on the inhabitants to meet the cost. The principal difference between the bridge and roadway laws was that liability rested with the county for bridges and the parish for roads.

The law remained virtually unchanged during Elizabeth's reign. General sessions were required to "inquire, hear and determine of all manner of annoyances of bridges broken in highways" and to take such action as was necessary for their speedy repair. This duty, however, was often delegated by the sessions to one or two justices living near to the bridge who inspected the site and gave such instructions as they deemed necessary to local workmen to carry out the repairs. It would appear that this was sometimes done without the appointment of surveyors.

As in respect of their other duties, the justices sometimes received peremptory orders to repair a bridge in their area. At the beginning of the reign, the Bishop and the other justices of Durham were told that

38.   5 Eliz. c. 13.
39.   18 Eliz. c. 10.

their bridges, especially at Newcastle, were in serious decay, and they were ordered to take immediate action.

The increase in traffic during the last half of the sixteenth century resulted in more bridges being built and in old ones being widened or replaced. There is, however, no evidence to suggest that the justices devoted a sizeable amount of time to the maintenance of bridges or that they found it onerous.

Trade and labour

The main sources of the country's wealth under Elizabeth were the same as under the earlier Tudors: agriculture, cloth and seafaring, all of which, especially the latter, increased in importance towards the end of the century. The significance of shipping was recognized in early Acts[40] of the reign which the justices were required to enforce. Among their provisions the Acts directed that cargoes be carried "in English Botomes" and, in the interests of the navy, that mariners should not be compelled to serve as soldiers. The JPs, most of whom were still drawn from the land-owning community, were naturally interested principally in agriculture, but the growing class of prosperous merchants whose wealth was derived from cloth and from overseas trade (the two were interconnected) were also securing appointment to the commissions after buying country estates and intermarrying with the less affluent squires.

Many of the Elizabethan Acts, both of Parliament and of the Privy Council, were directed to trade, industry and agriculture; but this was largely an extension of the process which had gone before and did not involve any striking innovation like the Poor Law, though it could be said that the Poor Law system itself was part of the government's economic strategy aimed at safeguarding and improving trade and employment.

The JPs were placed in a key position in virtually all new measures affecting trade and agriculture. They appointed searchers for the cloth trade,[41] and dealt specifically with the makers of defective cloth in the northern counties.[42] They supervised the manufacture of malt,[43] enforced the laws against the conversion of tillage into pasture,[44] and fixed the export quota of corn when there was a shortage.[45] At the same time they were required to carry out the Council's emergency orders whenever there was such an emergency.[46] They had to enforce

40.   1 Eliz. c. 13; 5 Eliz. c. 5.
41.   43 Eliz. c. 10.
42.   39 Eliz. c. 20.
43.   27 Eliz. c. 14.
44.   39 Eliz. c. 2.
45.   13 Eliz. c. 13.
46.   APC, September 1597.

laws restricting the import of certain foreign goods "for avoiding of divers foreyne wares made by Handye Craftsmen beyond the Seas,"[47] and they punished men of the lower classes who did not wear woollen caps on Sundays and holy days.[48]

The quality of workmanship was the subject of much attention and was assured by strict apprenticeship regulations. Previously, apprenticeship had been regulated by the guilds, but henceforth it was subject to legislation, which placed responsibility for supervision upon the justices.

Wages and conditions of employment
Responsibility for fixing wages rested irrefutably upon the justices and the mayors and officers in the corporate towns. A major Act of 1562[49] on "Artificers, Labourers, Servants of Husbandry and Apprentices" referred in its preamble to the serious inflation which had occurred since the passing of earlier legislation as a result of which wages were too low. The previous Acts were repealed and a new code, based mainly on the earlier provisions, was introduced. The justices were to meet each year within six weeks of Easter when they were to "call unto them such discreet and grave Persons ... as they shall think meet, and conferring together, respecting the Plenty or Scarcity of the Time, and other Circumstances" they were to assess and fix the rate for wages of all artificers, craftsmen, labourers, servants and workmen. The rates were to be for the year, the day, or any other period and might or might not include food and drink. Detailed provisions were made for the type of work as well as for the worker; for example "for ditching, paving, railing or hedging by the Rod, Perch, Lug, Yard, Pole, Rope or Foot." The justices' assessments and their reasons were to be sent to the Court of Chancery, and the Lord Chancellor or Lord Keeper might then order them to be printed and sent to the local areas where they were to be proclaimed and enforced by the justices. Any justice who failed to attend the annual meeting without good cause was to be fined £10 by his fellow justices.

The Act then specified the penalties to be incurred by employers who paid wages above the taxed rate and by employees who received them. The employee was to be imprisoned for 21 days. The employer was also to suffer imprisonment, though for only 10 days, but in addition he was to pay a fine of £5.

This lengthy Act, which provided an extensive code of practice, contained many other provisions. Workers for craftsmen such as weavers, hosiers, tailors and shoemakers must be employed for at least

47. 5 Eliz. c. 7.
48. 13 Eliz. c. 19.
49. 5 Eliz. c. 4.

a year, and any breach of this rule by either side was to be dealt with by either one or two justices. Workmen and servants who assaulted their masters were liable to imprisonment for a maximum of a year at the discretion of two justices. One or more justices could sentence an artificer to the stocks for two days and a night for refusing to work on the harvest. Two justices could order any unmarried woman between the ages of 12 and 40 to serve on such terms, including wages, as they thought fit. There were detailed provisions for apprenticeships, both in towns and the countryside. No one might "exercise any Craft ... or Occupation," unless he had served at least seven years as an apprentice. Anyone refusing to be apprenticed could be imprisoned by a single justice who was also empowered to resolve disputes between master and apprentice.

The whole of the execution of the Act was placed in the hands of the justices who were to meet twice a year in divisions for the purpose of checking that the provisions were being properly applied. To compensate them for their efforts the justices were to be paid five shillings a day, out of the fines and forfeitures imposed, up to a maximum of three days for each sitting.

Agriculture
Notwithstanding the increase in trade and industry, England and Wales remained predominantly agricultural and the justices continued to be involved to a considerable extent in enforcing the statutes of the previous reigns and in complying with an increasing number of directions from the Council, especially those aimed at securing an adequate supply of food.

When there was a surplus of grain the justices were required to fix an export quota (13 Eliz., c. 13), but more often there was a shortage, especially in 1586-87 following a particularly disastrous harvest in 1585. The justices received numerous directions from the Council on how to deal with the situation (most of them drafted personally by Burghley). They were obliged to see that there was an adequate supply of grain in the markets, that prices were fair and that there was no profiteering. In 1587 they were directed to arrange with the sheriffs for juries of local inhabitants to examine the quantity of corn available in each parish and the number of persons in every household. Households were then rationed and any surplus was sent to the market where the justices had to attend personally to ensure that reasonable prices were charged. During this period of acute shortage the Council supervised distribution on a national scale and ordered the justices to send supplies from one county to another according to where the need seemed to be greatest. For instance, in March 1587 the Cambridgeshire justices were reprimanded for restricting the regular supply of corn to Saffron Walden in Essex, while a few days later those in Hampshire were instructed to allow barley and malt to be moved to Carmarthen.[50]

These duties occupied a considerable amount of the justices' time. In addition to the inspections carried out by the juries in compliance with the 1587 Council directive, the justices themselves checked the stocks held by farmers (a task usually performed by a single justice in his local area) as well as arranging for supplies to be distributed to markets and elsewhere and for prices to be held at a fixed level. They then had to send a report to the Council on the action they had taken. The Calendar of State Papers contains many such reports which show the extent of the justices' involvement in this work. In 1587 the Gloucestershire justices reported that they had vistited the:

"markets, seen the poore relieved as we may, searched the barnes, storehouses and grenyers of farmers and others hable to furnishe the marketts with corne, and having consideration to theyr private families have in discretion appointed them a certeyne quantytie of certen kindes of graine to be by them brought weekelie to the markett accordinglie, and of such our appointments have kepte books in writinge and doe finde therepon, that as yet the said farmers and others doe fulfill our appointments in this behalfe without any disobedyence. And further according to the said your lettres we have sett downe several prices upon everie kinde of graine within the severall divisions of this Shire, as in respecte of the distaunce of the places and the present tyme of necessytie we have thought most convenyent, after which rate we will hereafter in our several limitts have care to see the same solde as may be beste for the relief of our poore neighbours."

The justices were also expected to spend their own money on buying corn in bulk and retaining it without profit, and they were required to persuade other wealthy people to do the same. This was made clear in the address, mentioned above, which was given by Lord Keeper Puckering in the Star Chamber in 1595. He also stressed the importance of the role of the justices in enforcing the laws governing the supply of corn. When handling farmers, marketeers and others they were to act "with a Hurculean courage."

In addition to their duties already described, the justices were given a peculiar task in 1589 which related to rural housing. A statute (31 Eliz., c. 7) prohibited the building of any new cottage unless it had at least four acres of land with it. If such a cottage were built it had to be

---

50.   APC, March 17, 20, 1586 (old style date).

pulled down unless a special licence were granted by the justices. Where it was demolished, the owner not only lost the house but was liable to a fine of £10 and a further £2 for every month that it remained standing. The object of this legislation was to limit the places in which paupers might live and so become a burden on the rate-payers. There are few records of such proceedings during the remainder of Elizabeth's reign but Quarter Sessions seem to have dealt with rather more in the following century. It would appear from the records that in the majority of these cases the justices allowed the cottage to remain on condition that security was given against the occupier or lodger becoming a charge on the parish. There were a few, on the other hand, where the justices appear to have applied the law with cruel harshness; though in doing so they seem to have acted with the approval of most of the population, and there were some instances where the inhabitants of a parish attacked a cottage and razed it to the ground without waiting for the justices to act.

Religion

The Roman Catholic domination of the country ceased with the death of Mary, but there was no immediate introduction of drastic countermeasures. Steps taken during the early years of Elizabeth's reign did little more than restore the position which existed under Edward VI. So far as the justices themselves were concerned, the Spanish ambassador reported that after some delay Catholic magistrates in certain areas had been removed and replaced by Protestants, but in 1565 there were still Catholic justices who did not make themselves conspicuous and who were allowed to remain on the commission.[51] Soon after Elizabeth's accession an Act[52] required all those who assumed public office, including Judges and JPs, to take the Oath of Supremacy. Under this oath they recognized the Queen as the only supreme governor of the realm in all temporal and spiritual causes and they swore to bear true allegiance to her, her heirs and successors and to do all in their power to defend these rights. Another decree[53] restored the Book of Common Prayer and penalized any priest who refused to use it or who made derogatory remarks about it (a first offence involved imprisonment for six months, a second for a year and a third for life). A single justice could impose a fine of 12 pence upon any person who failed to attend church, the money being collected by the churchwardens and given to the poor, but most offences against the Act were heard and determined at Quarter Sessions or Assizes. In either case the bishop of the diocese might join

51.   CSP, Spanish, 1558-67, 406, 416.
52.   1 Eliz. c. 1.
53.   1 Eliz. c. 2.

the court if he wished to do so. It would appear, however, that many who did not comply with the Act went unpunished.

The law, which was designed to support the Anglican church, was directed against Catholics and Protestants alike and there were many dissident JPs who became liable to prosecution and removal from the commission. In 1564 steps were taken, with the assistance of the bishops, to identify individuals, and any justices who did not actively subscribe to the church were liable to be dropped.54 The situation changed in 1569 and 1570 when the Northern rising and Catholic plotting on behalf of Mary Stuart coincided with the issue of a Papal Bull excommunicating Elizabeth. Harsher measures were taken against all Catholics, particularly during the war with Spain. Every justice was required to appear before a Judge of Assize and to take an Oath of Allegiance to the established church and of Obedience to the Acts establishing the new regime.55 A number of those who failed to comply were dismissed, but there seems to have been no thorough purge of all the commissions. This is surprising in view of the fact that the justices were both the organ of local government and a branch of the judiciary which had to be relied upon to enforce the policy of the central government in which religion and politics were closely intertwined. A possible explanation is the difficulty in finding enough persons who were regarded as suitable for appointment and were not already on the bench, and the need for the government to avoid antagonizing the gentry class to which all the justices belonged.56 In the 1570s the bishop of each diocese was required to report to the Council the names of all justices who failed to attend church services, and some were put out of the commission on the strength of such reports, but the numbers were small.57

An Act of 1570,58 extending a previous Act of 1562,59 forbad the importation of any Papal Bull, writing or token. Although the penalty was the same as for high treason (involving death and forfeiture) the justices were nevertheless empowered to hear and determine such cases. The Act also proclaimed that anyone receiving Papal objects should be guilty under the Statute of *Praemunire* unless he apprehended the person offering the object and handed him over to a justice or, if this were not possible, reported his name and address to a justice. The justice must then report the matter to the Privy Council

54.   J.R. Tanner, *Tudor Constitutional Documents,* Cambridge U.P.
55.   DP 1547-1580, 178, 324, 346-366; 1595-1597, 47.
56.   For an analysis of the extent to which the commissions were affected, see J.H. Gleason, *The Justices of the Peace in England,* 1558-1640, ch. V.
57.   APC, November 18, 1576.
58.   13 Eliz. c. 2.
59.   5 Eliz. c. 1. This Act also extended the Oath of Supremacy to, among others, all holders of local office.

within 14 days or he too would incur the penalties of *praemunire*.

Experience showed that there were means of circumventing the 1570 Act, and therefore another was passed in 1581[60] which declared that anyone who attempted to entice a subject of the Queen away from the established religion and anyone aiding or maintaining such a person was to be deemed a traitor and sentenced as in the case of high treason. Here again, the justices were empowered to hear and determine. The Act also strengthened the provisions of previous enactments for compulsory attendance in church, failure to comply leading to a fine of £20 which could be imposed by a single justice. In 1593, Popish recusants over the age of 16 were forbidden to move more than five miles from the place where they were born, on pain of losing all their lands and goods.[61] The Clerk of the Peace at Quarter Sessions was responsible for registering the names of those recusants who were obliged to move from elsewhere to their place of birth. The justices were required by the Council to inspect the homes of recusants and report their annual income. Sometimes, however, the laws against recusants were tempered by a spirit of compassion which was not so manifest in the treatment of other offenders such as vagabonds. When the recusants who were kept in custody at Ely suffered during the hot and pestilential summer of 1590, the Council instructed the justices to allow them to go out, accompanied by a gaoler, and they were not to be punished so that their health suffered.[62]

Under the Act of 1593,[63] those refusing to accept the church and the Queen's authority were to be imprisoned until they conformed, but if they would not conform they were to abjure the realm and must leave at such time and through such port as the justices at Quarter Sessions or the Judges of Assize should direct. In some instances the justices themselves failed to comply with the religious laws. A number were removed from the commissions for failing to attend church,[64] or even for the recusancy of their wives.[65]

The justices' responsibility for religious matters was not confined to dealing with offences against the criminal law and it extended to giving approval to the marriage of the clergy. Under a royal injunction to the Clergy of 1559 no priest or deacon could marry without the consent both of his bishop and of two JPs.

National defence
Under Elizabeth, JPs spent an unprecedented amount of their time on

60.   23 Eliz. c. 1.
61.   35 Eliz. c. 2.
62.   APC, 1590, 387.
63.   35 Eliz. c. 1.
64.   Sometimes they were reported to the Council by the bishop. APC, 1575-1577, 233.
65.   DP, 1581-1590, 449.

the defence of the realm. This arose to a large extent from the threat of invasion by a foreign power which became more acute than at any other time since the Normans.

The urgency of the situation required immediate action, necessitating the issue of innumerable Council orders direct to the justices. The Acts of the Privy Council during much of the period are full of correspondence on defence matters between the Council and justices, and the volume for 1588, the year of the Armada, is almost entirely devoted to this subject. The justices were occupied in raising, training and equipping levies, in securing transport, supplies and ammunition, supervising the firing of beacons, repairing fortifications[66] and maintaining watches on the coast and generally dealing with any emergency that might arise. Some of this work was the responsibility of the Deputy Lieutenants and Commissioners of Muster, but many individual justices also held these appointments[67] and, in any event, the Commission of the Peace was regarded as imposing a general responsibility for military matters in each locality.

A number of examples were given in the previous chapter of the correspondence which passed between the Council and local justices about military affairs. This did not consist solely of government orders, but sometimes involved an exchange of correspondence in the light of problems raised by the justices. Thus, the justices of Middlesex were directed to muster 1,500 men, but they explained that it was impossible to raise this number because of the commitments of many of the inhabitants elsewhere. The Council therefore told them to reduce the number to 1,000; but there were still problems as to where certain citizens were to serve. These were put by the justices to the Council and duly resolved.[68]

National defence remained one of the justices' principal concerns until the nineteenth century, but the volume of work it involved varied considerably. It did not again reach the proportions of the Elizabethan period until the Napoleonic wars imposed a new major threat of invasion.

Miscellaneous duties

By the end of the sixteenth century there were few if any matters affecting the people of England and Wales in which the JP might not find himself involved. The Privy Council seemed to have adopted the principle that anything requiring attention in a local area should be

---

66.   This might extend to fortifications overseas. In 1575 the Dorset justices were directed to arrange for masons and labourers to be assembled for transport to Guernsey where they were to repair the fortifications. APC, May 9, 1575.
67.   Sometimes every justice was included in the musters' commissions. SPD, Addenda, 1547-80, p. 488.
68.   APC, 1588, pp. 24, 25.

dealt with by the justices on the spot. At any moment justices might be surprised by the receipt of orders to take immediate action to solve some problem. Certain "Dutchmen" complained that they had been attacked and subjected to abusive words. The justices were to inquire and take what action they thought fit so that the Dutchmen should "have no further just cause of complaint."[69] Two JPs in Lincolnshire were told to hasten to the house of one John Bellowe, a suspected person, to take an inventory of all his goods and chattels which were then to be committed to the care of some honest and substantial person, while the inventory was to be sent to the Exchequer.[70] Two Gloucestershire justices were to examine one Anne Barnarde and others regarding the embezzled goods of Sir Anthony Kingston and to report to the Council.[71] Lord Mordaunt and other Bedfordshire justices were to call before them certain honest men from the town of Hockly to give evidence against certain offenders.[72] The justices   in several counties were told to make inquiries about outstanding bills for purveyances which had not been paid because of the default of the purveyors of the Queen's household. They were to report to the Council so that the accounts might be settled and the offenders punished.[73] When the plague struck London in 1592 the royal courts were moved from Westminster to the castle in Hertford. All JPs within 12 miles of the town were ordered to take steps to preserve the area from infection. They were to meet weekly and decide what best to do and to report to the Lord Keeper.[74] To avoid infection no plays were to be performed without a licence from the Lord Lieutenant or two JPs of the county.[75] In 1586, because of the scarcity and high price of corn, the poor in Devon were starving. The county justices were ordered to take corn from ships calling in the ports and to arrange for it to be distributed and sold at a reasonable price.[76] Disputes over land were frequent and the aggrieved parties often went straight to the Council who would then order the local justices to take such action as the Council thought right. The Sussex justices, for example, were told to put one Henry Shelleye in possession of a house of which his uncle Richard had taken forceable possession.[77] Kenilworth Castle was supposed to be "in the sole and quiet possession of Robert Dudley," but certain persons had entered the castle by force on behalf of the Countess of Leicester. The justices were to see that they were removed and did not return.

69.   APC, 1558-70, p. 334.
70.   APC, 1556-1558, p. 49.
71.   *Ibid.*, p. 119.
72.   *Ibid.*, p. 320.
73.   APC, 1586-1587, p. 45.
74.   *Tudor Proclamations* III, p. 114. P.L. Hughes and J.F. Larkin, Yale, 1969.
75.   *Ibid.*, II, p. 115.
76.   APC, 1586-1587, p. 59, 60.
77.   APC, 1581-1582, p. 117.

One of the justices' least pleasant duties was the enforcement of royal requests for funds. The Lords Lieutenant were asked from time to time to supply the Queen with the names of those in their counties who were likely to be able to supply her with a sum of money by way of a loan. The Lieutenant would then receive letters under the Privy Seal addressed to each of the persons named, and it was the duty of the Deputy Lieutenants and certain specially selected justices to distribute the letters and to persuade the recipients to comply. If any refused, the justice who had served the letter was usually directed to bind them over to appear before the Council.

The Tudor monarchs had established control over every detail of their subjects' daily lives, and this was achieved through a remarkable partnership between the government and the local gentry who comprised the Justices of the Peace - a body of wealthy, influential and independent-minded men who did not fear to express their own views, but who were generally in accord with the government and its policy. They were prepared, without any significant financial reward, to implement that policy and to accept constant interference from the Council because they recognized it to be in the interest of themselves and of the community in which they lived, and because they aspired to the status and power which the office brought them. Even the higher members of the nobility seem to have been convinced that there was advantage in being on the commission.

The comprehensive system of judicial administration and local government which had become firmly established by the end of Elizabeth's reign had grave defects which were probably unforeseen by its architects, the most serious being the inadequacy, both in numbers and ability, of the officials who operated the various schemes under the justices' supervision. In spite, however, of these handicaps, the system was a remarkable achievement and was generally regarded as being an outstanding success. It was to remain in operation for more than 300 years.

CHAPTER IX

THE SEVENTEENTH CENTURY 1603-1688

The first Stuarts - Civil War - Interregnum - Restoration

THE JUSTICES OF THE PEACE continued to be the principal organ of local government for nearly 300 years after the death of Elizabeth, and towards the end of the seventeenth century their influence rose to an unprecedented level in the political and national arena. This phenomenon can be studied in considerable detail, as more material is available to the historian on the lives and work of the JPs during the seventeenth century than for any earlier period. This is to be found in the surviving rolls, minute books and order books of the sessions and in numerous private papers.

Soon after the beginning of the century, Coke described the JP system as "such a form of subordinate government for the tranquility and quiet of the realm, as no part of the Christian World hath the like;" though he qualified this by adding "if the same be duly exercised."[1] Its effectiveness was soon put to the test, and the century proved to be one of the most crucial periods in the history of the justices as well as that of the nation as a whole. It began with the union of the Crowns of England and Scotland in 1603 (to be followed by the union of the two countries in 1707). It witnessed the demise of autocratic dictatorship and the establishment of democratic Parliamentary government. It saw the transformation of the country from a second-rate nation into a world power with a burgeoning overseas empire. In the course of these dramatic changes the realm was disrupted by a bitter civil war, followed by a spell of republican government under which the authority of the JPs sank to a lower ebb than at any other time in their history. Yet before the century ended they were approaching the zenith of their power. It was an era of expanding industry, trade and wealth, in the course of which society, politics, commerce and the economy abandoned the last vestiges of mediaevalism and began to assume a modern shape. In all these developments the JPs had a prominent role to play, and the widespread prosperity, increased secular education and the growth of a leisured middle class closely intermixed with the nobility, all contributed to the new type of squirearchy from which the JPs were drawn.

---

1.   *Institutes of the Laws of England,* 1797 ed., vol. IV, p. 170.

Significantly for the JPs, the century saw a shift in the distribution of wealth. As we have seen, the prosperity of the country gentry and the burgesses rose appreciably during the latter part of the sixteenth century. This process accelerated during much of the seventeenth. The fortunes of the burgesses advanced on the tide of expanding trade, while the wealth of the gentry increased spectacularly with the acquisition of land. From 1536 they had begun to purchase estates expropriated from the monasteries, but soon afterwards some of the nobility began disposing of parts of large estates, and so too did the Crown, ever desperate for funds. This land was bought up eagerly by the squirearchy and by some of the city magnates who soon turned their properties into profitable institutions. It was largely due to this that the gentry class more than trebled in size during the 100 years from the end of Henry VIII's reign while the rest of the population only doubled.

Many of the gentry became at least as wealthy as some members of the nobility, in some instances more so. An analysis of more than 300 manors in 1640 showed that 80 per cent were owned by squires, less than seven per cent by peers and only two per cent by the Crown. "The King of England now owned very little of England, and the squire had become the backbone of English rural life."[2] The shift of status was accentuated by the loss of prestige suffered by the nobility during the reign of James I, when the King trebled the number of peers by indulging in the sale of peerages. At the same time the families of the nobles and the squires became still more closely blended, and soon there was no clear-cut distinction between the lesser nobility and the leading gentry. It was from this fairly small section of the population that the JPs, Deputy Lieutenants and sheriffs were appointed and from which the Members of Parliament were elected. Most of them met together socially as well as at Quarter Sessions.

The assertion that the wealth of the JPs and their social class increased substantially during this period needs to be qualified, as there were some justices, even in the early seventeenth century, who did not comply with the £20 property qualification although there appear to have been few instances of removal on these grounds. The explanation seems to be that the individuals concerned were all men of some importance in the area, notwithstanding their lack of property,

2.   Herbert Heaton, *Economic History of Europe*, New York, 1948, pp. 310-311. Thomas Wilson gave the following figures for numbers of the top three sections of society in 1600 with their average annual income: 61 lay nobles, £3,607; 500 knights, £4,000 - £2,000; 16,000 gentlemen;, £1,000 - £500. See F.J. Fisher, ed., *The State of England, Anno Dom. 1600*, Thomas Wilson, Camden Soc. 3rd. Ser., L11, 1936, pp. 1-47. A detailed assessment of JPs in 1606 is given by J.H. Gleason in *The Justice of the Peace in England, 1558 to 1640*, App. G, based on a memorandum in the Ellesmere papers in the Huntingdon Libarary. A general note on the wealth of the gentry in five counties is given in the appendix to the same work.

and for this reason were allowed to remain.

The level of education among the justices continued to grow and by 1640 there were very few on the county commissions who had not studied at a university or an Inn of Court, but whereas in the earlier part of Elizabeth's reign more had attended one of the Inns rather than a university, under Charles I the position was reversed. The extension of educational experience was of the greatest importance in the development of the JP system because, as already remarked, it not only produced better educated magistrates but it broadened their outlook and brought them into contact with their fellows in all parts of the country. This was of special significance during the troublous times of the mid-century and in the new era of national politics which dawned soon after the Restoration.

In this climate it was natural that the landed gentry and the merchants in the towns, both enjoying rising political influence, should become predominant among the magistracy. Although the county commissions included almost all noblemen whose principal property lay in the county, it was usually the financially powerful knights and esquires, together with the lawyers, who were the most active JPs and, as Quarter Sessions became the focus of political debate, their impact upon national as well as local affairs assumed ever greater importance.

Membership of the commission was of even more significance than it had been in the previous century. The JPs were a select class even under the first Stuarts, and by the end of the century their élitism was a pronounced and established feature of society. The commission carried with it considerable influence and prestige and there is no doubt that it was generally regarded as an appointment which should be sought after, in spite of the heavy burden of work which it might entail. It is arguable that during Charles I's reign the onerous additional tasks imposed upon the JPs by the order books and the directions to collect ship money and other financial levies, which are mentioned later, made some of the gentry less keen to assume office than had been the case since the days of the Plantagenets. Enthusiasm for the office was, however, revived after the Restoration. From then onwards it became more sought after than ever before and the numbers who showed any hesitation in accepting appointment were negligible.

Except during the Interregnum, almost all the principal figures in national life were on the commissions. Most came from families of country gentry who had lived in the county for generations. Under James I and Charles I nearly half of the justices in most counties were from families which had been established in the area before 1500. Some were mere figureheads and took no part in the affairs, but many of the working justices were eminent men whose names appear in the *Dictionary of National Biography*. The commission contained more members of the nobility than previously, but this arose from James I's practice of creating more peerages.[3] Almost all spiritual peers were on the commissions and there was a tendency, especially under Charles I, to include some of the more junior clergy as well. Most of the latter had had legal training and they helped to make up the legal core of magistrates who regularly played the leading role at Quarter Sessions, where lawyers were among the most assiduous attenders. This group numbered between a sixth and an eighth of all those on the commission but, although it comprised most of the lawyers, it did not include all those who were in the *Quorum*. The latter had been growing in size since the beginning of Elizabeth's reign when already more than half the justices in most counties were members, many of them not being legally qualified. By the end of Charles I's reign barely a handful in each county were not of the *Quorum*. Earlier historians were, however, wrong in thinking that by 1689 all the justices on every commission were included in the *Quorum*. As will be shown later,[4] there were a few omissions from the *Quorum* until at least the 1720s. The last legislation to refer to the *Quorum*, however, was passed in 1664 when an Act against the holding of religious meetings other than those of the Church of England provided for searches to be made of private houses, but the houses of peers could be searched only under a warrant from the King or in the presence of two JPs, one of whom had to be of the *Quorum*.[5]

We have a full and continuous series of Quarter Sessions records for most counties from 1610, and these show that the total number of justices who attended varied greatly, both within each county and throughout the country as a whole. It is not possible, however, to give a precise figure for those who were present at any one time because the information is contained in the pipe rolls and the minutes and order books, none of which are entirely reliable for this purpose. Pipe rolls were used by the sheriff to claim for the wages he had to pay to the justices, but this did not include peers, who were not entitled to any pay and, as regards the sums payable to the other justices, these were usually put into a common fund and not distributed to individuals. The fund was then used to cover common expenses - usually the cost of dinners, as Lambard tells us. There is evidence that, for convenience, those justices who came to the first day of sessions were automatically credited with three days' attendance whether they were present for the whole time or not, while any who appeared only on subsequent days were omitted.[6] All that mattered was that the appropriate amount

3. Up to the beginning of the seventeenth century there were some counties in which there were no resident noblemen, and consequently none were on the county commission apart from the Lord Chancellor and other figureheads.
4. Vol. II, ch. I and vol. III, Appendix II.
5. 17 Charles II, c. 2, s. 14.
6. See Warwick RO, ed., S.C. Radcliff and H.C. Johnson, vol. II;

should be collected for dining and other purposes. Minutes and order books, on the other hand, which conflict greatly with the pipe rolls, contain lists of attendances compiled by the Clerk of the Peace and are more likely to be accurate, though even they are not always reliable as the clerk sometimes named only certain individual justices as being present and then added the words "and others." All that can be said with confidence is that in most counties those present at any one time were usually no more than a quarter of those on the commission (other than the figureheads). Sometimes the number was much lower, only two or three JPs being present, but these appear to have been occasions when there was little work to be transacted. It seems that a growing number of occasions were recorded which were not the ordinary Quarter Sessions but were adjournments, or were even what were becoming Petty Sessions. A few individuals never attended any meetings at all and this usually, though by no means invariably, led to removal from the commission.

As we have seen, the total number of justices became unduly large under Elizabeth and efforts were made to reduce it. Numbers increased again, however, under James I and in 1621 Parliament petitioned the King to reduce the size of the commissions and particularly to eliminate those who were thought to be too young. The youth and inexperience of many justices had been the subject of criticism for some time. It was due largely to the fact that, following a family tradition, the elder sons of justices were often appointed to their fathers' commissions at a young age. In 1608 Lord Ellesmere, when delivering the Lord Chancellor's customary address in the Star Chamber to the Judges about to depart on Assize - when many JPs were also present - rebuked the crowd of "New young knights who come in their braveries and stand there like an idol to be gazed upon, and do nothing." They were "not justices for their countenance only" but were to remember their oaths and duties which required them to stop all riotous assemblies and to see that the poor were provided for within their parishes.[7] Neither the Lord Chancellor's comments nor the subsequent petition of Parliament seem to have had much effect, although steps were taken on the King's orders to remove those who were "unworthy." In Charles I's reign, however, the commissions did tend to become smaller. They contracted further under the Protectorate but increased again after the Restoration.

The men who governed England as JPs differed in their social status, their personal wealth, their political involvement and in the manner in which they discharged their duties, from those who had similar responsibilities in any other country at that time. It is

---

7.   John Hawarde, *Les Reportes des Cases in Camera Stellata*, ed., by W.P. Baildon, 1894, pp. 367-368.

interesting to compare the system with that pertaining in France, whose history was closely intertwined with that of Britain during the seventeenth century. In England local government was in the hands of amateurs while in France it was directed through professionals. The reign of Louis XIII, who was the contemporary of the first two Stuarts, saw the introduction of the Intendants. They were under the direct and rigid control of the Crown, or rather of the King's Minister, Cardinal Richelieu while he was in office, and they conducted a highly efficient form of government but one which secured the absolute authority of the monarchy. In marked contrast, the JPs, while exercising royal authority on behalf of the Crown with a fair amount of competence and generally with complete loyalty, were also ready to show their independence when they thought that the King was exceeding his constitutional powers, and they played an important part in curbing royal supremacy and in ensuring that attempts by James I, and particularly Charles I, to establish a dictatorship were unsuccessful.

The justices were also unique in their close association with the country's legislative body, which was of prime importance as the authority of Parliament increased. As had been the case under Elizabeth, at least half of the Stuart House of Commons at any one time were JPs, and this interfusion between the magistracy and the legislature became of increasing consequence during the development of the political crisis in the first part of the century. The JPs' mounting opposition to the course adopted by the Crown was reflected in the conduct of the same individuals as MPs, and Holdsworth concluded that the peculiar characteristics of English local government through JPs, which were fatal to the success of a scheme of royal absolutism, were perhaps the most important cause of the ultimate success of the Parliamentary opposition.[8] The same phenomenon was of equal importance after the Restoration, when there was no longer any direct interference by Ministers of the Crown in local affairs. These were entirely in the hands of the JPs who became closely involved in the newly emerging national political parties.

The first Stuarts

When James I came to the throne he found that local government was firmly controlled by the local communities and that royal rule had to be conducted entirely through officers whose sentiments, although supportive of the monarchy, were not invariably in accord with the policy of the Crown. In spite of the new atmosphere of national pride engendered by the Elizabethan wars with Spain, national loyalty still

8.   HEL, vol. VI, p. 61.

tended to be subordinate to local loyalty. This attitude was to be found in all those responsible for the machinery of government in counties and towns and was shared by the lower officials - constables, overseers, surveyors and churchwardens - as well as by the governing oligarchy of JPs and Deputy Lieutenants, and even by the Lords Lieutenant who, although personal representatives of the King, had their roots in the community which they governed. It is true that at the beginning of the century the Crown was able to rely to a considerable extent upon the Lord Lieutenant to overcome local opposition, but this support weakened with the passage of time. Similarly the JPs, who had never been as closely identified with the Sovereign as the Lieutenants, became less ready to implement royal policy as the century progressed. As already mentioned, although they were in general loyal supporters of the Crown, they would not tolerate what they regarded as unconstitutional interference with the rights of the citizens, and whereas in the past they had been directly concerned in the political field only when serving as Members of Parliament, they now for the first time became involved as JPs. Under Elizabeth most JPs had generally exhibited dutiful obedience to the will of the Sovereign even when faced with forced loans, but the arbitrary methods adopted by James I and Charles I provoked a more critical attitude.

There was far less Parliamentary legislation affecting the justices during James's reign than there had been under the Tudors. This did not mean, however, that the justices were not encumbered with additional duties. They were bombarded with proclamations and orders from James and his government which both added to their tasks and also sought to ensure a more assiduous devotion to their existing functions. Within two years of James' accession a proclamation required the justices to be present throughout the whole of sessions and it directed Clerks of the Peace to record the time of arrival and departure of each justice and to report the result to the Judge of Assize, who in turn was to report non-attenders to the Chancellor. There was some justification for the order because of the small proportion of justices who performed a fair share of the work, but the autocratic manner in which the matter was handled aroused universal resentment. The instructions seem to have been ignored by the justices with impunity, as was usual when the whole body of justices was required to do something to which they objected, and the order did little more than arouse a sense of annoyance which made them the more ready to challenge any subsequent behaviour by the Crown.

This growing apprehension in the face of orders from the Crown made the justices react more readily than they might otherwise have done when the King started to direct them to deal with matters which were not covered by legislation through Parliament. He began by seeking to create new offences by edict, and he instructed the justices to dispose of them in the same manner as other crimes. The practice was challenged by the Commons in 1610 and was subsequently condemned by the Royal Judges. This put a stop to the creation of new offences by Royal Prerogative, but it did not diminish the King's inclination to govern through orders and proclamations. Soon he resorted to the same procedure in an attempt to raise revenue without Parliamentary sanction.

In 1614 a letter from the Council was addressed to the JPs and sheriffs in every county, lamenting the failure of Parliament to supply the King with the funds he needed and praising the readiness with which the lords spiritual and temporal and other gentlemen had "presented and given plate or money or both" to their Sovereign, thus showing their "dutiful love and affection". The letter continued:

"And therefore we, understanding the forwardness of your affections upon all occasions, have thought good to make the same known to you, wishing you to impart the same to other gentlemen and all such within that county that you shall discern to be persons of good ability or otherwise fit to further the service."9

Whatever was given was to be sent to Whitehall with the names of the givers so that his Majesty "may be pleased to take notice of their good affections." The letter concluded with the words "And so, leaving the carriage of this business to your discretions and wisdoms, we bid you heartily farewell."

It became clear that this did not mean that it was left to the justices' discretion as to whether or not contributions were made. In many counties the justices, faced with this unenviable and embarrassing task, were reluctant to comply with the request and, while giving assurances of their affection and desire to assist the King, returned evasive letters to the Council. The most common objection which they raised was that it was constitutional practice for all money to be supplied to the King through Parliament, and therefore the present proposal would set a precedent which would adversely affect the justices' successors. In the words of the Kent justices, their compliance with the letter would create "the danger of this precedent for which they had neither discretion nor warrant of Lawe." Those in Devon spoke of "the exceeding prejudice that may come to posterity by such a precedent."10 Warwickshire justices made it clear that they spoke as representatives of the county when they refused "on behalf of all men of ability" to contribute to the gift to the King; they offered to make payment but

9.	APC, July 4, 1614.
10.	A.H.A. Hamilton, *Quarter Sessions from Queen Elizabeth to Queen Anne*, 1878, pp. 42-44.

through Parliament only.[11] Other counties responded in a similar manner.

The reaction of the Council was to summon many of the justices to appear before them and to admonish them severely. In some cases a justice who had refused to make a contribution himself received a letter with a veiled threat as to what he should expect if he continued in his obstinacy. Some members of the nobility who were less forthcoming in their contributions than the original letter suggested were not exempt from rebuke. Lord St John of Bletsoe was informed by the Council that they had not yet heard from the Bedfordshire justices that he had sent anything. This, they said, set a bad example because he had attended their meetings and "many eyes were upon you." He was therefore required to attend to the matter "with all alacrity."[12]

There were, however, many justices who made a real effort to comply with the royal instructions, and it is probably largely for that reason that the outcome of the government tactics seem, at least for the time being, to have been reasonably successful. A fair though by no means abundant sum was realized. An even larger amount was produced when the same device, which came to be known as a Benevolence, was adopted again in 1622.

Although this may have appeared at the time as a significant victory for the Crown and its centralizing policy, it in fact marked the beginning of a new era in which the independence of the JPs was to become greater and more secure than before. Until then there had been little cohesion between the justices in different counties, but James' tactics served to unite them as a national force in the political sphere. From then onwards the impact of the justices on the affairs of the nation increased, while the influence of the Privy Council on local affairs gradually diminished.

Soon after Charles I succeeded to the throne in 1625, Parliament refused to grant him the funds he required. He accordingly decided to follow the precedent set by his father and to ask the justices, in somewhat more peremptory terms than those adopted in the previous reign, to persuade all those in a position to do so to make a donation to the royal purse. Accordingly, in July 1626, the Council issued a direction to the JPs and sheriffs in every county to collect free gifts in a similar manner to those which had been obtained in the previous reign. They were "forthwith to meet together and in our name to exhorte our people that they would not fail freely to give unto us a full supplye answerable to the necessity of our present occasions."[13] Lists

11.   APC, 1613-14, 655-6.
12.   *Ibid.*, October 9, 1614.
13.   "State Papers relating to Musters, Beacons, etc. in Norfolk from 1626 to beginning of the Civil War," Walter Rye, *Norfolk and Norwich Archaeological Society*, 1907, p. 25.

of donors, and also of those who refused to pay, were to be sent to the Council. This time the device met with stiff opposition throughout the country and proved to be totally ineffective. Its failure was due largely to the united front of resistance presented by almost all the justices, who were backed by the rest of the population. The King and his Council seem to have concluded that nothing would be achieved at that point by summoning the justices to Westminster to answer for their recalcitrance, and instead commissioners (some of whom were also JPs) were appointed under a royal patent of 1626 with the duty of raising the sum required by way of a loan from those who were of sufficient substance. The efforts made by the commissioners to fulfil their duties varied from county to county but, even where they strove to comply with their instructions, they usually met with firm refusal from the members of the population who were called upon to contribute. The attitude throughout the land was that the people were willing to help the King but only through Parliament. In some areas the commissioners refused to act. In Lincolnshire, where they took this course, ten commissioners, of whom four were JPs, were imprisoned and were not released until the King felt obliged to summon Parliament in 1628.

Once again the royal strategy had proved far less effective than had been hoped, thanks largely to the resistance of the JPs and their associates, who became ever more vigilant in scrutinizing the political manoeuvres of the Crown. In the absence of a professional bureaucracy backed by a strong standing army, the peculiar English system under the independent-minded JPs meant that local government was not always responsive to the wishes of the monarch and could ultimately become diametrically opposed to them. The possibility of tension between the justices and the central government grew with the increasing differences between the King and Parliament with its large JP element.

Attempts by Charles to increase administrative efficiency did not, however, go entirely unheeded. The foremost example of this was the issue, in January 1631, of Books of Orders, setting out the duties of the justices and other officers. Instructions on similar lines had been issued in the 1570s and 1580s, but these were less comprehensive than the Books, which laid down a clear procedural machinery and covered all areas of responsibility. Every justice was told exactly what he was required to do. The JPs were to meet monthly in each hundred to supervise the work of the subordinate officials and to make full reports, which were given to the sheriffs who submitted them to the Assize Judges on the circuit. The Judges were given the task by the Council of publicizing the contents of the Books and of explaining to the justices the more difficult points which they raised, including those relating to administration. It would be more than 300 years before the

Justices of the Peace again became subject to a centralized system of training. The Judges were also expected to collect four reports each year from the justices in each hundred and to forward them to Westminster. At first the response was not enthusiastic and, in 1633, when the Judges returned from the Trinity Assizes, it was found that reports had been submitted by only 18 counties. A further strong directive from the Council resulted in the procedure being followed more rigidily for a time.[14] Contemporary records are not sufficient to enable us to reach a firm conclusion as to the effectiveness of the Books, though it would seem that in general they had a beneficial effect. One undoubted result was to focus attention upon Petty Sessions[15] and to regularize their meetings, as later described. It also seems clear, however, that although the JPs accepted the need for these orders and made some effort to implement them, they resented the dictatorial interference in their affairs. The orders might have been more effective had not the justices become by now acutely apprehensive of government intervention. As it was the orders, although extending the role of magisterial meetings out of Quarter Sessions, fell far short of making the impact that was intended. This failure had a significant effect upon the Council and hastened the end of the Crown's attempts to modify the justices' independence in the control of local affairs.

In spite of these setbacks, however, Charles persevered in his efforts to raise money without the sanction of Parliament, and in 1635 he proceeded to levy ship money. This was a tax for the laudable purpose of repairing and maintaining the fleet, but it was imposed upon inland as well as upon seaboard counties which had borne the burden heretofore, and the extension of the catchment area was made without Parliamentary approval. The JPs and the sheriffs generally resisted, and where they did not do so the constables and bailiffs made collection of the tax impossible by refusing to provide returns of those liable, or to execute writs of restraint on the property of those who refused to pay. This local resistance was overcome for a time when the majority of the Exchequer Judges, in the case of John Hampden, saw fit to declare the collection of ship money legal even without Parliamentary sanction.

During the next few years the collection of ship money became ever less profitable, and in 1640 the need to deal with a Scottish invasion compelled the King, after 11 years of personal rule, to summon Parliament. From now on the Commons, most of whose members were opposed to the King's policies, played a dominant role and, in

14.   SP 16/259/88. An example is given by Professor Thomas Barnes in *Somerset 1625 -1640*, pp. 81-5.
15.   J.R. Tanner, *Constitutional Documents of the Reign of James I*, 1930, Cambridge U.P.

1641, an important Act was passed declaring ship money illegal. It also abolished the Star Chamber together with the prerogative jurisdiction of the Councils of Wales and the North and narrowly defined the jurisdiction of the Privy Council. The personal rule of Charles I broke down because it lost the confidence of the propertied classes, among them the JPs.

In addition to the efforts by the Crown to govern the justices through the Council there were attempts by the early Stuarts, and later by the Cromwellian and Parliamentary regimes, to control them through the Judges of Assize.

In addition to their responsibility for ensuring compliance with the Books of Orders the Judges reviewed the justices' decisions, both judicial and administrative. Many cases coming before Assizes arose from failure of the justices to discharge their administrative duties. An example appears in the Essex records of March 1629 when the churchwardens of Moulsham petitioned the Assize Judge regarding the number of alehouses in their village. Previous petitions had been referred by the Judges to "our next adjoining justices," but these had not only failed to reduce the number of licensed houses but had actually increased them. The Judge was therefore asked to take the matter "to your own breast, and so to order that this great grievance may suddenly be suppressed."[16] General instructions were sometimes issued to Judges to ensure that the justices dealt with some specific matter. Thus in 1641 Judges of Assizes were required to command the justices to cause constables to see that watch and ward be duly kept in all places for apprehending and punishing wandering soldiers and vagabonds.[17] Apart from the JPs themselves, the Judges were the only royal representatives of any importance seen in a county, where they appeared once or twice a year and delivered an address to the assembled justices. As had been the case under the Tudors, they themselves had been harangued previously in the Council chamber, usually by the Lord Chancellor, before leaving Westminster. Numbers of justices were also present in the chamber on these occasions to hear the Chancellor's charge which was sometimes directed at them, as we saw when Lord Ellesmere rebuked the young justices in their finery in 1608. Sometimes King James himself delivered the charge to the Judges. They were instructed to convey messages expounding government policy and also to report back to the King on the conduct of the JPs on the circuit. Their job was not only to try criminal cases but also to ensure that the justices were performing their administrative as well as their judicial duties. In the words of the King to the Judges before they began their Assizes in 1616, "You have

16.   ERO, Assizes 37/70/1.
17.   SP 16/483/36.

charges to give to the Justices of the Peace that they doe their duties when you are absent as well as present: take an accompt of them and report their service to me at your returne." The King attached great importance to this method of controlling local government for, as he also observed, "however godly, wise, righteous and just the King might be, if the subalterne Magistrates doe not their partes under him, the Kingdom must needs suffer." No matter how careful and industrious the Judges might be, "if the Justices of the Peace under them put not their helping hands, in vaine is all your labour. For they are the King's eyes and ears in the country."

On the same occasion, the King criticized some justices whom he described as "busy bodies who did so much, embracing many businesses for the enlargement of their private gain and profits." He was probably referring to what came to be known as "trading justices" in Middlesex, who will be described later. Generally he seems to have held a reasonably good opinion of the JPs whom he regarded as being of potential value both in maintaining law and order and as an instrument of local administration. As we shall see later, it was he who introduced the JP system into Scotland, and he observed that "Government by justices is so laudable and so highly esteemed by me that I have made Scotland to be governed by justices and constables as England is."[18]

The policy of governing the country through the Assize Judges proved as ineffective as that of direct intervention by the Council. The Assizes, with their limited duration, had insufficient time to scrutinize the activities of the JPs, and there was little they could do to stimulate those who were dilatory, apart from threatening the imposition of fines, which often proved ineffective. The height of the Assize Judges' responsibility for administration was reached with the issue of the Books of Orders; thereafter there was a gradual breakdown of their implementation of government policy and with it the government's influence over the justices diminished.

As will be apparent from what has already been said, the government was powerless without the willing co-operation of the JPs and other local officials. Although the justices were required to obey the government's orders, and might be summoned before the Council to be punished for failing to do so, the Crown, as we have seen in the Tudor period, had no means of enforcing its will against the concerted resistance of the whole body of magistrates. Under Charles I the justices were supported by all sections of the local population who were still imbued with the old communal spirit and who followed the tradition of the self-governing community. As Holdsworth points out, the JPs themselves were inspired by the ideas of the common law, and

18.   Record of Thirsk Sessions, October, 1640, North Riding QSR.

they were well aware that the King's current policy was to substitute the supremacy of the Royal Prerogative for the supremacy of Parliament. Every-day work was still done under judicial forms which left them free to act independently so long as they obeyed the rules of the law, unlike bureaucratic officials who always acted on detailed instructions from the government. Indeed there were occasions when justices sought the Council's directions on how to deal with an emergency only to be told to use their own judgment.

As tension grew between King and Parliament the justices still remained basically loyal to the Crown and blamed its counsellors for defects in government. Although there were considerable differences of view between individuals, most justices, including those in the Commons, hoped for the establishment of a democratic monarchy working through Parliament. Until 1640, records of sessions show little sign of any concern about the pending conflict. In 1639, however, there had been a change in the attitude of the public towards supporting the military forces which were beginning to assemble. Growing resentment was expressed at the obligation to defray the cost of munitions, supplies and the wages of the soldiers. Quarter Sessions' records in some areas were soon filled with entries relating to presentments of individuals and of whole parishes for refusing to pay their assessments. There was also opposition to billeting and increasing resentment at the crimes of violence committed by the soldiery, especially by the many deserters. This was most evident in areas which the King thought to be open to invasion by hostile forces and where he therefore tended to raise and quarter his troops. The sessions' records of the Northern counties from 1640 show the anxiety with which the justices regarded the deteriorating situation and there were occasions when Quarter Sessions had to be moved to another town because of the great disorder which was feared amongst the soldiers.

As the outbreak of hostilities approached, a feeling of alarm suddenly began to spread through all areas and the justices directed their minds belatedly towards the avoidance of hostilities. By 1642 the subject was debated at length at Quarter Sessions and at Assizes. Some of these gatherings sent messages to both King and Parliament urging them to compose their differences. It is doubtful whether these would have had any effect on the outcome even if they had been delivered earlier, but as it was they were too late. When Civil War began with Charles raising his standard at Nottingham in August 1642, the JPs in many parts of the country were deeply divided.

Civil War, 1642-1646

Before the Civil War, there had been peace in England, but almost continuous strife on the Continent, for more than 150 years. The work of the justices in most parts had proceeded regularly and in an atmosphere of greater calm than almost ever before. From 1642 the scene changed, and although the justices' routine functions continued to be performed in a more or less regular manner, except when they were disrupted by open warfare, their work generally was disorganized to an extent which had not occurred previously, even during the strife of the fifteenth century. It is sometimes assumed that those who were not directly involved in the opposing armies, or lived in the path of hostilities, were largely unaffected by the war. This had been true during the Wars of the Roses, but the conflict which took place two centuries later was a different affair. The cost of maintaining the armies had to be borne by everyone, whether they lived in a Royalist area or one controlled by Parliament. The damage to property and the pillaging by the ill-paid troops was enormous and compensation was seldom paid. Impressment by both sides removed the tradesmen and labourers from the village economy. There were many occasions when the justices were ordered by one side or the other to take some action in support of their respective armies. They were expected to raise troops and to produce supplies, or at least to assist others who were engaged in doing so. Thus in 1642 a Captain John van Haesdonck was appointed as commander of a troop with power to raise soldiers, and all JPs, mayors and certain others were directed to support him.[19]

Another difference between the two Civil Wars was that, whereas in the mid-fifteenth century only a small fraction of the population had any interest in the outcome of the conflict, in the 1640s Englishmen at all social levels and in all walks of life tended to favour one side or the other. This did not mean that they all gave active support. There were many who tried to adopt a neutral attitude while others were hostile towards whichever army happened to be plundering their neighbourhood at the time. Many justices had to make agonizing decisions as to the action they should take, especially when they lived in an area which was under the control of the party to which they were opposed. The situation was one which generated a disruptive atmosphere among all sections of the community. This was apparent at Quarter Sessions, where proceedings were thrown into turmoil, sometimes by the arrival of troops,[20] sometimes by disputes between the justices themselves. Buildings in which Quarter Sessions were held were often taken over by one or other of the armies, and when alternative accommodation was found the proceedings might still be disrupted and the justices intimidated. Soon after the outbreak of

19.   SP 16/4493/16.
20.   Sessions often had to be adjourned from one town to another. For instance the Devon July sessions in 1643 were adjourned from Tiverton to Topsham. Devon RO, pp. 128-9.

hostilities Warwick Quarter Sessions were disrupted by the noise caused by the arrival of 800 troops. The sessions adjourned to the Swan Inn, but this was filled with soldiers and no business could be transacted. No further Quarter Sessions were held in Warwickshire for three years.[21] This pattern extended to Assizes which sometimes had to be adjourned because "the Power of the Sword so prevailing that Public Justice cannot be administered."[22]

The position varied greatly from one area to another. In Norfolk, for example, which was firmly under Parliamentary control throughout the war and where most justices were Parliamentary supporters, the sessions' records show little disruption of work but in most counties the situation was different.

It is not surprising that many justices declined to attend sessions. Even before the outbreak of hostilities the number of absentees had grown as partisan divisions became more apparent - the absence being sometimes recorded as "he being a Parliament man." After the war began it was not uncommon for only two justices to be present at Quarter Sessions, and sometimes none appeared at all. Two centuries earlier the justices had sought to handle similar situations by meeting in their own houses. The same expedient was adopted in the 1640s and the number of sittings out of sessions increased significantly. There is reason to believe that when Quarter Sessions could not be held for a period of six months or more, the work in some counties was entrusted to a committee of JPs who met wherever a suitable venue could be found, but the outcome was not always satisfactory owing to the difficulty of enforcing decisions taken. The relationship between the justices and Assizes also became uncertain, at least in those places where there was extensive military activity. In some counties the JPs delivered the gaols themselves while in others they still sent prisoners to the Commissioners of Gaol Delivery for trial. Sometimes the gaols themselves could not be used and the prisoners had to be sent to the nearest garrison. Thus in 1646 the Wiltshire justices had to commit to the garrison at Malmesbury instead of to the gaol at Fisherton.

The pressure of work became heavier with growing lawlessness and with new responsibilities, such as the provision of pensions for wounded soldiers or their widows or orphans, all of whom were chargeable to the parish. Some of the earliest orders received by the justices from Parliament as it gained the ascendancy were to make a charge on local funds for the provision of relief to those who had suffered in the Parliamentary cause. The claims of these people were considered at each sessions in the face of mounting difficulty in raising the necessary sums.

21.   Warwick RO, QSOB, vol. II, Introduction, p. xxv.
22.   Ordinance of Parliament, July 1643.

By the end of the conflict there had been a noticeable effect on the composition of the commissions, though this was not as great as one might have expected. Surprisingly, Charles never resorted to a general purge of all justices who embraced the cause of Parliament, but towards the end of the war he did remove a number of those who were active in opposition to the Crown and replaced them with his own supporters.

Interregnum

Open hostilities had ended by 1648, apart from spasmodic outbreaks and the subsequent Parliamentary victories at Worcester in 1650 and Dunbar in 1651. Between 1646 and 1649 many people, including most of the JPs, seem to have hoped still to see the establishment of a constitutional monarchy. It is not within the scope of this work to discuss the reasons for the failure to reach a settlement between King and Parliament, which led to the execution of Charles I in 1649 and the establishment of a republican government which ruled for 11 years, but this had important consequences for the JPs.

When the fighting ended, many of the Royalist gentry who served on the commissions seemed resigned to a future under a constitutional monarchy, and there can be little doubt that they would have served as magistrates under such a régime. It was not until the King was executed and they themselves were subjected to punitive fines and confiscations that they were driven to vigorous opposition to the Commonwealth government and were imbued with a hatred of Puritanism which endured for the rest of the century. After the King's death many of them abandoned their role in local affairs. Parliament for its part, while prepared to build on the old foundations, came to rely upon novel institutions and upon the service of a new class of men who bore little resemblance to the knights of the shires of old. Its concern was to repair the wreckage of the war and to establish administrative machinery which would govern the country at all levels. The Long Parliament made the first change by excluding all members of the clergy, a few of whom had been included in most county commissions under Charles I. Among those removed was the Rev. Andrew Byng, Archdeacon of Norwich, who was one of the translators of the Authorised Version of the Bible. This was followed by the dismissal of numbers of Royalist sympathisers and their replacement by men likely to support the Parliamentary cause, even though many of them were not of the social status of their predecessors. Some of those now appointed had served previously as high constables.

In the result, the office of Justice of the Peace became debased and its work curtailed, while those appointed to the commissions were men of far lower social standing than their predecessors. Clarendon, in his *History of the Rebellion*, described the new justices by saying that "they who were not above the condition of ordinary inferior constables six or seven years before were now Justices of the Peace." Clarendon, who viewed the situation through the eyes of a staunch Royalist, probably exaggerated, but there was certainly a notable debasing of the coinage in the eyes of most contemporary observers. There were still some men of substance of the old type on the commissions but they were comparatively few in number and, for the first time, merchants and tradesmen appeared on county benches.[23] The disapproval of the gentry was exacerbated when the Commonwealth government made the mayors of some towns justices *ex officio* of their adjoining counties.

Attempts were made from time to time to bring the commissions into line with the views of Parliament, but these had only limited effect. The extreme radical dissenters, known as the Levellers, tried to have the office of JP made elective, but were defeated. Purges of the commissions in 1650 and 1651 removed prominent opponents of the Rump Parliament, but in fact only the most outspoken were dismissed. The same occurred in further purges in 1652 and 1653. Nevertheless, the commissions did become filled with those dedicated to the Parliamentary cause.

From the end of the Civil War until the death of Charles I, Commissions of the Peace were issued under the authority of Parliament but were addressed to the justices in the King's name, each beginning with the words "Carolus Rex." During the republic they were issued in the name of the "Keepers of the Liberty of England," and under the Protectorate of "Oliver Cromwell, Lord Protector." By an ordinance of 1650 all writs, processes and other proceedings in courts of justice were to be in English, and thereafter English replaced Latin in the Commissions of the Peace until the Restoration, when they reverted to Latin for a further 73 years.

The quality of the justices became of less importance than it had been previously because their powers were curtailed by new bodies with authority equal to, and in some cases exceeding, those of the JPs. Before the war, the justices had gained a virtual monopoly of authority in provincial areas and were the sole and undisputed local governors. In those parts of the country which had been dominated by the Royalists this situation persisted for a time after the end of hostilities, but elsewhere Parliament began to set up various local bodies charged with the administration of the area according to government directions. This system was gradually extended to all areas, thus undermining the position of the justices. Among the first of these

23. The number of noblemen on the commissions dropped by about 85 per cent and that of knights and baronets (who had been created for the first time by James I) fell by nearly 75 per cent.

bodies were commissions, first established during the war (by an ordinance of February, 1643) to collect money for the maintenance of the Parliamentary army. These were soon followed by others responsible for a wide variety of matters many of which had been dealt with traditionally by justices. Moreover, the local officials, such as the constables who previously reported only to the justices, were now required to assist the new commissioners. Even the justices themselves were sometimes ordered to act in a subordinate role. It is true that many of the JPs also served on one or more of the new committees or commissions, but the significance of the change was that the justices as such no longer enjoyed exclusive control of local affairs, and their status was accordingly debased in the public eye.

In spite, however, of the tendency to usurp their powers, the JPs remained responsible for many of their former local duties which they were able to perform with remarkably little interference. The Star Chamber having been abolished, they were not subjected to constant scrutiny by the Council of State, which was the successor to the Privy Council. They exercised a fairly wide criminal jurisdiction with little supervision, though most cases were minor ones, the majority being stealing and assault, and there were also many charges of recusancy arising from failure to attend church or to take the sacraments. During the Commonwealth, jurisdiction in certain ecclesiastical offences was transferred from the church courts to Quarter Sessions, the most frequent being failure to repair a church or churchyard, adultery and fornication. The justices spent a considerable amount of time on the maintenance of highways, the fixing of prices and wages and above all on the administration of the Poor Law. In this context they were required to see that pensions were paid to disabled soldiers of the Parliamentary army, which caused deep resentment among the former Royalist troops who received nothing under the government ordinances. (The Royalists got their own back after the Restoration when an Act restricted pensions to those who had fought for the King). Cromwell himself took a personal interest in these matters and there is a letter of January 12, 1651,[24] addressed to the justices of Caernarfonshire and signed by him, directing them to levy a rate to provide for the "widowes and orphans of those whose husbands have died and such soldiers as have been maymed in the service of Parliament" so that they might not be exposed "to misery and ruin." The amount awarded to those permanently maimed in the Parliamentary cause varied considerably. For the loss of a limb it was usually between 30 shillings and 50 shillings per annum. The widows of soldiers who had been killed often received substantially more if they had dependent children, sometimes as much as £4 per annum. This

24.   Caernarvonshire RO.

placed a heavy strain on county funds, and sessions' minutes deplored the lack of sufficient money to meet the claims. This drain on resources was increased by the needs of the poor whose numbers were swollen by destitute Royalist soldiers and their families.

It is generally believed that the care of the poor, aged, sick and infirm and the education and apprenticing of children was carried out by the justices during this period at least as efficiently and possibly more so than at any other time. There is, however, evidence that, at least in some areas, the administration of the Poor Law was harsher than it had been before and that the justices, probably under government pressure, were more concerned with suppressing vagrancy than the relief of the impotent poor. This was certainly the case under the Major Generals, who are mentioned later.

The horror with which the authorities regarded any form of public gathering is illustrated by many records of proceedings at Quarter Sessions. What are seen today as harmless rural festivities were treated as grave sources of crime. For instance, in 1655, the Warwickshire justices, meeting at Henley-in-Arden, were informed of "unlawful meetings of idle and vain persons ... for erecting of may-poles and may bushes, and for using of morris dances and other heathenish and unlawful customs, the observations whereof tendeth to draw together a great concourse of loose people ... to the hazard of the public peace." The justices ordered the bailiff and constable of Henley to prevent and suppress such activities in future.[25]

Among the many odd jobs which rested with the Cromwellian justices were some which one might have expected to be viewed unfavourably by the new régime, such as the preservation of game on private estates; their power to deal with poachers was confirmed by an ordinance of 1647. (In the seventeenth century the expression "poaching" was beginning to replace the earlier term "unlawful hunting"). On the other hand, the justices were saddled with a number of new duties which obviously reflected Puritan opinion. Some were aimed at ensuring the proper observance of the Lord's Day. In 1644 an ordinance had directed them to burn publicly all copies of the book on sport which encouraged sports on Sundays, and other rigid measures followed. JPs also had to execute the laws against Jesuits and Popish priests.[26] Their responsibility for church affairs included the supervision of parochial elections of clerks and churchwardens, and they intervened in disputes over churchwardens' accounts and levies for church repairs.

The JPs continued to have responsibility for the militia, and they sometimes received other military assignments. For example, under an

25. Warwick RO, QSOB, vol. III, QSOB, 271-2.
26. AOI, 1642-1660, vol. II, p. 1427.

sometimes received other military assignments. For example, under an order of the Council of 1651, they were directed to demolish the fort at Christchurch.

The Acts and ordinances of the Interregnum contain numerous directions to the JPs on a variety of matters. Two or more justices were to suppress stage plays. They were to enter premises for this purpose and to commit the actors for trial at the next general sessions.[27] They were to adjudicate on the non-payment of wages and regulate differences between master and servant. They surveyed the state of repair of churches, punished blasphemy, issued licences for the sale of corn, examined the officers of captured ships and suppressed vagrancy, horse-racing and cock-fighting. They were ordered to assist other officers, from the Commander-in-Chief of the army to the surveyors of lands confiscated from the bishops. Their jurisdiction was extended for certain purposes; in 1654, JPs of "the greatest ability and integrity" in a county were to be appointed Masters in Chancery Extraordinary.[28]

The task of dealing with profiteers was entrusted to the JPs by an ordinance of 1657. "Divers lewd and dissolute Persons" were living "at very high Rates and great Expences, having no visible Estate, Profession, or Calling." Every JP was given the power to send for such persons and take sureties from them to appear at the next general sessions. If they could not find sureties they were to be imprisoned in the common gaol. If convicted they were to be sent to the house of correction and set to work for three months. On a second conviction they were to be committed to a house of correction until they were discharged by the justices in open sessions.[29]

One entirely new duty was entrusted to the JPs at this time and that was to perform the marriage ceremony. Under a Parliamentary ordinance of August 1653,[30] civil marriages replaced those in church, and between then and 1657 the justices had a monopoly of this function. The ordinance established registers of marriage in parishes, and those who wished to marry had to register the particulars, which were then published, either in the church on three Sundays or in the market place on three market days. When that had been done, the parties came before a JP who examined them and if he found no cause to the contrary he declared them to be henceforth man and wife. The ordinance declared that the marriage should be legally binding and it also decreed that there was to be no other form of marriage according to the laws of England. Like most Parliamentary ordinances, it went into considerable detail, even providing that "In the case of persons that have no hands the Justice of the Peace may dispense with joining hands." If the parties were deaf he could dispense with the words.

27. *Ibid.*, vol. I, p. 1027.
28. *Ibid.*, vol. II, p. 925.
29. *Ibid.*, vol. I, p. 1249.
30. *Ibid.*, vol. II, p. 715.

The marriage ceremony proved to be a new source of revenue to the justices who were entitled to take a fee. Not all of them did so, but there were some, at least among the new justices, who charged excessive amounts.

The banning of church marriages aroused considerable resentment and there were instances of the ordinance being disregarded to the extent that a religious service was held after the civil ceremony, often with the connivance of a justice who sometimes performed his part of the ritual in the church. Feelings became so strong that the prohibition of church marriages was lifted in 1657, but the JPs' power to solemnize marriages remained and was not abolished until after the Restoration. Even then, under an Act of 1660, marriages previously celebrated by JPs remained valid. The authority was never restored to justices in the United Kingdom but, as we shall see, it was adopted in some colonial territories and today is still one of the principal functions of JPs in the United States of America.

The various routine functions which the justices had been performing with little interference were interrupted between 1655 and 1657 when Major Generals were appointed to govern the 11 military districts into which the country was then divided. This was an attempt by Cromwell to introduce direct rule from Westminster through the army. The Major General took the place of the Lord Lieutenant, but he was much more than a military commander. He was also a civilian governor with responsibility, according to the instructions of the Council of State:

"to inquire into idlers that may be compelled to work or banished and the poor better provided for and execute the law in such cases. To make the highways safe from daily robberies and burglaries by finding out and apprehending thieves and dangerous persons."

The justices found themselves subject to the overall authority of the Major Generals, who were appointed to the Commissions of the Peace and were required to report to the Council the names of justices "who are remiss that they may be dismissed."

The rule of the Major Generals was short-lived. It aroused great resentment in local areas and soon the whole country was outraged by this blatant example of military intervention. During the two years that the Generals governed the country they came to rely to a considerable extent upon the support of the JPs, and they recognized that, in order to make this effective, the commissions needed to be strengthened by men of substance and that the door must be opened wider to the squirearchy. It came to be realized that the new men on the commissions were unable to govern the countryside and that effective control could be exercised only through the old established landed gentry. Gradually, members of this class were again appointed justices, though their numbers were at first small, partly because the gentry themselves were still reluctant to accept office. It could indeed be said with some justification that the leading families had contributed to the decision to appoint the Major Generals by their unwillingness to continue to exercise the office of JP under the Protectorate, thus leaving a gap which had to be filled.

Some of the Parliamentary leaders, like Sir Thomas Fairfax and Oliver Cromwell himself, had always been prepared to accept that the gentry had a useful role to play. They were willing to leave them with some authority provided that this did not conflict with the radicalism of the new régime. It is unlikely, however, that they appreciated the effect that the debasing of the magistracy had upon the attitude of the propertied classes in town and country, and it could be argued that failure to gain and hold their support was a contributory factor in the fall of the Protectorate.

During the last few years of the Protectorate a number of prominent men were placed on the commissions. Very few of them were dedicated republicans and most favoured a constitutional monarchy. At first some were not averse to the establishment of a kingship in the person of Oliver Cromwell, but from an early stage most of the land-owner JPs seem to have looked towards a restoration of the Stuarts. After the death of Cromwell in 1658, the justices in their Quarter Sessions meetings became ever more critical of the régime, and when Charles II landed in May 1660, they were prominent in welcoming the new King. They looked forward eagerly to a resumption of their old authority and to the return of the days when the JPs were the élite rulers of the countryside. To a large extent their hopes were realized, but in some respects they were to be disappointed.

Restoration

It has been remarked that in the years immediately preceding the Civil War a picture emerged of England resembling a "union of partially independent shire-states, each with its own distinctive ethos and loyalty."[31] The isolationism which characterized that and earlier periods was eroded during the Protectorate, particularly under the regional government of the Major Generals, and from the Restoration onwards the common interests of the counties became stronger and there was a greater consciousness of England as a nation. Although government was decentralized and although the JPs who administered it at local level were still primarily concerned with the affairs of their

31.   A.M. Everitt, "Social Mobility in Early Modern England, Past and Present," 1966, No. 33, p. 59.

own county and neighbourhood, they were far less localized in their outlook than they had been before, and they became involved to a much greater extent in matters concerning the nation as a whole.

The victory of Parliament in the Civil War meant that in future the localities were assured of a large measure of independence in the conduct of their domestic affairs but, whereas under the Protectorate the JPs had occupied a subordinate position, from 1660 onwards both the JPs and the squirearchy as a whole regained their influence and became of even greater significance than before. The Stuarts and the Commonwealth had tried to override the squires and the chartered corporations and had failed. The central government's authority in local affairs declined throughout the period and by the end of the century was far weaker than it had been under Elizabeth.

After the Restoration, many of those justices who had been Parliamentary supporters were removed and replaced with Royalists, but this process was less thorough than might have been expected, and numbers of those appointed during the Protectorate were left in office. The first commissions issued by Charles II contained up to a third of those who were on the Cromwellian commissions. The most noticeable feature of the new commissions compared with those of the previous régime was a great preponderance of landed gentry and a paucity of the merchant class who had figured prominently before. The landed gentry, however, now included some former Roundheads, many of them townsmen who had acquired estates during the Interregnum. Although the lands of Cavaliers which had been confiscated by the government in this period were restored to their former owners, those which had been sold by Royalists to pay their fines were left in the possession of their purchasers, many of whom were wealthy townsmen. The Royalists looked with contempt upon the townsmen, and their feelings were behind legislation passed by the new Parliament which disqualified non-landowners from hunting. The prosperous bankers and merchants, however, who had bought estates, were now among the land-owners themselves, and they were therefore qualified to join the squire both at the hunt and on the commission. Nevertheless the majority of the landed gentry were of the old school who were obsessed with memories of the war and the Commonwealth. Some had been in exile, many had had their estates confiscated or heavily taxed, and they all resented the humiliation of the usurpation of their dominant social position during the Interregnum by men of lower degree. It was from this time that Parliamentary political parties began to develop. The former Roundhead supporters became the nucleus of the Whig Party, while the Tories were centred on the old Cavalier squires and nobles. These divisions became marked among the justices and, as we shall see, party politics became a dominant feature of Quarter Sessions from the late seventeenth century onwards. In 1679, two justices, Sir

Richard Newdigate and Thomas Mariet, were removed from the Warwickshire commission after they had contested Parliamentary seats in opposition to candidates favoured by the court. In the 1680s, the commissions were purged of Whigs in the wake of the Exclusion crisis, while in 1715 they were to be purged of Tories with equal vigour.

The Restoration commissions resembled those of the pre-war period. The ban on the appointment of anyone in holy orders was removed in 1661 and bishops and other clergy were again appointed. Most peers and a large proportion of baronets and knights were included. In addition to local men, many national figures, such as Prince Rupert, were added to a number of commissions, though few of these ever attended sessions and the proportion of absentees was greater than it had ever been. In some counties those who never appeared were twice as numerous as the working justices. Much of this was due to the prestige attaching to the office, which has been mentioned. It was sought after by all who had ambition - which accounted for most of the upper classes in the Kingdom - but many of these were reluctant to do their share of the work. Edmund Bohun who, as we have seen, wrote the leading textbook for justices at the end of the century, strongly disapproved of those who benefited from the prestige conferred by the office without sharing the responsibility. In 1693 he wrote that some JPs "look to nothing but the Credit, Honour and Reputation they shall gain by it, and if they can gain the Title of Right Worshipful and have their neighbours stand bare-headed to them, they have their Designs."[32] Samuel Pepys, the diarist and secretary to the Navy Board, who was appointed a JP in 1660, recorded in his diary "With which honour I find myself mighty pleased, though I am totally ignorant of the duties of a Justice of the Peace." Pepys proved to be more conscientious in the performance of his magisterial duties than some of his colleagues.

One of the causes of absenteeism was the renewed lure of London, which had had no attraction for the JPs during the Interregnum. With the return of the court and the social life of the city, the justices flocked to the capital and some bought town houses. London's attraction was enhanced by the reopening of the theatre, which had been banned under the Protectorate but which became a feature of upper-class life after 1660. The Restoration comedy, beginning with Etherege and developed by Congreve, Dryden and others, depicted the selfish society, bent on sensual pleasures, which pervaded the fun-loving members of the Establishment. We shall see later that one of the best known dramatists of the next generation, Henry Fielding, was

32.   E. Bohun, *The Justice of the Peace, his Calling and Qualifications* London, 1693, p. 135. In Warwickshire there were 190 justices on the commission between 1674 and 1682 but 72 of these never attended a single Quarter Sessions nor are they recorded as having performed any other duty as a justice. WCR, QSOB, vol. VII, Introduction, p. xxxvi.

to become chief magistrate at Bow Street.

In spite of the enticement of London, there was still an appreciable number of justices who devoted the whole of their time to country pursuits and who seldom, if ever, left their counties. A typical example of a country JP immediately after the Restoration was Sir Peter Leicester of Cheshire, whose life and character have been described in a work by Miss Elizabeth Halcrow.[33] Born in 1613, Sir Peter was descended from a long line of Cheshire squires, lords of the manor of Nether Tabley, and could trace his descent for over three centuries. He was a student at Oxford and later at Grays Inn. In 1642 he married the daughter of Lord Gilbert, who lived in a neighbouring county, and had four children. His whole life was that of a country gentleman and he spent most of it on his estate, except when he was campaigning in the Royalist army or undergoing imprisonment by the Roundheads. They permitted him to return to his home at the end of the war on payment of a fine of £747 10 shillings, but he was too suspect to be allowed to hold office under the Protectorate. In 1660, however, he was duly rewarded by the new King when he was created a baronet and appointed both a Deputy Lieutenant and a JP for his county. He was more assiduous in his duties than many of his colleagues and delivered as many as nine charges to the jury at Quarter Sessions. The first of these, delivered soon after his appointment to the commission, while outlining all the types of offence with which the sessions had to deal, referred at some length to treason and regicide, showing that the events of the past 20 years were uppermost in the justices' minds. It may seem surprising that a newly appointed justice should deliver the charge at sessions, but this was often the case, especially when the justice concerned was considered to be particularly competent. There was no regular chairman, and apart from the Lord Lieutenant and the *Custos*, no justice occupied any special position. The chairmanship of Quarter Sessions was not established as a permanent office until the eighteenth century.

The total number of justices on the commissions throughout most of the country increased considerably after 1660, in some cases by as much as 50 per cent. Such evidence as is available supports the estimate of the Webbs that by 1687 there were about 3,000 JPs, of whom between 700 and 800 were active, in a total population of some four million.

The high hopes of many of the justices at the Restoration of the monarchy were realized to some extent by the regaining of their position as the undisputed centre of local government. Their authority was even greater than before as all intervention by the Council had virtually ceased and was never resumed. Such supervision as there was came through the courts which scrutinized their judicial proceedings

33.   Elizabeth M. Halcrow, *Sir Peter Leicester's Charges*, Cheetham Soc., Manchester U.P.

but did not interfere in their administrative or executive functions. The justices' feeling of satisfaction was no doubt heightened by the universal air of euphoria which engulfed the country under its hedonistic King, after being released from the austerities of the previous two decades. They soon found, however, that they were saddled with various unpalatable tasks, especially in the enforcement of religious practice. This arose under the Clarendon Code, so called after Edward Hyde, Earl of Clarendon who, as both Lord Chancellor and Chancellor of the Exchequer, was head of Charles II's government immediately after his accession. In fact, the code was not the work of Clarendon, still less of the King, who sought religious toleration, but of the Cavaliers in Parliament who were obsessed with a bitter hatred of their former enemies and a determination for revenge. The code aimed at maintaining the supremacy of the Church of England. Anyone practising any other form of worship was subject to severe penalties, and there was no tolerance shown to either Catholics or dissenters. Responsibility for enforcing the law rested naturally with the justices.

In the Declaration of Breda of 1660, Charles promised religious freedom provided that this did not disturb the peace. Many of his subjects, however, were not prepared to tolerate any sect which did not subscribe to the Church of England, and this attitude was shared by the Cavalier Parliament which, in May 1662, passed an Act of Uniformity which required every holder of a benefice to declare his acceptance of the Book of Common Prayer and to repudiate other forms of worship. Many clergy refused to conform and were dispossessed. This in itself presented the justices with new problems, especially where livings were left unfilled, and in some instances the justices allowed a dispossessed incumbent to continue to conduct services. The situation became more complicated when Charles persevered in his support of religious toleration, thus causing confusion in the minds of the JPs as to how they should act. It also created friction between different groups and individuals on the commissions.

A notable victim of the repressive ecclesiastical laws was the poet John Bunyan who, as a nonconformist and an advocate of religious liberty, suffered long periods of imprisonment notwithstanding the obvious desire of the JPs to show leniency. He was tried at Bedford Quarter Sessions in 1661 and, although he stated emphatically that he would continue to preach in defiance of the Act, was given a mild sentence of three months' imprisonment. Towards the end of this term he was visited by the Clerk of the Peace who had been delegated by the justices to endeavour to persuade him to conform. He staunchly refused to do so and ultimately remained in prison until he was released following the Declaration of Indulgence in 1672, but was imprisoned again for two years from 1675. His confinement was not very arduous and during the first spell he wrote his autobiography and during the second he completed the first part of *The Pilgrim's Progress.* An account of his meeting in gaol with the Clerk of the Peace of Bedfordshire, John Cobb, on April 3, 1661 is given by Bunyon in his *Grace Abounding to the Chief of Sinners* which he wrote during the first part of his imprisonment and was published in 1666.

In 1664, the first Conventicle Act[34] empowered JPs to impose penalties on anyone over the age of 16 who attended a meeting of more than five persons for religious worship other than in accordance with the Book of Common Prayer. Two justices of the division in which the offence had been committed could convict and commit to gaol or to a house of correction without bail for any period not exceeding three months, unless the offender paid a fine imposed by the justices of not more than £5. The money was to be paid to the churchwardens "for the reliefe of the Poore of the Parish where such offender did last inhabite." For a second offence, the fine was £10, or six months. For a third offence, the accused had to be committed to prison until the next Quarter Sessions who might impose a fine of £100 or order seven years' deportation.

In the following year an Act[35] required persons in holy orders to take an oath that they would not take up arms against the King and would not endeavour to make any alteration to the government of the church or of the state. A person preaching in conventicles might not come within five miles of any corporate town which sent a Member to Parliament until he had taken the oath. Two justices could commit an offender for six months unless he took the oath before them.

Although these Acts, like the Act of Uniformity, were the work of a Parliament which contained many JPs, they caused even greater confusion among the general body of justices, many of whom neglected to enforce them, notwithstanding a warning from the Lord Chancellor in a letter of March 1665, addressed to the JPs in every county. There are few records of proceedings being taken before justices under the Act.

Some justices delighted in prosecuting anyone who did not conform strictly to the doctrine of the Church of England,[36] but the majority did not and, with a view to persuading them to be more assiduous in applying the law, a further Act, of 1670,[37] imposed a penalty of £100 upon any justice who did not implement the Act. This statute was stated to be "to prevent and suppress Seditious Conventicles" and was

34. 16 Charles II, c. 4.
35. 17 Charles II, c. 2.
36. An intriguing account of the activities of one such justice in 1675 is given in the March 1988 number of *The Magistrate,* p. 50.
37. 22 Charles II, c. 1.

to provide "further and more speedy remedies against the growing and dangerous Practices of Seditious Sectaries." The Act empowered a single justice to deal with those who attended a meeting of non-conformists or dissenters. He might impose a fine of five shillings for a first offence and 10 shillings for every subsequent offence. A third of the fine was to go to the King, a third to the churchwardens for the poor, and a third to the informers. A person preaching in defiance of the Act could be fined £20 for the first offence and £40 thereafter. If he escaped, the JP was to levy the amount of the fine on the goods and chattels of the other persons present. The Act also contained an early example of a right of appeal. There was an appeal to Quarter Sessions against conviction if the penalty exceeded 10 shillings. In such a case the appeal was to be made in writing within one week, and the justices must then return any fine which had been collected and certify under their seals the evidence upon which they had convicted. There then followed a jury trial at Quarter Sessions. If the applicant did not proceed, or if he was not acquitted, Quarter Sessions were to order him to pay treble costs. The Act also stipulated that there was to be no further right of appeal to any other court. The fact that JPs were also police officers was shown by the power they were given under the Act to break open and enter any house or other place where they were informed that a conventicle was being held and to seize persons assembled therein. They could call upon such help as they required for this purpose including the militia. The application of this enactment varied considerably from one area to another, but nowhere was there any conspicuous prosecution of justices for not complying, although it is obvious that many of them failed to do so. There were, however, many occasions when a justice might find himself involved in additional work in consequence of the new religious laws. For example, he often had to intervene in disputes as to who was to be the incumbent in a particular parish. In 1661, the vicar of Farnham complained to a justice that four men had dispossessed him of his church. The justice proceeded to arrest them.[38]

Not only was no work to be done or business transacted on the Lord's Day but no one might travel by boat or barge on a Sunday except with a permit from a JP. The Act[39] imposing this restriction was another which contained an inducement to potential prosecutors. At the discretion of the justices they might be awarded up to a third of the penalty imposed.

The justices' predicament regarding the enforcement of the religious laws was aggravated by a further intervention by the King on behalf of nonconformists and recusants. In 1672 he issued a

38.　Surrey RO, XXV, p. 127.
39.　29 Charles II, c. 7.

Declaration of Indulgence which enabled anyone who wished to do so to escape the penalties of the law by obtaining a licence from the King. As this seemed to be contrary to the Act passed by Parliament it resulted in much confusion. Justices who ignored a licence and tried to enforce the Act were liable to be reprimanded by the Lord Chancellor, while those who failed to apply the law against dissenters who held licences were open to prosecution. A justice in Northampton was threatened by an informer with prosecution and the recovery of the £100 fine because he had not acted against dissenters (named by the informer) who were in possession of licences. He wrote to the King's secretary saying: "I desire your advice, for I am very unwilling to offend the King and yet loth to venture the knave."[40]

Charles, faced with the need to obtain a subsidy from Parliament, was obliged to withdraw the Declaration a year after it had been issued, but there continued to be uncertainty as to whether the licences which had already been granted were still effective. The question was not resolved until an Order in Council of 1675. Even then, many justices, disturbed by the confusion of the previous years and with personal doubts as to the justification for the religious laws, were reluctant to proceed against offenders.

In 1673 the Test Act excluded Roman Catholics from holding any office under the Crown. In addition to the Oaths of Allegiance and Supremacy, justices were required to produce a certificate authenticated by two witnesses and signed by the minister and churchwarden that they had taken the sacrament according to the usage of the Church of England. As time went by, the failure of these laws to achieve their purpose became apparent. In 1678 there was a temporary renewal of hostility towards all who supported religious views other than those of the Church of England when Titus Oates claimed to have uncovered the Popish Plot. The number of prosecutions before the justices increased substantially for a short period and some Papist suspects were executed. Most of the justices themselves, however, do not appear to have been greatly impressed by Oates' revelations, and allegations were made to the Council of their failure. This was one of the rare occasions after the Restoration when some justices were ordered to appear before the Council to answer for their neglect.[41] (The JP before whom Oates made his depositions was later found murdered). Feeling against Roman Catholics became so strong that an Exclusion Bill was introduced in 1679 to bar the Duke of York from succession to the throne. It was unsuccessful but many members who supported it were removed from the commissions.

40.   SP Dom. 1672-3, p. 613. The justice, Peter Whalley, also told the secretary: "The reports that the declaration is made by the House of Commons to be of no effect in law has set the informers to work again." (February 26, 1673).
41.   The Lancashire justices, for example, were ordered to do so in 1680. HMC. Kenyon, p. 114.

At the end of 1679 a change took place in the selection of appointees to the commissions. A number of committees were set up, composed of members of the Council, whose duty it was to scrutinize the membership of every commission, each committee being assigned a number of counties for this purpose. A new commission was then issued for each county as soon as the committee had completed its inquiries, and by the end of 1680 every county had been dealt with in this way. The disturbing feature of this operation was that the committees appeared to have been strongly biased towards those in favour at court. Numbers of conscientious and efficient JPs, including in some cases the *Custos Rotulorum*, were removed and replaced with others of no special merit and sometimes of questionable reputation. This applied not only to the working justices but also to distinguished national figures who headed the commissions, such as the Duke of Buckingham (a former member of the Cabal and intimate of the King) who happened to be out of favour with the court. It was also observed that the Crown's distaste for Parliament was reflected in the removal from the commissions of many members of the Commons while no new appointments of members were made. There was widespread concern, and near the end of the year the House of Lords set up its own committee to investigate the matter. The committee's inquiries supported the allegations of abuse and suggested that many of the new JPs had been chosen because they were all disposed towards the Papists. The Lords' committee had completed barely half its examination when its work was abruptly terminated by the prorogation and subsequent dissolution of Parliament, and the position remained largely the same during the remaining years of Charles II's reign. There continued to be much criticism. The gentry resented the inclusion of men whom they regarded as unsatisfactory and they were incensed by the exclusion of some of their own number. They and the county nobility also resented what they saw as a transfer of control from themselves to the central government. Most of the justices were Tory (that is members of the party that opposed the exclusion of the Duke of York) although there were still a few Whigs, and by the end of Charles's reign in 1685 the Tory party was firmly in control of local affairs through the commissions. As the justices were mainly men well disposed towards the court and the High Church they readily accepted the decisions of the King and implemented the policy of suppressing both Whigs and dissenters.

James II, an avowed Roman Catholic, came to the throne in February 1685 and immediately summoned Parliament; but although more Royalist than ever, it was not willing to turn the country into a Catholic state, nor were the Justices of the Peace. Soon after the accession, the Duke of Monmouth landed in Somerset and claimed the throne, but was defeated at Sedgemoor. Although a champion of those who opposed a Catholic regime, Monmouth received no backing from the local justices. This was probably due to their refusal to accept a revival of Puritanism rather than because they viewed Roman Catholicism with favour. This lack of support for the invader, however, from those responsible for local government may have encouraged James in his determination to crush all opposition to his religious policy. He recognized the importance of the JPs in local affairs and seemed to be satisfied that he had their support, at least since the commissions were revised by the Council in 1680. At that time he wrote to Prince William of Orange, with whom he was still on good terms, expressing the view that the commissions had been greatly improved by the removal of "all disaffected people" who had encouraged the King's "old friends of the Cavaliers and Church party."[42]

Monmouth's rebellion was followed by the "Bloody Assize" in which Judge Jeffreys ordered the execution of large numbers of those who were alleged to have taken part. To enable him to accomplish this work he was placed on the commissions for the South Western counties. Immediately on his return to Westminster he became Lord Chancellor and one of his first duties, in 1686, was to head a committee of the Privy Council to review the state of the JP commissions throughout the country. New commissions had been issued to every county in England and Wales during the four months following the demise of the Crown in 1685, but after Jeffreys' review others were sealed in 1687. These included large numbers of Roman Catholics, most of them men of substance, but although some of the former non-Catholic justices were dropped, many were retained and by the end of the operation there was still a majority of Anglicans on the commissions. What seems to have been overlooked at first was that all justices were still required by the Test Act of 1673 to take the Anglican sacrament before they could act; so the new Catholic justices could not take up their duties. To remedy this new commissions were issued in 1687, which included a dispensation clause exempting all those named in a commission from the obligation to take the statutory oaths and from having to obtain a certificate that they had taken the Church of England sacrament.

James was sufficiently impressed with the need to have the justices' support to make an effort to obtain their views, particularly on the removal of disabilities from those who did not support the established church. In 1687 he ordered all Lords Lieutenant to consult with the JPs and Deputy Lieutenant and to submit a report. The result was not encouraging to the King. Some Lord Lieutenants declined to co-operate and it was clear that, with but a few exceptions, justices throughout the country were not prepared to support a relaxation of

42.   F.C. Turner, *James II,* Eyre & Spottiswoode, 1948, p. 178.

the laws excluding Roman Catholics. As was to be expected, James reacted by dismissing numbers of Lieutenants and JPs, many of them among the most senior and effective members of the commissions, and reacted by dismissing numbers of Lieutenants and JPs, many of them among the most senior and effective members of the commissions, and replacing them with men whom he considered to be more amenable. These included some dissenters. He expected them to support the policy of toleration towards religious minorities but he gained little in this direction, and the presence of dissenters on the commissions merely added to the apprehension of those who recalled with foreboding the years of the Commonwealth. Even the Catholic gentry were not as supportive as he had expected, largely because they were not prepared to risk another Civil War which, they could see, was likely to be the outcome of the King's extreme policies.

It was certainly the case that James could not find a sufficient number of co-operative recruits to pack the commissions, and those whom he did appoint made little impression. By 1688 he recognized his error in alienating the JPs and attempted to recover their support by reappointing some of those he had dismissed.[43] In Norfolk more than 40 justices who had been dismissed earlier in the year were offered reappointment in October, but all refused. In any event it was too late, William of Orange landed at Torbay in November 1688. Unlike Monmouth, he was accompanied by a fair-sized army and he received the support of all sections of the local population, including most of the justices. Some of the latter seem to have had doubts as to the course they should pursue, but the matter was soon resolved for them by James' decision to flee the country. It has been rightly said that the massive changes made by James in the Commissions of the Peace undoubtedly played a significant part in achieving the "Glorious Revolution" of the winter of 1688-9.[44]

Routine duties

This chapter has necessarily been dominated by the political events of the century. These had a profound effect upon the Justices of the Peace, yet throughout most of the period their day-to-day work proceeded with remarkable regularity along similar lines to what had taken place before. Only during part of the Cromwellian interlude and when life was disrupted by open hostilities during the Civil War was there any serious break in the continuing process which gradually advanced the justices still further along the road they had been

43.   It has been estimated that by the summer of 1688 24 per cent of JPs and DLs were Roman Catholics and that three-quarters of the Anglican justices who had been on the commissions in 1685 were no longer there three years later. J. Miller, *Popery and Politics in England, 1660-1688,* 1973, Cambridge U.P., pp. 270-272.
44.   Glassey, *Politics and Appointment of Justices of the Peace 1675-1720,* p. 91.

following in the previous century. By the end of the Tudor era they had been transformed from essentially judicial and police officers into administrators responsible for virtually every aspect of local government. It remains therefore to record the few further changes, other than those already mentioned, which took place in the traditional work of the JPs during this period.

Judicial business

In the trial of criminal offences the work of the justices' courts, which was procedurally the same as that of Assizes, remained largely as it had been in the Middle Ages, being focused upon the charge to the grand jury followed by presentment and indictment and by trial before a petty jury. The day-to-day records of Quarter Sessions show that many matters were sent down to be dealt with by one or more JPs in their respective divisions, while on the other hand some were reserved for the Judges of Assize, the minutes commenting "because this is a case of difficulty." The sessions themselves, however, spent a good deal of time dealing with minor offences and the enforcement of law and order. The records contain a rather monotonous list of penalties imposed, often with no description of the offence, but one can see that they meted out rough justice. Much time was also spent dealing with petitions, about half of which were complaints by one individual against another, and they included many accusations of ill-treatment of servants by their masters and of wives by their husbands. There were but few changes in this side of the justices' work, but the following need to be noted.

First, the practice of reserving capital offences for trial at Assizes was extended during both the seventeenth and eighteenth centuries and it was rare for such cases to be tried at Quarter Sessions after 1650. The extent to which this was done varied from county to county, depending to some extent upon the readiness of the justices to handle these cases. Although many instances are recorded in county archives of the death sentence being imposed by Quarter Sessions during the first half of the seventeenth century, a large proportion of these cases had been to Assizes and were remitted to Quarter Sessions only because the Judge had not completed his list before he was obliged to move on to the next county. It seems fairly certain that from the second half of the century capital offences were almost always committed to Assizes, though there were still occasions when they were tried at Quarter Sessions because the Assizes ran out of time. As most of the more serious crimes involved the death penalty, the scope of criminal work at most Quarter Sessions was considerably reduced.

Secondly, with the establishment of overseas colonies, a new type of sentence became available in the form of transportation. This became established by the end of the century when prisoners began to be sentenced to penal servitude in North America and the Caribbean. A century later, when the American colonies had gained independence, the flow of convicts was switched to Australia. Sentences of transportation were used extensively by Quarter Sessions as a treatment for even minor offences, particularly petty theft. It was a penalty which could even be imposed in some circumstances by justices out of Quarter Sessions. Under an Act of 1671, for example, three justices could order up to seven years' transportation for rick burning or for killing or maiming cattle by night, if the accused, to avoid the risk of a death penalty, elected to be tried summarily.45 So far as the county was concerned, the cost of transportation was considerably less than that of hanging. The latter could amount to nearly £10 for each sentence. The hangman's fee was usually four guineas with a further 15 shillings for refreshment, on top of which was the cost of a horse and cart to "hale him to the gallows" and then to remove the body. Compared with this, the cost to county funds of transportation was only five guineas on average. Cheaper still were whipping and the stocks which amounted to only one pound, while a fine would obviously result in a profit. A capital sentence was mandatory in many cases, but it is clear from the evidence available that the cost of the punishment had some influence on the justices' choice of sentence in cases where they had a discretion. Likewise, we find examples of Quarter Sessions trying to avoid a death sentence by undervaluing articles stolen. (Theft of goods above the value of 12 pence from the house of the owner was a capital offence; below that amount it was not). The motive for devaluing was sometimes compassion for the prisoner, as mentioned elsewhere, but undoubtedly the cost of the punishment to the county was usually also in the justices' minds.

Imprisonment was still not used extensively except for those who failed to pay their debts. In these cases the prisoner had to provide for his own upkeep. There were many who had difficulty in avoiding starvation and large numbers lingered in the gaols indefinitely because they were unable to raise the sums to pay. In 1670 an Act authorized the justices to release from gaol those imprisoned for non-payment of debt who were worth less than £10 and could not pay. The prisoner had to swear on oath to this effect and was then taken before Quarter Sessions where his creditors were also summoned to appear. If the debtor's statement was not challenged he could be released. On the other hand, if it were decided that he should remain in custody the creditors could be ordered to contribute a reasonable sum to his maintenance not exceeding 18 pence a week.

Mention has already been made of the growing amount of work done by justices out of sessions. For some time pairs of justices had

45.   22 & 23 Charles II, c. 7.

met at irregular intervals to pass accounts, and in the early seventeenth century the practice began of assigning certain justices to groups of hundreds into which the county was divided. This divisional arrangement was extended to the whole country by order of the Privy Council in 1631, and justices were required to meet monthly. The object was primarily to deal with the poor and distressed on these occasions but the justices soon began to take the opportunity to discuss other matters as well. These meetings were the forerunners of Petty Sessions, but the term, which had been applied for some time to sessions held by high constables, was not extended to the justices until the latter part of the century by which time their regular meetings out of sessions had become well established and came to be known as Petty Sessions. The term was applied to regular meetings of the justices in a division. These were concerned especially with the Poor Law but also with other questions, as described below. There were also special sessions, which were not held on a regular basis and which dealt with a variety of business such as highways and licensing. Most minor offences, such as assault and petty larceny, still had to come before Quarter Sessions, but an increasing number of criminal charges could be tried under various Acts by two justices sitting together whenever they might think fit. Statutes enacted during the century for this purpose empowered two justices to imprison for three months or to fine any person killing game or taking eggs;[46] to commit the mother of a bastard child to a house of correction for one year;[47] and to confiscate the goods of runaway parents of a bastard child.[48]

Reference has also been made to the extension of the powers of a single JP during the century. He continued, as before, to issue summonses to appear at sessions, to bind over to keep the peace and to imprison for default. He retained his authority to deal with vagrants and could order them to be whipped or placed in the stocks and returned to their place of settlement. He could also commit anyone who opposed his authority when performing his magisterial duties.

Under Charles I, one justice was empowered to deal summarily with breaches of the Sunday observance laws.[49] A single justice acquired further powers to fine (with imprisonment in default) and in some cases to send to the stocks. This included anyone who, to his personal knowledge, uttered a profane oath, tippled in an alehouse, or was drunk.

Much time at sessions was spent, as before, in dealing with those who failed to perform some public duty. In these cases the prosecution was often undertaken by a private individual who was induced to

46.   1 James I, c. 27; 7 James I, c. 11.
47.   7 James I, c. 4.
48.   14 Charles II, c. 12, s. 19.
49.   1Charles I, c. 1; 3 Charles I, c. 1.

assume the task by being entitled to receive a portion of the fine if he was successful. As regards personal actions, the institution of proceedings rested, as it had always done, with the aggrieved party who was obliged to conduct the case at his own expense. The risk of losing both case and costs deterred many victims from pursuing their claims in the courts and, as an incentive, the government introduced in 1669 what was called a Tyburn Ticket. This was issued by a judge or JP to anyone who prosecuted a felon to conviction, and it provided lifelong exemption from service in any parish office, including that of constable. In 1698 the ticket received statutory recognition when an Act (10 William III, c. 12), which was designed to encourage the prosecution of burglars and housebreakers, provided for the issue of certificates of excusal from public office within the parish in which the offence had been committed. The ticket was transferable, once only, and was therefore a valuable acquisition. Many people were prepared to pay substantial sums to avoid service in these offices.[50]

The first moves to protect the JPs themselves from prosecution for acts done in the course of their duty were made at the beginning of the century. An Act[51] of James I introduced procedure which made it easier for a JP and certain other officers to defend actions when they were sued, and where a verdict was given in their favour they were to receive double costs.

Administrative duties

The seventeenth century did not see as rapid an increase in the JPs' administrative commitments as had occurred under Elizabeth, but this side of their work continued to occupy the greater part of their time. Throughout most of the period their meetings were habitually concerned with administering the Poor Law, repairing highways and bridges, maintaining and supervising prisons and houses of correction, fixing prices and wages, licensing alehouses and a wide variety of trades (such as drovers, pedlars and chimney sweeps) and raising rates on parishes to meet local needs. We have already referred to some of the additional duties placed upon the JPs during this period, including the novel function of performing the marriage ceremony. Except during the Interregnum the justices were clearly regarded as the proper authority to deal with virtually all government administration and law enforcement in a county and therefore, as yet more matters required regulation and as new laws were introduced, so further duties were entrusted to them.

The need to raise revenue was reflected in new taxes for whose

---

50.   The price might vary considerably according to the area. Thus in Gloucestershire a ticket might cost £30 in a Bristol suburb but as little as five shillings in some rural parishes.
51.   7 James I, c. 5; made perpetual by 21 James I, c. 12.

collection the JPs were responsible to a varying degree. A particularly unpopular tax was the Hearth Tax, first introduced in 1662. This was under an Act entitled: "For establishing an additional Revenue upon His Majesty."[52] It provided an illustration of the difficulties which could arise when the government sought to introduce an unpopular measure without the full support of the justices. This Act decreed that anyone who owned property worth 20 shillings a year or more was liable to annual payment of two shillings for every fireplace or stove in his house. (There had been a precedent for "chimney money" tax in England since Norman times). Returns were made to the JPs by the constables and tithingmen, listing the householders who were liable to pay the tax, with statements of the number of fireplaces in each house. These returns were delivered by the constables to Quarter Sessions and were enrolled by the Clerk of the Peace who sent a duplicate to the Exchequer. If a constable was not satisfied with the householder's statement he was entitled to search the house. The occupiers bitterly resented this intrusion and did their best to obstruct it. A further Act[53] therefore provided that the JPs were to issue warrants to the high constables, who were to issue like warrants to the petty constables, to give notice in church that every occupier must give a true account of the number of his fireplaces within 10 days. Then the constables with two other substantial inhabitants were to enter all premises and compare the accounts with what they found and forward the result to the high constable who, in turn, transmitted it to the Clerk of the Peace for forwarding to the Exchequer. Those who gave false returns, or none at all, were to be fined by the justices; and so too were any constables who failed to implement the Act. This also proved to be unsatisfactory, largely because of the "negligence" of those required to enforce the law. The constables, in particular, were unenthusiastic because they were often assaulted by the householders and their servants, while the justices found little in the tax to commend it, especially as they were among those with the largest number of hearths. Yet another Act[54] was therefore passed empowering the King to appoint such officers as he should "think meete" to search buildings and to collect the tax; and if any violence were offered to them, a single justice was to commit the culprit to prison on the oath of a witness. These new measures met with little better success, and the whole scheme was finally abandoned. Undoubtedly, the justices' disapproval of the tax and their reluctance to enforce it were major causes of its failure.

The greatest increase in the volume of the JPs' work arose in the field of trade and industry. Until the outbreak of the Civil War the

52.   14 Charles II, c. 10.
53.   15 Charles II, c. 13.
54.   16 Charles II, c. 3.

country enjoyed a growing boom, the principal industrial growth being in the cloth trade. The economy of the nation, however, was still agrarian, a fact which was of prime importance to the JPs as landowners. In this context, a new type of crop appeared in the English countryside at this time. Tobacco, which had been imported from America by the Elizabethans, began to be grown in England, but this could not be done without express authority, and the JPs were ordered to sequester all tobacco which people had presumed to grow "contrary to His Majesty's proclamation."[55] In 1608 there was an abortive attempt to introduce the silk trade into the country. Previously all silk had been imported, but it was planned by the Council to breed silk worms in the southern counties and to feed them on the leaves of mulberry trees which were to be brought in from the Continent. The JPs were considered to be the obvious authority to take charge of this venture and they were instructed to make the necessary arrangements. They seem to have responded fairly readily, at least in some counties like Devon,[56] and individual justices bought large numbers of trees. It has been suggested that this was done through purely selfish motives as they hoped to benefit personally from entering the market at an early stage; but if that was the case they must have been disappointed for the project came to nothing.

At the end of the Civil War the whole national economy was in a precarious state with trade at a standstill. One of the most urgent tasks facing the Cromwellian government, and later that of Charles II, was to rebuild the economy and to restore trade and industry. The JPs were to play an important part in achieving these objectives, especially after the Restoration.

High unemployment and rocketing prices, combined with the return of great numbers of discharged soldiers, led to riots and general disorder requiring firm action by the authorities. Even before the war there were many unemployed workers. In 1622, those in Gloucestershire went in groups to the houses of the wealthy demanding money and seizing provisions. For several years after 1640 there were riots by those thrown out of work by a further extension of enclosures. During the Interregnum, there was greater freedom in relationships between employer and workmen and, for the time being, the government ceased trying to regulate wages. After the Restoration, however, with the return to power of many of the old landed gentry, an attempt was made to reverse the trend and the regulation of wages again became an important part of the justices' functions. It was in the

---

55.   APC August 6, 1621, sets out letters addressed to the Lord Mayor of London and the justices of Kent, Essex and Surrey, ordering them to investigate and to seize the crops. For another example of restrictions on the growing of tobacco see Gloucestershire QSR for Trinity, 1682.

56.   Devon County QSR, p. 95.

justices' own interest to fix the rate as low as possible as this was what they themselves would have to pay to their employees. They were also encouraged to keep the wage level low because the poor relief was raised from taxes on all ratepayers, and therefore the JPs' wage bills might be supplemented by the taxes paid by all the householders in the area. In consequence of this the justices acquired a reputation for exploiting the workers who were treated as having no rights whatever, but although there were undoubtedly some who fully deserved this criticism there were also many who contributed large sums to poor relief. They resented having to pay a poor rate but were ready to give voluntarily to charity. During the sixteenth and seventeenth centuries a number of JPs and other gentry and merchants also endowed schools and scholarships.

The rate of wage for different types of work was decided at Quarter Sessions and a tariff was then delivered to the high constables for proclamation at the hiring sessions which they conducted. In many instances a separate rate was declared for work with or without refreshment, and sometimes also for different seasons of the year. The following is an example of a typical list which was agreed at Oxfordshire Quarter Sessions in 1687.[57]

Rate of wages agreed upon at the general Sessions of the Peace for the said County ... Delivered to the Sheriff to be Proclaimed according to the Statute in such cases made and provided.

	£ s. d.
For a Bailiffs Wages for Husbandry for a yeare	6 0 0
For a Chief Carters Wages for a yeare	5 0 0
For a Under Carters Wages for a yeare	3 0 0
For a Shepherds Wages found in the house for a yeare	3 15 0
For a Chambermaids Wages for a yeare	2 10 0
For a Young Maids Wages for a yeare	1 6 8
For a Mowers wages with meat & drinks a day	0 0 10
For a Mowers wages finding himself a day	0 1 4
For a Reapers wages finding himself a day	0 1 6
For a Labourers Wages for making hay and raking barley a day	0 0 10
For a Womans wages for the same work	0 0 6
For a Plowright Carpenter & Masons Wages in winter finding themselves a day	0 1 2
in summer finding themselves a day	0 1 4

---

57.   Gretton, *Oxfordshire Justices in the Seventeeth Century*, p. lxiii, which gives the full list, the above being an abbreviated version.

Throughout most of the century the value of money decreased and
prices rose by several hundred per cent. This, added to the restrictions
on wages, brought the poor to starvation. On the occasions when the
situation became particularly serious, as it did whenever there was a
bad harvest, the government made some effort to alleviate it by
ordering the justices to buy up corn and to sell it below cost price. They
were also told to control its consumption, which included reducing the
number of alehouses and restricting the making of malt. They also
fixed minimum wages. In times of plenty, the justices were ordered to
arrange for corn to be stored against further shortages. Occasionally,
however, the JPs reported that there was no corn left. The reason
sometimes given was that there had been too much conversion of
arable ground into pasture and of barley into malt.58

The JPs continued to spend an appreciable amount of their time
dealing with the twin problems of poor relief and vagrancy, a task
which would remain with them into the nineteenth century. An
indication of the number of paupers in the kingdom in the seventeenth
century is given by the fact that in 1670 about 30 per cent of the
population was deemed to be too poor to pay the Hearth Tax, though
the proportion varied between counties. Although begging was illegal
without a licence, there were many who were permitted to do so. If a
man suffered some great loss, as by having his house burned down, he
could petition the justices for a brief, and if he obtained it he could
then wander around the county begging. Sometimes the justices also
engaged in raising subscriptions for the relief of the destitute. All this,
together with the care of the ordinary poor of the parish, became a
heavy burden upon local funds, especially in Charles I's reign when
large numbers of soldiers returned from overseas and again when
troops were disbanded after the Civil War. The plight of disabled
soldiers was often the subject of discussion at Quarter Sessions, not
only as to their initial qualification for a pension but sometimes as to
whether they should receive additional relief because of their
circumstances. An example is recorded in Norfolk Quarter Sessions
Order Book for 1650.

> "Petition of Edward Appleby, a poor old soldier. Had pension for
> many years, now almost blind. Cottage decayed & likely to be forfeit
> to Lord of Manor. Referred to justices ... to call Potterheigham
> Overseers before them & make such order as they think fit."59

There were frequent disputes between parishes as to which one was
responsible, and until these were settled the unfortunate paupers were

58.   SP Dom., 1631, December, p. 213.
59.   Norfolk QSOB, 1650-57, 4.

driven from one parish to another. Disputes often centred upon an interpretation of the law governing settlement. An attempt to define this was made in the Settlement and Removal Act of 1662, though without conspicuous success.

This Act was the only further piece of legislation to make any significant change to the Elizabethan Poor Law before 1834. Its main provision was that anyone found in a parish who was likely to become chargeable to the poor rate could be forcibly returned to his parish of settlement, which was generally defined as his place of birth. The object of the Act, as explained in the preamble, was to protect the more generous and philanthropic parishes to which the poor tended to emigrate, but it has usually been criticized as marking the beginning of a harsher approach towards the poor.[60]

A type of case which appeared frequently at Quarter Sessions was bastardy. The main concern of the justices in handling these cases was that the bastard might become a charge on the parish. This was shown by the differing treatment of the parents according to whether the child was alive or dead. If it had died, the case was closed, apart from an order on the father, if he could be found, to repay any money spent by the parish on the care of the mother or child. If it was alive, the mother was sent to prison for a year and a day and the father fined. In 1652 some of the parishioners of Lea Marston in Warwickshire, "observing a vagrant woman great with child, barbarously carried her in a chair to a tree supposed to be the bounds of the two parishes of Cudworth and Lea Marston." They did this on the assumption that her offspring would then be the liability of Cudworth. The justices in Quarter Sessions ordered that she should be returned to Lea Marston.[61]

It was not uncommon for the justices to show compassion when dealing with the impotent poor. On another occasion, in 1656, Warwickshire Quarter Sessions, "upon reading the humble petition of John Sargent, a poor inhabitant of Tysoe ... setting forth that he having been a long time afflicted with lameness in his limbs is altogether unable to maintain himself and is advised by those that are learned in 'physic' and 'chyrurgery' to go to the Bath for the cure of his said lameness, and also upon reading a certificate of divers of the inhabitants of Tysoe testifying the same," the court gave Sargent a certificate to enable him to go to Bath and sent a recommendation to the master of the hospital.[62]

The general operation of the Poor Law was left, as in Elizabeth's reign, to the overseers who were appointed by the justices to act with the churchwardens and to collect the poor rate, which was usually done once a week after the church service. The justices themselves might

60.   See Webbs *English Poor Law History I,* "The Old Poor Law," 1927.
61.   Warwick RO, QSOB, vol. III, p. 96.
62.   *Ibid.,* p. 316.

also be involved, not only in general supervision of the system but in various routine matters. A single justice could order the parish authorities to find accommodation for a family turned out of their home. Quarter Sessions had to deal with petitions from parishes and individuals. The able-bodied had to be provided with work. Children were apprenticed to employers who were paid for taking them. Where an employer was unco-operative the sessions could order him to accept an apprentice or to give work to the adult poor. Earlier legislation on apprenticeship was re-enacted in the Poor Relief Act of 1601, under which the overseers of the poor could, with the consent of two justices, apprentice boys until they were 24 years of age and girls until they were 21. The intention of the Act was to ensure that poor children were taught a trade and so were less likely to become destitute and a liability to the parish.

In 1623 there was an interesting early example of the government trying to solve an unemployment problem. The Privy Council called upon the justices in 10 counties which were involved in the clothing trade to do what they could to dissuade the clothiers from dismissing any of their employees. The reason given was that the sacked workers would be likely to "disturb the quiet and government of those parts wherein they live." At the same time, the government was endeavouring to increase the market for cloth so that in due course more workers would be needed in the industry. The JPs duly summoned the clothiers to appear and urged them to retain their workers. The clothiers explained why it was not possible for them to comply. This answer was passed back to the Council by the justices who, acting as they usually did as the mouthpiece for all those in the county, pointed out that the clothing trade was in a state of depression which affected industry in general. The Gloucestershire justices, who were among those approached by the Council, explained that:

> "All trade besides this is much decayed, money grown scarce, the yearly profits of livings much fallen and our whole county greatly impoverished."

As expected, rioting broke out and the justices had to face the problem of keeping order. The government, as it did frequently throughout history, responded by assuring the people that everything was well in hand, that new measures had been introduced which would cure all ills, and that returning prosperity was just around the corner. "His Majesty, in his princely commiseration for his people's wants, hath directed a course for restoring the trade of clothing to as good and flourishing an estate as these times will any way admit."[63] None the

63.   APC, 1621-23, pp. 224-25.

less, the depression continued, and was still as bad as ever 10 years later when we see one of the many examples of the government carrying out an inquiry into local problems through the JPs. The Council ordered the Gloucestershire magistrates to investigate the state of the spinners who supplied the clothiers with yarn and whose conduct had been the subject of complaint. The justices produced a report which supported the spinners and which the Council seem to have accepted.

A duty which had long rested with the JPs was to assist the Crown in reaping the greatest benefit from its monopolies. Not only were the justices obliged to ensure that there was no interference with such royal rights, but they might even be required to mount an advertising campaign. One such occasion, which shows that modern media advertising has historical precedents, occurred in 1633. Soap was a monopoly which could be sold only through licensed agents. In 1631, a new type had been introduced but it did not meet with immediate success. The JPs were therefore urged to take action to boost sales. The Lord Mayor of London and other commissioners were asked to conduct an examination and to report on the effectiveness of the new product. Their certificate, which was distributed to the justices, stated:

"We caused two laundresses indifferently chosen, to wash therewith, and we did plainly perceive that the new white soap, with a very small difference, lather much better than the old Crowne soap did, and that the clothes washed with the said new soap (being dried) were as white and sweeter than the clothes washed with the old Crowne soap."

The certificate also stated that "four countesses, five viscountesses and divers other ladies and gentlemen of great quality" had confirmed that the new soap "neither fretteth the maids' hands nor spoileth the linen." The justices were told to publicize these findings.[64]

The JPs' responsibility for regulating the sale and consumption of alcoholic liquors underwent few changes during this period, but their duties were more clearly defined. Whereas the length of time for which a licence should be granted had not been specified by any statutes, it became customary by the beginning of the seventeenth century for each licence to be granted for one year only, and this was confirmed by a royal proclamation of 1618. Nor had statutes set any limit upon the number of alehouses that might be allowed in any area, but a council letter of 1604 told the justices that there should be no more than were required for the needs of travellers and of poor people who were unable to provide victuals for themselves. We have seen that the

---

64.   SP Dom. 1633, December 29, p. 337.

justices did not always take steps to comply with these instructions but it is clear from references in the State Papers that they often did so. Thus, in 1623, the mayor and aldermen who composed the magistrates for Ripon in Yorkshire refer to the directions they have received and inform the Council that, having examined the position, they have found "the number to be great" and have "reduced them to half the number."[65] Dalton also makes it clear that the JPs in some counties fixed hours of closing at night and forbad alehouses to open on Sundays.[66]

We have seen that the use of the roads began to increase at the end of the sixteenth century. It grew more rapidly during the seventeenth and eighteenth with expanding trade and increasing travel by individuals. Roads were used to a far greater extent by long-distance travellers and carriers of merchandise, and the majority of users were no longer the local farmers and landowners who were responsible for the maintenance. This responsibility still rested upon the inhabitants of the parish and was carried out under the directions of the surveyors nominated by the parishioners and then appointed by the JPs to whom they were responsible. In spite of the improvements made in the Acts of 1555 and 1563,[67] the system was incapable of keeping pace with the new developments and the state of the roads deteriorated further. Little was done to remedy this situation during the first half of the century, though rebukes to the JPs from the Council were not uncommon. The criticism tended to centre on areas in which the King was wont to travel. Thus, in 1622, the JPs of six counties were admonished for omitting to repair highways, with the comment that their failure was taken by His Majesty as "a great omission of your duties" especially "in those parts where His Majesty and his carriages doe usually Passe." Therefore they must attend to this without delay and "for the better effecting whereof," they were not only to rely on ordinary day labour, but they might tax townships within which the roads passed, and if the township could not support the charge, they were to tax the hundreds or if necessary the whole county. Furthermore, they were to report within 20 days on what had been done.[68]

In 1627, the justices of Middlesex and three neighbouring counties were told that the Queen, "being advised for her health to take the waters of the wells at Wellenborough in the county of Northampton," was to leave London on the following Tuesday, spending four nights on

65. CSP Dom., James I, vol. 137.
66. M. Dalton, *The Country Justices,* 1618, pp. 333-334. This also mentions other conditions imposed by justices in some areas.
67. 2 & 3 Philip & Mary, c. 8; 5 Eliz. c. 13.
68. APC, May 13, 1622. To JPs in Middlesex, Kent, Essex, Hertfordshire, Surrey and Buckinghamshire.

the way - at Barnet, St Albans, Dunstable and Bedford. The "immoderate heat" and the stress of the highways constituted a hazard to her health, and it was therefore proposed that "the most comodious wayes and passages" should be found through fields. The JPs were therefore "to take such speedie and effectual course as you in your discretions knowe best for expediting this service." Anyone offering resistance to the justices was to be bound over to appear before the Council.[69]

Parishioners were still under an obligation to provide workmen and materials, and could be fined for failing to do so, the proceeds being payable to the parish officers "for bestowal on the highway" under the 1555 Act. We have also seen that justices could levy a rate to pay for hired labour. Neither of these methods, however, worked smoothly, especially as the farmers and landowners tried stubbornly to avoid providing either labour or money, and as traffic increased the condition of the roads continued to deteriorate. It was not until the new broom of the Commonwealth administration that an attempt was made to tackle the problem. As the Webbs point out:

"The student who will examine the records of the Commonwealth from the standpoint of economic and social development will find in these troublous years the beginnings of many of the institutions of our own time. Among these is the Highway Rate."[70]

At the end of the Civil War some surveyors asked the JPs in Quarter Sessions to assess the inhabitants of the parish for the repair of the highways, and in a few areas the justices complied with the request, although they had no statutory authority to do so. In 1654, however, an ordinance of Parliament[71] provided for parishioners to meet and fix a rate, not exceeding a shilling in the pound, for "making and repairing and cleansing roads and pavements." If a shilling in the pound was insufficient the justices in Quarter Sessions were empowered to levy a rate in aid on adjoining parishes. If the parishioners failed to fix a rate this might be done by the surveyors, but it then had to be confirmed by the JPs. The funds raised by these rates were to be used by the surveyors to hire labour and to provide the necessary equipment.

Communications did improve noticeably during the Interregnum. The first regular coach service dates from this period, and with it a postal service was introduced which provided for private as well as public customers. A letter posted in London was delivered in

69. APC, July 8, 1627. To JPs in Middlesex, Hertfordshire, Bedfordshire and Northamptonshire.
70. ELG, *The Story of the King's Highway*, p. 21.
71. Ordinance for the Better Amending and Keeping in Repair the Common Highways within this Nation.

Winchester the following day. All legislation during this period became invalid, however, on the Restoration of the monarchy, and in many instances it was not replaced effectively by new enactments. Highway maintenance was one of the areas which suffered. In 1662 a temporary Act,[72] which was to last for three years, empowered each surveyor, "together with two or three substantial householders," to assess every inhabitant rated under the Poor Law for the cost of repairing, maintaining and enlarging the highways. The rate had to be approved and signed by a JP and was not to exceed sixpence in the pound per year. It had to be levied in every parish unless Quarter Sessions or two JPs decided that it was not required.

After the 1662 Act expired no further step was taken by Parliament to deal with the problem until 1670 when another temporary Act[73] of three years' duration was passed, under which a fixed payment could be ordered in default of the obligatory service. This was set at one shilling and sixpence for a day's work of one man, three shillings for a man and a horse, and 10 shillings for a cart with two men. If the justices in Quarter Sessions decided that a highway could not be properly maintained by other means, they could also levy a rate on all parishioners not exceeding sixpence in the pound on lands or on every £20 worth of personal estate in any one year, and the money was to be spent on repairing the roads at the justices' direction. This Act, like its predecessor, does not seem to have been implemented with any great enthusiasm, partly perhaps because it was known to be of short duration, and it was not until after the Revolution of 1689 that, as we shall see in a later chapter, any further action was taken by the legislature. In the meantime the JPs, while frequently voicing indignation at the intolerable state of the roads, were unable to achieve any improvement in their condition.

There was, however, one other way in which road travel came to be improved and whose beginning can be found in the seventeenth century. This was the turnpike road, whose birth in the middle of the century has been described at some length by the Webbs.[74] Under the Protectorate, the JPs in some areas had sought power to levy tolls for the repair of unusually busy highways, like the Great North Road whose traffic increased considerably after the Union of the Two Crowns. After the Restoration, Acts were passed giving authority to the JPs to erect gates and levy tolls for this purpose. The first, in 1663,[75] was in response to a petition from the justices in Cambridgeshire, Hertfordshire and Huntingdon, who claimed that "the ancient highway and post road leading from London to York, and so into Scotland" was

72.   14 Charles II, c. 6.
73.   22 Charles II, c. 12.
74.   ELG, *The Story of the King's Highway*, ch. VII.
75.   15 Charles II, c. 1.

becoming almost impassable by reason of the great increase in wagons, especially those engaged in transporting barley and malt, and that "the ordinary course appointed by all former laws and statutes of the realm is not sufficient for the effectual repairing of the same." The Act entrusted the power to levy tolls to the Quarter Sessions in each of the three counties. There was, however, much local opposition, and only the gates at Wadesmil in Hertfordshire were effective. Later, another three Acts extended similar powers to some other counties, though the precise arrangements differed. In some cases the powers rested with Quarter Sessions, in some with the justices of a specified division of the county in special highway sessions, and in others with a number of justices from different counties. From the early part of the eighteenth century, the system was changed by the introduction of Turnpike Trusts, and responsibility was placed upon new statutory bodies as we shall see in another chapter.

The JPs' omnifarious duties ensured that any form of disaster, whether national or local, was bound to have an impact upon them. Throughout their earlier history they were constantly involved in attempts to alleviate the effect of events which had been outside their control: war, famine, fire, the plague and others. The Restoration period had more than its fair share of major disasters in the space of less than three years between 1665 and 1667, the last two of which were the subject of Dryden's *Annus Mirabilis*. In 1665 the country was devastated by one of the worst visitations of the plague in its history. In the following year most of London was destroyed by fire, while in 1667 the Dutch fleet sailed up the Thames and destroyed the English ships in the Medway. It is clear from contemporary documents that the JPs were preoccupied with all these events; sometimes raising and training the militia and preparing defences, sometimes raising funds and providing for the needy, almost always dealing with an upsurge of theft, looting and other crimes. This trilogy, however, was only a major illustration of the problems which were constantly facing the justices. Fires occurred frequently, and with most houses being built in wood it was not uncommon for a whole town to be destroyed. The plague was a frequent visitor, and so too were other diseases, and the justices were involved in efforts at prevention as well as cure, the most frequent being the restriction of movement into and out of threatened areas. War, or the threat of armed conflict, was seldom absent and the justices were regularly concerned not only with the militia but with the provision of troops for overseas service. The fact that a large proportion of those in the armed forces were compelled to serve against their will added to the difficulties, and much time was spent arresting deserters and returning them to their units. In 1627, for example, the Earl of Suffolk, Lord Lieutenant of the county, was told by the Council that many soldiers impressed for service had run away and numbers were believed to be hiding in Suffolk. He was to instruct the Deputy Lieutenants and the JPs to search the county, to apprehend the fugitives and to bring them to Harwich for embarkation for service abroad.[76]

The justices' officers

There were no important changes in the infrastructure of the justices' courts in the seventeenth century. The work of the existing officers, from Clerk of the Peace to petty constable, increased with the growth of the justices' duties during much of the period, but as yet there were no additional new appointments. The greatest development was to be seen in the position of the clerks employed by justices out of sessions. The growing importance and recognition of their work was shown in the manual *Cabinet of the Clerk of the Justice of the Peace* by W. Sheppard which was first published in 1641 and reprinted in 1654 and 1660. There were as yet, however, no statutory regulations governing their appointment, duties or qualifications and they were still only personal employees of individual justices; but the considerable increase in this side of the justices' work made it almost essential that they should have clerical assistance.

In some counties the position of the high constables was also enhanced. From the beginning of the century the Assize Judges sometimes required them to supply answers to inquiries put to them, and there is reason to believe that some Judges were inclined to attach considerable weight to their reports, even regarding them as a valuable alternative source of information to that of the Justices of the Peace. At the same time, however, a suspicion was aroused among the justices that high constables who served for a long time became corrupt, and therefore some counties placed a limit on the length of their appointment. In 1610 the West Riding fixed the term at three years and Suffolk did the same a few years later. In Lancashire they were always appointed for one year only from 1600 when they first appear in the county records. The appointment was made at a meeting of the county justices, but at the beginning of the century there were instances of it being made at Assizes.

It will have been seen that various statutes authorized the raising of rates for specific purposes and that their collection was usually the task of the constables or churchwardens. As yet there was no county treasurer, and sums collected were normally paid to the Clerk of the Peace. Sometimes, however, a treasurer was appointed for a specific job. This occurred most often in connexion with the repair of a highway or bridge where some person living in the neighbourhood,

76.   APC, April 29, 1627.

usually but not always a justice, was appointed to act as treasurer and to see that the work was done.

JPs in other lands

It will be seen from what has already been said that the seventeenth century was one of particular significance in the history of the Justices of the Peace in England. There was an extension of the picture in some ways just as intriguing as that which has already been described. The first half of the century saw the introduction of the JP system into countries beyond England and Wales. An unsuccessful attempt was made to establish it in Scotland in 1587, but from 1609 Commissions of the Peace were issued there in the English fashion. At the same time, the search for new trade routes was resulting in the founding of trading ports and colonies and the creation of an overseas empire, beginning with the establishment of the East India Company in 1601. Generally, however, it was only in those places where large numbers of British settlers took up residence as landowners that the office of JP was introduced, notably in North America and later in the West Indies, Australia and New Zealand. These experiments, each with its own peculiar characteristics, will be described in vol. III.

CHAPTER X

THE CITIES AND BOROUGHS

Evolution of the English boroughs - Keepers and justices appointed under charters - Differences between borough and county magistrates - Municipal reforms of the nineteenth century - Removal of justices' administrative functions by Municipal Corporations Act 1835 - The twentieth century; assimilation of borough and county justices - The unique position of the City of London

Justices of the Peace in towns prior to 1835

JUSTICES OF THE PEACE were to be found in towns as well as in the rural areas of England from the fourteenth century, but until the nineteenth there was considerable diversity in the method of their appointment, in the scope of their authority and in the manner in which they performed their duties.

There is still much uncertainty about the development of English towns. They usually began as part of a manor or hundred, where they were governed by a feudal lord or by the church or directly on behalf of the King, and they were entirely under the jurisdiction of the old customary courts or moots which, according to the circumstances, might be presided over by the sheriff, the bailiff or the portreve. All the freeholders owed suit and were obliged to attend. Often the town court was combined with a court of piepowder associated with a market or fair.

There is no clear definition of the term borough which came to be applied to many towns in the Middle Ages. Coke and Littleton both regarded the essential qualification as being entitlement to send a representative to Parliament, but any vil which had obtained a certain degree of independence could be regarded as a borough. At the time of the Norman Conquest there were between 60 and 70 towns (mostly very small) which could be described in this way.

In the late twelfth century Hubert Walter who, as we have seen, placed his confidence in the "middle classes" of the shires by entrusting them with the maintenance of the peace, adopted the same policy in the towns and began to issue charters which *inter alia* conferred similar powers on some of the leading citizens. In granting these powers the charters did not always give exclusive jurisdiction to the burgesses, and after Justices of the Peace were introduced into the counties in the fourteenth century these usually exercised their authority in the municipal areas to the same extent as elsewhere. A town was subject to the authority of the county Quarter Sessions unless its charter contained a *non intromittant* clause which gave its magistrates exclusive jurisdiction.

In the Middle Ages there were few centres of population which amounted to more than large villages, and the number of people who lived in the towns was very small indeed compared with the rest of the country. They were not regarded therefore as being of great significance but, as the wealth of the citizens increased, their ability to provide revenue began to be appreciated. The removal of the threat of foreign invasion was followed by increasing prosperity, which was considerably greater in the towns than in the rural areas, and this coincided with a decline in feudalism. By the thirteenth century, therefore, the townsfolk became better able to make their voices heard. They made frequent attempts to arrogate the function of the county officers, and from the end of the twelfth century a number of towns bought various independent privileges under charters, some of which were granted by feudal lords, some by the church and others by the King. Hubert Walter had raised money in this way by granting charters on behalf of Richard I, and when John came to the throne in 1199 his financial needs induced him to adopt a still more active policy of augmenting his revenue by this means. This trend was continued by later monarchs who were usually in dire need of funds.

A charter did not necessarily mark the beginning of independence. In many cases various rights had been acquired by prescription and these were merely confirmed by a charter. In a number of instances a town received a charter under which it was incorporated and then, at a later date, another which converted it into a county. For example, Southampton was incorporated in 1445 and made a county two years later. It was then separated from Hampshire whose sheriff no longer had power to arrest and imprison its citizens as he could do before 1447.

Only in a very few cases (Haverfordwest, Oxford and Poole) were Commissions of the Peace issued to towns. In most cases the charter named certain leading office holders, such as the mayor and aldermen, who were made magistrates *ex officio*. The few commissions which were issued to towns were similar to those of the counties. They were addressed to various dignitaries, who took little or no part in the proceedings, as well as to leading citizens who did all the work. Names were placed in the commission by the Lord Chancellor who might be moved by political considerations as in the case of counties, and he often followed local advice, sometimes from Members of Parliament, but the majority of nominations came from the mayor and his caucus.

Towns with a corporate existence, including a mayoralty, were developing in the thirteenth and fourteenth centuries, and the formal incorporation of boroughs on a large scale occurred during the fifteenth century. Many of the charters,[1] however, did not give the town county status, and the citizens still had to attend the courts operating in the county and submit to the jurisdiction of the county Justices of the Peace.

It was only where the charter expressly excluded the county justices by a *non intromittant* clause that the borough justices were able to exercise exclusive jurisdiction within their own area. Thus, the charter of Charles II which was granted to Wigan in 1674, made the mayor a Justice of the Peace during his term of office and for one year thereafter and also stated that the Justices of the Peace for the county of Lancaster were excluded from "entering or in anywise intromitting themselves within the Borough." A later charter, granted by James II in 1685, made the mayor of Wigan a justice also for the county of Lancaster. A few of the largest boroughs came to be accorded county status. This meant that county Quarter Sessions and its officers no longer had any jurisdiction within the borough, apart from the fact that when Lords Lieutenant were introduced they were responsible for the militia in corporate boroughs as well as in the county. The borough's own officials were employed to deal with all matters arising within the borough boundary. Under the charter, the borough also acquired the right to pay annually the *firma burgi*, which was a lump sum in lieu of various payments which would otherwise have been collected by royal officials. The burgesses elected a sheriff who with the mayor had power to inquire into all disturbances within the town, to arrest offenders and to hold them in custody pending trial before the Justices of Gaol Delivery of whom the mayor was usually one. The borough sheriff also held a court which could deal with titles to land within the area. The powers of a borough sheriff, however, were less extensive than those of a county sheriff, and these officers came to be largely administrative agents of the borough authorities and spent much of their time collecting fines and maintaining order.

At the beginning of the fifteenth century charters began to provide expressly for the appointment of Justices of the Peace. For instance in 1409 a charter which granted county status to Lincoln stipulated that the mayor, sheriffs and four citizens should be Justices of the Peace. A similar charter was granted to Nottingham in 1413. The powers which the borough justices could exercise were defined in the charter but they could also act under the statutes which applied to county justices. These justices gradually ousted the older courts of which the principal were the tourn and the leet. Previously the courts leet had exercised

---

1.   Examples of charters are to be found in Stubbs, *Select Charters.*

most of the criminal jurisdiction in the town but by the end of the
seventeenth century the justices had taken over much of the leet's
work, as they had wider powers and acted with greater speed and
efficiency.

Wide differences between boroughs
There was a wide range of levels between those boroughs at the top of
the scale which were counties in themselves and those at the bottom
which merely enjoyed minor privileges, such as the right to hold a fair
or to be free of certain tolls. Often there was considerable variation
within the geographical area of a single county, as is shown by the
following examples which, with the exception of London, are taken for
comparison from the territorial region of Gloucestershire.

From early times London had had its own courts, and because of its
exceptional and predominant position it will be considered separately
at the end of this chapter, but it was often used as an example for the
grant of a charter to another borough. Thus in 1155 a charter granted
by Henry II to Oxford merely conveyed to that city the customs already
enjoyed by London. This did not, however, provide for the
appointment of Justices of the Peace or Keepers of the Peace, and in
1236 commissioners were sent to Oxford to ensure its "peace and
tranquility," but two years later 24 of the burgesses were sworn *ad
pacem conservandum.*[2]

Apart from the exceptional position of London the first town to
receive special county recognition was Bristol which, in the fourteenth
century, was the chief port of the west. At the beginning of the
thirteenth century the burgesses of Bristol had been given the right to
choose their own mayor, and the old manorial authority which, as in
other towns, had governed Bristol until then gave way to communal
government. It was a great inconvenience to the citizens to have to
seek justice at the two nearest county towns - Gloucester for
Gloucestershire and Ilchester, which was then the county town of
Somerset. This led Bristol to seek a charter, which was granted in 1373.
It raised the city to the status of a corporate county with its own
Assizes. The mayor and sheriff became Justices of the Peace, *virtute
officii,* and so too did the aldermen from 1499. The mayor and sheriff
were given the power to:

> "inquire, hear and determine ... concerning all manner of evil doings,
> transgressions, disturbances against the peace, champerties,
> conspiracies, confederations, ambidextries, extortions, oppressions,
> falsifications and other misprisions whatsoever done or to be done

2. CPR 1232-47, pp. 139 and 217.

within the town, suburbs and precinct aforesaid and concerning victuallers, workers, labourers and artificers within the same town, suburbs and precinct, as often as they shall see it right to be done and to punish such transgressions by fines and amerciaments and imprisonments of their bodies and to make due execution of judgments given by them hereupon."

The mayor and sheriff sat as Justices of the Peace almost every weekday to try minor offences. This arrangement changed in 1499 when the six aldermen, one of whom was made the recorder, became *ex officio* Justices of the Peace. Each of the aldermen, whose number was doubled to twelve two centuries later, was responsible for a ward. There was no Commission of the Peace for the city and a man became a justice solely through assuming one of the designated offices which automatically made him a magistrate *ex officio*. From 1373 onwards, therefore, although Bristol lay geographically within Gloucestershire, it was totally independent of the county authorities and it had its own court of Quarter Sessions. It was not unusual for a borough to introduce some novel arrangements of its own, particularly in the administrative sphere, and Bristol was noteworthy in introducing its own system of poor relief. As we have seen, responsibility for administering the Poor Law was placed on the Justices of the Peace in 1597, but in 1696, following the proposals of John Cary, Bristol introduced a sophisticated scheme which was later copied by other boroughs. A body called the Incorporation of the Poor was formed, comprising the mayor, aldermen and 48 elected representatives of the twelve city wards.[3] They administered a system under which the able-bodied were compelled to work, the young were trained and the infirm cared for.

Bristol retained its county status until county boroughs were abolished in the twentieth century. It continued to grow in importance and by 1700 it had become, after London, the largest city in England and the largest port. It derived its wealth from foreign trade, particularly in tobacco, sugar and slaves.

Gloucestershire was a typical English county and its towns provide a good illustration of the varying degrees of independence which were to be found among municipal authorities throughout the country. As already mentioned, the county town was the city of Gloucester, whose earliest charter of liberties was granted by Henry II in 1155. Fifteen years later Henry suppressed an attempt by the citizens to claim greater self-government, but in 1483 Richard III granted Gloucester a further charter which conferred county status and permitted the election of a mayor, sheriff and coroner, and the establishment of the

---

3. The scheme was confirmed by statute; 7 & 8 William III, c. 32.

city's own courts of law. The city was given power to make its own bye-laws and soon such laws were promulgated which regulated weights and measures, prices and the quality of goods. There were various rules to ensure cleanliness throughout the city; for instance, "no swyne nor dukkes goo in the open stretes." Immorality was regarded as a serious offence and, with a view to discouraging others, those convicted were drawn through the town in an open cart in addition to suffering other punishment.

The municipality of Gloucester covered a large surrounding territory in addition to the built-up areas of the city. This included the hundreds of Dudstone and King's Barton which were called the "in-shire." In 1662, however, Charles II, mindful of the city's defiance of his father, deprived it of this territory which was then restored to the county. For the same reason he also deprived it of its county status which it was not to regain until it became a county borough in the nineteenth century, but in spite of this it retained most of its privileges including the right to hold its own Quarter Sessions.

The 1483 charter incorporated Gloucester under the style of "the mayor and burgesses of the town of Gloucester." Among the offices performed by the mayor were those of clerk of the market, steward and marshal of the King's household and escheator. The office of sheriff was held by the two bailiffs. The governing body of the city was a common council which was not mentioned explicitly in the charter but seems to have been implied as it existed by at least 1484. It comprised the mayor, 11 aldermen, two sheriffs, four stewards and 22 other burgesses. The mayor was president of the council and he and the aldermen were Justices of the Peace *virtute officii*. It was largely a self-perpetuating body as the mayor was chosen from the aldermen by the other aldermen and by 12 leading burgesses who were all council men. The aldermen themselves held office for life and when vacancies occurred they were filled by the surviving aldermen from among the senior common council men who were also elected for life by the full council. There was a rather larger electorate for the bailiffs who were chosen by "the burgesses of the town," but it appears that in the course of time they too came to be chosen solely by the common council. The sheriffs became mainly executive officers and were subject to the discipline of the common council. There was a single coroner who was elected by, and held office during the pleasure of the mayor and aldermen, and who by the mid-sixteenth century was always chosen from among the aldermen. The entire government of the city therefore came to be controlled by a small oligarchy.

By the early sixteenth century Gloucester had a recorder whose position was confirmed by a charter of 1561. He was principally concerned with criminal trials but assumed an increasingly important role as adviser on all legal matters affecting the city. He was an important figure in the life of the borough, and William Lenthall, who became recorder in 1638, was later the Speaker of the Long Parliament.

The office of town clerk was also established after the 1483 charter and became increasingly important during the following century. He was usually a lawyer and was appointed for life. In addition to being town clerk, he acted as clerk to the hundred court, to the court of piepowder and as Clerk of the Peace, as well as holding other lesser appointments.

The charter of 1483 had therefore concentrated power in the hands of the leaders of Gloucester city, headed by the mayor and aldermen who were automatically Justices of the Peace for the borough. There were no justices appointed by commission. The mayor and aldermen exercised exclusive jurisdiction over the city and also the in-shire area, the latter causing considerable friction with the Gloucestershire county justices.

Gloucester had a number of different courts for which the mayor and aldermen were responsible. The hundred court tried civil actions involving citizens, but from the mid-sixteenth century it was in decline. The court of piepowder was held by the mayor at the Tolsey on market days, and that was the main court of pleas in the city. In 1561 an orphans' court was established at which the mayor and aldermen administered the estates of freemen whose heirs were minors, but this court fell into disuse in the early part of the following century. In 1605 James I granted the aldermen authority to hold Quarter Sessions for the city and the in-shire. Within 30 years Quarter Sessions had become both the principal court of the city and also the centre of government, controlling public order and administration, including such matters as relief of the poor, suppressing vagrancy, setting up workhouses and regulating apprentices.

During the Civil War Gloucester supported the Parliamentary cause. Most of the aldermen were appointed by Parliament as Deputy Lieutenants and played a leading part in the defence of the city. After the Restoration a new charter was granted in 1664 confirming the privileges granted by the earlier charters, but the further charter of 1672, which deprived the city of the in-shire areas, brought a number of county landowners into city affairs, several of whom became mayors. A similar change took place in the city's representation in Parliament. During the Civil War and the Interregnum only city men had been elected, but from 1660 until 1715 most of the Members were landed gentry from the county. This also resulted in the introduction of party politics and for a long time the city was divided between feuding Whigs and Tories.

By the 1720s the Gloucester hundred court only held one session a year and, although this continued until 1796, the only business transacted there was the taking of oaths of new officers of the trade companies. Views of frankpledge were still held twice a year in the Boothall before the sheriffs, now two in number. The only presentments made by the jury at the sessions were in respect of minor nuisances, but these seem to have been dealt with effectively. By the end of the century only one such session was held a year and they had ceased entirely by 1820. The piepowder court remained in operation until nearly the end of the century and was used by tradesmen to recover debts up to £10. In addition to this, some of the aldermen sat monthly at the Tolsey in a court of conscience which dealt with actions for debt up to 40 shillings.

The relief of the poor became one of the major administrative problems in Gloucester as elsewhere. Various schemes for establishing and maintaining workhouses were unsuccessful, partly due to financial problems although they received generous subscriptions from private individuals. Another problem which illustrated the difficulty which could arise, for which two different bodies of justices were responsible, was the raising of rates in parishes outside the city boundary. These parishes were served by the Gloucester workhouse and were therefore required to contribute to the cost, but they were within the jurisdiction of the county magistrates who were responsible for authorizing and enforcing the collection of the rate.

Vagrancy was a major problem in the eighteenth century and various steps were taken by Quarter Sessions to deal with it including the provision of a house of correction (described in ch. VIII). It was also assumed that the large number of alehouses in the city was an encouragement to vagrants and a cause of disorder. The city magistrates therefore reduced the number of licences and also urged the Gloucestershire county justices to take similar action to reduce alehouses in the suburbs.

Gloucester Quarter Sessions imposed the same type of penalties as the justices at the county sessions. Persons convicted of vagrancy and other minor offences were usually whipped publicly through the streets on market days. The extent of the whipping, however, varied according to the severity of the offence. The idle and disorderly were usually whipped from the prison, which was at the North Gate, and round the wheat market, which was no great distance, but for a more serious offence, such as obtaining money by false pretences, the offender would be whipped the whole length of Westgate Street and back. Persistent offenders were given hard labour in the house of correction. The pillory and the stocks in Southgate Street were still used occasionally in the early nineteenth century. In 1781 a new city gaol was built in Southgate Street which replaced the old prison in the castle, and from then onwards the most frequent punishment for petty crime was imprisonment in the gaol.

As in all other parts of the country the city magistrates were responsible for policing the area. This was always a greater problem in the cities than in the rural counties. In Gloucester the police force was composed of 12 ward constables in addition to various minor officers and they were controlled by the city magistrates who met twice a week for the purpose at the Tolsey. In 1786 a nightwatch was instituted, though it was never very effective, and a system of rewards for arrest was introduced. Here again, difficulties arose from lack of co-operation between the city and the county magistrates. Many criminals escaped beyond the city boundary where no action was taken against them, partly because county justices did not live in the immediate vicinity.

In the nineteenth century the history of Gloucester is similar to that of other contemporary boroughs which are described generally in the later part of this chapter. Following the Municipal Corporations Act of 1835, described later, it was granted its own Commission of the Peace and the city was enlarged to cover the same area as the Parliamentary borough. The old borough authority was abolished and was replaced by a council composed of six aldermen, of whom three were elected triennially in rotation by the council, 18 councillors, of whom six relinquished office each year, and the mayor who was elected annually by the council from among its members. Gloucester remained a county and as such it retained one sheriff, chosen annually by the council. Administrative matters were the responsibility of the new council, except for a number which came under various independent bodies. Criminal jurisdiction, however, was completely removed from the council and entrusted to new courts of Quarter Sessions and Petty Sessions, although the council appointed the Clerk of the Peace and the coroner. Quarter Sessions were held by the recorder who was now appointed by the Crown and not elected by the council as previously. Civil matters continued to be dealt with by the court of conscience, but this became the county court under the County Courts Act of 1846.

When the Justices of the Peace Act, which implemented the recommendations of the Royal Commission of 1946-48, was passed in 1949 Gloucester city had a population of 53,000 and it was therefore able to retain its county borough status, its separate Commission of the Peace and its court of Quarter Sessions - as did Bristol with its much larger population of 403,000. It was not until 1971 that, together with all other cities and boroughs except London, Gloucester lost its Quarter Sessions which were merged in the new Crown Court. Similarly, in 1973, its Commission of the Peace was combined with that of the county.

Gloucester and Bristol were the only centres in the Gloucestershire area which had county status. At the other end of the scale there were many towns with no municipal status, but in between there were a few which had obtained privileges to a varying degree. The hundreds of Cheltenham and Slaughter were liberties upon which the privilege of separate Quarter Sessions had been bestowed. The origin of these special courts is to be found in a grant of 1247 when the Abbey of Fecamp received the hundreds from the Crown in exchange for Rye and Winchelsea. Some records of proceedings before the Cheltenham sessions of the peace in the fifteenth and sixteenth centuries have been preserved in the Public Record Office.[4] Records of the Slaughter sessions, which were held at Stow-on-the-Wold, are in the Gloucester Record Office.[5] The Cheltenham sessions do not seem to have survived the Reformation, but the Slaughter court continued to sit until the Civil War. Neither Cheltenham nor Slaughter has ever had its own Commission of the Peace.

Somewhat different circumstances applied to Tewkesbury which had its own Justices of the Peace and Quarter Sessions under a Royal Charter of 1605. The charter provided that the two bailiffs and two other burgesses were to act as justices, but five years later the number of burgesses was increased to four, while in 1686 a charter provided that the mayor, the chief steward or his deputy and three aldermen should be justices. Finally, under a charter of 1698 the justices comprised the two bailiffs, the recorder and four burgesses. The administrative powers exercised by these magistrates were more limited than in the case of Gloucester. Many administrative functions were performed by statutory bodies.

From 1610 Tewkesbury's charters contained clauses forbidding the county justices to interfere in the town or parish of Tewkesbury. There was uncertainty, however, regarding liability for the payment of rates, and this was a constant source of dispute between borough and county until the borough's claim to exemption from county rates was declared to be void in 1708.

In 1836 Tewkesbury obtained the grant of a new court of Quarter Sessions under the provisions of the Municipal Corporations Act 1835, together with a recorder appointed by the Crown. The court was finally abolished under the Justices of the Peace Act 1949, and its archives were transferred to the Clerk of the Peace for the county in 1951.

The above description of the various courts in Gloucestershire is given as an illustration of the situation which was to be found in all

4.   PRO, SC 2/175/25-27.
5.   Gloucester RO, D 45.

parts of the kingdom. Boroughs in the other counties of England and Wales varied in a similar manner in the extent to which they acquired their own exclusive rights of jurisdiction under individual charters prior to 1835. The paragraphs which follow immediately hereafter describe in greater detail those who were responsible for operating the courts within the borough areas during this period.

Composition of borough benches until the nineteenth century
A marked difference between the magistrates in the boroughs and those in the counties was that most of the former were Justices of the Peace because they held certain offices such as mayor, recorder or aldermen, and not because they had been specifically chosen to administer justice. They were all officials of the town and remained magistrates only so long as they continued to hold these posts. Another difference was that the county magistrates were composed almost exclusively of landed gentry whereas those in the boroughs were tradesmen and shopkeepers. In cathedral cities bishops and some other clergy came to be included among the magistrates, and in Oxford and Cambridge a number of members of the universities were justices.

The borough magistrates tended to become an even closer oligarchy than those in the counties. It may seem at first sight that the system was democratic in that the burgesses of a town would elect, usually annually, a certain number of capital burgesses who in turn elected the mayor and aldermen for the ensuing year, but in practice only a fraction of the population had a vote and there was little if any choice of candidate. Consequently the governing body of a borough became self-perpetuating and the result was corruption and tyranny. They also proved to be incapable or unwilling on many occasions of performing their duties effectively. They did not command the respect among the rest of the population which was enjoyed by the county justice who was usually a man of greater calibre. The borough magistrate sought to emulate his opposite number in the county, but he did so by neglecting his own duties and seeking an entrée into county society by purchasing an estate where he spent much of his time. The deficiencies of borough magistrates were particularly noticeable in times of industrial unrest. Not only did they fail to deal effectively with the mass of minor crimes but they were unable to cope with the major disturbances which occurred during the earlier part of the nineteenth century, examples of which will be mentioned later. Another disadvantage was that the borough justices usually served for much shorter terms than those in the counties. Throughout most of their history the majority of county justices remained on the commission for life. In the boroughs there were also some who died in office, but the usual practice was for a man to serve for some time as alderman, then to be elected mayor and to remain a magistrate for one year after relinquishing the mayoralty.

The result was that many did not serve long enough to gain sufficient experience and to follow a consistent policy.

The situation was to change after 1835 when, as explained later, the borough benches though remaining independent became analogous to those of the counties.

Recorders

An exception to the general climate of incompetence was the borough's recorder who was a lawyer and who normally presided over Quarter Sessions with some efficiency as well as advising the corporation on legal matters.

The origin of recorders is one of some antiquity. In some places there were officers analogous to recorders before a town received a charter, but a recordership was invariably the creation of a charter which provided for their election by the burgesses and declared that they should be Justices of the Peace for the town or borough. They normally presided at Quarter Sessions, sitting with two or three other town justices. The extent of their jurisdiction, like that of the other justices, was specified in the charter and usually extended to all felonies, trespasses and misprisions, and also "for all manner of other causes, suits and misdeeds whatsoever that in any way chance or arise within the said town or borough." In the case of felonies many recorders as well as the mayor and aldermen were excluded from trying cases of counterfeiting, clipping or otherwise falsifying coins. This was probably because coinage offences were regarded as being particularly heinous and the penalty allowed by law could involve unbearable torture. In some instances the recorder also presided over the borough civil courts, but this was rare. There were a few boroughs, such as Kingston-upon-Thames, which ultimately acquired separate Commissions of the Peace but were not granted separate Quarter Sessions. These boroughs acquired honorary recorders who exercised no jurisdiction and received no financial reward, but the borough usually made them an annual gift in kind such as two sugar loaves in the case of Kingston-upon-Thames.

Recorders were usually competent lawyers and sometimes they finished their legal careers in high judicial office. In the nineteenth century it became customary for virtually all those appointed to the High Court to have served for a time as a borough recorder. From the sixteenth century a number of recorders also became Members of Parliament. This meant that they were often absentees and their work had to be conducted by other justices of the borough. This coincided, however, with an influx of lawyers into the borough oligarchies which mitigated to some extent the absence of the recorder at Quarter Sessions.

The corruption and inefficiency of borough administration led to the reforms of the 1830s which are described later. These included a realignment of the position of the recorder.

Court clerks

The town clerk of a borough was appointed by the corporation and until the eighteenth century, usually held office for life. He also acted as Clerk of the Peace and of the other borough courts such as the hundred court, orphans' court and court of piepowder. From the early seventeenth century he became an important figure in urban life and politics. He had usually studied at the Inns of Court and had become a barrister. The choice of a new town clerk, and consequently of Clerk of the Peace, was often the outcome of a heated contest. After 1835 when boroughs were granted their own Commissions of the Peace, the council appointed a separate Clerk of the Peace for Quarter Sessions and the magistrates appointed another clerk to deal with their affairs at Petty Sessions.[6]

Subordinate officials

The subordinate officials in boroughs differed from those in the counties in that they were more numerous and occupied a greater variety of posts, and also that the majority were paid for their work and were not required by law to perform public duties gratuitously. They included beadles and nightwatchmen and also a number of deputy constables who provided a somewhat ineffective police force. They were all under the control of the city magistrates.

Judicial functions

The distinction between the jurisdiction of the various courts in the boroughs was less clear than in the counties, and sometimes it was far from obvious in what capacity the magistrates were sitting. There was sometimes confusion between a market court of piepowder and an ordinary session to deal with minor crimes in the town, and there were occasions when the same court dealt with a civil dispute. Generally speaking, however, cases coming before the borough courts were similar to those in the county at large. We have seen earlier that many Acts of Parliament which applied to Justices of the Peace expressly included the borough magistrates. Crimes of violence were the most frequent, but many other offences, especially relating to streets and highways, were almost as numerous. So too were those arising from trade - false weights and measures, forestalling, regrating and usury - which arose more often in the towns than in the rural areas as one

6.   Confirmed by Municipal Corporations Act 1882, s. 59(1).

would expect in a mercantile community. Some boroughs had their own courts of Oyer and Terminer and Gaol Delivery, but these were not always regarded as unmixed blessings, and some boroughs sought to relinquish these privileges. Southampton, for instance, did so in 1725 because it was short of funds and regarded this as a means of reducing its expenses. Thereafter Southampton was included in the Western Circuit of the Assize Judges. In any event, borough Quarter Sessions were required to send their more difficult and serious offences to Assizes for trial. If the borough did not have its own Quarter Sessions those of the adjoining county had jurisdiction over the borough area. Even where a borough did have its own Quarter Sessions with exclusive jurisdiction over the borough it was not unusual for both the borough and the county sessions to sit in the borough, sometimes in the same building.

Administrative functions
Whereas the borough magistrates had the same judicial functions as those in the counties, the extent of their administrative duties and the time spent on them were even greater because a thickly populated urban area engendered more numerous and frequent problems than a rural district, and consequently the mayor and the other members of the corporation who were magistrates were engaged daily in matters of town government. The Justices of the Peace in the towns came to assume authority in their sessions for all local government matters, most of which had previously been the responsibility of some other body. When performing these administrative duties the mayor and aldermen were acting as magistrates and not as part of the corporation. There were some towns, however, where the common council and not the city magistrates controlled certain fields of public life. At High Wycombe in Buckinghamshire, for example, most matters which came within the jurisdiction of Justices of the Peace in the counties, including the Poor Law, were supervised by the council. Generally, however, local government was clearly in the hands of the borough justices. The town usually had its own gaol, which was under the direct authority of the magistrates, though administered by a salaried gaoler. The cleansing and maintenance of the streets, the control of alehouses and the supervision of the watch were matters to which they were constantly giving their attention. Poor relief, which occupied as great a proportion of the magistrates' time as it did in the counties, had been provided in the boroughs before it became the subject of national legislation for the country as a whole. In the fourteenth and fifteenth century, town guilds, in addition to the municipal government, had played a prominent part in the relief of the poor, and wealthy members of the guilds endowed almshouses, hospitals and

schools. As regards bridges, it was not at first clear where responsibility lay for the upkeep of bridges and therefore in 1531, 22 Hen. VIII, c. 5, provided that where no other liability could definitely be proved, responsibility for maintaining bridges should fall on the county for bridges outside corporate towns and on the towns themselves where the bridges were situated within the town area. This responsibility also applied to the highway within 300 feet from the end of the bridge. In some cases where there was a common interest - not only in respect of highways and bridges - the justices from both a borough and a county would decide the proportion of the amounts to be paid by each authority. Joint meetings of this kind continued to be fairly common into the nineteenth century. In 1855, for example, two justices each from Bristol, Tewkesbury and Gloucestershire met to award the amounts payable from each authority for the provision and repair of militia storehouses which became necessary under an Act of 1854 (15 & 16 Vict., c. 50).

Most of the local Acts at the end of the seventeenth and beginning of the eighteenth centuries were passed to give increased powers to the governing bodies of towns. Thus we have the city of Bristol acquiring "power to pave, light, watch and cleanse" the town and to regulate the market and also to have control over the rivers Avon and Frome,[7] and Yarmouth was given power over its harbour and docks.[8]

Statutory bodies[9]

The pressure arising from local administration in the large urban areas became so intense that the existing machinery under the supervision of the mayor and other town officers proved to be totally inadequate. Consequently although many local Acts increased the powers of the governing bodies of the towns to enable them to deal with the new demands, the government tended to an increasing extent to place the burden of local administration in specific areas upon independent commissioners. Resort was had to *ad hoc* bodies in order to meet the increasing demands of town government, and these bodies were given power to deal with such matters as lighting, sanitation, drainage, paving, police and the poor. They varied greatly from one place to another, in some cases being autonomous bodies while in others they were virtually special committees of the municipal corporation. Almost all operated in the boroughs, though there were a few in the country districts.

The earliest of these bodies were those of Poor Law Commissioners

7.   11 William III, c. 23; 28 Geo. II, c. 32; 6 Geo. III, c. 34; 28 Geo. III, c. 65.
8.   10 & 11 William III, c. 5.
9.   These bodies, which were established in counties as well as in boroughs, are described at
      length by Sidney and Beatrice Webb in *ELG, Statutory Authorities for Special Purposes.*

but these were closely followed by others designed to improve conditions generally in the towns. The first of the poor law bodies was the Corporation of the Poor of the City of London (described below), created by a Parliamentary ordinance of 1647, confirmed by a statute of 1662,[10] and similar systems were soon adopted elsewhere, each under a local Act of Parliament. These corporations of the poor, although separate bodies, were not always completely independent of the magistrates and leading officers of the town. Thus in Bristol, as mentioned above, and many other towns they were subject to the management of the mayor, the aldermen and the churchwardens of the parish together with representatives (usually four in number) elected at a public meeting in each ward. In some cases the corporation consisted of all the owners of property above a certain value. Thus in Shrewsbury, under an Act of 1783, it included all owners of freeholds and copyholds of £30 a year and the occupiers of premises rated at £15 a year. The duties performed by these bodies were the same as those of the justices in the counties. They maintained the destitute, apprenticed children and built workhouses in which the aged and infirm could obtain relief and the able-bodied put to work. The idle could be forced into employment. Although the workhouses and other institutions began well they fared no better in the long run than those used by the justices in rural areas which, as we shall see in a later chapter, failed to achieve their purpose and were ultimately abandoned.

Relief of the poor was by no means the only problem which required special attention in the boroughs. Recognition of the squalor in urban areas and the intolerable conditions under which the citizens lived gave rise to an increasing demand during the eighteenth century for special remedial measures. The Webbs give a vivid description of the appalling conditions of the streets[11] at this time, where there was no sanitation, no lighting at night, no police and where even main thoroughfares were blocked by filth. In 1714 and 1736 general Acts gave borough authorities power to cleanse and repair streets and to appoint scavengers to carry out the work. They could also levy a rate to cover the cost. Local Acts also established improvement commissioners to devise and introduce essential remedies. They could eliminate nuisances, remove obstructions including unnecessary signs, regulate traffic, carry out street improvements such as widening, and purchase land compulsorily for the purpose. They could also give names and numbers to the streets. Street lighting did not become usual until the middle of the eighteenth century. Until fairly late in history,

10.   13 & 14 Charles II, c. 12, made perpetual by 12 Anne, st. 1, c. 18.
11.   *Statutory Authorities*, p. 344.

persons wishing to have light to enable them to move about by night carried their own lanterns, but by the late seventeenth century some borough authorities had power to compel householders to fix lamps to the outside of their premises. There was also increasing awareness of the nuisance caused by smoke, especially with the increase in coal fires, and clauses were included in local Acts giving the authorities power to remove chimneys which were causing particular offence. These clauses were largely superseded by an Act of 1821 which strengthened the law on causing a nuisance by smoke. Commissioners also had powers regarding sewers, but these referred almost entirely to drainage of surface water, and not until well into the nineteenth century was provision made for the disposal of sewage in the modern sense. As the Webbs comment in this context, until as late as 1835 "it never occurred even to the most enlightened local authority, that it had any responsibility for the freedom from noxious filth of the town as a whole."

Borough magistrates were particularly concerned with the detection and punishment of criminals and with the maintenance of order, and from the 1730s it was normal for local Acts to provide for some form of borough police to replace or augment the ancient watch.

Power to deal with these matters was at first given to the magistrates and other officers of the boroughs, but the results were unimpressive, and as urban problems became more acute responsibility was transferred to independent *ad hoc* bodies. By the beginning of the nineteenth century they numbered about 300, including those in the London area. Their composition and functions varied greatly. In most the mayor and aldermen were commissioners *ex officio*, but they shared office with numerous other persons, some of whom were elected while some comprised all citizens who had property of a specific value or above. A serious weakness of the commissioners was that they were severely limited in the amount of money they could raise either by borrowing or by levying a rate.

With a few exceptions, borough magistrates did not exhibit the same concern for the welfare of the population as did the justices in the counties. They were interested in matters affecting their own welfare and that of their close associates, but they took a myopic view of all else. It is true that the county justices were primarily concerned in maintaining their own privileges, but they also took a close interest in the welfare of the community as a whole. Borough magistrates who served as improvement commissioners, as many did, devoted some time to improving amenities of the area in which they resided but they mainly ignored the other parts of the town which were usually in a far worse state. This irresponsible attitude was to be found both in the corporations and in the statutory bodies, but it must be said in favour of the latter that they did achieve many reforms which would never have been introduced if the affairs of the towns had been left solely in the charge of the corporation.

Although the statutory bodies, or something similar, were essential to save the life of the boroughs, they ultimately failed because many were totally independent of outside supervision. There was no other authority, either local or national, which could effectively scrutinize their work and compel them to discharge their public duties as there had been in Tudor times when the Council was constantly intervening in borough affairs as well as in those of the counties. Sometimes there were even directions under the Tudors as to who should become mayor or town clerk. Again, when a borough corporation appeared to be exceeding its powers it was kept in check. For instance, in 1575 Poole was forbidden to levy new import duties and in 1597 Shrewsbury was not allowed to impose unreasonable market tolls.[12] The absence of any supervision in the eighteenth century resulted in the administration of both the borough authorities and the improvement commissioners becoming lax and ineffective. The reforming legislation of the 1830s sounded the knell of the statutory bodies as well as of the old-style corporate bodies. The Municipal Corporations Act of 1835 did not itself abolish improvement commissioners, nor other *ad hoc* bodies, but the efficiency of the new municipal authorities which the Act established was such that the work of all *ad hoc* bodies was gradually absorbed into the new local government machinery.

Municipal reform of the nineteenth century

By the eighteenth century the boroughs had come to be governed by a small co-optive circle of prominent citizens, and the vast majority of the inhabitants had no chance of playing any part in the management of their affairs. The administration became incompetent and the leaders of the boroughs refused to undertake any additional functions which were required by the new conditions arising from the Industrial Revolution and other causes. Some of these had therefore been given to the *ad hoc* bodies but, as already explained, even they became ineffective and the central government had no means of ensuring that local administration was properly conducted.

Fundamental reforms were needed to solve this crucial problem. There could be no hope of a revolution in local administration without an equally drastic reform of the national legislature. The old system had been bound up with the rotten boroughs which returned Members

12.　Dasent, viii, 375 & xxviii, 360.

to Parliament at the behest of local magnates and without any democratic election. As soon as the new "ten-pounder" householders were given the Parliamentary vote following the Reform Act of 1832, they set about obtaining government by popular election in their own towns. This was achieved in the Municipal Corporations Act of 1835 which gave all ratepayers the right to vote for the new municipalities. The Act applied to all the principal towns except London, but smaller districts were still left to the county justices until elected county councils were established in 1888. In the meantime, however, all the corporations of the old boroughs were abolished and were replaced by new municipal bodies based on election by the ratepayers. These new authorities were entrusted with the administrative functions of their predecessors but judicial work, and also the licensing of public houses, were given to borough magistrates who were now completely separated from the corporation. The radicals would have liked the elected councils to have dealt with these matters as well, but the prevailing view was that the administration of justice and the granting of licences were incompatible with party politics which were likely to dominate local as well as national elections, and therefore the judiciary at all levels must be non-elective. The Act anticipated the reform of the county commissions by more than 50 years, but it established the principles on which these were to be based - a democratically elected body in charge of administrative matters and the total separation of administrative from judicial functions. The new municipalities were empowered to levy a rate and they gradually assumed the various functions which had previously been exercised by the *ad hoc* bodies.

For half a century between 1835 and 1888 the differences between the counties and the towns increased further the social and political divergence between the two. The new urban authorities were imbued with the democratic spirit of the age and were dominated by the new middle class, whose political views were influenced by socialist philosophy. Rural England, on the other hand, remained subordinate to the squire and the landed gentry with their roots firmly implanted in the past. They were prepared to move with the times but only in so far as this did not interfere with their vested interests.

All charters and customs inconsistent with the 1835 Act were repealed. The Act provided that the body corporate of every borough was to consist of the mayor, aldermen and burgesses, and the governing body was to be a council. Every burgess who was enrolled on the burgesses' roll was entitled to vote for councillors who were to hold office for three years, but each year there was to be an election of one-third of the total. The number of aldermen was to be one-third of the number of councillors, and the mayor was to be elected annually by the aldermen and councillors.

Effect of the 1835 legislation on the Justices of the Peace

The 1835 Act provided that everyone holding office of Justice of the Peace at the time of the passing of the Act should continue in office until May 1, 1836, but no longer. Thereafter the mayor was to be a justice during his mayoralty and for one year thereafter. The only other person who could become a justice *ex officio* was the recorder if one were appointed for the borough. Apart from these provisions no borough Justices of the Peace were created automatically under the Act, but provision was made for each borough to have a separate Commission of the Peace which would be identical with those issued to counties. Schedule A to the Act set out the names of boroughs, numbering 128 in all, which were to be entitled to receive a separate commission in any event. Schedule B gave the names of 50 boroughs which were not to have their own commissions unless they petitioned the Crown and duly received a grant. Section 98 of the Act empowered the King to grant commissions to the cities and boroughs set out in the schedules and, having done so, he might "from time to time appoint as many persons as he shall think proper to be Justices of the Peace in the borough." No one could be appointed a borough justice unless he resided in or within seven miles of the borough (s. 101), and the same section disqualified borough justices from sitting in courts of gaol delivery. It was the duty of the council for every borough to which a separate commission had been granted to provide one or more suitable police officers for the purpose of transacting the work of the borough justices (s. 100).

The Act also enabled a borough to obtain a stipendiary magistrate. Under s. 99 the council could petition the Secretary of State for the appointment of "a salaried magistrate or magistrates," and they had to state the salary which they were prepared to pay to the stipendiary magistrate, which was to be fixed by bye-laws. The King might then at his discretion appoint one or more "police magistrates" to serve at his pleasure.

If a Commission of the Peace were not granted to a borough the justices for the neighbouring county would exercise jurisdiction over the borough area, but once a commission had been granted the borough justices would hold their own courts of Petty Sessions, and they were required (s. 102) to appoint a clerk who must not be Clerk of the Peace or alderman or councillor, nor be concerned in the prosecution of offenders committed by the borough justices.

Reference has already been made to the provisions of the Act regarding courts of Quarter Sessions. Quarter Sessions which were in existence before the passing of the Act were abolished and if a borough wished to have a separate court it had to petition the King in Council (s. 103). If it did not do so the justices for the adjoining county sitting in their county Quarter Sessions had jurisdiction within the borough. If the borough council were successful in its petition the King might grant a separate court and appoint a salaried recorder. The sessions were to be a court of record but they did not have jurisdiction over treason, capital felonies and certain other crimes. Appeals against summary conviction by the justices within the borough might go either to the borough Quarter Sessions or to those for the county. Under s. 132, no conviction or other matter might be quashed for want of form or be removed by *certiorari* or otherwise to any of Her Majesty's courts of record at Westminster.

The year 1835 therefore saw a complete revolution in the position of Justices of the Peace in the boroughs. From then onwards there was little difference between the borough justices and those in the counties. There were, however, two dissimilarities of some significance. First that borough justices could not sit at Quarter Sessions, and this applied whether the borough had its own sessions or was subject to those of the county. Secondly, the borough justices were confined to judicial work whereas, for the next fifty years, the county justices continued to be in charge of local administration. Borough justices, like those in the counties, were appointed by having their names entered in the commission at the direction of the Lord Chancellor, who sought advice on candidates from a number of quarters, sometimes from Members of Parliament, and did not normally consult the Lord Lieutenant of the county.

The Municipal Corporations Act, 1882 re-enacted the provisions of the 1835 Act and provided (s. 156) that "It shall be lawful for the Queen, on the petition of the Council of a borough, to grant to the borough a separate Commission of the Peace." The Crown was advised on such applications by the Home Secretary until this function was transferred to the Lord Chancellor in 1949. The form of both borough and county commissions, which had remained unaltered since 1590, was changed in 1878 under rules made in pursuance of the Crown Office Act, 1877. The commissions for counties and boroughs were identical save for the salutation which, in the case of counties, was addressed to the Lord Chancellor, the Lord Lieutenant, the Lord Chief Justice and a number of members of the Privy Council and of the higher judiciary, as well as to the Attorney and Solicitor General. Borough commissions were addressed only to the mayor, and in later years to the county court Judge, in addition to the body of justices named in the Schedule (see *post*, vol. III, Appendix I).

Recorders and Borough Quarter Sessions after 1835
All the old charter recorderships were abolished by the Municipal Corporations Act 1835 which repealed all charters and customs which

were inconsistent with its provisions. Under the Act, any borough which wished to have a separate court of Quarter Sessions and a recorder could petition through one of the principal Secretaries, setting out the salary which it was prepared to pay. The Crown was then empowered to grant a separate court of Quarter Sessions and to appoint a recorder who had to be a barrister of at least five years' standing and who, while in office, took precedence within the borough next after the mayor. He was a Justice of the Peace *ex officio* for the borough. The previous right of the corporation to appoint the recorder was removed. Until 1949 the Crown made the appointment on the advice of the Home Secretary but thereafter of the Lord Chancellor. Unlike the recorders who had previously been appointed by the borough, the new-style recorder was disqualified from serving in Parliament or as an alderman, councillor or police magistrate for the borough. Before he could act as recorder he had to take the oaths required of a Justice of the Peace, except the oath as to qualification by estate. Both he and the Justices of the Peace were required to declare before the mayor or two or more aldermen or councillors that "I will faithfully and impartially execute the office of recorder [or Justice of the Peace] for the Borough of ... according to the best of my judgment and ability."

After 1835 borough Quarter Sessions consisted of the recorder sitting alone and no other justices were empowered to participate. The only exception to this rule was introduced in 1963 by the Children and Young Persons Act which required recorders to sit with two justices as assessors when hearing appeals from juvenile courts. This was a concession to the view held by many Justices of the Peace at that time that those who had served in juvenile courts had experience and understanding of juvenile problems which were not possessed by a recorder. No such exception was made, however, in respect of appeals from the adult courts, notwithstanding the claim by many justices that the recorder also lacked an understanding of local problems which led him to reduce the sentences they imposed. The recorder was required to hold sessions once in every quarter or at such other and more frequent times as he in his discretion might think fit or Her Majesty might direct. Borough Quarter Sessions were confirmed as being a court of record.

If a recorder could certify that the work of his forthcoming sessions was likely to occupy more than three whole days he could enlist the temporary services of an assistant recorder who had to be a barrister of five years' standing, so that two courts might be held at the same time and the work of the sessions completed expeditiously. If a recorder found that owing to illness or some other unforeseen reason he was unable to attend in person at Quarter Sessions he might appoint a deputy recorder (who must also be a barrister of five years' standing) to act in his absence but only at that particular session. If neither the recorder nor a deputy recorder was present the mayor of the borough might open and adjourn the court.

Throughout most of their history borough courts of Quarter Sessions, like those in the counties, were not in permanent session, and only a limited amount of the recorder's time was spent in court. The City of London, however, as we shall see later, had a whole-time recorder who also exercised the jurisdiction of a commissioner of Assize. After 1956, Liverpool and Manchester also had whole-time recorders who were appointed by the Crown on the Lord Chancellor's recommendation under the Criminal Justice Administration Act 1956.

Under the charters it was usual for a recorder to hold office for life, but after 1835 he served *quamdiu se bene gesserit*. The Criminal Justice Administration Act 1956, however, gave the Lord Chancellor power to dismiss a recorder for inability. This authority was never exercised, but there were occasions when a recorder was admonished by the Lord Chancellor, usually because he had shown excessive leniency. An unduly severe sentence could be cured by the Court of Appeal but there was no remedy for a grossly inadequate sentence, and most Lord Chancellors considered it to be their duty to "educate" a recorder who exhibited such a weakness.

The remuneration of recorders was the salary which the borough had indicated its willingness to pay pursuant to the Act of 1835. It could be increased by resolution of the borough council approved by the Secretary of State. In most cases the salary was little more than nominal and was in no way comparable with the fees which the recorder would have received during a similar period of time in practice. In spite of this, there was no shortage of candidates - it was customary for members of the Bar to apply for appointment and there were few of the more successful practitioners who did not do so. They regarded appointment as an honour and an opportunity to render public service as well as a possible stepping-stone to permanent judicial office. The salary was paid by the borough council but the amount varied considerably, depending more upon the council's generosity than upon the size of the borough or the volume of the work. From 1962, however, under the Criminal Justice Administration Act (s. 8), the remuneration was fixed by the Lord Chancellor after consultation with the council, the rate being based on the borough's population. In most cases the amount still fell far short of compensating the recorder for what he lost in brief-fees while attending sessions. He was also penalized under the rule established by the decision of the House of Lords in the case of *Ricketts* v.

Colquhoun,[13] upholding the Inland Revenue's contention that a recorder did not begin to act as such until he was seated on the bench. This meant that he was obliged to pay his own travelling expenses without income tax relief even though he would have been entitled to tax reimbursement had he attended the same sessions as counsel. In 1955 the Royal Commission on Taxation of Profits and Income recommended that this inconsistent rule should be abrogated, and so too did an Interdepartmental Committee in 1961,[14] but the Revenue's dogged refusal to capitulate succeeded in maintaining the *status quo* until the old-style recorderships together with all courts of Quarter Sessions were abolished by the Courts Act 1971. In the circumstances it is not surprising that most recorders devoted the minimum amount of time to the work of their Quarter Sessions. From 1835 borough justices could commit cases for trial at either borough or county sessions and recorders tended to select dates for holding their sessions immediately after those of the county when there would be little work left over.

The Justices of the Peace Act 1949 sought to eliminate those recorderships which were unproductive and it made provision for the abolition of every borough Quarter Sessions serving a population of less than 20,000, of which there were 31. The Act contained a saving clause, however, which enabled the Lord Chancellor to retain a recordership if he was satisfied that this was desirable for historical or geographical reasons and having regard to the assistance which the court had given or was likely to give to the administration of justice in the county. Responsibility for deciding the fate of the smaller boroughs was entrusted to a committee of three[15] which had a long and laborious task in assessing the claims of each of the boroughs concerned. Their recommendations, which were implemented by the Lord Chancellor, retained eight of the small recorderships and

13. 1926. AC 1; 10 TC 118, HL (E).
14. *Final Report of the Royal Commission on Taxation of Profits and Income,* Cmnd 9473 (HMSO, 1955) paras. 238-40; and *Report of the Interdepartmental Committee on the Business of the Criminal Courts,* Cmnd 1289 (HMSO, 1961) para. 208.
15. The members were: Sir Hartley Shawcross (the Attorney-General, later Lord Shawcross), Philip Allen of the Home Office (later Lord Allendale) and the author.

abolished the remaining 23.[16] This left 93 boroughs with separate Quarter Sessions from then until 1971.

In 1966 the Royal Commission on Assizes and Quarter Sessions was appointed. Its report, published in 1969, will be discussed in greater detail later, but its recommendations included the abolition of all existing recorderships and the replacement of all courts of Quarter Sessions and Assizes by a new Crown Court. At that time there were still only three whole-time recorders - at the Central Criminal Court in London and the Crown Courts at Liverpool and Manchester. In addition to the recorder of London there were several other whole-time Judges at the Central Criminal Court, one holding the title of common serjeant and the others were called additional Judges. They, like the recorder, were appointed and remunerated by the City Corporation. The offices of recorder and common serjeant were not affected by the Royal Commission's recommendations, but the additional Judges, together with the recorders of Liverpool and Manchester and the full-time chairmen of county sessions who held office at that time, were all transformed into the new category of Circuit Judge which was created in accordance with the Commission's recommendations. Thereafter there were no recorderships of the old kind other than for the City of London, but the title was retained and conferred upon a new type of part-time Judge who was appointed by the Queen on the Lord Chancellor's recommendation from among barristers and solicitors of not less than 10 years' standing.[17] The Royal Commission lamented the loss of the old-style recorderships and commented (para. 239):

"It is understandable that members of the Bar attach considerable importance to the title of recorder, to the association of their

16.   Boroughs with populations under 20,000 which lost their recorderships were:

Berwick-upon-Tweed	Maldon
Bideford	Oswestry
Bridgnorth	Richmond (Yorks)
Carmarthen	Rye
Chichester	Saffron Walden
Faversham	Sandwich
Hythe	South Molton
Ludlow	Stamford
Sudbury	Tiverton
Tenterden	Warwick
Tewkesbury	Wenlock
Thetford	

Those which were retained were:

Abingdon	Bury St Edmunds
Andover	Devizes
Banbury	Lichfield
Barnstaple	Newbury

17.   Courts Act 1971, s. 21(1), (2).

recordership with a particular borough, and to the civic status their position gives them within the borough. It was with great regret, therefore, that we concluded that the title could not be perpetuated with anything like its present significance. What we propose is that all the part-time Judges shall be called recorders, but, since borough Quarter Sessions will disappear as a distinctive form of court under our proposals, the new recorders will have no affiliation with particular boroughs by virtue of their judicial appointment. Existing recorderships' will necessarily lapse with the institution of the new system."

The twentieth century

Advisory committees

The position remained virtually the same until 1949, save for the establishment of advisory committees on the appointment of justices following the recommendations of the Royal Commission of 1910. In accordance with these recommendations the Lord Chancellor appointed a committee for each area having a separate commission.[18] The chairman, in the case of counties, was the *Custos Rotulorum* who was also invariably the Lord Lieutenant; in the case of borough committees the Lord Chancellor selected some suitable person to take the chair. The introduction of the advisory committee system had the effect, as it was intended, of broadening the social and political spectrum of the benches, though this was less noticeable in the boroughs whose benches already tended to be more representative of the local population as a whole than did those in the counties.

The arrangement of having a separate advisory committee for every area having a separate Commission of the Peace and for none other continued until 1973 when, as we shall see later, all borough commissions were abolished and were merged in those of the adjoining counties. The old borough advisory committees were abolished at the same time, but it was thought that some of the new commission areas were so large and populous that a single committee would be inadequate. The Lord Chancellor therefore decided to establish some committees to advise him on appointments to the largest benches even though their justices formed only part of a county commission. Accordingly, as from 1973, a separate advisory committee was set up for each district in a metropolitan county. This was in

18.   In 1949 there were 251 boroughs with separate Commissions of the Peace (this did not include the City of London which had no commission at that time). Fourteen of the boroughs had stipendiary magistrates (who were still appointed on the advice of the Home Secretary) and 61 had separate courts of Quarter Sessions (whose recorders were also appointed on the Home Secretary's advice).

addition to the committees for areas which had separate commissions, *ie,* each county, each of the four commission areas of Outer London and the City of London.

The mayor
Since time immemorial it had been customary for the mayor as first citizen to preside when present over borough courts. Although his jurisdiction at Quarter Sessions was largely removed by the 1835 Act, it nevertheless provided that, in the absence of the recorder or of a deputy recorder, the mayor might open and adjourn the court. At Petty Sessions his pre-eminent position remained intact. The Municipal Corporations Act 1882, confirmed not only that the mayor should, by virtue of his office, be a justice for the borough and should continue to be a justice during the year after he ceased to be mayor, but also that (s. 155(2)):

> "The mayor shall have precedence over all other justices acting in and for the borough, and he be entitled to take the chair at all meetings of justices held in the borough at which he is present by virtue of his office of mayor ..."

The subsection went on to say that the mayor should not have precedence over justices for the adjoining county except where the court was dealing with borough business. Again, he was not to take precedence over a stipendiary magistrate who was engaged in administering justice - though he did so on all other occasions. These provisions were confirmed by the Local Government Act 1933 (s. 18(9)). The Act also stated (s. 18(8)) that the mayor of a non-county borough should during his term of office be a justice for the county in which the borough was situated. The Departmental Committee on Justices' Clerks (the Roche Committee) in their Report published in 1944,[19] strongly condemned the mayor's right to preside. Their words implied that the individuals who occupied the office of mayor at that time were not of the quality required of a Justice of the Peace. The Justices' Clerks' Society had found on inquiry that less than a quarter of the mayors in office had been on the Commission of the Peace before their election as mayor, yet in a large number of boroughs it was the practice for the mayor to sit regularly as chairman of the bench, in some cases wearing his insignia of office. In some places the mayor sat and took the chair only on formal occasions, but in only two instances did he vacate the chair in favour of the senior magistrate present. The Departmental Committee commented (para. 217):

19.   Cmd. 6507.

"Under this system it is a matter of accident whether the bench obtains a suitable chairman. In many cases the mayor has had no experience as a magistrate before his appointment, and where he is already on the bench he is not necessarily the most suitable member to act as chairman. He may be unavoidably prevented by his other duties from giving all the time required to the work which should be performed by a good chairman out of court, and it is generally undesirable that the head of the local authority should also be chairman of the borough bench before which the local authority is frequently appearing. In some areas it is the practice for the mayor to vacate the chair when cases in which his council is interested are being heard, but this does not wholly remove the difficulty. The fact that the mayor is elected annually leads to a discontinuity in the chairmanship which is also unfortunate."

The Departmental Committee therefore recommended that borough justices should elect their own chairman. This proposal was brought to the notice of the boroughs and in many cases the mayors voluntarily refrained from taking the chair at ordinary sittings of the court, but others continued to preside as before. No amending legislation was introduced at that time because of the War, and the position of the mayor remained unchanged until 1949 when fundamental reform of the whole system was introduced as described in the following paragraphs.

Reform of 1949
The circumstances which led to the appointment of the Royal Commission on Justices of the Peace in 1946 are described later, and so too are the provisions of the Justices of the Peace Act 1949 which implemented most of the Commission's recommendations as well as those of the Roche Committee. Most of the changes had equal effect on the justices in counties and in boroughs, but there were a few which applied only to the boroughs. Those relating to recorders and Quarter Sessions, which resulted in the elimination of 23 borough sessions together with the borough commissions, have already been described. When the Royal Commission was appointed there were 251 boroughs having separate Commissions of the Peace, which was the same as there had b.en when the previous Royal Commission reported in 1910. The figure was, however, considerably larger than it had been shortly after 1835 because a growing number of boroughs successfully petitioned for a commission under the 1835 Act. The Royal Commission of 1946 pointed out that the possession by a borough of a separate commission depended "more on the course of past history than upon considerations of its real desirability" and it

drew attention to the substantial number of small boroughs with separate commissions which existed at that time. There was then a total of 114 such boroughs with populations under 25,000, of which 28 had populations of less than 5,000.[20] As the Commission explained, if a borough having a separate commission was unduly small a number of disadvantages followed. In particular, there was the difficulty in finding sufficient suitable candidates for appointment to the bench when the choice was restricted to a relatively small body of local inhabitants. In addition to this, those who were appointed in these circumstances did not have sufficient work to enable them to gain adequate experience. Furthermore, it was often difficult to form a court at all because most of the justices tended to be disqualified from adjudicating in a substantial proportion of cases, especially if they were members of the borough authority. The situation was particularly unsatisfactory when, as often happened, there was a county Petty Sessional division whose justices sat in the same town, sometimes in the same building on the same day, while the total volume of work could easily have been handled by a single court. The Commission agreed with those who claimed that the retention of separate commissions for areas of small population was detrimental, but it refrained from suggesting a figure for the minimum size as, for some reason which is not entirely clear, they did not think it "within our province to make a detailed examination of the precise test that can be applied." They contented themselves with referring to the Report of the Roche Committee which suggested a minimum of 25,000. The government, after considering the Report, decided that the smaller boroughs should be eliminated subject to certain qualifications, and accordingly the Justices of the Peace Act 1949 provided (s. 10(1)) that there should be a separate commission for every county, for every borough and for such non-county boroughs as satisfied one of the following conditions:

"(a) that at the end of December 1948 the borough had a separate Commission of the Peace and a population of 35,000 or over;
(b) that at the end of that month the borough had a separate Commission of the Peace and court of Quarter Sessions and a population of 20,000 or over;
(c) that at the end of that month the borough had a separate Commission of the Peace and court of Quarter Sessions, and the Lord Chancellor makes an order under subs. (5) of this section saving the grant to the borough of its commission and Quarter Sessions;

20. Cmd. 7463, para. 52.

(*d*)   that after the passing of this Act His Majesty grants a separate Commission of the Peace to the borough under s. 156 of the Municipal Corporations Act 1882, on a petition made by the Council at a time when the borough has a population of 65,000 or over."

There was to be no Commission of the Peace for any other area.

The Royal Commission was also critical of the law which made the mayor a justice during his mayoralty and for one year thereafter and also gave him the right to preside, but although they recommended that the chairman of county and district councils should cease to be justices *ex officio* they considered that special conditions applied to the mayor because of his peculiar relationship with the borough. They therefore recommended that he should remain a justice *ex officio* but should no longer continue to be a justice for a year after relinquishing office. They also recommended that if the borough had no separate commission the mayor should be a justice *ex officio* for the county. As to the mayor's right to preside, they thought that this should be restricted to formal and ceremonial occasions. The County Council's Association, in its evidence to the Royal Commission, had supported the view that all justices *ex officio*, including the chairmen of county councils, should cease to hold office on the grounds that "the qualities which enable the chairman of a local authority to perform his duties with success are not of necessity those requisite for the office of Justice of the Peace." The boroughs, on the other hand, while content to witness the disappearance of other justices *ex officio*, were strongly opposed to any interference with the rights of the mayors. The government finally accepted the Royal Commission's recommendations with amendments. Under s. 2 of the 1949 Justices of the Peace Act a mayor no longer remained a justice during the year next after he ceased to be mayor. Where a borough had no separate Commission of the Peace the mayor became a justice for the county but not for the borough, whereas when it did have its own commission the mayor became a justice for the borough and not for the county. The Act did not implement the Commission's recommendation that chairmen of county and district councils should cease to be justices, and these officers continued to be on the county commission for a further 19 years. During the passage of the 1949 Bill through the House of Lords an amendment was moved by Lord Merthyr, who had been a member of both the Roche Committee of the Royal Commission and had signed a minority report for the latter, strongly advocating the removal of all justices *ex officio*. His amendment sought to achieve this object but was heavily defeated and it appeared at that time that mayors at least would remain Justices of the Peace for all time in view of the strength of the boroughs' resistance to any proposal for abolition. As we shall see in a later chapter, however, Lord Gardiner, when Lord Chancellor, was also convinced that all justices *ex officio* were an encumbrance to the administration of justice and, in spite of opposition from many quarters, he succeeded in the Justices of the Peace Act 1968 in bringing to an end the long association of borough mayors with judicial office. Under that Act mayors and chairmen of county, urban and rural district councils, together with almost all others who were justices by virtue of their office ceased to be magistrates. The only exceptions were recorders, chairmen and deputy chairmen of Quarter Sessions, stipendiary magistrates, the Lord Mayor and Aldermen of the City of London and the Commissioner and Assistant Commissioner of Police for the Metropolis, most of whom will be referred to more fully elsewhere.

The right of the mayor to preside at the sittings of a court was also abolished by the 1949 Act (Schedule 7) which repealed s. 18(9) of the Local Government Act 1933.

The 1949 Act also contained certain innovative provisions regarding stipendiary magistrates which are described in a later chapter. So far as borough magistrates were concerned, s. 29 provided that the council of any borough having a separate Commission of the Peace could petition the King for a stipendiary who was to be a barrister or solicitor of not less than seven years' standing. On appointment he was to become a justice *ex officio* for the borough. Whereas previously the appointment was to be made by the Crown on the recommendation of the Home Secretary this responsibility was now transferred to the Lord Chancellor, and likewise a stipendiary could be removed only on the Lord Chancellor's recommendation. There was, however, some confusion because the Act seemed to contemplate that the petition had to be submitted to the Home Secretary in the first instance and it was not clear to what extent he could influence the decision to grant a stipendiary. In any event the position remained unsatisfactory in that it still rested with the local authority to decide whether or not it was to have a stipendiary magistrate, and as the borough council remained responsible for paying the salary the decision might well turn upon the cost rather than upon the need for the appointment. The only new provision relating to this point which was introduced by the Act was a requirement that the council, before presenting a petition, must consult the Magistrates' Courts Committee for the area (a new administrative body described in a later chapter). Borough councils regarded it as their inalienable right to have a stipendiary magistrate when they wished to do so; usually for reasons of prestige or because the council was on bad terms with the justices. In view of the strength of the borough lobby it is unlikely that this privilege would have been removed, at least in the foreseeable future, had it not been for the local government reforms of the 1970s which resulted in the abolition of boroughs as local government bodies and in all areas other than counties losing their Commissions of the Peace in 1973.[21] As explained later, the Lord Chancellor was then given power to appoint stipendiaries at his discretion where, and only where, he thought they were required.

Final assimilation of boroughs and counties
The final act in the saga of the borough justices had begun in 1971 when, following the recommendations of the Beeching Royal Commission, the Courts Act abolished all Assizes and Quarter Sessions and transferred their jurisdiction to the new Crown Court. Section 5 of the Act provided that Justices of the Peace should be empowered to sit in the Crown Court to hear appeals, committals for sentence and trials at first instance. Details of these provisions are given in a later chapter, but from the point of view of the borough justices the important point was that the provisions applied equally to them and to the county justices. Whereas the latter had always sat at Quarter Sessions, borough justices had been disqualified from doing so, even in their own borough sessions, since the Act of 1835. Now they were on precisely the same level as the county justices. The assimilation became virtually complete in 1973 with the merging of the borough and county commissions under the Administration of Justice Act of that year.

The assimilation of the borough and county magistrates is an illustration of the ability of the system to adapt to changing times, though once again this was the outcome of chance rather than of any conscious design. Borough magistrates of the old school might have survived indefinitely had the borough authorities not reached a state of corruption and incompetence which aroused the zeal of the reformers of the nineteenth century. Once the decision had been taken to abolish the old system of borough government the course might well have been adopted of replacing the former magistrates with stipendiaries. In 1835, however, those serving in both Houses of Parliament were well disposed towards the traditional county Justices of the Peace, and so it was decided to extend this to the boroughs. Even so, the boroughs were given a discretionary option to adopt a stipendiary system, and had they done so it would probably have flourished with little

21.   Boroughs ceased to exist as municipal authorities in consequence of the Local Government Act 1972 which implemented the recommendations of the Royal Commission on Local Government in England 1969, Cmnd. 4040. Section 1(1) of the Administration of Justices Act 1973 limited commission areas to counties, the four London commission areas and the City of London.

alteration to the present day. There was, however, a curious aversion on the part of borough councils to professional magistrates, probably because the councillors enjoyed the prospect of serving on the borough commission themselves. It was only when the Lord Chancellor omitted to appoint aspiring councillors and a feud developed between the council and the town bench that thoughts turned to undermining the authority of the lay justices by the appointment of a stipendiary. Apart from this, it was only on rare occasions when the borough authorities thought that the town's standing was enhanced by having a stipendiary that it was decided to submit a petition. In either case, when the current situation changed with the passage of time, enthusiasm for a stipendiary waned, and sometimes on the retirement of the incumbent no steps were taken to obtain a replacement.

An entirely new vista appeared with the establishment of borough commissions after 1835. The new borough justices were not tainted with the discreditable reputation of their predecessors, and moreover they were divested of almost all the administrative functions which had brought the previous system into disrepute. It was another 50 years before the same applied to the county justices. There were still defects in the borough system which attracted increasing criticism, such as the smallness of some of the catchment areas and the peculiar position of the mayor, but as we have seen they were duly corrected. As usual this was done in the teeth of opposition from those directly concerned, but successive governments took the opportunity presented by major reforming legislation to introduce the necessary remedies. It is true to say that some of these changes would not have been made had it not been for certain chance phenomena such as the enthusiasm for reform of Lord Chancellor Gardiner and the local government philosophy of the 1970s. By 1980 there was a uniform system of Justices of the Peace for the whole of England and Wales, and this was no doubt conducive to the continuing strength of the office. There was, however, one remarkable exception to the uniform pattern - the City of London.

The City of London
From the Conquest onwards London stood apart from the rest of English towns in the size of its population and in the volume of its trade. Nor did any of the other towns have the same influence on national affairs; an example of London's unique importance being the fact that its mayor was with the 25 barons at Runnymede who were elected to carry out the terms of Magna Carta in 1215. A charter of Henry I in 1132 had given the citizens the right to appoint their own sheriff and justiciar to keep the pleas of the Crown.[22] These privileges

22.   For the texts of the City charters see Birch, *Historical Charters of the City of London,* revised
        ed. 1887.

were lost under Stephen but were restored by Henry II and extended by a charter of John in 1199. The mayor and aldermen, however, exercised judicial functions long before these were confirmed by a charter. London had its own courts similar to the rest of the country but with some peculiarities of their own. The London folkmoot was the equivalent of a shire court at which every citizen was required to attend. It became merged in the thirteenth century with the court of husting, which was a court in which the citizens came to transact all their civil litigation. The husting court probably dated from the Danish occupation in the ninth century but it was not prominent until the twelfth. It was presided over by the sheriff until London was granted a mayor in 1193, and thereafter the mayor or an alderman presided at the husting, which was held weekly at the Guildhall. If not satisfied with a judgment given by the mayor and sheriffs a party might obtain a writ of error to have the record brought before a session of royal justices who were appointed *ad hoc*. In the course of time two types of husting sessions developed; the husting of common pleas where the mayor, aldermen and sheriffs "did the citizen's right in the King's name and on his writ in respect of their lands," and the mayor's court where the mayor enforced public order and commercial and trade regulations and where he punished offenders. From 1327 the mayor's court could inflict capital punishment. By the reign of Henry I London was divided into wards where wardmoots performed the functions of the hundred courts elsewhere. The aldermen presided at the wardmoots for their respective wards, which settled small disputes and punished minor offenders.

It seems fairly certain that the aldermen discharged the duties of Keepers of the Peace from the time of Hubert Walter's proclamation in 1195. By the latter part of the thirteenth century the mayor and aldermen were performing the judicial duties of the later keepers, and the first records of peace-keeping proceedings by the mayor appear in 1281. These show that at least by that date he was trying and punishing offenders. In 1298 the aldermen are formally described as justices and keepers - *Justiciario et Custodi*.

Apart from charters, the Crown issued many commissions to the mayor, aldermen and others which conferred various judicial and executive powers upon them, and these were supplemented by large numbers of writs. In 1327 the mayor and aldermen were given the right to be placed on all Commissions of Oyer and Terminer and Gaol Delivery for the city. The effect of all these instruments was to confer on the mayor and other officers extensive powers to arrest suspected offenders and to try and punish them, not only for breaches of statutes but also of the laws of the City. The result was that the mayor and aldermen in addition to being *Custodes Pacis* from the early part of the thirteenth century were also authorized to hear and determine and to impose sentences long before these judicial functions were extended to keepers in the rest of the country. These privileges were not conferred without a struggle on the part of the City which sometimes lost all the ground it had gained; as, for instance, in 1265 when, having supported the cause of Simon de Montfort and the barons, London was deprived by the King after the Battle of Evesham of all its privileges and liberties. London, however, was too rich and important to be ignored for long and it soon regained all that had been lost. It was jealous of its independence and the citizens were determined to secure their own courts with as wide a field as possible of remedies and the means of enforcing them, so that no one need look for justice beyond the City boundaries.

In 1444 Henry VI granted a charter to London under which the mayor, recorder and those aldermen who had served the office of mayor became Conservators of the Peace *ex officio*. This was confirmed by further charters of 1462, 1550 and 1608. The charter also formalized the issue of a Commission of the Peace[23] to the City, a step which was opposed unsuccessfully by some of the City authorities on the ground that it tended to place London on the same level as counties in the rest of the country instead of allowing it to remain in a special and unique position of its own. In fact, the charter clearly treated the City as a special case. It was worded in very wide terms. After declaring that the mayor, recorder and aldermen should be *Custodes Pacis* within the City and its liberties and suburbs, it went on to say that these officers, or four of them of whom the mayor and recorder must be two, should be justices to hear and determine all things which by ordinances and statutes ought to be discussed and determined by *Custodes Pacis,* and they were also to chastise and punish all offenders against the said ordinances and statutes; "providing always that the city always enjoy and use her ancient liberties, anything herein notwithstanding." To remove any doubt, the further charter of 1462 confirmed that the mayor and commonalty and citizens should forever "have and hold all and singular their liberties and authorities, acquittals and franchises as freely as in the time of our progenitors ..." It added that the mayor, recorder and aldermen, or any any four of them, of whom the mayor should be one, should be "justices to inquire, hear and determine all manner of felonies, trespasses, forestallings and regratings, extortions and other misdemeanours done or committed within the city or the liberties or suburbs thereof and also to hear and determine and execute all and

---

23.   This was a standing commission addressed to the Mayor, recorder and aldermen for the time being and it did not contain the names of individuals.

singular other things which shall pertain to our Justices of the Peace within our realm of England."

In 1550 a charter of Edward VI made the mayor, recorder and those aldermen who had served as mayor Justices of the Peace for Southwark. Yet another charter was granted by James I in 1608, which extended the area of these officers' authority by including a number of additional liberties in which they were to have exclusive jurisdiction.

The process of expansion, both territorially and as regards the number of persons who could hold the office of Justice of the Peace in the City, continued steadily for more than a century. In 1638 a charter provided that the three senior aldermen who had held office longest but had not yet served as mayor, should also be Justices of the Peace so long as they should remain aldermen. It also empowered the mayor to nominate to the Lord Chancellor one alderman to be inserted in the Commission of the Peace for Middlesex and one in the commission for Surrey. For some reason which is not entirely clear the Lord Mayor[24] did not exercise this power after 1678. A charter of 1692 extended the number of city justices by adding six more aldermen "who have borne the office of sheriff, next below the three senior aldermen who have not yet served the office of Mayor." It was not until 1741 that all aldermen were made Justices of the Peace for such time as they held their municipal office. This charter remains operative to the present day and, as we shall see later, the city justices now comprise the Lord Mayor, recorder, common serjeant, 25 aldermen and a number of justices appointed by a Commission of the Peace issued to the city in 1969.

In 1575 London was described as:

"an ornament of the realm by the beauty thereof, and a terror to other countries by reason of the great wealth and frequency [population]. It spreadeth the honour of our country far abroad by her navigations, and maketh our power feared even of barbarous princes."[25]

Proceedings before the mayor and aldermen were subject to Royal Prerogative writs, but they were not subjected to scrutiny to as great an extent as might have been expected. There was, however, some interference with the exercise of summary jurisdiction by the mayor

24.   The Mayor began to assume the title Lord Mayor soon after the beginning of the sixteenth century. No precise date can be ascribed to the change of name because it was made without any express authority, and even at the present day some official documents, such as those relating to Parliamentary elections, refer to the "Mayor." The term Lord Mayor was, however, in general use in the seventeenth century.
25.   *An Apology of the City,* in John Stow's Survey of London.

and aldermen in consequence of the City's close proximity to the royal palace at Westminster. All civil disputes between members of the King's household were heard by the steward and marshal of the household who also tried cases of trespass within the "verge of the palace" which extended to a distance of 12 miles from the King's person. It also heard prosecutions of those who resisted the compulsory purchase of supplies at reduced prices for the King's use known as purveyances, which was a matter of major concern for the City. The marshal's court, commonly known as the Marshalsea Court, sat within the precincts of the Marshalsea prison in Southwark and it sometimes exercised wider jurisdiction than was intended. There were numerous complaints by the City that it was usurping the jurisdiction of the City courts.

The recorder

Originally the recorder of London was a person having legal knowledge who was appointed by the mayor and aldermen to record their proceedings and to keep a note of their customs. The office can be traced to at least the thirteenth century, though the term recorder was not used formally until the beginning of the fourteenth. In 1298 Geoffrey de Norton was given an office which was virtually a recordership, but the title was first used for his successor, John de Wengrave, in 1304. Both of them were aldermen, and so too were all their successors until 1376. The recorderships were partly political appointments and several of the holders were returned to Parliament for the City.[26] The recorders were remunerated, though not as well as they would have been in practice for they were chosen from the most eminent lawyers of the day, and the post was probably looked upon as a stepping stone for further advance. Some of them later became Chief Justice of the King's Bench and of the Common Pleas, Chief Baron of the Exchequer, Master of the Rolls and even Lord Chancellor. They included Sir Edward Coke and Judge Jefferies.

As early as 1365 the recorder was named, together with the mayor, as Justice of Gaol Delivery. (The gaol which had to be delivered was that at Newgate which was the principal prison for the Queen's Bench). He also sat to deal with civil cases in the mayor's court. Although the mayor and aldermen were Judges in this court the work was carried out in practice by the recorder until his criminal work became so heavy that a separate Judge was appointed for the mayor's court. He has always played a prominent part in city ceremonials and he takes precedence over those aldermen who have not served as mayor.

26.   Of the 28 recorders who served between 1442 and 1628, 19 were Members for the City during their recorderships. Until 1885 the City was represented by four Members in Parliament.

Unlike all other recorders (except those for Liverpool and Manchester after 1956) the recorder of London was appointed from an early stage on a full-time basis and exercised the jurisdiction of a Commissioner of Assize. His appointment as recorder has always been made by the court of aldermen, but since the Local Government Act of 1888 he has not been able to exercise judicial functions until appointed to do so by the Crown. He is today the only Judge to be appointed by a municipal authority under its charters, but under the City of London (Courts) Act 1964 (s. 12(1)) he may not exercise any judicial function unless "appointed by Her Majesty to exercise such functions." The effect of this provision is that the City, in choosing its recorder, must first seek the approval of the Lord Chancellor.

The common serjeant
The origin of the office of common serjeant of the City is obscure owing to the number of posts which were described as serjeant in early times. It probably dates from before the fourteenth century but the first holder who can be positively identified was Geoffrey de Norton, who was appointed common serjeant and pleader by the mayor, aldermen and commonalty in 1319. The common pleader became a separate appointment from the sixteenth century when it was applied to those who had the right to plead in husting and the mayor's court. Geoffrey de Norton later became recorder but this was not the regular practice.

After the Restoration the common serjeant came to be included in the Commissions of Oyer and Terminer and Gaol Delivery. His judicial work did not, however, occupy the whole of his time, and he continued to practise as a lawyer. This met with the disapproval of the City as the work of its courts increased, and in 1803 the Court of Common Council resolved that it was inconsistent with the dignity of the City and with the proper administration of justice for him to practise in any inferior court of criminal jurisdiction. In 1834 the common serjeant was named in the Central Criminal Court Act as one of the Judges of the court and in 1856 it was decided that he should assist the recorder in the mayor's court. He became obliged to devote the whole of his time to judicial work. By the Mayor's and City of London Court Act, 1920 which amalgamated the mayor's court and the City of London court, he was named as a Judge of the combined court.

The common serjeant was appointed by the Court of Common Council until 1888 when the Local Government Act vested the appointment in the Crown. The City of London (Courts) Act 1964 (s. 12(2)) provided that: "The Common Serjeant shall be a person appointed by Her Majesty but no person shall be qualified to be appointed ... unless he is a barrister of not less than ten year's standing." Like the recorder, the common serjeant has always been paid by the City.

In 1969 the Royal Commission on Assizes and Quarter Sessions recommended in para. 241 of their Report: "Because of their special position as the senior members of a court of Assize, we recommend that the existing holders of these two Judgeships (recorder and common serjeant) shall remain more or less unaffected by our proposals." The Commission also recommended that the Lord Chancellor should review the position when the existing holders vacated them. Meanwhile they both became Circuit Judges by virtue of their office under sch. 2 to the Courts Act 1971. Their salaries, however, have continued to be fixed and paid by the City. The position was allowed to remain unaltered when the existing recorder and common serjeant respectively retired and were replaced.

Appointment of Justices of the Peace in the City
Until 1969 the City of London was unique in that, from 1835, although other boroughs had Justices of the Peace appointed by commissions in addition to those who held office *ex officio,* London had no Commission of the Peace and its justices were only the Lord Mayor, recorder, common serjeant and the 25 aldermen. This meant that whereas the Crown could dismiss most of the justices in all other parts of the country by removing them from the commission, it had no such power in respect of the City. It is claimed that this never had a detrimental effect on the administration of justice because aldermen, when nominated by a ward, were always carefully scrutinized by the court of aldermen before their election was confirmed, and if they proved to be undesirable after assuming office they were invariably persuaded to resign by their colleagues. There is certainly no recorded instance of an alderman continuing to administer justice when generally regarded as being unacceptable. An alderman could also be removed from office under the London Reform Act 1849 if he became bankrupt or insolvent, was absent from his duties for more than six months otherwise than through ill health or other reasonable cause or was found guilty of fraud or any other crime.

The City had been made exempt from the more drastic measures applied by the Municipal Corporations Act 1835 because, with its ward representation, it was thought to be already a more democratic institution than other cities and boroughs. Moreover, the City was again singled out for special treatment when the Indictable Offences Act 1848 and the Summary Jurisdiction Acts 1848 and 1849 empowered the Lord Mayor or any aldermen sitting at the city justice rooms to do any act that elsewhere required two or more justices. The effect of these Acts was therefore that, unless there was an express enactment to the contrary, the Lord Mayor or one of the aldermen alone could constitute a court of summary jurisdiction and exercise the powers of Petty Sessions in cases which would otherwise require at least two justices. Even the Royal Commission of 1946-8 did not include in its far reaching Report any recommendation that any change should be made in the unique position of the Lord Mayor and aldermen. They commented, in para. 283 "The traditions and practice of the City have resulted in a high standard of administration of criminal justice and we do not recommend any change for the adult court."

The Royal Commission did propose, however, that the aldermen should no longer sit alone to deal with juvenile cases, as they had been able to do under the Children and Young Persons Act 1933 which had established special juvenile courts composed of three justices throughout the rest of the country. The second schedule to the Act provided that "Juvenile courts for the City of London shall be constituted in such manner as the Court of the Lord Mayor and Aldermen of the City may from time to time determine," and s. 48(6) provided that "such a juvenile court shall have all the powers of a petty sessional court notwithstanding that the juvenile court is constituted only of the Lord Mayor as a single alderman." The Royal Commission stated, in para. 284 of their Report: "We think that an ordinary juvenile court is a more satisfactory body than a single alderman, and we recommend that in future such cases should be tried by a county of London juvenile court." A further reason for making the change, which was not mentioned in the Report, was that juvenile courts included both men and women justices, whereas there were no women aldermen until 1975. The Commission's recommendation was implemented by the Justices of the Peace Act 1949 which declared (s. 11(5)): "The Justices of the Peace for the City of London shall not exercise any jurisdiction which is required to be exercised by a juvenile court," and it went on to apply the same provision to matrimonial proceedings which since 1878 had been dealt with in special courts in the rest of the country but by aldermen sitting alone in the City. The 1949 Act therefore provided, in the same subsection, that metropolitan stipendiary magistrates and other Justices of the Peace for the county of London should exercise jurisdiction within the City for these purposes "as if the City were included in the county of London."

By the end of 1949 it was generally supposed that the City had adapted sufficiently to the reforming climate of the time and that no further changes would occur, or indeed be justified, in the foreseeable future. The Royal Commission had confirmed that the machinery operating in the City was satisfactory and required no amendment, apart from modifications to juvenile and matrimonial proceedings, and there were no complaints from the public about the way in which justice was dispensed in the City.

An unexpected turn of events occurred in 1968 which threatened to alter the whole complexion of the City magistracy. This arose from the determination of the Lord Chancellor, Lord Gardiner, to introduce further reforms in the magisterial system in general which will be recounted in another chapter. They included the total abolition of all Justices of the Peace *ex officio* which would annihilate the City's individuality.27

A Bill was introduced in Parliament which sought to abolish all local government justices *ex officio* without exception and provided that in future no one might become a justice unless appointed by name (and not by office) by a Commission of the Peace for the area. The Bill provoked a stiff reaction from the City which proceeded to an impressive mustering of its resources. The Report of the Royal Commission was cited in the City's defence, and so too was the support for the *status quo* which had been voiced by the Lord Chief Justice, the Magistrates' Association and the London solicitors. It was also pointed out that the City courts had given general satisfaction - there being few appeals from their decisions and most of these were unsuccessful - and that the Lord Mayor and aldermen were exceptionally well qualified to adminster justice, not only because of the method of their selection but because they underwent a thorough course of training. These arguments did not impress the government, still less the House of Commons many of whose Members represented boroughs which were jealous of the City's privileges. In particular, the court of aldermen was criticized for being undemocratic and not representative of all cases of society (which was the criterion for the rest of the country) and that it did not include any women. This attack had the effect of driving the City to still greater defensive effort. They gathered their supporters in preparation for a spirited counter-attack in the Lords, and when the Bill reached the upper House it was met by the massed forces of the Guildhall which appeared to be overwhelming. To avoid defeat the government were obliged to retreat and to accept a compromise amendment moved by a former Chancellor, Lord Dilhorne. The effect of this was that the Lord Mayor and aldermen remained justices *virtute officii* but they were joined on the bench by a number of justices appointed by name in the normal way. To achieve this a Commission of the Peace was issued to the City for the first time. Thereafter a number of Justices of the Peace were appointed for the City by the Lord Chancellor in the usual way on the advice of a separate City advisory committee, and this has remained

27.   See Skyrme, *The Changing Image of the Magistracy,* 2nd. ed., p. 39.

the position. From then onwards the City's summary courts were composed of two or more justices, as elsewhere. The Lord Mayor and aldermen could no longer sit alone, but when present the Lord Mayor retained the right to preside. He was therefore the only mayor to enjoy this privilege after the Justices of the Peace Act of 1968.

These amendments to the Bill were accepted reluctantly in the Commons, and the City became the only local authority in the country to have justices *ex officio* and the only one where the mayor had the right to preside. It was a remarkable illustration of the City's continuing ability to preserve its traditional institutions and it was all the more notable coming at a time when the City and its traditions were out of favour with a large proportion of the House of Commons and of the population as a whole and when it could expect no support from the Labour government of the day. Its success was due to its ability to enlist powerful support and particularly to gain the backing of a large element in the Lords, especially among the hereditary peers.

The City's capability of survival was to be demonstrated once more in 1973. A year earlier the Local Government Act had replaced all the old administrative counties and municipal boroughs with metropolitan and non-metropolitan counties divided into districts. With the demise of all the cities and boroughs their separate Commissions of the Peace disappeared with them. The lacunae were filled by the Administration of Justice Act 1973 which provided that in future there should be commissions only for the administrative county areas, with one exception - the City of London. From then onwards there was a commission for each county, for each of the five areas of Greater London and for the City, and for no others.

Quarter Sessions

Quarter Sessions for the City were held under the charters of 1462, 1608 and 1638 and were composed of the mayor, recorder and aldermen. They had power to try felonies, trespasses and other misdemeanours committed within the City and its liberties, and also to transact all business usually dealt with at Quarter Sessions. In order to form a quorum the mayor, recorder or one of the aldermen who had passed the chair had to be present. The Central Criminal Court, which was established by the Central Criminal Court Act in 1834, had concurrent jurisdiction with the City Quarter Sessions which by then was dealing only with criminal work, and for convenience most indictable cases arising in the City were thereafter taken by the new court sitting at the Old Bailey.[28]

---

28.   Under the 1834 Act (s. 17) the City Quarter Sessions were restricted from trying most offences, but this provision was repealed by a later Act of 1851 (14 & 15 Vict., c. 55, s. 13).

When all courts of Quarter Sessions were abolished by the Courts Act 1971, the City sessions and the Central Criminal Court were merged in the new Crown Court. By that time the City had its own Commission of the Peace and a number of justices appointed under it, as we shall see later. Appeals from the City's courts of summary jurisdiction were heard at the Crown Court, sitting at the Old Bailey, and on these occasions the court consisted of the recorder, common serjeant or another circuit Judge sitting with two of the City justices, whereas before that appeals had been heard by the recorder or one of the other Judges sitting alone.

Administrative functions

As elsewhere in England and Wales the City Quarter Sessions were responsible until 1835 for much of the City's administration, and in some spheres they led the way in making innovations.

The Poor Law. The City were clearly in the lead in their arrangement for poor relief. We shall have seen above how Justices of the Peace in all the counties were placed in charge of schemes for the relief of the poor and the punishment of vagabonds and idle labourers. We have already noted that poor relief was provided in boroughs from early times, particularly through charitable organizations like the merchant guilds. The first steps of this kind which were taken in London occurred so early in the City's history that no clear record survives, but London was the first to adopt a system which was defined by statute.

Local legislation for dealing with the poor began in London with a Commonwealth ordinance of 1647 which established the "Corporation of the Poor of the City of London." This was confirmed by an Act of 1662.[29] It was copied by other authorities, though not to as great an extent as the Corporation established by Bristol in 1696. The object of the Corporation was to give relief to the poor, to provide work for the able-bodied and to punish vagrants and other disorderly persons in the City. It established a workhouse in which the able poor were put to work and orphan children were maintained and taught a trade. It also supplied materials to enable people to work in their own homes. Sometimes it found work for the poor further afield as by sending them to serve in fishing boats. The Corporation was under the supervision of the mayor, aldermen and 52 other citizens chosen by the Common Council, and it was administered by a president and governors. It continued in existence throughout the eighteenth century, by which time some of the City parishes had also established similar schemes with their own workhouses under local Acts. As we shall see,

29.   13 & 14 Charles II, c. 12; made perpetual by 12 Anne, st. 1, c. 18.

the functions of Justices of the Peace in respect of the Poor Law were removed when a national system was introduced in 1834. This applied equally to the City of London.

Prisons. London had its own prisons from the earliest times, but as in other boroughs these were no purpose-built structures. It was usual in walled cities to house prisoners in the gatehouses, and London used Ludgate, Cripplegate and Newgate for this purpose. In none of these were conditions any better than in the prisons throughout the rest of the country, and in the case of Newgate, to which the worst criminals were sent, they were probably worse than the average. Newgate was notorious for its epidemics of gaol fever which brought death not only to the prisoners but to the Judges, lawyers and others attending the courts. In the 1750s two of the mayors died of the fever after attending the sessions. The old gatehouses were totally inadequate to cope with the increasing number of prisoners and they had to be extended or rebuilt. Newgate in particular was rebuilt on several occasions; on one of these, in about 1425, part of the cost was borne by a bequest from the famous mayor, Richard Whittington.

The Marshalsea prison, which became notorious for its scandalous conditions, was also situated within the purlieu of the City in Southwark. It was, however, principally a gaol for the Court of King's Bench and was under the control of its marshal. Responsibility for prisons was transferred to the prison commissioners who were appointed under the Prisons Act 1877, but the Justices of the Peace retained an inspectorate role and in this context six City aldermen are appointed annually together with justices of neighbouring counties to serve on the visiting committees of Brixton and Holloway prisons.

Other administrative duties. The City led the way in establishing improvement commissions which were first appointed under an Act of 1662.[30] They were charged with cleansing and lighting streets, the repair of roads and sewers and the abatement of nuisances. It would be superfluous to describe the other administrative functions of the City justices as they were largely the same as those performed in other county areas, though they were usually more intensive. They were separated from the judicial work of the Lord Mayor and aldermen by the local government legislation of the nineteenth century, except for licensing. The City was deemed to be a county borough for licensing purposes under the Licensing (Consolidation) Act 1910 (s. 2(4)).

Apart from the duties normally performed by Justices of the Peace the mayor, and sometimes the aldermen, were occasionally given peculiar extraneous functions. We have seen, for instance, that in the

---

30.   13 & 14 Charles II, c. 2; followed by 22 Charles II, c. 12; 2 William & Mary, sess., 2, c. 8; 8 & 9 William III, c. 17.

seventeenth century the Lord Mayor was required to conduct an inquiry into the merits of different brands of soap for the benefit of the government's soap monopoly. In 1555 an Act required the mayor and aldermen to establish a system for licensing boatmen on the Thames.31

Assizes and the Central Criminal Court
The Lord Mayor and aldermen acted under Commissions of Oyer and Terminer and Gaol Delivery long after Justices of the Peace ceased to do so in other parts of the country and they continued to be named in these commissions until the latter part of the twentieth century. When exercising these powers they usually sat with one of the Royal Judges. Sometimes there was a disagreement on sentence. A notorious instance of this occurred in the trial of Elizabeth Canning in 1753. This case is also of interest because of the intervention by the Lord Mayor in earlier proceedings at the Old Bailey which had a crucial effect on the issue. Two women who ran a brothel had been convicted of abducting Miss Canning and stealing her clothes, for which one was sentenced to death and the other to be burned on the hand and imprisoned for six months. The Lord Mayor, Sir Crisp Gascoigne, who was present at the trial, was disquieted by the verdict and carried out a private investigation involving the interrogation of witnesses. This led to a subsequent inquiry by the law officers, and ultimately to a pardon for the two accused followed by the arrest and trial of Miss Canning. She was convicted and sentenced to seven years' transportation to New England. Some of the aldermen who sat with the Judge sought to modify the punishment and the sentence proposed by the Judge, who was Chief Justice Wilkes of the Queen's Bench, was carried only by a majority.

As already mentioned the Central Criminal Court (commonly called the Old Bailey) which became the Assize Court for the London area, was established in 1834. The Judges sat by virtue of a commission which was also addressed to the Lord Mayor and aldermen, but in practice trials were conducted by Judges of the Queen's Bench, the recorder, common serjeant or one of the additional Judges. All of these, except the Queen's Bench Judges, were appointed and paid by the City. It was a requirement of the charter of 1462 that the mayor should always be present in the City court, and this was extended to the Lord Mayor or recorder in 1638 and to the Lord Mayor, recorder or senior alderman in 1741. After 1834 the Lord Mayor or one of the aldermen attended each day and presided in court, but the Judge sitting at his right hand conducted the proceedings. The court also acted as Quarter Sessions for the City.

31.   2 & 3 Philip & Mary, c. 16.

Under the 1834 Act the court's jurisdiction extended to parts of Essex, Kent and Surrey as well as London and Middlesex, and by an Act of 1862 the King's Bench Division was given power to order the trial of any person subject to military or naval law and accused of murder or manslaughter to be transferred to the court. Under the Supreme Court of Judicature Act 1873 the Old Bailey became a branch of the High Court of Justice, but the Judges remained the same. The court's jurisdiction was further enlarged by the Criminal Justice Act 1925 under which any cases might be sent there for trial from outside its normal district. At the time of the Royal Commission on Assizes and Quarter Sessions of 1966-9 there were 14 or 15 courts sitting at the Old Bailey every day and the professional Judges included 10 additional Judges and a varying number of part-time commissioners drawn from the Bar. Apart from the High Court Judges and the recorder and common serjeant they were replaced by Circuit Judges and the new types of part-time Judge under the Courts Act 1971, though the existing additional Judges were allowed to remain in office until they retired. The Old Bailey had then become part of the Crown Court, which it still remains.

Justice rooms

From early times courts were held at the Guildhall, and the City Justices of the Peace still exercise summary jurisdiction in a court house adjoining the old building. After the Mansion House was built as the Lord Mayor's official residence a similar court was held there from about 1750. It continued to be used until 1988 and was the only remaining court to be held in a private house. Both justice rooms had concurrent jurisdiction over the whole of the City, but for convenience the area was separated, divided into two divisions by a line running along Gresham Street and continuing east and west to the City boundary. All cases arising north of this line were taken at the Guildhall and those to the south by the Mansion House, though there were a few exceptions. Customs cases for instance were always taken at the Mansion House as the Customs House was in the southern part of the City.

Cases tried summarily by the City justices

Most of the cases coming before the City justices have long been similar to those in other cities but an exception can be seen in the large number of important cases involving large sums of money which come before the City courts in consequence of London's position as the financial and commercial centre of the country. Examples are share-pushing, customs offences and tax evasion. These cases often involve large monetary penalties which are not subject to the normal limits imposed on fines in magistrates' courts. In the case of *DPP* v. *Stanley and Others,* which was heard by three City justices sitting at Guildhall in 1973, the court imposed fines of £300,000 (£200,000 on one charge and £100,000 on a second) on two companies whom they convicted of offences under the Exchange Control Regulations, the financial penalty in such cases being limited only by the sums involved in the illegal transaction. At that time the maximum fine allowed by statute for most offences in magistrates' courts was only £400. Proceedings in the *Stanley* case could have been brought in the Crown Court but it was thought that the expertise of the City magistrates made them the better tribunal. Many of them were, and still are, drawn from the leading financial experts in the country.

Remaining differences between borough and county benches

The past six centuries have seen first, a period of deviation between the justices in the boroughs and those in the counties followed by a close assimilation of the two systems which, save in the case of London, was completed in 1973. This did not mean, however, that the composition of the benches became identical. In the twentieth century there remained wide differences in the social and political background of the justices themselves. Benches in rural areas continued to be dominated by landowners who supported the Conservative party. This was due largely to a shortage of suitable candidates from other sections of the community who were able and willing to serve. In urban districts, on the other hand, there was a wider spread. The majority of the justices were drawn from trade and industry at different levels, from management to factory worker, and a far greater proportion supported the Labour and other parties than did their colleagues in the countryside. In consequence their attitudes also differed towards their duties. This was apparent in their approach to social problems, but there was also marked disparity in the level of sentences imposed for a range of offences, which was not due to the justices' political philosophy but to the diverse conditions to be found in rural and urban areas. As would be expected, street offences and crimes of violence were usually dealt with more severely in the cities; on the other hand there was a curious relic of the past in the policy applied to poachers. Few of the offenders against the poaching laws in the latter part of the twentieth century were any longer the local labourers of former generations, who usually stole to feed their families, but were members of organized gangs from other areas who made a substantial income out of their activities. When caught, those appearing before the urban benches were treated leniently as they had been in the past, whereas those tried by the country justices were likely to be punished severely and their equipment was confiscated, including their lurcher dogs which, as the local justices well knew, were used for the brutal hunting of deer.

From the middle of the century groups from the two sections of the magistrates were brought together in sentencing conferences and other meetings at which differences of outlook could be discussed with a view to achieving reasonable uniformity, yet the divergence remains. This must be attributed not only to the different circumstances which pertain in the countryside and the built-up areas but also to the different types of individual who still occupy the office of Justice of the Peace in the two kinds of locality. It does not follow that the justice administered in one area is inferior to that in another, but rather that it is adapted to local requirements. As to the quality of the magistrates themselves, it could be said with some truth that in the 1980s benches throughout the country have generally conformed to the Lord Chancellor's requirement that they should represent a microcosm of the local community.

INDEX

(Page numbers in italics refer to footnotes)

Abbey of Fecamp 265
abbots 71, 117
Abergavenny, Lord (Lord Lieutenant of
    Kent) *169*
absence or attendance of justices 46, 112,
    118, 209-10, 212, 230, 267
    during Civil War 221
    at Quarter Sessions 79, 171, 209-10
affray 84, 129
agriculture 141-2, 196, 198-200, 244
aldermen 257, 277
    boroughs 266, 267, 269, 271-2, 274-5
    Bristol 259-60
    Chester 76
    Gloucester 261-4
    London 286, 289-300
    Tewkesbury 265
alehouses 126, 132, 140, 217, 241, 263,
    269
    disorderly 170
    games 143-4
    licensing 83, 142-3, 179, 242, 249-50,
    274
    reduction in numbers 246, 250
Allen, Sir Carlton 33
Allen, Philip (later Lord Allendale) *279*
Ambrose, William (justice in Lancaster) 91
amerciaments 29, 37, 76, 132, 157, 175,
    260
    Duchy of Lancaster 89, 91
    source of remuneration 46, 123
    see also fines
Anderson, Sir Edmund (Chief Justice of
    Common Pleas) 185
Anglicans 96-7, 237, *238*
Anglo-Saxon times 25, 33
apparel 50, 59-60, 139, 197
appeal 137-8, 276, 277, 287
    Court 278

London 296, 298
    Quarter Sessions 192, 234
appointment of justices 5, 19-21, 47, 74-5,
    121
    Duchy of Lancaster 96, 98, 101-6
    Elizabethan 180-1, 183, 201
    London 294-7
    quality 69-70, 254
    towns 256, 258, 259, 281
apprenticeships 57-8, 144, 147, 175, 197-8,
    262
    beggars 150
    children 191, 192, 225, 248, 271
    disputes with masters 131, 173, 198
approvements 62
archbishops on commissions 71, 117
archdeacon's court 192
archery 58, 143, 162
Armada (1588) 203
armies, private 18, 158-9
arms 8, 11-12, 17, 24, 46, 59, 143
    see also weaponry
arrest 1-2, 64, 90, 129-31, 147
    by constables 41, 157
    by justices 32, 37, 56-8, 63, 164, 172
    by keepers 9, 13, 15-16
    by sheriffs 2, 39, 40, 62, 257
arrow-smiths 52
arson 63
assault 26, 63, 84, 129, 179, 224
    Quarter Sessions 170, 241
assistant recorders 104, 277
Assizes and Assize Judges 12, 129, 176,
    177
    appointment of justices 180
    Bloody 237
    Books of Orders 215-16
    Bristol 259
    church law 153
    Civil War 221
    Clarendon (1164) 2, *27*

commission 21-2, 21, 117
Commission of Peace 69, 117, 186
Crown Court 280, 287
disruption 182
Duchy of Lancaster 90, 91-4
Durham 84-6
extortion 39
Eyre 29
gaming laws 162
Great Sessions 78
highways 60-1
and justices 34, 64, 110, 113, 114, 138, 165, 212, 217-18
keepers 17
labour laws 24
London 278, 293, 294, 300-1
Lord Chancellor 210
murder 35, 84-5, 170
Northampton (1176) 27
oaths 40
Quarter Sessions 134
Quorum 39
recusants 112
religion 200-2
remuneration 46-7
serious cases 22, 39, 62, 172, 239
Southampton 269
Star Chamber 111
treason 170
Atlee, Clement (Chancellor of Duchy of Lancaster) 94
Attorney-General 82, 118, 276
Australia 240, 255
Aylesford, Lord 97

Bacon, Sir Nathaniel (of Norfolk) 179
Bacon, Sir Nicholas (Lord Keeper 1571) 183
bail 37, 55, 62, 132-3, 137, 233
bailiffs 8, 11, 26, 53, 76, 178, 225, 256
attacked and intimidated 63, 65
boroughs 50, 56
discretionary sessions 134
extortion 114
gaols 157
labour laws 55-8
Quarter Sessions 40, 136, 261, 265
wages 245

weights and measures 145
Baneret (knight) *46*
Bar 100, 165, 178, 278, 280-1, 301
Barnes, John (Clerk of the Peace, Durham) 85
Baronets *46*, 78, *223*, 230, 231
barons 6, 8, 9, 13, 19, 288, 290
barratry 170
Barrington, Bishop Shute (of Durham) 83
barristers 268, 277-8, 280, 286, 293-4
writing textbooks 166, 167
basket justices 182
Bath 190
Bathurst, Lord (Chancellor of Duchy of Lancaster) 98
Bayley, Thomas Butterworth 100
beadles 268
Bedfordshire 43, 66, 184, 204, 214, 232-3
Beeching Royal Commission 287
beggars 57, 113, 147, 150, 246
Poor Law 188, 189-90, 191
Bek, Antony (Bishop of Durham) 80
Benevolence 214
Bexley, Lord (Chancellor of Duchy of Lancaster) 98
binding over 33, 63, 68, 133, 145, 205, 251
church laws 153, 154
single justice 129, 241
bishops 153, 179, 180, 188, 200-1, 226, 266
Chester 78
on Commissions of Peace 71, 117, 230
Durham 80-5, 88, 117, 195-6
as justices 177
marriage of clergy 202
Black Death 22-4, 56
see also plague
Black Prince 76, 87
Blackstone, Sir William 33, 111
Bletsoe, Lord St John of 214
Blount, Sir Walter (later Lord Mountjoy, Lord Treasurer 1464-66) 69
Bohun, Edmund *The Justice of the Peace, his Calling and Qualification* 166, 230
Boke of Justyces of Peas (Anon) (1506) 165
Bolingbroke, Henry *see* Henry IV
bonds 112, 113

Book of Common Prayer 153, 200, 232, 233
Books of Orders (1631) 215-16, 217, 218
Booth, Henry (later Earl of Warrington) 78
boroughs 49, 57, 70, 107, 256-303
  benches 266-7
  bridges 154
  Cheshire 79
  difference from shires *4*, 259-66, 302
  Durham 84, 86
  ex officio justices 50
  gaming laws 144
  letters from Privy Council 111
  London 288-302
  palatinates 75
  Parliament 108
  poor relief 188, 298
  prison 299
  Quarter Sessions 170, 276-81
  reform 283-7
  stipendiary magistrates 100-1, 102, 104
Boundary Commission (1972) 105
bows and arrows 58
Bradshaw, John (Chancellor of Duchy of Lancaster 1649) 95
branding 23, 57, 149, 153, 174, 176, 192
Brandon, Lord (later Earl of Macclesfield, Lord Lieutenant of Lancashire) 97
brawling 26, 41
Brewster Sessions 83
bribery 171, 182
Bridewell 193
bridges 60-1, 154-7, 194-6, 270
  inspected 126, 131, 132
  repair 93, 136, 242, 254
Bridgewater 169
Bristol 259-60, 265, 270, 271, 298
Bristowe 161
Brixton prison 299
Brockholes, Robert (justice in Duchy of Lancaster) 91
Brown, John 160
Buckhurst, Lord (Lord Lieutenant) 159
Buckingham, Duke of 236
Buckinghamshire 43, 161, 269
Buckstone 190
building restrictions 168, 199-200
Bunyan, John (poet) 232-3

burgesses 16, 43, 60, 207, 261, 265
  boroughs 266, 267, 274
  Henry VII 107, 108
  Parliament 9, 12-13, 20
  towns 256-9
Burghley, Lord 163, *169*, 176, 180, 182, 186, 198
burglary 63, 242
Burgoine, John of (justice in Bedfordshire) 184
Burn, Rev. Richard *The Justice of the Peace and the Parish Officer* (1755) 167
burning
  of ears 189
  of hands 300
  at stake 174
bye-laws 275
Byng, Rev. Andrew (Archdeacon of Norwich) 222

Cabal 236
Cade, Jack (rebellion 1450) 41, 44, *67*
Caernarfonshire 224
Cambridge 178
  university 118, 266
Cambridgeshire 43, 198-9, 252
Canning, Elizabeth (tried 1753) 300
Canterbury, Archbishop of 117
capital punishment 172, 173-4, 176, 194, 239, 289
  see also death penalty
Capitalis Constabularius see constables
Caribbean 240
Carlisle, Chancellor (Rev. R. Burn) 167
Carmarthen 199
carpenters 23, 55
Cary, John (of Bristol) 260
Catholics *see* Roman Catholicism
Cavaliers 229, 232, 237
Cavendish, John de (Chief Justice of King's Bench) 43
Cecil, William (later Lord Burghley)
  see Burghley, Lord
Central Criminal Court 280, 297-8, 300-1
Chancellor 39, 43, 65, 114, 212
  appointment of justices 47, 69
  see also Lord Chancellor

Chancellor of Duchy of Lancaster 87-8, 91-2, 94-8, 100-6
Chancellor of the Exchequer (Edward Hyde) 232
Chancery 65, 89, 91, 104, 141, 197
   Durham 85-7
   Master (Lambard) 166
Charles I (r.1625-1649) 208-12, 214-18, 222, 223, 241, 246
Charles II (r.1660-1685) 95, *96*, 228-9, 236, 244, 258, 261
   religion 232, 235
charters 274, 276, 278
   Bristol 259-60
   corporations 229
   Gloucester 259-62
   London 288-91, 293, 297, 300
   Tewkesbury 265
   towns 256-61, 266-7
Chatham 118
Chaucer, Geoffrey (justice for Kent) 72
Cheltenham 170, 265
Cheshire 77, 78, 231
Chester 69, 74, 75-80, 82, 86, 87
Chief Justices 78, 110
children 150, 191, 241, 247
Chipping Sodbury 170
Cholmondeley, Earl of *78*
Christchurch 226
church 82, 126, 152-4, 166, 177, 233-4, 237
   appointment of justices 47
   class distinction 59
   damaged 66, 130
   duties of justices 71, 225
   ecclesiastical courts 26, 224
   ex officio justices 117
   marriages 226-7
   obligatory attendance 143, 153, 173, 182, 200-2, 224
   poor relief 147, 187
   taxes 243
   towns 256, 257
   violence during services 45
Church of England 232, 233, 235, 237
Churchill, Sir Winston 94, *107*
churchwardens 130, 154, 171, 212, 217, 225, 235

collecting rates 190, 192, 254
   fines 195, 200, 233, 234
   poor relief 150, 191, 247, 271
Cinque Ports 7
Circuit Judges 79, 87, 105, 280, 294, 298, 301
Cirencester 170
City Corporation 280
civil suits *16*, 25, 77, 84, 132, 134, 262
   husting court 289, 292
   single justices 131
Civil War 5, 8-9, 67, 121, 206
   Duchy of Lancaster 93, 95
   Quarter Sessions 35, 85
   Stuarts 219-22, 223-4, 228-9, 231, 238, 243-4, 246, 251, 262, 265
Clarence, Duke of 66
Clarendon Assize 2, 27
Clarendon Code 232
Clarendon, Earl of 232
   History of the Rebellion 223
class 23, 30, 72, 181-2
   apparel 59-60, 197
   commissions 117-18, 229
   distinction 53, 59-60, 175-6
   gentry 49, 217, 228
   hunting 144-5
   juries 136
   justices 70, 177-8, 181, 228
   lower 34, 67, 70, 144-5
   middle 4-5, 11, 108-9, 118, 206, 256, 274
   upper 65, 128, 144-5, 164, 230
clergy 34, 46, 109, 150, 153, 222, 232
   assaulted 66
   clothing laws 60
   on commissions 71, 117, 209, 230
   Durham 82, 83
   Egyptians 152
   Jesuits 112
   as justices 98, 100, 167, 177, 266
   marriage 202
   universities 178
Clerks of the Peace 41-2, 119-20, 122-4, 243, 265, 268, 275
   attendance lists 210, 212
   Bunyan, John 232-3
   Chester 76

collector of rates 254
Custos Rotulorum 71
discretionary sessions 134
Duchy of Lancaster 91, 92, 96
Durham 85
Gloucester 262, 264
Quarter Sessions 137
religious offences 202
remuneration 46-7
textbooks 165, 166-7
vagrants 149, 189
clothing and cloth trade 50-1, 63, 139, 196, 197, 244, 248-9
laws 59-60
Cobb, John (Bedfordshire) 233
Cobham, Lord (Lord Lieutenant) 171
coins and coinage 13, 54, 223, 267
Coke, Sir Edward 166, 206, 256, 292
Colchester 157
colonies 227, 239-40, 255
comes palatinus 74
Commissioners of Array (Durham) 81
Commissioners of Assize 29, 101, 165
commissions of the bishop (Durham) 80-2, 83
Commissions of the Peace 38-40, 43, 68-72, 165, 205, 276
ability 179, 183, 184
appointment of justices 180, 182, 281-2, 294
Assize Judges 21-2
boroughs 267-8, 270-3, 275-6, 283-8, 297
Civil War 222-4, 228
class 59, 108, 177, 182, 208-9
clerical justices 167
constables 125
Duchy of Lancaster 88-90, 95-9, 102, 104-5
Durham 84, 86
Edward I 12
Edward II 13
Elizabeth I 185-6, 200-1
Eyre 30
juries 65
keepers 15-18, 20-1, 33-4
Kent 166
knights 4

labour laws 24
lawyer justices 176
London 289, 290-1, 294, 296-8, 300
Major Generals 227
merchants 196
national defence 203
palatinates 74, 76-9
prestige 182, 205, 208
Privy Council 110
Quarter Sessions 34-5
reduction in size 210
religion 202, 235-8
removal of justices 114, 115, 171, 181, 184
Restoration 229-31
Scotland 255
sheriffs 3-4
in towns 257, 260, 264-6
Tudor times 116-20, 122, 124
Wars of the Roses 66-7
William I 28
common-law courts 65, 110
common pleader 293
Common Pleas 39, 41, 64, 91, 101, 165
Chief Justice 185, 292
common serjeant 280, 291, 293-4, 298, 300, 301
Commons, House of 41, 43, 82, 94, 108, 213, 219
justices 47-9, 62, 69, 114-15, 211
London 296, 297
Members 70, 211, 236
ship money 216-17
Commonwealth 72, 163, 222-4, 229, 238, 298
roads and highways 157, 251
Commonwealth Judicial Journal 168
Commonwealth Magistrates' Association 168
communal courts 62, 168
commune, la 9, 15, 16, 18, *19*, 20, 28
compensation 220, 224-5
Congreve, William (playwright) 230
conscience, court of 263, 264
conscription 174
Conservative party 302
conservators 3, 11, 31, 33, 61, 165, 173
appointment 7-8, 19

Chester 76
Durham 81
London 290
conspiracy 175
constables 130, 154, 156-7, 166, 212, 225, 264
  attacked 63
  church damage 130
  Civil War 222-4
  Clerk of the Peace 123
  Cornwall 161
  discretionary sessions 134
  exemption 242
  gaol 157-8, 194
  head or high (*Capitalis Constabularius*) 7-8, 93, 124-6, 179, 190, 241, 243, 254
  juries 37
  labour laws 57, 58
  petty 80, 124-6, 179, 195, 243, 254
  police role 164, 268
  Quarter Sessions 40, 41, 136, 137, 169
  Rockingham Castle 45
  Scotland 218
  support for justices 128, 131
  under (*Custodes Pacis*) 3, 5, 7-10, 12, 20, 76, 81, 289, 290
  vagrants 147-9, 189, 192, 217
  wages 245
contempt 113, 152
conventicles 166, 233-4
cordwainers 52, 140
corn *39*, 55, 140, 193, 226, 246
  shortage 111, 112-13, 139, 142, 196, 198-9, 204
Cornwall 118, 121, 161
coroners 62, 76, 81, 90, 134
  Gloucester 260, 261, 264
  Quarter Sessions 136, 137
  shire courts 19, 25
corporal punishment 173-6, 194
Corporation of the Poor
  Bristol 298
  London 271, 298
corporations 271-4
corruption 185, 266, 268, 287
  constables 254
  justices 100, 107, 176

King's Bench 43
  sheriffs 20, 107
  trade and industry 49-50
  cotton industry 98-9
Council 18, 176, 203, 213-15, 244, 273
  appointment of justices 47, 180
  Books of Orders 215-16
  fines 46
  grain shortage 198-9
  local government 218, 231, 274-7
  London 171-2
  orders to justices 138-9, 183, 219, 226, 235-7
  Poor Law 186
  power 138, 139
  prices 146
  religion 152, 202
  removal of justices 184
  shipping 140
  vagrants 147
  see also Privy Council
Council of the Duchy of Lancaster 90, 92
Council of the King 110
Council in the Marches 77, 78
Council of the North 83-4, 217
Council of State 224, 227
counterfeiting 71, 267
County Council's Association 285
county courts 77, 84, 86, 124, 130
Court of Common Council 293
courts of summary jurisdiction 37, 67, 132, 295, 297-8
cows 141
Crakenthorp, Robert (Westmorland justice) 65
Crécy 18
Cripplegate 299
Cromer 179
Crompton, Richard (author) 165
Cromwell, Oliver (Lord Protector) 217, 223-4, 227-9, 238, 244
Crook, Dr. David 43
Crown Court 280, 287
  Chester 79
  Duchy of Lancaster 91, 104, 105
  Durham 86
  Gloucester 264
  London 298, 301

Cumberland 167
curia regis 5, 28, 109
customary courts 25-7, 36, 41, 75, 155, 256
Customs House 301
customs offences 85, 301
Custodes Pacis 3, 5, 7-10, 12, 20, 76, 81
    duties 9-10
    London 289, 290
Custos Rotulorum 39, 71, 111, 134, 177, 231, 236
    appointing justices 132, 281
    Chester 77, 78
    Clerk of the Peace 96, 122-3, 185
    Commissions of the Peace 119-20
    Duchy of Lancaster 92, 97, 105
    Durham 83, 85
    Lord Lieutenant 121-2, 281
    sheriff 40

Dalton, M. *The Country Justice* (1618) 166, 250
Danelaw 27
Darlington 84
death penalty 57, 66, 152, 189, 201, 239-40
    see also capital punishment
Declaration of Breda (1660) 232
Declaration of Indulgence (1672) *96*, 232, 235
Dedimus Potestatem 40
deodands 80-1
Departmental Committee on Justices' Clerks (the Roche Committee) 282-5
deportation 233
Deputy Lieutenant 122, 205, 207, 212, 231, 237, 262
    deserters 254
    training military 143, 159, 160, 203
deputy recorder 278, 282
Derby 159
    Earls of 78, 96-7
Derbyshire 43, 69
d'Eresby, Lord Willoughby (later Duke of Ancaster) 97
deserters 160, 219, 253-4
Devon 111, 118, 160, 204, 213, 244
Dilhorne, Lord 296
discretionary sessions 133-4
disseisin 130-1
Domesday 28

doomsmen 25
Dorset *203*
Dover 140
Drake, Sir Francis (Devon justice) 118
Dryden, John (playwright) 230, 253
ducking-stool 175
Dudley, Robert 109, 204
Dufferin, Lord (Chancellor of Duchy of Lancaster) 101
Dunbar (1651) 222
Dunkirk 160
Durham 96, 101, 119
    Bishops 80-5, 88, 117, 195-6
    bridges 195-6
    county palatine 74, 75, 80-7
Dutch destroying ships (1667) 253

Eagle, William *Magistrate's Companion* 167
ear, loss of 147, 149, 153, 154, 174
East India Company 255
ecclesiastical matters 71, 112, 126, 164, 224, 232
    courts 25-7, 152-3, 170
    see also church; clergy
edict of Hubert Walter (1195) 6, 7, 32, 33
Edward I (r.1272-1307) 10-13, 17, 27, 29, 76
    when Prince 9
Edward II (r.1307-1327) 13-16, 29, 81
    when Prince of Wales 76
Edward III (r.1327-1377) 16, 40, 45, 62, 76, 87, 133
    accession 15
    conservators 31
    Eyre 29
    labour laws 56
Edward IV (r.1461-1483) 58, 67, 76
Edward VI (r.1547-1553) 118, 129, 132, 149, 151, 291
    religion 153, 200
Egerton, Lord *78*
Egyptians (gipsies) 119, 151-2
Eirenarcha see Lambard
Elizabeth I (r.1558-1603) 109, 130, 138-9, 206, 210-12, 229, 244
    appointment and removal of justices 180-1, 184

Assizes 172, 176
Cheshire 78
commissions 177, 178
constables 124
Durham 81
duties of justices 131, 172-3, 179, 182, 183, 186, 195, 242
government 164
highways 157
House of Commons 108, 211
local government 135
Lord Lieutenant 122
military 160
Poor Law 148, 150, 158, 186, 191, 193, 247
poor relief 151
Privy Council 111
Quarter Sessions 132, 135, 200
recusancy 116
religion 126-7, 152, 154, 174, 200-2
trade and labour 196
wage fixing
Ellesmere, Lord (Lord Chancellor 1608) 210, 217
Ely 74, 117, 202
Ely, Bishop of 117
Ely, Isle of 74
embezzling by Clerks of the Peace 123
emigration to England 50
Empsom (lawyer) 109
enclosure of land 116, 128, 141, 147, 244
engrossers 39, 171
escheators 19
Essex 43, 112, 118, 157, 176, 217, 301
corn shortage 199
tobacco *244*
ession 7
Etherege, Sir George (playwright) 230
Europe (Continent) 2, 18, 107, 135, 148, 220, 244
poor relief 186-88
wool trade 50, 139
Evershed Committee (1952) 86
Evesham, Battle of 10, 290
exchange control regulations 302
Exchequer 64, 172, 185, 216, 243
Chief Baron 185, 292
exclusion Bill (1679) 235

export 50, 139, 142, 179
extortion 2, *34*, 39, 114, 170, 171, 290
Eynesham 45
Eyre 6, *7*, 16, 21, 26, 36, 61
history 28-30
supervision of justices 64, 109

fairs 27, 256, 259
Fairfax, Sir Thomas 228
Far East 139
Farnham 234
Fell, Thomas (Chancellor of the Duchy of Lancaster 1655) 95
felonies 20-2, *29*, 32, 34, 37, 39, 114
Assizes 22, 39, 62-4, 170
bail 62, 133
death penalty 173
Durham 80, 81
Egyptians 151-2
keepers 13, 16, 17
London 290, 297
Quarter Sessions 267, 276
feudalism 2, 4, 26, 65-8, 147, 155, 256-7
courts 2, 25-7, 41, 62, 71, 125, 168
gaols 194
honour 76
nobility 109, 110
Fielding, Henry (playwright) 230-1
fines 76, 80-1, 175-6, 182, 229, 240-3, 260, 302
church law 153, 154, 200, 202
collected by sheriffs 124, 258
disseisin 131
Duchy of Lancaster 89, 90, 91
Egyptians 151-2
forcible entry 63
gaming laws 58-9
hunting 145
imposed by keepers 13
on juries 137
on justices 37, 64, 175-6, 184, 191, 218, 233-4
for non-attendance 46, 114, 137, 197
labour laws 23, 57, 58
non-payment 194
on parishes 150, 154, 156, 157
prices breach 55
religion 233-5

Royalists 222, 231
on sheriffs 130
source of remuneration 46, 123, 242
thoroughfares 60, 61, 156, 157, 195, 251
on tithings 2
trespass 32
wages breach 23, 54-5, 146-7, 197
weights and measures 50-1, 53, 145
firma burgi 258
fishing industry 61, 140-1
Fitzherbert, Sir Anthony *L'Office et auctoryte des Justyces de peas* 165
Fitz-William, Ralph (Conservator) 81
Flanders clothmaking 50
folkmoot 289
Folville family (robbers) 45, 65
Forbes, William (book on justices in Scotland 1707) 167
forcible entry 63, 65, 130, 170, 172
forestalling 39, 146, 171, 173, 268, 290
Foster, David 98-9
Fox, Robert (Bishop of Winchester) 109
France 4, 17-18, 211
franchises 26-7, 46, 69, 70
Frankish empire 74
frankpledge 2, 26, 263
fraud 170, 294
Froissart, Jean 66
Frowyck, Chief Justice (Middlesex) 165

galleys 174
game laws 84, 145, 172, 225, 241
games (unlawful) 41, 58-9, 114, 142-4, 162, 170
Gaol Delivery 4, 37, 40, 133
Commission 4, 7, 21-2, 29, 35, 77, 221
court 269
Durham 81, 85
Justices 67, 258
keepers 13
knights 10
London 289, 292, 293, 300
vagabonds 57, 188
gaolers 55, 57, 63-4, 172, 174, 190, 269
gaols 157-8, 172, 190, 226, 233, 269, 292
Civil War 221
fever 299

for forcible entry 63
Gloucester 263-4
paying for upkeep 194, 240
rate 155
by single justice 129, 130
see also imprisonment; prisons
Gardiner, Lord (Lord Chancellor) 286, 288, 296
Gascoigne, Sir Crisp (Lord Mayor of London) 300
gentry 33, 49, 65, 128, 147, 178, 207
appointment of justices 98-9
appointment of keepers 19
charity 245
class 59
commissions 29, 70-1, 97, 116-18, 223, 229, 236
Deputy Lieutenant 122
enclosures 116
Gloucester 262, 266
Henry VII 107-9
hunting 59, 144, 145
as justices 177, 184, 201, 205, 208, 266
and lawyers 12, 20-1
local peacekeeping 4, 13, 15, 16, 18
and magnates 16-17, 20
Parliament 9, 25
Peasants' Revolt 43-5
plague 23, 24
private armies 158
religion 238
Royalists 222
wages 244
Walter, Hubert 6-7
Wars of the Roses 67
gentz des contes 19
gipsies 119, 151-2
Gladstone, W.E. (Prime Minister) 101
Glanvill, Ranulf (Chief Minister to Henry II) 6
Glascock, Mr. (Member of Parliament 1601) 182
Glassey, Lionel 97
Gleason, J.H. *The Justices of the Peace in England* 177-8, *180, 207*
Gloucester 259, 260-5
Gloucester, Earl of 8
Gloucestershire 160, 170, 204, 244, 270

boroughs 259-60, 262, 265
clothing trade 248-9
Commissions of the Peace 68-9
corn shortage 112-13, 199
Gneist 109
gold 139
Gower, Sir John Leveson (later Lord Gower) 97
graft 185
grand larceny 173
Grantz 17, 20, 44
Great Charters 36
Great Seal 31, 38, 118, 119, 180
Duchy of Lancaster 88, 95
Great Sessions 78, 79
Green, Henry (King's Bench) 43
Guernsey *203*
Guildhall 289, 296, 301, 302
guilds 269-70, 298

Halcrow, Miss Elizabeth 231
Hampden, John (ship money) 216
Hampton, John (Clerk of the Peace) 124
Hampshire 199, 257
hands cut off 154, 174
Harding, Prof. Alan 7, 12, 44
Hastings, Sir Francis (Member of Parliament 1601) 182
Hatfield, Bishop (Durham) 81
Hatton, Sir Christopher (Lord Chancellor) 185
Haverfordwest 257
Hawkins, Sir John (Devon justice) 118
Hearth Tax (1662) 243, 246
Heaton, Herbert *Economic History of Europe 207*
hedgebreaking 170
Henry I (r.1100-1135) 28, 288, 289
Henry II (r.1154-1189) 2, 4, 6, 28, 259, 260, 289
Henry III (r.1216-1272) 1, 8, 10, 13, 87
Henry IV (r.1399-1413) 49, 58, 87, 89, 90
Henry VI (r.1422-1461) 128, 132, 158, 290
Henry VII (r.1485-1509) 68, 72, 114, 129-30, 182, 188
archery 143
bail 133
enclosures 141

hunting 145
installing order 107-9
military 158, 161
parishes 126-7
vagrancy 148
wages 146
Henry VIII (r.1509-1547) 81, 113, 128, 130, 149, 164, 207
bridges 195
Chester 78
Durham 83
Egyptians 151
ex officio justices 117, *118*
gaol 158
Lord Lieutenant 120, 121-2
military 162
parishes 126-7
poor relief 188
religion 152
Wales 78, 162
heresy 71-2, 152, 174
Hertford 204
Hertfordshire 159, 161, 252-3
Hexhamshire 74
High Court 86, 267, 301
Lancaster 101, 104
High Wycombe 269
highways and roads 60-1, 164, 169, 194-6, 268, 270, 299
Durham 85
maintenance 154, 155-7, 224
repair 127, 136, 250-4
special sessions 241, 242
see also bridges
Holdsworth, Sir William 108-9, 126, 132-3, 135, *138*, 163, 211, 218
Holland, Lord 98
Holloway prison 299
Home Secretary 101, 276, 277, *281*, 286
houses of correction 136, 173, 191-4, 226, 233, 241-2
Duchy of Lancaster 91, 92, 93
Gloucester 263
housebreaking 63, 170, 242
hue and cry 2, 6, 123, 125, 164
hunting 59, 144-5, 229, 303
Huntingdon 252
Huntingdon, Earl of (1428) 65-6

hurdle 174, 175
Husey, Chief Justice (1485) 73, 127
Hussey 183
hustling court 289, 293
Hutcheson, Gilbert (Scottish justice 1815) 167
Hyde, Edward (Earl of Clarendon) 232
Hylton, Robert (*Custos Pacis*, Durham) 81

Ilchester 169, 259
imports 139, 141, 197, 244

impressment 160, 220
imprisonment 2, 23, 41, 154, 198, 202, 226
    Bristol 260
    Bunyan, John 232-3
    church law 152-3, 200
    disseisin 131
    Egyptians 151
    fishing 61
    gaming laws 58-9, 144
    gaols 157, 194
    Gloucester 263
    hunting 145
    labour law breach 57-8
    London 300
    for non-payment 188, 189, 215, 240, 241
    parents of illegitimate children 191, 247
    pending trial 63
    powers of justices 31-2
    as a punishment 175-6
    Royalists 231
    Shakespeare, William 179
    wage breach 55-6, 147, 197
    weights and measures 36
Incorporation of the Poor 260
indictments 67, 85, 89, 112, 123, 132, 152
    justices' procedure 36, 39, 61-2, 114, 239
    Peasants' Revolt 41, 42, 44
    Quarter Sessions 136, 137
    textbooks 165, 166
Industrial Revolution 98, 273
inflation 23, 24, 116, 128, 145, 197
informers 234, 235
Inland Revenue 279

Inns of Court 78, 117, 177-8, 208, 268
Intendants (France) 211
Interdepartmental Committee (1961) 279
Interregnum 84, 95, 208, 222-30, 242, 244, 251, 262
Ireland 112, 189
Isabella (wife of Edward II) 15-16

James I (r.1603-1625) *46*, 121, 174, 207-14, 242, 262, 291
    sale of peerages 207, 209, *223*
James II (r.1685-1688) 85, 96-7, 236-8, 258
James, William (Dean of Durham) 83
Jefferies, Judge 292
Jeffreys, Judge 237
Jesuits 112, 225
John (r.1199-1216) 1, 5-6, 257, 289
John of Gaunt 43, 49, 87-91
Jowitt, Lord (Lord Chancellor) 102-3
judges 16, 33-5, 37, 166, 176, 182, 210
    appointing justices 180
    Cheshire 78-9
    commissions 29, 71, 103, 185
    common pleas 21, 39
    Duchy of Lancaster 87, 91-3, 103
    Durham 81
    ecclesiastic 152
    King's Bench 21, 39
    London 280-1, 299, 301
    Middlesex 69
    Oath of Supremacy 200
    see also Assizes
juries and jurors 25, 42, 173, 183, 186, 263
    Assizes 176
    attacked 63, 66
    church law 152-3
    corn shortage 198
    corruption 114
    disseisin 131
    Duchy of Lancaster 90
    empanelled by sheriff 39-41, 136
    Grand 37, 136-7, 239
    intimidated 65, 66, 114, 158, 182
    packed 110
    petty 37, 239
    presentment 12, 27, 36-7, 126, 134, 136

Quarter Sessions 134, 136, 137, 170, 231, 234
   textbooks 165, 166
jurisdiction 65, 142, 164, 217, 224, 226
   Assizes 29
   Chester 76-9
   City of London 291-3, 295, 297, 300, 301
   civil 105, 132, 173
   Commissions of Peace 71
   County Court 124
   court leet 168
   criminal 33, 35, 61-3
   Crown Court 287
   Duchy of Lancaster 87, 95, 105
   Durham 80, 82-4, 86
   ecclesiastic 224
   feudal courts 26
   franchise courts 26-7
   Gloucester 262-4
   hundred courts *26*
   King's Bench 64
   manor courts *26*
   mayor 282
   Privy Council 10
   Quarter Sessions 134, 276
   Queen's Bench 172
   rates 263
   recorder 278
   Royal Courts 30
   single justice 131
   towns 256-9, 262, 266, 267-9, 276
justices 5, 10, 13, 131-2, 203-5
   absence 112, 118, 221, 230
   agriculture 141-2, 196, 198-200, 244
   apparel 59-60, 248-9
   appeal 137-8, 277
   appointment 5, 19-21, 47, 69-70, 74-5, 96, 98, 101-6, 121, 180-3, 201, 254
   in towns 256, 258, 259, 281, 294-7
   arrest 32, 37, 129-31, 164
   Assizes 34, 64, 110, 113, 114, 138, 165, 212, 217-18
   attendance 46, 79, 171, 209-10, 212, 267
   authority 114, 115
   bail 132-3, 137
   boroughs 50, 256-303

bridges 60-1, 154-5, 194-6
Bristol 259-60
Chancery 65
charters 256-62, 265-7
Chester 75-80
Civil War 219-22
class 70, 177-8, 181, 228
clergy 98, 100, 117, 167, 177, 266
Clerk of the Peace 41-2
colonies 186, 227, 239-40, 255
commissions 21, 33, 38-40, 68-72, 74, 116-20, 185-6
complaints against 114
conscription 174
conservators 3
constables 12, 124-6, 131
corn 246
corruption 100, 107, 176
counties 177-81
counties palatine 74-106
criminal jurisdiction 61-3
death penalty 173-4
differences between boroughs and shires *4*, 259-66, 302-3
disasters 253-4
Duchy of Lancaster 87-106
Durham 80-7
ecclesiastical matters 112
Edward III 16
Egyptians 151-2
Elizabethans 163-205
emergence of name 1, 17
Eyre 28-30
fined 37, 64, 175-6, 184, 191, 218, 233-4
fluctuating fortunes 16, 17, 48
funds for the King 213-15
game laws 58-9
games 142-4, 170
gaols 157-8, 194
gentry 5, 7, 10, 49, 116-17
Gloucester 259-64
highways 60-1, 155-7, 164, 169, 194-6, 250-3
House of Commons 47-9, 62, 69, 108, 114-15, 211
houses of correction 193-4
hundred courts 27-8

hunting 144-5
Interregnum 222-8
intimidation 66, 110
itinerant 2, 28, 29, 64
James II 236-8
juvenile courts 277
keepers 5, 7, 28, 30, 31
knights 13, 181, 208, 210, 222
labour laws 54-6, 67, 164
labour shortage 48
lawyers 21-2, 40, 117, 176, 177, 208
licensing 140, 142-3
local administration 13, 27-8, 30, 128, 132, 242-54, 269-76
local government 107, 109, 135, 205-6, 211-12, 215, 218, 223-4, 231, 237, 239
  in boroughs 269-74, 287-8, 296
London 288-302
Lord Lieutenant 120-2, 177
Magna Carta 8, 288
marriages 226-7
mayors 50, 56, 172, 177, 223, 257-8, 275-6, 285-6
military 158-62, 169
misconduct 113, 116, 138
Municipal Corporations Act (1835) 273-6
national defence 202-3
officers 254-5, 268
overseas 255
parishes 126-7
Parliament 108, 118, 182-3, 211-12
Peasants' Revolt 42-6
Petty Sessions 126, 132
policing 37, 128-31, 138, 158, 163-4, 168, 234, 239
Poor Law 186-93, 224-5, 246-8, 298-9
Possessory Assizes 8
prices 54-5, 137, 145-6
Privy Council 14, 111-13, 115-16
procedure 36-8
punishments 50, 54, 55
qualification 70, 117, 165, 166, 207, 254
Quarter Sessions 34-6, 40-1, 60-1, 133-8, 169-72, 209-10, 276-81
rates 190-4

recorders 267-8, 275, 277-81, 282, 286
reform (1949) 283-7
religion 152-4, 173, 174, 181, 200-2, 232-8
removal 96, 102-3, 104, 171, 181, 184, 207, 236, 294
remuneration 46-7, 90-1, 100, 119, 198
Restoration 228-38
retirement 104
Royal Charters 12
Saxon 109
sentencing 131, 173-6, 240, 302-3
Shakespeare 178-80
shipping 140-1, 208
single 129-31, 173, 241
Star Chamber 14, 110-11, 116
status 155, 205, 224
Statutes of Westminster 15-16, 31-4
statutory bodies 270-3
stipendiary 100-1, 103, 275
Stuarts 211-19
supervision 14, 64, 109-11, 224
taxes 242-3
Tewkesbury 265
textbooks 3, 164-9, 230
town clerks 268
trade and industry 49-53, 68, 98-100, 139-40, 164, 186, 196-7, 218, 223, 243-4, 302
  in Elizabethan times 169-71, 173
training 103-4, 176, 216
transportation 239-40
Tudors 72-3, 107-27, 128-62, 168
vagrants 147-51, 172, 179, 186-93, 241
wages 54-6, 137, 145-7, 197-8, 244-6
Wars of the Roses 66-8, 72-3
weights and measures 35-6, 49-53, 145
work out of sessions 63-4, 67, 129-33, 172-3
Justice of the Peace, The (periodical first published 1837) 167
Justices' Clerks' Society 282
justiciar 6, 76, 77, 288
juvenile courts 277, 295

Keepers of the Peace 1, 7, 33, 133, 162, 204
  appointment 5, 9, 15, 18-20, 259

commissions 15-17, 38
development of office 10-14, 48
Duchy of Lancaster 105
Durham 81, 82
lawyers 21-2
local administration 30
London 289-90
military duties 10, 18, 24, 40,
policing 9, 24
transition to justices 28, 30, 31
ways fixed 23-4
Kenilworth Castle 204
Kent 29, 69, 72, 166, 213, *244*, 301
Lord Lieutenant *169*, 177
Peasants' Revolt 43
Kett (peasants' rising in Norfolk 1549) 141
King's Bench 21, 45, 73, 159, 177, 185-6,
` 301
appeal 138
church law 152, 173
corruption 39, 41, 42, 43
London 292, 299
Middlesex 136
supervising justices 64
Westminster 85, 174
Kingston-upon-Thames 267
knights 4-8, 11-13, 16, *46*, 65, 136
appointment of keepers 19
Chester 78
clothing 59-60
commissions 4, 230
conduct 181-2
coroners *25*
Custos Rotulorum 120
gentry 49
as justices 181, 208, 210, 222
Parliament 13, 70, 108, 124
peacekeeping 4-7, 18, 32
private armies 158
Knutsford 79

Labour party 297, 302
labour and labourers 76, 164, 220, 260,
298
Commons 22, 24
games 144
hunting 59
justices 24, 42, 54, 88, 89, 91

laws 34-5, 39, 41-3, 54-8, 67, 119
movement 23-4, 56-8
ordinance 23
plague 23-4, 48
price fixing 54
shortage 24, 30, 56, 57
vagrancy 149
wages 23, 54-6, 146-7, 187, 197, 245

Lambard, William *131*, 134-5, 138, 185,
209
Eirenarcha (1581) 1, 3, 7, 73, *119*,
120, 172
Ephemeris 166, 171
punishments 173, 175
Quarter Sessions 170
textbooks 165-6, 169
Lancashire 78, 116, *235*, 254
Lancaster 119, 169, 258
Duchy 74, 87-106
Duke 87-9, 90, 91, 94
house of 66-8
palatinate 69, 74, 75, 82, 86
Seal 95-6
Lanfranc, Archbishop 26
Langele, Thomas de 45
Langland, William, *Vision of Piers
Plowman* 72
language (of the law) 72, 185, 223
latin 72, 185, 223
lawyers 42, 70, 78, 109, 163, 167, 262
Assizes 21-2, 39, 40
attendance 71, 171
commissions 29
common serjeant 293
gaol fever 299
gentry 12, 16, 20-1, 22
as justices 117, 176, 177, 208
Peasants' Revolt 42, 43
Quarter Sessions 209
recorders 267, 292
sitting with justices 34

Lea Marston 247
leather 52, 140, 179
Lee, Bishop Rowland (*Custos Rotulorum*)
77
Leeds 87

leet, court 26, 125, 168, 258-9
  thoroughfares 60-1, 154, 156
Leicester 167
Leicester, Countess 204
Leicester, Earl (Simon de Montfort) 8-10, 290
Leicester, Earl (conflict with Lord Burghley) 182
Leicester, Sir Peter 231
Leicestershire 45
Lenthall, William (Speaker of Long Parliament) 262
Levellers 223
Lewes (victory by Simon de Montfort 1264) 9
libel 170
licences and licensing 85, 123, 132, 137, 235, 241
  alehouses 83, 179, 217, 242, 249-50, 263, 274
  boatmen 299, 300
  building 200
  corn 226
  liquor 142-3
  plays 204
  soap 249
  trade 140, 142, 242
  vagrants 149, 188, 189, 246
lighting in the streets 270-2, 299
Lincoln 258
Lincoln's Inn 166
Lincolnshire 204, 215
Littleton 256
Liverpool 100, 278, 280, 293
  Court of Passage 105
livery 114, 182, 183
Llewellyn (invasion of England) 9
local government 36, 206, 211-12, 215, 223-4, 231, 287-8
  boroughs 269-74
  counties palatine 75
  courts 24-5, 30
  France 211
  James II 237, 239
  by justices 5, 47, 107, 109, 135, 205, 211, 218, 223
  London 296, 299
  parish 41, 87

Peasants' Revolt 44
Quarter Sessions 169
Lollards 44, 71-2
London 112, 184, 193, 271, *281*, *287*
  absent justices 118, 171-2, 230, 231
  aldermen 140, 286
  appointment of justices 76, 282, 294-7
  City 288-302
  Commissions of Peace 79, 105, 282
  common serjeant 293-4
  fire 253
  local administration 272, 274, 298-300
  mayor 140, 286
  Peasants' Revolt 50
  plague 204
  Quarter Sessions 297-8
  recorder 278, 280, 292-3
  silver 53
  special courts 259, 260, 264
  stipendiary magistrates 100
Long Parliament 222, 262
Lonsdale Hundred 92, 94
Lord Chancellor 138, 177, 185, 210, 232, 303
  appointing justices 74, 101-5, 180, 281
  Chester 77
  Commissions of Peace 118, 119, 121, *209*, 257, 276, 284
  Custos Rotulorum 119-20
  Duchy of Lancaster 88, 96
  Durham 83
  Gardiner, Lord 286, 288, 296
  instructions to judges 117, 134, 217
  London 291, 294
  recorders 277, 278-80, 292, 293
  religion 233, 235
  Star Chamber 111
  stipendiary magistrates 286-8
  wages 197
  see also Chancellor
Lord Keeper 77, 96, 118, 177, 197
  Bacon, Sir Nicholas (1571) 183
  Puckering (1795) 184, 199
Lords Lieutenant 161, 171, 205, 212, 231, 253, 258, 276
  appointment of justices 101-2, 281
  canvassing justices 237-8
  Cheshire 78

Custos Rotulorum 121, 281
Duchy of Lancaster 95-7
Durham 85, 86
Essex 112
as justices 177
Kent *169*
licence 204
Major General 227
private armies 159
riots and rebellions 128
Tudor times 120-2
Lord Treasurer 83, 96, 177, 180, 184
Lords, House of 236, 278, 285, 296, 297
Louis XIII 211
Lucy, Sir Thomas 179, 180
Ludgate 299

magistrates 1, 75-6, 166, 218, 250, 263-5, 271
ability 179, 303
boroughs 268, 269, 272, 274, 287
class 5
courts 98, 302
Custos Rotulorum 71
Duchy of Lancaster 105
Durham 84, 86
education 208, 209
Fielding, Henry 231
gentry 222
mayors 283, 286
pay 1, 183-4, 275
religion 200
Shakespeare's father 178
stipendiary 86, 100
textbooks 168
towns 257, 260, 266
from trade and industry 98-9, 249
wage fixing 56
Magistrates' Association of England and Wales 168, 296
Magistrates' Courts Committee 286
Magistrate, The (journal) 168, *233*
magnates 7, 13, 74, 171, 176-7, 182, 207
appointment of justices 47
Chester 76
Durham 81, 82
gentry 16-17, 20, 44-5
keepers 17, 18

Parliament 16, 274
private armies 158-9
Star Chamber 110
Wars of the Roses 67, 72-3
mainprize 32, 55, 62, 133
Maitland 67, 163
Major Generals 225, 227, 228
Man, Isle of 189
Manchester 87, 99, 100, 105, 278, 280, 293
manor courts 26, 27, *43*
Mansion House 301
manslaughter 301
Manwood, Sir Roger (Chief Baron of Exchequer) 185
Mariet, Thomas 230
markets 27, 256, 262, 263, 270
Marowe, Thomas (lecturer on duties of justices 1503) 165
marriage ceremonies 226-7, 242
marshal 292, 299
Marshalsea Court 292
Marshalsea Prison (Southwark) 292, 299
Mary I (r.1553-1558) 109, 113, 151, 153-4, 174, 200
Mary Stuart 201
masons 23, 55
Master of the Rolls 292
Masters in Chancery 226
matrimonial proceedings 295
Maurois, André 107
mayors 118, 220, 258
boroughs 50, 56, 266, 267, 269-74, 277-8, 282-3, 288
Bristol 259-60
Chester 76
Cornwall 161
gaming laws 144
Gloucester 260-2, 264
as justices 50, 56, 172, 177, 223, 257-8, 275-6, 285-6
labour laws 57, 58
London 112, 165, 172, *244*, 249, 286, 289-300
at signing of Magna Carta 8, 288
poor relief 187
Tewkesbury 260-2, 264
trading standards 53, 289, 292, 293

vagrancy 188
wages breach 56, 57
weights and measures 145
Meetings of the Sheriff's Table 93-4
merchants 4, 24, 32, 108, 187, 208, 245
    clothing laws 59-60
    commissions 196, 223, 229
Merseyside 87, 105
Merthyr, Lord 285
Middle Ages 1, 44, 49, 59, 158, 239, 256-7
Middle Temple 165, 167
Middlesex 69, 116, 136, 165, 203, 218
    highways 250-1
    London 291, 300
    plague 112
    trading justices 100
Middlewich 79
military affairs 75, 128, 158-62, 219, 234, 270, 301
    Civil War 221
    cost of war 18
    Custodes Pacis 10
    Durham 81
    duties of justices 169, 225-6, 253
    keepers 11-12, 24, 40
    Lord Lieutenant 120-2, 258
    national defence 203
    roads 195
    weaponry 143
misdemeanours 22
misprisions 267
Moleyns, Lord 66
Molyneux, Viscount (Lord Lieutenant) 96-7
monasteries 26, 187, 207
    dissolution 128, 147
Monmouth, Duke of 78, 236-7, 238
Montfort, Simon de (Earl of Leicester) 8-10, 290
moots 256
Mordaunt, Sir John 159
More, Sir Thomas (Lord Chancellor) 118, 188
mort d'ancestor 10
Mortimer, Roger (lover of Queen Isabella) 15-16
murder 1, 45, 63, 133, 153, 158, 301
    Assizes 35, 170

Durham 84-5
    vagrants 149, 188
Musters, Commissioners of 122, 159, 179, 203

Nantwich 79
national defence 202-3, 112
negligence by justices 110, 113, 114
Nelson, W. *Justice of the Peace* 167
Nessefeld, William de 89
Neville family of Durham 82
New England 300
New Zealand 255
Newcastle 87, 196
Newdigate, Sir Richard 230
Newgate prison 292, 299
nightwalkers 170
nobles and nobility (including lords) 31, 34, 65, 78, 128, 214, 229, 297
    appointment of justices 180-1
    class 59, 70
    Commissions of Peace 39, 46, 68, 71, 117, *223*, 230
    conduct 181-2
    Custos Rotulorum 120
    disruption 20
    education 178
    feudal courts 26
    Henry VII 107-8
    as justices 177, 205, 206-9
    Lords Lieutenant 121
    Parliament 13
    Peasants' Revolt 44
    plague 23
    powers 17, 107, 109, 236
    private armies 18, 158
    Privy Council 110
    Quarter Sessions 171
    Wars of the Roses 67
Norfolk 43, 161, 179, 221, 238, 246
    The Paston Letters 66
    Peasants' Rising (1549) 141
Norfolk, Duke of (1428) 65-6
Norman Conquest 1, 5, 76, 256, 288
Normandy 7
Normans 1-2, 4, 25, 26, 144, *150*, 203, 243
North America 139, 227, 240, 244, 255
Northampton 235
Northern Rebellion (1569-70) 164

Northumberland 80, 83, 159
Northwich 79
Norton, Geoffrey de
    recorder of London (1298) 292
    common serjeant of London (1319)
        293
Norwich 139
Norwich, Archdeacon of (Rev. A. Byng)
        222
Nottingham 159, 258
Nottinghamshire 111, 112
novel disseisin 10

Oates, Titus 235
oaths 8, *16*, 32, 71, 83, 233, 237
    Allegiance 201, 235
    fealty 6
    frankpledge 2, 26, 263
    jury *27*
    by justices 40, 42, 79, 183
    Obedience 201
    Supremacy 200, *201*, 235
*Office of the Clerk of the Assize, together
    with the Office of the Clerk of the
    Peace* (Anon) 166-7
Old Bailey 297-8, 300, 301
Ormskirk 169
orphans 298
    court 262, 268
outlaws and outlawry 6, *16*, 77, 175-6
overseers of the poor 125, 171, 190-2, 212,
        247-8
Owen, Robert (Member of Parliament
        1601) 182
Oxford 257, 259
    Provisions 8
    university 118, 178, 266
Oxfordshire 45, 245
oyer and terminer 21, 32, 44, 89, 259
    commissions 29, 35, 39, 45
    justices 81, 110
    London 289, 293, 300

palatinates 69, 118, 169
    Lords 74-5, 80, 87
pardon by the King 87, *90*, 91
Parliament 5, 11-13, *34*, 38, 62, 131, 161,
        230

appointment of justices 47, 98
burgesses 9, 12, 13
Canterbury Tales 72
Cavaliers 232
Charles I 219
Charles II 235, 236
Chester 76
Civil War 220-2, 229
class 59, 108, 207
Clerk of the Peace 124
commission 210, 224, 276
common law 75, 81
democratic government 206, 273-4
Duchy of Lancaster 94, 95
Edward III 15
empowering justices 31-2, 48-9, 132,
        155, 217, 287
Eyre 29
gentry 16, 18, 228
Henry VII 107, 111
hunting 59
Interregnum 222-3
James I 213-16
keepers 19, 20
knights 9, 13, 70, 124
local government 223, 296
marriage 226-7
Members 19, 65, 256-7, 262, 267, 277,
        292
    as justices 108, 118, 182-3, 211-12
pensions 224
Poor Law 186-8, 270
prelates 71
Quarter Sessions 135
religion 233
roads and highways 156, 251-2
sheriffs 13
shire courts 19, 25
stipendiary magistrates 100
trade and industry 196
vagrancy 147-8
violence in society 44
Paston Letters (ed. James Gairdner) 66, 67
Patent Rolls 18
peasants 26, 30, 65, 141
Peasants' Revolt (1381) 24, 42-6, 50, *67*
Peel, Robert 99
Pembroke, Earl of 177

Pembrokeshire 74
pensions 191, 192, 193, 221, 224, 246
Pepys, Samuel (diarist) 230
perjury *16*, 118
Peterborough 69
petty larceny 170, 241
Petty Sessions 67, 79, 132, 168, 216, 241
  beginning 189, 210
  boroughs 268, 275, 282, 284
  constables 126
  Durham 84, 86
  Gloucester 264
  London 295
Philip of Spain 154
piepowder courts 27, 256, 262, 263, 268
pillage 18, 31
pillory 147, 149, 154, 174, 175, 263
pipe rolls 209-10
pirates 161
plaque 22-4, 48, 56, 88, 112, 204, 253
Plantagenet, Edward (Earl of Lancaster) *87*
Plantagenets 4, 65, 208
Pleas, Court of 85, 86, 262
Plymouth 118
poachers 225, 302
Poitiers 18
police and policing 1, 115, 163-4, 168,
    239, 286
  boroughs 263, 270, 271-2, 275
  Cheshire 80
  constables 125, 268
  Custodes Pacis 9, 10
  Gloucester 263
  justices 37, 47, 63, 128-31, 138, 158,
    234
  keepers 9, 12, 24
  Lancashire 99
  Lord Lieutenant 121-2
  recorders disqualified 277
  sheriffs 3
poll tax (1380) 43
Poole 257, 273
Poor Law 127, 148, 150-1, 158, 186-93,
    196, 241-2
  altered 247
  boroughs 269, 270-1
  Bristol 260
  commissioners 270-1

Durham 85
  justices' time spent on 224, 225
  London 298-9
  Quarter Sessions 137
  rate 252
poor relief 128, 210, 245-6, 260, 262-3,
    298
  rate 92, 138, 155, 245, 247
  towns 269, 270, 271
Pope 113, 152, 235
portreve 256
Portsmouth 118
posse 63, 67, 129-30, 148
  comitatus 9, 13, 41, 158
Possessory Assizes 8, 10
postal service 251-2
Powell, Edward 21
prelates 13, 26, 31, *34*, 71, 177
presentment 36-7, 41, 85, 166, 219, 263
  church law 152
  constables 125
  enclosures 141
  highways 60, 157
  justices 61-2, 239
  Quarter Sessions 134-7
Preston 92, 93, 94, 98, 169
prices 10, 54-5, 112, 128, 137, 261
  fixed 140-2, 145-6, 171, 224, 242
  grain 198-9, 204
  keepers 13
  plague 23
  purveyancing 62, 292
  rocketing 244, 246
priests 45, 130, 200, 225
  hunting 59, 145
  see also clergy
printing 165, 168
prisons 137, 190, 242, 292, 299
  see also gaols; imprisonment
Privy Council 127, 177, 193, 203, 217,
    224, 240
  Commissions of Peace 118-19, 237,
    276
  clothing trade 248-9
  deserters 253-4
  Duchy of Lancaster 92, 93, 96, 97
  Durham 83, 96
  highways 195, 250-1

letters 111-13
local administration 203-5, 214
Lords Lieutenant 121-2
military matters 159, 160, 161
religion 201-2
supervision 14, 109-11, 114-16
trade and industry 196
see also Council
Privy Seal 205
profiteers 226
Protectorate 95, 210, 223, 228-31, 252
Protestants 153, 200-1
Puckering, Lord (Lord Keeper 1795) 184, 199
Puiset, Bishop Hugh du *81*
punishment 157, 187, 194, 263, 302-3
   conservators 81
   costs of 240
   dictated by Henry VIII 113-14
   discretion of justices 20, 31-2, 36-9, 50, 54-5
   Elizabeth I 173-6
   Eyre 29
   fishing laws 61
   gaming laws 58
   for immorality 192-3, 261
   for justices' misconduct 116, 138
   labour laws 56-8
   London 289, 300
   for negligent collectors 151
   Quarter Sessions 31-2, 36-9
   for sheriffs 133
   trade offences 52, 55
   vagrants 147-50
   see also capital punishment; corporal punishment
Puritanism *178*, 222, 225, 237
purveyancing 62, 292
Putnam, Prof. Bertha 17, *18*, 21, *23*, 32, *33*, 34, 48, 64, 165

qualifications for justices 70, 117, 165, 166, 207, 254
quarantine 85
Quarter Sessions 34-6, 40-1, 118, 166, 182, 216, 228
   abolished 279, 287
   appeal 138, 192, 234

Assizes 164, 239, 269
attendance 79, 171, 209-10
Bedford 232
boroughs 257-8, 267, 268, 275-81, 283-4
Bristol 260, 264
building in rural areas 200
chairmanship 231, 286
Cheltenham 265
Chester 78-80
church law 153-4, 173, 224
Civil War 220-1, 224, 225
Clerk of the Peace 123, 124
constables 125, 126
crimes dealt with 241
disrupted 158, 219, *220*, 221
disseisin 131
Duchy of Lancaster 90, 91-3, 98, 100, 104
Durham 82-6
Elizabethan 169-72
Gloucester 261-4
illegitimacy 247
lawyers 209
licensing 142, 143-4
Lollards 71
London 297-8, 300
misdemeanours 22
party politics 207-8, 229
pensions 246
poor relief 187, 247-8
procedure 135-8
religion 200, 202, 233
remuneration 46, 119
taxes 243
Tewkesbury 265
textbooks 167, 168
thoroughfares 60-1, 154, 156, 251-3
transportation 240
Tudor times 128, 129, 132, 133-8
wages 245
Wars of the Roses 67
Queen's Bench 172, 300
Quorum 20-2, 34, 39, 71, 117, 120
   Chester 77
   church laws 152-3
   Duchy of Lancaster 93, 96
   illegitimacy 191

(justices as members 131-3, 135, 177-8, 209)
licensing 142, 188, 190
Marowe 165
military laws 158
poor 189
revision of commissions 185-6
Shelley, R. 181

Radeclyve, Richard de (sheriff of Duchy of Lancaster) 90
Raleigh, Sir Walter (Lord Lieutenant of Cornwall) 121
rape 63
rate 191, 192, 242, 254, 263, 265
  on alehouses 140
  boroughs 271, 272, 274
  for bridge repairs 154-5, 195
  for gaols 158, 190, 194
  for militia 161
  for pensions 224
  for poor relief 92, 190-2, 193
  Quarter Sessions 137
  for roads 251-2
recognizances 119, 123, 137, 143
recorders
  appointment 104
  boroughs 266, 267-8, 275-83
  Bristol 260
  Chester 76, 79
  Durham 84
  ex officio justices 275, 277, 286
  Gloucester 261-2, 264
  juvenile courts 277
  Liverpool 105
  London 290-1, 292-4, 297-8, 300, 301
  Manchester 105
  Quarter Sessions 277-83
  salary 276, 277, 278-9, 280
  Tewkesbury 265
recusants 112, 116, 122, 166, 179, 202, 224, 234
Reform (of 1949) 283-7
Reform government 98
Reformation 109, 126, 265
regicide 231
regrators 39, 146, 171, 268, 290
religion 112, 140, 152-4, 170, 200-2

duties of justices 173, 181, 232
James II 236-8
Restoration 233-6
see also clergy; Roman Catholic
removal of justices 102-4, 171, 181, 207, 236, 294
remuneration
  not for constables 125
  for justices and clerks 46-7, 90, 100, 119, 198
  for recorders 278, 292
republican government 206, 222
Restoration (1660) 78, 79, 208, 223, 228-38, 253, 262, 293
  commissions 210, 230
  Duchy of Lancaster 93
  local government 211
  marriage 227
  roads 252
  Royalist pensions 224
  trade 244
  wages 244
retirement 118, 121
Revolution (1689) 78, 97, 238, 252
Rich, Lord (Lord Chancellor) 118
Richard I (r.1189-1199) 1, 5-6, *81*, 257
Richard II (r.1377-1399) 36, 49, 54, 69, 87
  labour laws 57, 58
  price fixing 145
  trade and industry 50-1, 139
Richard III (r.1483-1485) 68, 69, 72, 260
  when Duke of Gloucester 82, 90
Richelieu, Cardinal 211
riots and rioting 31-2, 37, 67, 112, 114, 161, 172
  Lords Lieutenant 128, *130*
  Manchester (1819) 99
  Quarter Sessions 170
  South England (1715) 97
  unemployed 244, 248
Ripon, Yorkshire 250
river conservancy 61
roads *see* highways and roads
robbery 1, 6, 24, 31, 63, 67, 144
  in church 13
  by Egyptians 151
  by Folville family
  on the highway 128, 148

sheriff's tourn 26
    see also theft
Robert the Bruce 13
Roche Committee 282-5
Rockingham Castle 45
Roman Catholicism 153, 174, 176, 200-1,
        232, 235, 236-8
    Lancashire 96, 116
Roundheads 229, 231
Royal Charters 12, 76, 87, 170, 265
    see also charters
Royal Commission (1910) 102, 291, 283
Royal Commission on Assizes and Quarter
        Sessions (1966-9) 280, 294, 301
Royal Commission on Justices of the
        Peace (1946) 102-4, 264, 283-5,
        295, 296
Royal Commission on Local Government
        in England (1969) *287*
Royal Commission on Taxation of Profits
        and Income (1955) 279
Royal Courts 28, 30, 62, 71, 81, 300
Royal Liberty of Durham 81
Royal Prerogative 121, 213, 219, 291
Royalists 95, 220, 223-5, 229, 231, 236
Rule Committee 104
Rump Parliament 223
Rupert, Prince 230
Rutland 116, 159
Rye 265

Sadberge 81, 83
St. Aidan of Lindisfarne 80
St. Albans 8
St. Cuthbert 80
salary
    for justices 100, 275
    for recorders 276, 277, 278, 294
    stipendiary magistrates 286
    see also remuneration
Salford 100, 105, 169
Saxon 1, 25, *150*
Scilly Isles 161
Scotland 1, 167, 218, 252, 255
    border *3*, 75, 83, 159
    Durham 80, 81, 83
    invasion 85, 216
    union (1707) 206

Scrope, Geoffrey (Chief Justice) 16
security 81, 152, 200
    for good behaviour 32, 39, 89, 129
Sedgemoor 236
sedition 112, 154, 173, 174, 183
sentencing 173-6, 287, 289, 300
    costs 240
    differences 302-3
    by justices 131
    by keepers 13
    by recorders 278
    transportation 239-40
Serjeants-at-Law 62, 82, 117, 165
servants 158, 182, 183, 192, 198
    disputes with masters 131, 171, 173,
        226, 239
    games 58, 144
    hunting 59
    movement of labour 56-8
    wages fixed 23, 54-6, 146-7, 171, 197
Shakespeare, William (playwright) 178-80
share-pushing 301
Shawcross, Sir Hartley (later Lord
        Shawcross) *279*
sheep 141
Shelley, Richard 181
Shephard, W. *Sure Guide for his Majesties
        Justices of the Peace* 166
Sheppard, W. *Cabinet of the Clerk of the
        Justice of the Peace* 254
sheriffs 61-2, 128, 132, 164, 209, 257
    appointment of keepers 19
    arrest 39, 57, 62
    authority 2-4
    bail 132-3
    Books of Orders 215
    Canterbury Tales 72
    Chester 76, 77
    Civil War 8, 9
    class 207
    constables 7, 8
    corn shortage 198
    corruption 20, 107
    County Court 124
    discretionary sessions 134
    Duchy of Lancaster 90, 91
    Edward I 11-13
    extortion 114

fines 46, 55, 57
funds for the King 213, 214
gaols 157, 194
jurors 39, 136, 137, 186
knights 6
labour laws 57, 58
London 288-9
Lord Lieutenant 120
malpractice 2-3, 130
Meetings of the Table 93
military duties 10, 160
moots 256
pirates 161
Quarter Sessions 40, 41
recusants 112
riot 64
Saxon courts 25
tourn 2, 26, 41, 62
towns 258-60, 260-1, 263, 264
ship money 208, 216-17
shipping 140-1, 196
shoemakers 52, 140, 197-8
shopkeepers 266
Shrewsbury 271, 273
Shrewsbury, Earl of 159
signal beacons 161
silk 139, 244
silver 50, 53, 139
Simnel, Lambert 108
Slaughter 170, 265
slave trade 260
Smith, Sir Thomas *De Republica Anglorum* 163
smoke 272
soap 249, 300
social services beginning 186
socialists 274
Solicitor General 82, 118, 276
solicitors 280, 286, 296
Somerset 160, 169, 236, 259
Somerville, Sir Robert 87
Southampton 257, 269
Southwark 170, 291, 292, 299
Spain (at war) 121, 161, 164, 201, 211
Speaker of the Commons 108
squirearchy 206-7, 227, 229
standards 49, 53
Stangford, Earl of 78

Stapleton, Henry (County Court Judge and Recorder of Durham) 84
Star Chamber 83, 110, 111, 116, 183, 184
  abolished 217, 224
  corn shortage 199
  Lord Chancellor's address (1608) 210
  Tudor times 14
  status and prestige 155, 205, 224
  statutory bodies 270-3
Stephen (r.1135-1154) 289
stewards 57, 69, 136, 137, 261, 265, 292
  Bishop of Durham 82, 85
  Duchy of Lancaster 90
stipendary magistrates 275, *281*, 282, 286-8, 295
  appointment 103, 104
  introduced 100, 101
stocks 41, 57, 174, 198, 240, 241, 263
  vagrancy 148, 150
Stockton-on-Tees 84
Stone, John *The Practice of the Petty Sessions* 167
Stone, Samuel *The Justices' Pocket Manual* (1842) 167-8
Storey, R.L. 65
Stratford-upon-Avon 178-9
Strayer, J.R. *The English Government at Work* 4
Stuarts 56, 167, 177, 208, 211-19, 228, 229
Stubbs, William *Select Charters* 258
subpoena 65
Sudbury, Archbishop (Chancellor) 43
Suffolk 160, 161, 253, 254
Suffolk, Earl of 253
sugar 260
sumptuary laws 76
Sunderland 84, 86
supervision of justices 14, 64, 109-11, 224
sureties 32, 33, 57, 113, 144, 164
  to appear at court 113, 226
Surrey 170, *244*, 291, 301
surveyors 154, 158, 212, 226
  highways and roads 125, 156, 195, 250-2
Sussex 159, 204

Taunton 169
tax 6, 10, 24, 28, 49, 242-3, 301

Civil War 229
 poor relief 189, 245
 relief for recorders 279
 road repairs 250
 ship money 216
tenure 26, *43*
Tewkesbury 265, 270
textbooks 3, 72, 164-9, 230
theft 6, 22, 26, *39*, 63, 84, 179
 punishment 173, 240
 vagrants 149, 188
 see also robbery
Third Crusade 6
Thomas à Beckett *34*
Thorpe, William (King's Bench) 43
tilers 23, 51-2, 54, 63
tithings 2, 189, 243
tobacco 244, 260
Tolsey 262, 263, 264
tolt 7
Torbay 238
Tories 97, 229, 230, 236, 262
torture 267
tourn 2, 26, 36, 41, 62, 258
town clerks 262, 268, 273
trade and industry 10, 97, 139-42, 164,
 206-7, 243-4, 288-9
 apprenticeships 57-8, 298
 boroughs 108, 266, 268
 class 4
 constables 126
 controls 68
 expansion 47, 49-53
 Elizabeth I 169, 171, 173, 196-7
 impressment 220
 labour 54
 licensing 242
 overseas 196, 255, 260
 pay for justices 119
 prices 54, 146
 providing justices 98-100, 218, 223,
 302
 roads 156, 195, 250
 wages 54
 Wars of the Roses 67
Trailbaston *29*, 35, 44
training 125, 296
 clergy 209

levies 122, 203
 for magistrates 103, 104, 176, 216
 of militia 158-60, 161, 253
transportation 175, 239-40, 300
treason 78, 153, 174, 201-2, 231
 not at Quarter Sessions 35, 134, 170,
 276
treasure trove *25*
Treasurer 39, 47, 85, 94, 123, 254-5
trespass 12, *29*, 63, 90, 128, 132, 267
 commissions 20
 keepers 13, 16, 17
 local courts 21
 London 290, 292, 297
 powers of justices 31-2
 weights and measures 50, 51
Trevelyan, G.M. 2, 163
 History of England 2
Tudor times 14, 47, 107-27, 128-62, 273
 Chester 76
 Duchy of Lancaster 92
 dynasty 68, 71-3
 powers of justices 168, 172, 218
 roads and waterways 60
 textbooks 167
 trade 198
tumbrel 174, 175
Tunstale, Sir William and Sir Richard 67
Turnpike Trusts 253
Twynyho, Ankerrette (wrongly hanged) 66
Tyburn Ticket 242
Tyler, Wat (leader of Peasants' Revolt) 24,
 43
Tyne and Wear 86

under-conservators 61
under-sheriff 64, 76, 90, 130
unemployment 128, 141, 187, 193-4, 244,
 248
Union of the Two Crowns 252
unions 24
United Provinces 160
university 118, 148, 178, 208, 265
usury 268

vagabonds and vagrancy 24, 57, 112-13,
 128, 147-51, 172-4, 246
 Civil War 225, 226

constables 126, 217
Durham 81, 85
enslaved 132
Gloucester 262, 263
justices 172, 179, 241
London 298
Lord Lieutenant 122
Poor Law 186-94
punishment 174
Quarter Sessions 170
whipped 126
van Haesdonck, Captain John 220
Vaughan, Sir John (Judge) 42
venality 182
verderers 19
Victoria (r.1837-1901) 101
Vinogradoff, Sir Paul 165
violence 18, 128, 129, 147-8, 268, 302

wages 171, 209, 226
fixed 54-6, 58, 137, 145-7, 187, 197-8, 224, 242, 244-6
for various jobs 245
Wales 1, 73, 93, 203, 237, 298
appointment of justices 101, 102
border *3*, 75
boroughs 266
Chester 76, 77, 78
Council of Marches 78
counties palatine 74
courts 79
first appearance of justices 1, 162-3
invasion by Llewellyn 9
Poor Law 186, 188
textbooks 168
trade licence 140
uniformity of justices 255, 288
vagrancy 189
war 11
Waller, Sir Walter *169*
Walter, Hubert (Archbishop of Canterbury) 6, 7, 32, 256, 257, 289
wapentake 25, *27*, *81*
war 30, 158, 253
Eyre 29
with France 17-18
inflation 24
knights 19

Napoleonic 203
with Spain 121, 161, 164, 201, 211
weapons 58
World I 104, 283
see also Civil War
Wars of the Roses (1455-85) 66-8, 72, 220
wardens 7, 33
wardmoots 289
warrants 243
Warrington, Earl of *78*
Warwick 221
Warwickshire 213, 225, 230, 247
waxchandlers 53
weaponry 58, 130, 160, 162
see also arms
weaving industry 140, 141
Webb, Sidney and Beatrice 135, 163, *188*, 231, 251-2, *270*, 271, 272
English Poor Law History 187
weights and measures 13, 145, 261, 268
cloth trade 51
wool trade 50
justices 24, 35-6, 39, 88, 89, 132
Wells 169
Wengrave, John de (recorder of London 1304) 292
Wentworth, Lord 160
West Hartlepool 84
West Indies 255
West Riding 169-70, 254
Western Europe 135, 187
Westminster 14, 28, 74, 86, 216, 237, 292
courts 42, 64, 80, 91, 117, 204
Parliament 12
Star Chamber 111
Westminster, Duke of *78*
Westminster, Marquess of *78*
Westmorland 65, 167
Westmorland, Earl of (Lord Lieutenant) 159
Whalley, Peter *235*
Whigs 97, 229, 230, 236, 262
whipping 174, 175-6, 179, 240, 241, 263
vagrants 126, 148-50, 189, 192
Whittington, Richard (Lord Mayor of London) 299
Wigan 100, 169, 258
Wilkes, Chief Justice 300

William I (the Conqueror) (r.1066-1087) 4, 25, 26, 28
William of Orange, Prince 237, 238
Willoughby, Richard (King's Bench) 43
Wiltshire 124, 221
Winchelsea 265
Winchester, Bishop of 8
Windsor 8
witchcraft 63
witnesses 133, 153, 182, 235, 243, 300
    attacked and intimidated 65, 66
Wolsey, Cardinal 109, 116
Wolverhampton, Lord (Chancellor of the
        Duchy of Lancaster) 102
women
    none as aldermen (until 1975) 295, 296
    juvenile courts 295
wool trade 4, 50, 139, 179
Worcester 222
workhouses 262, 263, 271, 298
Worth, Sir Robert (Member of Parliament
        1601) 182
Worth, Symon 160
Wray, Sir Christopher (Chief Justice of the
    King's Bench) 185
Wray, Rev. W.R. 100
writs 8, 11, 13, 36, 39, 165, 223
    appointment of conservators 19, 31
    certiorari 85, 110, 276
    Dedimus Potestatem 40
    Durham 80, 81
    error 138, 289
    justices 39
    Lancaster 87, 91
    mandamus 110
    oyer and terminer 32
    palatinates 77
    praemunire 152
    prerogative 138
    restraint 216
    revolt (1265) 10
    sheriffs 41
    terminariari 65
Wycliffe, John (and the Lollards) 71, 72

Yarmouth 270
York 170
York, Archbishop of 117

York, Duke of 235, 236
Yorkists 66-8, 108, 128